THE ECONOMY AND POLITICS OF THE NETHERLANDS
SINCE 1945

THE ECONOMY
AND POLITICS
OF THE NETHERLANDS
SINCE 1945

edited by

Richard T. Griffiths

1980
MARTINUS NIJHOFF – THE HAGUE

ISBN 90 247 9049 2 (gebonden)
ISBN 90 247 9019 0 (ingenaaid)

PREFACE

There is relatively little information on The Netherlands written in the English language which is easily accessible to social science students and even less which is systematically assembled between the covers of a single book. This is unfortunate not only because The Netherlands is an important part of Western Europe but because the experience of The Netherlands in the way in which it has attempted to resolve the economic and political problems confronting it may help to shed valuable light on similar issues facing other European countries. The contributions for this volume were chosen with these considerations in mind. On the one hand the selection of topics was intended to provide an overall impression of the political and economic development of The Netherlands since the Second World War. Thus separate chapters are devoted to an examination of economic development; counter-inflation, energy, regional and planning policies; pressure groups, electoral performance, cabinet formation and colonial and European policies. On the other hand, these areas for investigation were chosen to invite specific contrast with the experience of other European nations or to illustrate certain problems of political or economic theory.

It is my pleasure to thank, first of all, the contributors themselves for the conscientious way in which they prepared their drafts which made my task as editor so much easier. Secondly, it will be apparent to even the most casual observer that I have contributed two chapters. This was not an attempt to grab the limelight or even to earn some extra cash but because the original authors of the EEC chapter were unable to submit a manuscript in time for publication. I happened to have prepared a chapter on the same subject for a book by Ken Twitchett and Carol Cosgrove Twitchett and I am grateful for their permission for it to appear in this volume. I hope their book, *Building Europe: The Member States of the European Communities*, enjoys the success it deserves. I would also like to thank Liz Diggle, Elly Molendijk and Marijke Kreuze for preparing the entire manuscript for press so efficiently, and uncomplainingly. Finally I must thank my wife Janet for the time spent rechecking the drafts for accuracy. She undertook the task with great good humour and the final manuscript has benefitted immeasurably from her help.

Amsterdam, April 1980   Richard Griffiths

LIST OF CONTENTS

3. Counter-Inflation Policy in the Netherlands   61

C.J. van Eijk

4. The Influence of Natural Gas on the Dutch Economy   87

R.F.M. Lubbers and C. Lemckert (translated by R.T. Griffiths)

5. Sectoral and Regional Imbalances in the Dutch Economy

G.A. van der Knaap

6. The Netherlands Central Planning Bureau   135

R.T. Griffiths

7. Interest Groups in Dutch Domestic Politics   163

J. de Beus and H. van den Doel

8. Patterns of Voting Behaviour in the Netherlands 199

G.A. Irwin

9. Government Formation in the Netherlands 223

R.B. Andeweg, Th. van der Tak and K. Dittrich

LIST OF TABLES

LIST OF FIGURES

ABBREVIATIONS USED IN TEXT

AKZO   *Algemene Koninklijke Zout Organon* (General Royal Salt Company).

ARP   *Anti-Revolutionaire Partij* (Anti-Revolutionary Party).

AVRO   *Algemene Vereniging Radio Omroep* (General Society for Radio Broadcasting).

BEB   *(Directoraat-Generaal voor) Buitenlandse Economische Betrekkingen* (Directorate-General for Foreign Economic Affairs).

CAO   *Collectieve Arbeids Overeenkomst* (Collective Labour Contract).

CAP   Common Agricultural Policy.

CCEIA   *Coördinatie Commissie voor Europese Integratie en Associatie Problemen* (Coordinating Commission for European Integration and Association Problems).

CDA   *Christen Democratisch Appèl* (Christian Democratic Appeal).

CEC   *Centrale Economische Commissie* (Central Economic Commission).

CED   *Commissie van Economische Deskundigen van de SER* (Commission of Economic Experts of the Social-Economic Council).

CEP   *Centraal Economisch Plan* (Central Economic Plan).

CHU   *Christelijk Historische Unie* (Christian Historical Union).

CNV   *Christelijk Nationaal Vakverbond* (Christian Dutch Trade Union).

CPB   *Centraal Plan Bureau* (Netherlands Central Planning Bureau).

D '66   *Democraten '66* (Democrats 1966).

DS '70   *Democratisch Socialisten '70* (Democratic Socialists 1970).

DGES   *Directoraat-Generaal voor Europese Samenwerking* (Directorate-General for European Cooperation).

DM   Deutsche Mark.

DSM   Dutch State Mines.

EAGGF   European Agricultural Guidance and Guarantee Fund.

ECSC   European Coal and Steel Community.

EDC   European Defense Community.

EEC   European Economic Community.

EMU   (European) Economic and Monetary Union.

EPC   European Political Community/Cooperation.
FNV   *Federatie Nederlandse Vakverenigingen* (Federation Dutch Trade Union Movement).
GNP   Gross National Product.
HVA   *Handels Vereniging Amsterdam* (Trading Company Amsterdam).
IGGI   Inter-Governmental Group for Indonesia.
KVP   *Katholieke Volks Partij* (Catholic People's Party).
MCA   (European) Monetary Compensatory Amount.
MEV   *Macro Economische Verkenning* (Macro-Economic Survey).
NAM   *Nederlandse Aardolie Maatschappij* (Netherlands' Petroleum Company).
NATO   North Atlantic Treaty Organisation.
NCRV   *Nederlands Christelijke Radio Vereniging* (Dutch Christian Radio Organisation).
NCW   *Nederlands Christelijk Werkgeversbond* (Dutch Christian Employers' Organisation).
NHM   *Nederlansche Handels Maatschappij* (Netherlands' Trading Company).
NNP   Net National Product.
OECD   Organisation for Economic Cooperation and Development.
PPR   *Politieke Partij Radicalen* (Radical Party).
PR   Proportional Representation.
PTT   *Post, Telegraaf, Telefoon* (Post, Telegraph, Telephone).
PvdA   *Partij van de Arbeid* (Labour Party).
REZ   *Raad voor Europese Zaken* (Council for European Affairs).
SER   *Sociaal Economische Raad* (Social Economic Council).
VNO   *Verbond van Nederlandse Ondernemingen* (Union of Dutch Enterprises).
VAT   Value Added Tax
VOC   *Vereenigde Oost-Indische Compagnie* (United East Indies Company).
VVD   *Volkspartij voor Vrijheid en Democratie* (Party for Freedom and Democracy; Liberals).
WEU   Western European Union.
WIC   *West-Indische Compagnie* (West Indies Company).

1. THE FOUNDATIONS OF DUTCH PROSPERITY

P.W. Klein

During the quarter of a century that followed the end of World War II the Netherlands experienced a remarkable process of economic growth. Its continuity, its stability and its high rate were unique in the country's history. In a seemingly effortless manner, levels of prosperity were reached that in former times had been unattainable. The annual average growth of domestic product rose to well over 4,5 percent during the fifties and sixties, comparing favourably with other West-European countries like Belgium, Denmark, Norway and the United Kingdom, displaying growth rates of less than 4 percent or even 3 percent.

Moreover, this economic growth was achieved within a social framework reputed for its absence of internal strife. There were hardly any labour conflicts to speak off. In the field of domestic politics the harmonious cooperation and peaceful compromising among parties precluded any tendency towards polarisation. Any discontent with the prevailing conditions that might have existed did not surface into public consciousness until the second half of the sixties. In the field of international relations the Dutch were determined to live up to their reputation of reliable partners in the Western alliance.

The economic performance of the Dutch was of course to a very large extent part of the general post-war economic upswing all over the world. The economic expansion of Western Europe, especially served as a direct and decisive pre-condition to the Dutch achievement. But however favourable the international conditions may have been, they cannot explain why and how the Dutch succeeded in exploiting them to such a large and satisfying extent. Considering the problem that had to be overcome the success actually came as a surprise. The long-term economic development of the past certainly did not indicate a rich future. The perennial shortage of the domestic natural resources had always been a serious obstacle to the industrialisation of the economy. The long-lasting depression of the thirties and the disastrous war damages had created formidable barriers to economic development. The immediate post-war period was not without new impediments and setbacks. Taking these circumstances into account it is clear that the new economic growth did not arrive as a spontaneous and automatic process. A deliberate and careful policy as well as specific qualities and skills had to be applied in order to overcome the difficulties and in order to grasp the opportunities which circumstances offered. It took some trial and error before the correct policies were discovered. Some of them were failures even before they started, others miscarried as time proceeded. It was soon realised, however, that the nation's economic chances in the last resort stood or fell with industrialisation. At the end of the 1940's an ambitious programme of industrialisation had been launched and in 1950 it could be said that the country had entered into a new and prosperous phase of its economic history. The Dutch post-war achievement cannot be appreciated without an understanding of the earlier developments that actually had shaped the chances and opportunities of economic growth available in 1945. Some of these factors dated far back into pre-industrial times, others had a more recent origin. Where necessary they will be considered in the rest of this chapter, which will also look for the specific bottlenecks and obstacles which had to be removed before a process of self-sustained economic growth could begin. This process started somewhere in the early fifties. What means and measures led up to this development and what course had the economy taken during the immediate post-war years? The story would not be complete if no mention was made of the failures and mistakes which preceded the years of continuous growth.

1.1 Economic Development in the nineteenth century

From a long-term point of view the Netherlands had never served as an impressive example of modern, industrial economic growth. It is true that the country once had been one of the most industrialised centres of Europe. But even during the 17th century commerce, shipping, finance and agriculture had characterised the economy more than manufacturing industry. Because of its dependance on the dominating entrepot trade, taking care of a relatively abundant overseas supply of raw materials, the latter had never been able to develop as a growth factor in its own rights. When during Napoleonic times the entrepot trade fell into definite decline, manufacturing practically came to a standstill. It never recovered in its traditional forms.

During the first half of the 19th century the Dutch economy continued in its decline and stagnation as other West-European countries like Belgium,

Germany and France began to follow the British model of modern indust-rialisation. The Dutch just seemed unable to do likewise. During the second half of the century, however, the economy began to show some substantial advance. Commerce revived, shipping increased, agriculture expanded, banking and finance moved into new fields of enterprise and activity. It would seem as if the traditional, rather slow and fitful economic progress of earlier times had been resumed. For the time being industrial manufactur-ing remained a somewhat reluctant straggler, apart from some haphazard and incidental innovations. This was hardly surprising in view of the unfavourable relations of supply and demand. Inadequate, inferior tech-nologies, unskilled labour, lack of natural resources, together with prevail-ing entrepreneurial attitudes, giving preference to short run investment in commercial enterprise to the exploitation of industrial opportunities, formed substantial obstacles on the side of supply. They prevented a vigorous approach to the problem. In theory a sufficient amount of capital would have been available even though Dutch investors were mainly inte-rested in investment abroad. As the industrial investment opportunities were small, there was, however, hardly any capital demand for industrial purposes. The industrial development was severely limited by demand factors as well, as the home market was relatively small and poor.

After 1895, however, modern industrialisation began to develop as a result of a favourable turn in international economic affairs. As domesic agri-culture recovered from the long-drawn international depression of the 1880's, the home market now began to carry weight for a more or less general and balanced development. All sorts of industrial enterprises were to profit from this general rise. During the earlier decades technological improve-ments had been slowly introduced in a wide variety of industries. These innovations now began to bear fruit. So did the improvement of the system of waterways and railroads that had been effected in the 1860's and 1870's. The colonial market in the Dutch East Indies suddenly developed as a vigorous factor of growth owing to the expansion of private enterprise in tropical agri-culture. The colonial contribution to the Dutch national income seems to have increased from about 3 percent before the 1890's to approximately 10 percent in 1913.

The most impressive advance was realised by the sector of light industries producing consumer goods like textiles and foodstuffs rather than capital goods. The light industries could profit particularly from the rapid population increase from 5,2 million people in 1900 to 6,2 million in 1913. At the time real income per capita tended to rise. In this way the growth of domestic pruchasing power became a forceful stimulant. The development of interntional trade remained of decisive importance, however. Formerly Dutch exports had been of a mainly agricultural origin, serving the requirements of the neighbouring countries which had already become industrialised. As a consequence foreign markets generally had been receptive. The position of the newly emerging manufacturing sector, also dependent on the importation of raw materials, fuel and capital goods, was considerably less secure.

1.2 Economic performance between the wars

The vulnerability of Dutch industry was to be demonstrated during the First World War. It caught the Dutch economy by surprise at a time when its transformation from a traditional society into a modern industrial one had been far from completed. Under these circumstances it was of little avail that the Netherlands managed to maintain a strict neutrality. Industrialisation and economic growth were interrupted. The living standard of the majority of the population deteriorated severely. The peace did not bring a resumption of the pre-war development. During the twenties the economy was subjected to fitful and short-lived revivals, alternating with recessions and slumps. This was, however, nothing peculiar to the Netherlands; the same precarious state of affairs existed all over Europe. The structure of the Dutch economy, however, was possibly much more affected than was the case elsewhere. Very significantly, the modernisation of the Dutch agricultural sector was even reversed. It had been steadily progressing since the 1880's but during the 1920's the Dutch farmer returned once again to more traditional methods. Production actually became more labour intensive and productivity declined. The continuing population growth – up to 7.9 million in 1930 – and a decline of employment opportunities in the sector of industry seem to have been responsible. In fact the country was trying to readjust to the change for the worse in interntional economic relations. It did so by a gradual and more or less automatic switch to a less advanced stage of structural economic development. The conditions of the market for Dutch products and services just did not seem to allow for more. The rate of industrial investment and technological innovation actually slowed down.

The depression of the 1930's thus caught an economy well out of its road towards balanced economic growth. The consequences were disastrous. The Netherlands suffered to a large extent and for much longer from the depression than any other West-European country. During the thirties real per capita income continued to decline at an annual rate of almost 1 percent. Such a development stood in sharp contrast to what happened elsewhere. Great Britain for instance reassumed its regular growth pattern of about 2.5 percent as soon as 1933. As British unemployment finally began to fall after 1932, Dutch unemployment kept increasing until 1936 when it had surpassed the British rate. Dutch international trade registered a disastrous fall of no less than 65 percent in comparison to the late twenties. British trade, which had declined considerably less, recovered as early as 1933. The Dutch fall continued until 1936 and recovery lagged behind the British revival. And when British investment was in full rally, the Dutch investment rate continued to level off.

The very poor performance of the Dutch economy during the thirties was partly the result of wrong economic policy. The monetary policy especially was at fault, as the government stubbornly refused to abandon the gold standard. It did so against all economic reason and just for the sake of prestige. As a consequence Dutch exports were needlessly impeded. The sector of international transport, which had been one of the main traditional pillars of the economy, was also damaged very heavily as it became almost impossible for Dutch shipping to compete with other flags. The government, however, just insisted on economising in the confident belief that a further adaptation and adjustment to the severity of times was the best way out. Some day better times would arrive. It was a passive and uninspiring course to take. Its traumatic experience left a deep and lasting impression, that to a large extent conditioned the firm determination after the second world war to tackle things differently. Yet it is difficult to see what other policy would have achieved better results. The main economic problem of the thirties could certainly not have been solved by short run government policies. It was caused by structural developments. The Dutch economy had enjoyed too little for its modernisation. Its chances for self-sustained, long-time economic growth therefore had not developed sufficiently.

1.3 The economy during the Second World War

The economy had far from recoverd at the outbreak of war. The country became involved in 1940 when the real per capita income still fell short from the level that had been reached in 1929. During the war matters deteriorated further. At the end of the war public affairs had been thrown into a complete disorder. In pre-war times annual public expenditures had amounted to about one billion guilders. During the first four years of war public

expenditure accumulated to an amount of 18 billion guilders and worse was
to follow. As economic activity kept declining, for a variety of reasons,
taxation was more than doubled. It nevertheless fell far short of covering
public expenditures. The national debt was therefore ruthlessly increased
from 4 to 20 billion guilders. It was not sufficient. The issue of paper notes
was responsible for a five-fold increase of the monetary stock. The government instituted rigid controls in order to prevent an excessive rise of prices.
These controls had a large measure of success. They protected not only low
income consumers, but also German enterprise which provided itself
cheaply with all sorts of materials in the Dutch market. Actually, the process
of hidden inflation created enormous problems for the future: how to
operate with the considerably increased stock of money when international
trade would have to be reassumed in peace time. The international transfer
of payments had become completely disrupted. A starved economy ran the
danger of ravenous buying in the world market, causing severe dislocation.
A balanced recovery, which would be a condition to the return of economic
stability, might have been prevented. A large reserve of domestic unspent –
and for the time being unspendable, purchasing-power would have to be
kept under control. The danger was increased by the fact that even Dutch
solvency was put at stake. As the national debt increased to 20 billion
guilders, the national capital stock was reduced from 35 billion to 27 billion
guilders. At the same time current national income fell from 5 billion
guilders to less than 4 billion guilders. In this way the international credit of
the Dutch had been reduced to almost nil. It was even questionable whether
the income would be sufficient for debt servicing, considering the pressing
needs of the society. Substantial credits would be required for the reconstruction of the economy.

Especially during the last phase of the war consumption had fallen well
under the level of subsistence. Raising consumption was a sheer necessity
and there would be little left for saving. A more or less acceptable standard of
living had to be restored. It could even be considered as a basic investment in
the nation's productive resources. And a broad and extensive investment in
these recourses was certainly required in view of the serious losses that had
occurred. Worst of all, war damages had not been distributed evenly over the
economy. This implied a further structural dislocation, impeding the return
to normal conditions. The most vital sector of transport and communications had lost 55 percent of its productive capacity through bombing, other
fighting activities and German requirements. The merchant marine was
reduces to half of its pre-war tonnage. The rolling stock of railroads had been
practically devastated. Of its most modern equipment -- 300 electric engines

– only five were still fit for use.

Manufacturing industry had also been hit heavily. About 40 percent of its capital stock had been lost. The greater part of the loss had been caused by eating into inventories, but the fixed capital had also been depleted through plunder, destruction, obsolescence and wear and tear. Agriculture and horticulture had suffered least. Even so, no less than 10 percent of the cultivated area had been inundated. For the time being it was lost for productive purposes. Cattle breeding had sustained qualitative and quantitative losses, weakening the country's position as an exporter of dairy-products.

A different but extremely difficult set of problems was caused by the serious deterioration of living accommodation. Before the war the annual production of the building industry had amounted to about 40,000 dwellings. During five years of war no more than 60,000 new houses had been finished. Losses had been accumulating at the same time to a staggering number of 165,000, leaving a shortage of some 300,000 houses. More than one million people – of a total of 9.3 million in 1945 – were deprived of proper living accomodation. A tremendous effort would be required in order to catch up with the backlog. The problem was aggravated as the 9 million population of 1945 multiplied to 14 million within the next 30 years. Dutch post-war population growth had in fact accelerated in comparison to the interbellum and it easily surpassed the growth rates elsewhere in Western-Europe.

1.4 Economic recovery

In 1945 it seemed almost impossible that the economy would be ready in the near future to provide an adequate livelihood and sufficient employment to these fast rising numbers. Small wonder, that Dutch self-confidence during the immediate post-war years was slow in reasserting itself. This was evinced by the high and rising rates of emigration to overseas countries. The exodus reached its peak in 1952 when 76.000 people left. Since then the emigration figures have kept declining. The same years also saw the end of rationing, coffee being the last article to be freed. The nation had come a long way since V-day when the weekly diet per person had been limited to 1 kg of potatoes, 900 gr. of bread, 1 liter of milk and 100 gr. of cheese.

In 1948 real per capita income surpassed for the first time its pre-war maximum of 1929. At the same time the unemployment had declined to less than 2 percent. As far as is known it had never been at such a low level. In 1949 the deficit on the current account of the balance of payments was reduces to the mere trifle of 300 million guilders, comparing favourably to the deficits of the previous years which had been 5 or 6 times as high. During the early fifties the deficit even turned into quite satisfying surplusses. The international credit of the Dutch had been obviously restored.

These were impressive achievements in view of those factors obstructing development and policy failures. In the early fifties the plan for industrialisation for example was upset by the outbreak of the Korean war. The military budget was suddenly increased by no less than 25 percent. It required an unexpected and unsettling reallocation of national resources. This was barely accomplished when the country was struck by disastrous floods in 1953. In a single night 2000 people were drowned. The material damage amounted to about 5 percent of the national income. As a consequence the nation burdened itself with the construction of a completely new system of sea-defence. Putting it into operation required billions of guilders. It has still not yet been quite completed.

The Indonesian struggle for independence, which was finally granted at the end of 1949, seemed to be a double disaster. First there was the loss of a market of 80 to 100 million people. It was expected that the Dutch national income would sustain a loss of 10 to 15 percent . In the meantime the impoverished Netherlands kept a large and expensive army of more than 100,000 men in its colony, where it failed to achieve any permanent results whatsoever.

Other adventurous dreams floundered to their fruitless end at the same time. Such was the case with the idea of the annexation of large German territories, coal and iron mines preferably included. One famous plan envisaged the enlargement of the Netherlands by at least 80 percent. The German population concerned would have to find its abode somewhere else, of course, as Dutch workers and farmers moved in. The international political situation made short work of these wild ideas. Anyway, a sober Dutch government had soon realised that annexation was no means to economic recovery. It tried to shelve all territorial ambitions. It was, however, unable to withstand all pressure. In the end some 70 km² of German territory were annexed in 1949, fortunately under the cover of technical reasons. This made it easier to return the annexated areas as soon as feelings had calmed down. This actually occurred in 1960. A great debate of the first post-war years was then brought to end.

Another great debate of the late forties and early fifties concerned the fundamental reorganisation of the economic order. Actually the discussion had already started well before the war. This was not surprising because it was widely held that the poor performance of the economy during the interbellum period had been occasioned by serious shortcomings in the institutional framework of the economy. The discussion was of a mainly political character, however, and the argumentation was chiefly ideological in kind. Socialists, roman-catholics, protestants and liberals all had more or less differing opinions. It is therefore not surprising that nothing much was really accomplished in the end. When the bill on public industrial organisation was finally passed in 1950, it was a complicated compromise. The law provided for the establishment of public corporations of employers and employees, which would regulate the affairs of their trade or branch of industry. A number of industrial councils were indeed founded but they generally enjoyed no great influence. An exception must be made, however, for the Social Economic Council at the head of public industrial organisation. It developed into an authoratative, able and important advisor to the government. The Council had a tripartite constitution of employers, employees and independent experts. It became one of the main cornerstones of the well-balanced, delicate frame-work of Dutch post-war industrial relations, to which the economy certainly owed much of its development.

Even before the Social Economic Council was instituted the Central Planning Bureau had been established in 1945. The Bureau's function was economic forecasting and testing. Dutch planning was intended to be indicative, offering the government various models and instruments to chose from. Planning was actually most effective thanks to its common sense approach to problems. Another cornerstone of the new economic system had in fact already been erected during the war. The Foundation of Labour had been the result of the cooperation of employers and employees in the underground resistance movement. After the war the Foundation was established as a body of private law. As such it became the focal point for the co-operation and negotiation amongst the Unions of employers, employees, trades people and farmers. All collective bargaining was centralised in the Foundation, taking on itself the publication of general guidelines and rules for the regulation of wages and other labour conditions. The Foundation stood in close consultation with the Minister of Social Affairs, who held the final authority through means of a committee of experts putting all labour agreements to the test of general government direction. The system distinguished itself by its careful balancing of power. It was intended for harmonising industrial relations and it actually succeeded to a very large and remarkable extent in preventing polarisation and social strife. It was unique in the world.

Its successes were not to be continued indefinitely, however. As the growth of the economy proceeded the system was put under increasing stress. Sectoral differences and discrepancies occurred in all-important variables such as productivity, prices and the latitude for wage increases. It became increasingly difficult to control these divergent developments from one central point. The differentiation of wage policies became a necessity. The resulting strains were too much for the system which collapsed in 1963. Government controls had to be relaxed and the Foundation of Labour lost its dominating influence. It was nevertheless evident, that improvements in the economy's institutional framework during 1945-1950 had born rich fruit in the meantime.

Another renewal of decisive importance had occurred in the government's policies. They contrasted sharply with the policy during the thirties, when the government had tried to remain passive. The experiences of the 1930's had taught that a simple reconstruction of the pre-war economy would not suffice by far. A progressive renovation of the economy was necessary and it became more or less accepted that the government should assume a large degree of responsibility for following such a course. As a matter of fact it is difficult to see what other course could have been taken. The mere danger of imminent monetary chaos called for a strong and speedy government action. The uncontrolled accumulation of monetary stock during the war implied a process of hyper-inflation which would wreck all chances of recovery and future economic development. The situation was resolved by a single and daring stroke in September 1945. All money in circulation was declared of no value. For a whole week all monetary transactions were stopped. Then the government allowed the gradual introduction of new money, the old values being held in frozen accounts. So-called black money was confiscated. The money of legitimate origin could gradually be used again, but only for certain purposes like capital investment or government bonds. In this way it was possible to keep the inflation under control. At the same time the government was in the unique position of controlling the flow of expenditures, whether for consumptive or productive purposes. In this way it became possible to deal most effectively with all sorts of problems related to the economic recovery. It was already perfectly clear in 1946 and 1947 that the monetary policy of the government was a tremendous success. The final settlement of the monetary purge, however, was delayed until 1950.

In the meantime the government had defined the aims of its general economic policy as a 'magic triangle' of purposes: stability of prices, equilibrium in the balance of payments and full employment. It is interesting to note that economic growth had not yet been defined as a separate goal. It was only added later as were the equalisation of the income distribution, regional development and protection of the natural environment. These were the goals an affluent society could permit itself. But during the first post-war years a more modest approach to fundamental economic issues was indicated. Common sense dictated that priority should be given to the development of key sectors, which would stimulate economic growth in the long run. Since both agriculture and industry depended on the importation of raw materials, machines and fuel, the most fundamental bottle-neck in the short run was caused by the large deficit in the balance of payments. Under these circumstances priority was given to transport and communication and coal mining as these would either earn or save foreign currency.

In the meantime the nation exerted itself in rebuilding its capital equipment. This would have been an almost impossible task had not foreign aid intervened. Between 1945-1950 Dutch net investment amounted to about 10 billion guilders. Only half of it was financed through national savings. The rest was obtained through loans and gifts from abroad, mainly from the United States. Again priorities were defined. The greater part of foreign aid was used for restoring and extending the capacity to export in order to earn foreign currency. By 1948 the immediate war shortages and damages had been conquered. It was time for a second phase in the recovery. Again it was launched by the government when the first of a series of impressive plans for the industrialisation of the economy was introduced. This first plan mainly served for maintaining full employment but it was also intended as a relief for the troubles in the balance of payment. Actually the plan lay the foundation of long-term economic growth. The four year plan was an immediate success. Investment proceeded as intended. It was highly significant that the most modern industrial sectors – chemicals, metallurgy, electro-technical industries and energy works – yielded the best results. Their growth rates and productivity rises were highest. The older and more traditional branches of light industry did not do so badly either. In fact, it was mainly thanks to their expansion that the employment opportunities increased according to plan. The industrialisation plan of 1948 had predicted a rise of 30 percent in the production of manufacturing in four years. But the industrial production had already increased by about 15 percent in the middle of 1949. By 1950 the economy was in full swing. The solid foundations of the future development had been laid in a surprisingly short period of less than five years and against overwhelming odds. After an interruption of more than thirty years, and after having suffered substantial losses, the Dutch economy had returned on its way to modernisation and economic growth.

Select Bibliography

J.G. Abert, *Economic policy and planning in the Netherlands 1950-1965.* New Haven, 1969. (over de rol Centraal Planbureau).

J.M.W. Binneveld, P.W. Klein, H.H. Vleesenbeek, 'De groei van de welvaartsstaat' in P.W. Klein (ed.), *Van Stapelmarkt tot welvaartsstaat.* Rotterdam, 1970, p. 109-134.

P. Boomgaard, 'De havenstaking van 1946 in Amsterdam en Rotterdam. Confrontatie met conflict- en stakingstheorieën. *Economisch- en Sociaal-Historisch Jaarboek.* Jg. 40 (1977), p. 242-312.

W. Brakel, *De industrialisatie in Nederland na 1945.* Leiden, 1954.

P. Coomans, *De Eenheidsvakcentrale (EVC) 1943-1948.* Groningen, 1976.

G.C.J.J. Harmsen/L. Noordegraaf, 'Het ontstaan van de Eenheidsvakcentrale'. - *Te Elfder Ure.* no. 14 (december 1973), p. 791-852.

G.C.J.J. Harmsen/B. Reinalda, *Voor de bevrijding van de arbeid. Beknopte geschiedenis van de Nederlandse vakbeweging.* Nijmegen, 1975.

F.van Heek, *Van hoog kapitalisme naar verzorgingsstaat. Een halve eeuw sociale verandering 1920-1970.* Meppel, 1973.

Herwonnen Welvaart. De betekenis van het Marshallplan voor Nederland en de Europese samenwerking. Den Haag, 1954.

E.W. Hofstee, 'Arbeid op de tweesprong' in W.J. Wieringa (ed.) *Arbeid op de tweesprong.* Amsterdam, 1965, p. 95-135.

F. de Jong, *Om de plaats van de arbeid. Een geschiedkundig overzicht van ontstaan en ontwikkeling van het Nederlands Verbond van Vakverenigingen.* Amsterdam, 1956.

Th. L.M. Thurling/J.H. Lubbers, *Bedrijvig Nederland, een studie over Nederlands economische structuur.* Amsterdam, 1948.

Tien jaar economisch leven in Nederland. Herstelbank 1945-1955. Den Haag, 1955.

Joh. de Vries, *De Nederlandse economie tijdens de 20ste eeuw. Een verkenning van het meest kenmerkende.* Antwerpen/Utrecht, 1973. English translation *The Netherlands Economy in the Twentieth Century. An examination of the most characteristic features in the period 1900-1970,* Assen, 1978.

Joh. de Vries, 'De twintigste eeuw' in J.H. van Stuijvenberg (ed.), *De economische geschiedenis van Nederland.* Groningen, 1979² (1977¹), p. 261-308.

M. Weisglas (ed.), *Nederlands economisch herstel.* Amsterdam, 1946.

J. Wemelsfelder, *De Duits-Nederlandse economische betrekkingen na 1945.* Leiden, 1954.

J.P. Windmuller, *Labor relations in the Netherlands.* Ithaca (NY), 1969.

2. A DESCRIPTION OF POST WAR ECONOMIC DEVELOPMENTS AND ECONOMIC POLICY IN THE NETHERLANDS*

P. de Wolff and W. Driehuis

During the post war years the Netherlands have undergone strong structural developments which in many respects influenced the inflationary process and employment growth during the period. In order to understand the underlying forces it will be necessary to describe these developments in some detail. However, such a description has the disadvantage of treating the different aspects consecutively although it is clear that they form part of a system of interrelations. Therefore, the order of presentation does not necessarily reflect a chain of causal relations, it is mainly chosen for reasons of convenience.

This chapter is divided into two parts. Section 1 gives a description of the post-war development[1]. Section 2 contains a description of goals and instruments of economic policy. It deals only with the most important economic policies pursued so far, i.e. wage and price policy, fiscal and monetary policy. Exchange rate policy (see Kessler 1978), labour market policy and sectoral policies are not discussed since discussion really only strongly focussed on them after the mid-seventies. Moreover, the developments of the second half of the seventies are largely outside the scope of this chapter.

2.1 Production and production capacity

At the end of the World War II the country found itself in a deplorable state. Stocks were depleted, the transportation systems partly destroyed, large parts of the industrial enterprises dismantled and the inhabitants of the most densely populated western provinces were on the brink of starvation. Therefore, the first five years after the war were a period of reconstruction during which, due to a combined effort of all remaining available resources, considerable foreign aid (loans, Marshall aid) and a stringent governmental economic policy, a more normal situation was attained. The developments have been described in Chapter One.

During the quarter of a century which passed since then the level of production and production capacity increased very strongly. The rate of growth
of total production, on the average equal to 4.8 percent p.a., showed fluctuations of a cyclical nature. The years 1952, 1958, 1967 and 1975 can be
considered as years in which capacity was under utilized, whereas the years
1955, 1964 and 1970 were years of high capacity utilization. Apart from the
cyclical movements, characteristics of a more structural nature can be
discerned. For analytical reasons we distinguish three subperiods, 1951-
1960, 1961-1970, 1971-1977[2]. The fifties can be considered as years with a
shortage of capital in which potential employment was below potential
labour supply, a moderate rate of production growth, a relatively high
unemployment rate and a moderate rate of inflation. The rate of growth of
production and prices were higher in the sixties, whereas unemployment
was lower and the capital shortage has been replaced by a capital surplus.
The seventies again show a lower production growth, higher unemployment, a capital shortage, but now also a higher rate of inflation (see table
2.1). These developments are also clearly demonstrated by figure 2.1 in
which the percentage of registered unemployment is shown together with
the degree of unused capacity of enterprises. As the fluctuations of the latter
are much more pronounced than those of the former – the ratio of their
standard deviations over the period is about 2:4 – the scales are adapted
accordingly. One percent of unemployment corresponds to 2.4 percent of
unused capacity.

Table 2.1. Key data for the Dutch economy 1951-1977

	1951-'60	1961-'70	1971-'77
		annual averages	
Growth rate of production capacity	4.4%	5.6%	3.9%
Growth rate of production of enterprises	4.6%	6.0%	3.2%
Rate of change of consumer price	3.1%	4.1%	9.0%
Balance of payments on current account as % of NNP	2.6%	0 %	2.4%
Utilization rate of labour	97.4	98.6	96.3
Utilization rate of production capacity	95.5	96.2	96.4

Figure 2.1 Unused production capacity (right scale) and unemployment rate (left scale)

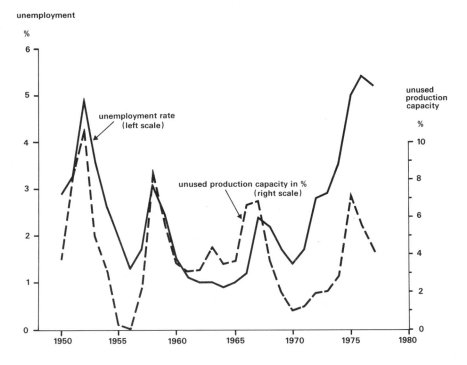

2.2 Expenditures

In this section the main components of national expenditure will be described, viz. private consumption, private investment, autonomous expenditure and exports.

From the seventh line of table 2.2 it can be seen that the volume of consumption increased rather rapidly during the whole period. The increase in the rate of growth from the first period to the second reflects not only the increased rate of growth of disposable income (= total income inclusive of income transfers but net of taxes, and of premiums paid to social security-, pension- and life insurance funds), but also the increasing share of labour income in it[3].

During the seventies and particularly during the recent recession the growth rate was maintained at a relatively high level as the gross labour income continued to rise considerably and the net transfers from social security funds were high.

2.2.1 Private consumption

Table 2.2 Net disposable income and consumption

	1953/62	1963/70	1971/77	1971	1972	1973	1974	1975	1976	1977
Net disposable income										
(1) From labour (in bill. gld.)	15.97	40.48	102.28	67.54	76.02	85.81	98.78	115.12	129.39	143.31
(2) From other sources (in bill. gld.)	8.58	13.07	19.40	15.29	17.55	22.33	21.81	14.57	21.45	22.82
(3) Total	24.55	53.55	121.68	82.83	93.57	108.14	120.59	129.69	150.84	166.13
(4) (2) as % of (3)	34.9	24.4	15.9	18.5	18.8	20.6	18.1	11.2	14.2	13.7
(5) Private consumption (in bill. gld.)	20.99	46.32	109.15	73.19	82.21	93.29	105.45	120.74	136.78	152.36
(6) (5) as % of (3)	85.4	86.5	89.7	88.4	87.9	86.3	87.4	93.1	90.7	91.7
(7) Annual growth rate of the volume of consumption (in %)	4.1	6.4	3.5	3.0	3.2	3.9	2.7	3.4	3.8	4.3
(8) National savings rate	19.5	19.5	18.4	19.7	20.2	21.9	20.5	15.2	16.1	15.1

The shift in the distribution of disposable income between labour and other income is very marked. It explains the increasing part of disposable income spent on consumption as the marginal savings rates of the two categories are very different (5-10 percent for the former and 70-80 percent for the latter, if it is diminished by a 'substance' allowance based on the number of independants and as average imputed allowance per capita equal to the average labour income).

The complements with respect to 100 of the figures on line (6) of table 2.2 obviously represent the savings rates from the net disposable income. The decline in recent years is in agreement with the development of investments during the same period, as these are to a large extent financed from these savings (together with depreciation funds).

However, the figures do not represent total national savings. Considerable contributions are also provided by the so called institutional savings funds (social security-, pension- and life insurance funds). Moreover, savings arise out of the budgets of the public authorities (government and lower authorities). A considerable part of their investments are financed out of surplusses on current account. Therefore, table 2.2 also mentions the total national savings rate. It shows a decline similar to the one mentioned above.

2.2.2 Private investment

Table 2.3 Private investment, labour productivity and relative factor prices

	1953/62	1963/70	1971/77	1971	1972	1973	1974	1975	1976	1977
(1) Volume of investment in equipment and transportation (average percentage change)	10.7	7	1.5	− 2.8	− 7.4	9.4	7.3	− 7.6	− 1.1	9.7
(2) Volume of investment in non-residential construction (average percentage change)	6.5	9	− 0.9	− 2.3	− 10.3	4.5	− 6.6	− 7.5	1.3	14.4
(3) Sum of (1) and (2)	9.2	7.5	1.3	0.8	− 8.9	10.7	− 0.3	− 7.5	− 3.7	15.5
(4) Private investment in % of production of enterprises	21.7	23.4	21	23.9	22.2	22.1	20.8	19.6	17.9	20.5
(5) Labour productivity (%)	3.9	5.3	4.0	4.2	5.0	6.5	4.0	− 0.4	5.4	3.0
(6) Private investment in 1970 gld. per unit of labour in enterprises	215	345	439	437	407	454	453	424	414	481
(7) Idem., percentage change	7.8	6.5	1.8	0.5	− 6.9	11.6	− 0.2	− 6.4	− 2.4	16.2
(8) Ratio of wage rate to user cost of capital (index 1970 = 100)	52	70	131	106	112	121	130	139	149	159
(9) Share of non wage income in value added	28	20.4	11.3	14.2	14.9	15.0	12.1	6.2	8.3	8.6

At present 75 percent of private investment consists of investment in equipment and transportation, whereas in the beginning of the period considered it had been about two thirds. Especially after 1970 the ratio of non-residential construction to investment in equipment has decreased, the main reason being the fall in construction for health care and the shift from building intensive to building extensive industries. The growth of demand for goods and services, in which exports played an important role, was the main stimulus behind investment in equipment and transportation. Moreover, especially in the second and the third period the user cost of capital (reduced by special tax facilities) in comparison with strongly rising wages, stimulated investment in a labour saving direction. This is reflected in the acceleration of investment per worker and the growth of labour productivity. The reduction in the growth rate of investment after 1970 is partly the consequence of the slower expansion of production. But in addition the low level of profitability and the low degree of capacity utilization were responsible for a decline of the investment ratio.

2.2.3 Autonomous expenditure

Table 2.4 Volume of autonomous expenditure

	1953/63	1963/70	1971/77	1971	1972	1973	1974	1975	1976	1977
			average percentage change							
government consumption of goods and services	6.0	6.1	3.2	3.7	− 1.9	− 1.4	2.6	8.3	5.6	5.3
gross government investment	10.2	6.5	− 2.3	4.8	− 9.3	− 8.8	− 0.8	7.7	− 1.9	− 7.5
investment in dwellings	4.7	9.1	3.4	8.7	14.7	2.0	− 12.5	− 7.5	2.5	15.9
total	6.5	7.0	1.5	5.9	1.9	− 2.1	− 4.9	1.8	2.3	5.6

These expenditures are entirely or largely under control of the government. There is a significant fall in growth after 1970. Important herein is the slowing down of residential construction as a consequence of equilibrating tendencies in the housing market, which had been characterized by a quantitative shortage of houses in the first and the second period. The development is also reflected in government investment which is largely complementary to investment in housing. Furthermore, the figures reflect the diminished elbow room of the government in real terms because of the decline in the rate of growth of production and the decrease of the profit share in output.

2.2.4 Exports

The Netherlands is a very open country, heavily depending on foreign trade. The value of exports of goods and services amounts to about 45-50 percent of the G.N.P. (in market prices). During the period 1953-1962 the percentage was equal to 47.9, during the next 10 years it was slightly less, 45.6. During 1974 and 1975 it even rose above 50, partly due to the export of natural gas which increased in volume as well as price. Apart from the last 4 or 5 years foreign trade prices have risen much less than the internal price level and, hence, the volume of exports (and of imports) increased much more than that of the G.N.P. From 1950 until 1974 when this volume reached a peak it nearly increased tenfold! Therefore, an increasing part of the volume of the national product had to be exported to pay for the imports but this unfavourable development was balanced by the fact that import prices almost rose pari passu with those of the exports. Nevertheless, it will be clear that the country's economy is rather sensitive to changes in the terms of trade.

The very strong growth of exports closely follows the developments of world trade which in turn was caused by the economic development during the post-war period supported by the trade liberalisation of the fifties and the establishment of the Common Market in 1957, to mention the most import factors. This is illustrated by table 2.5.

Table 2.5 Development of the Netherlands' export in relation to prices

		average percentage change		
		1953/62	1963/70	1971/77
(1)	Volume of world imports	7.9	9.6	6.9
(2)	Volume of Dutch exports	8.3	9.6	6.7
(3)	(2) minus (1)	0.4	0	− 0.2
(4)	Competing export prices (in guilders)	− 0.7	1.9	5.8
(5)	Dutch exports prices (in guilders)	− 1	1.7	7.4
(6)	(5) minus (4)	− 0.3	− 0.2	1.6
(7)	Appreciation of the guilder with respect to $ (in %)	0.6	0	5.8

The volume of world imports in this table is measured by an index computed by the Central Planning Bureau and derived from the volumes of imports of the most important sales markets weighted with their shares in Dutch exports. The index of competing export prices is computed by the same Bureau and is a correspondingly weighted index of the export price indices of the most important competing countries.

During the first period the Netherlands' exports took the lead because of the fact that their prices declined more than those of their competitors, notwithstanding a revaluation of the guilder by 5 percent in 1961. During the second period volumes and prices almost rose at the same rate. The same conclusion holds for the third period, although in the beginning a deterioration of the competitive position took place. Although there has been a considerable appreciation of the guilder resulting from the favourable balance of payments position connected with the exports of natural gas, the growth of unit wage costs in domestic currency slowed down. It is therefore a striking development that Netherlands' export growth after 1975 cannot keep up with the growth of world trade. Some preliminary studies by the Central Planning Bureau seem to point to a maladjustment of Dutch production capacity to World demand. Moreover Dutch exports are relatively energy intensive which has given rise to difficulties.

Shifts in exports did not only occur with respect to commodities. There is also an important shift between services and goods. In the fifties the share of the former was about 25 percent, during the sixties it gradually declined to some 20 percent whereas at present it is of the order of 16 to 17 percent. The relative deterioration of the position of shipping and the deterioration in the balance of tourism are the main factors behind this development.

To complete the description of the national expenditures a few words may be added on imports. From the fact that the balance of payments on current account showed only relatively moderate fluctuations it can already be inferred that imports rose more or less *pari passu* to exports. Nevertheless it is interesting to observe that the ratio of imports of goods and services to production of enterprises rose considerably during the period under consideration. More particularly the Central Planning Bureau has observed a sharp increase in the marginal import quote of consumption goods (cars, oil, alcohol, tourism).

2.3 Production structure

The development of expenditure is also reflected in the composition of the total product. They are clearly shown in table 2.6. Manufacturing production in particular showed the strongest and almost equal increases in the first two periods. But within manufacturing widely diverging trends can be observed. The weaker industries, such as textiles, clothing, shoes and paper, subject to heavy foreign competition, lag behind or even show a decline. They were also very seriously hit by the 1975 depression.

The chemical industry on the other hand increased its growth rate, which was already rather high, still more during the second period, although after 1973 a much weaker development has taken place.

A really spectacular development is shown by the mining industry. Coal mining was subject to a rapidly increasing decline during the whole period and was entirely closed down in the course of 1974. This process has no doubt been accelerated by the discovery during the second half of the fifties of very large deposits of natural gas in the Northern province of Groningen which shortly afterwards started to supply considerable quantities of cheap

Table 2.6 Gross value added by sectors in volume (average annual percentage change)

	1953/63	1963/73	1973/77
Agriculture	2.9	3.6	1.7
Food – animal products	5.1	3.9	0.9
– other products	3.2	3.5	1.6
Beverages and tobacco	6.2	7.6	4.4
Textiles	3.3	0.8	− 4.5
Clothing and shoes	3.1	− 3.4	− 8.7
Paper	8.6	5.7	4.1
Chemicals	9.6	13.5	2.6
Petroleum refineries	10.8	9	− 3.0
Basic metal industry	10.2	9.3	− 2.6
Metal products and machinery	6.6	5.5	1.4
Electrotechnical industry	14.0	7.9	2.1
Transport equipment	3.1	4.4	− 2.1
Other industries	6.4	4.2	− 0.7
Manufacturing	6.1	5.9	0.8
Coal mining	− 0.1	− 17.3	⎫
Other mining (natural gas)	8.8	26.5	⎬ 5.7
Public utilities	8.8	12.3	3.7
Manufacturing, mining and public utilities	5.9	6.5	1.3
Construction	2.4	2.9	− 0.7
Trade	6.4	5.5	4.2
		.5	
Exploitation of dwellings	2.5	3.1	2.6
Shipping and aviation	3.3	4.2	1.5
Other transport	6.0	5.6	3.2
Other services	3.5	4.9	6.3
Services	4.7	5.1	3.6
Enterprises	4.7	5.9	2.2

energy. The size of this development which has reached its peak recently and which now supplies about 50 percent of the total home consumption of energy can clearly be seen from the table. This source of energy has had an important impact on the economic development since the early sixties and its effects will still be met with at various places in this paper and it is fully discussed in Chapter Four of this volume. However, it should be added that it was not the only reason to stop coal mining. The geological structure of the Netherlands' coal deposits are very unfavourable compared to those in other countries and it seems improbable that the activity will be taken up again in future even if energy prices rise still more and the gas deposits become depleted, unless entirely new technologies become available.

The rate of increase of the production in the building industry was moderate throughout the whole period, but still some 20 percent higher during the second period compared with the first. This is largely due to the development in the construction of dwellings. During the war a large number of dwellings have been destroyed whereas production was virtually nil. For a considerable part of the post-war period the construction of dwellings had to compete with other urgent building activities and, therefore, during these years building was subject to a system of permits, the only type of rationing remaining in force after the reconstruction period. At the same time government developed exclusive programs of subsidies to restrict the effect of rising building costs, whereas rents were and still are under control. As the population increased rather rapidly (1.3 percent p.a. during the fifties) and the size of families continuously tended to decrease it was very difficult to reduce the gap between demand for and supply of dwellings. Therefore, in 1963/'64 a sort of 'crash' building program was initiated which increased the level of production of dwellings in a few years by some 50 percent whereas the share of non-subsidised construction also went up considerably. Due to this upsurge and also as a consequence of a declining rate of growth of the population (0.85 percent during 1973/75) the quantitative shortage has now largely been covered. But as the depression also led to a reduction in the rate of industrial building, the government now strongly supports a program of qualitative improvement of the existing stock of dwellings. This renovation programme was intensified during the second part of the seventies. Nevertheless the building industry could not maintain its growth rate during these years.

The heavy volume of house building since 1963 undoubtedly has had a very positive result as it led to the solution of an urgent social problem. But, undoubtedly, it also reinforced the inflationary pressure. During the whole period the price of the output of the building industry rose more than the average. For the period 1963-1973 for example the figure was 7.2 percent per annum as compared to 5.4 percent for all enterprises.

Finally, as in many other countries, services increased considerably during the whole period, although their growth rate is normally lower than in the manufacturing industries. On the other hand it was one of the few sectors which even maintained growth during the seventies. The share of services in total production is thus constantly increasing, as well as their share in employment.

2.4 Wages, prices and labour productivity

In table 2.7 a few characteristics referring to the development of prices, wages and related data are brought together. From these data it is clear that there is a marked difference before and after 1963. After this year prices and wages rose considerably more than before. After 1975 the wage-price development weakened considerably due to the appreciation of the guilder.

Table 2.7 Wages, prices, disposable income and labour productivity

		1953/ 62	1963/ 70	1971/ 77	1971	1972	1973	1974	1975	1976	1977
(1)	Wage rate %	7.2	11.7	12.6	13.1	12.6	15.6	15.7	12.8	11.0	7.8
(2)	Consumer price index %	2.8	4.6	9.1	8.3	8.8	9.3	10.1	10.7	9.2	6.8
(3)	Real wages: (1)-(2)%	4.4	7.1	3.5	4.8	3.8	6.3	5.6	2.1	1.7	1
(4)	Real disposable income Labour productivity %	3.5	5.0	2.2	2.0	2.9	0.9	2.7	3.8	0.9	2.4
(5)	Labour productivity in manufacturing %	5.0	6.9	5.0	4.9	6.6	9.0	3.3	− 3.8	11.6	3.5
(6)	in all enterprises %	3.9	5.3	4.0	4.2	5.0	6.5	4.0	− 0.4	5.4	3.0
(7)	'Wage-earners share' corrected for natural gas, public utility and rents.	72.0	79.6	88.7	85.8	85.1	85.0	87.9	93.8	91.7	91.4

(1)-(6): average annual percentage change
(4)   : referring to a married worker with two children and an income just below the lowest premium-income level of the social security system (cf. section 1.5)
(7)   : share of labour income (increased by labour income imputed to independents) in the net national income (cf. the text).

An interesting conclusion to be drawn from table 2.7 is that until 1971 real wages rose almost as fast as labour productivity in the manufacturing industries. During the last years of the boom period they lagged behind but as the depression set in and productivity slowed down and even declined, real wages increased again so that during these years as a whole real wages surpassed productivity. But the means available for distriburtion are largely determined by the rate of growth of total productivity and this quantity increased considerably less (the difference being of the order of 1 - 1.5 percent per annum). Therefore it will be clear that the share of labour in total income gradually went up. This is a phenomenon which can be observed in many other countries, but, particularly, in 1975 when total productivity declined whilst real wages still went up, the labour share in income reached an unprecedentedly high level.

The concept 'wage-earners share' has been introduced in the early fifties by the Social Economic Council as a tool in the Netherlands' income policy which will be described in some detail in Section 2.4. It is defined as total labour income, increased by labour income imputed to independants on the basis of an average income equal to that of employees, divided by the net national income. The concept defined in this way does not give a sufficiently clear picture of the shift of the income distribution in the private sector.

In recent years, a correction has been introduced by deducting from the numerator and from the denominator of the fraction the following three sectors. The production of natural gas (as it hardly employs labour and as its profits to a very large extent run into the treasury), public utilities (as they are all publicly owned in the Netherlands) and the exploitation of dwellings. The corrected share is shown in table 2.7.

As a consequence of the surge of the wage-earners' share the rate of return on private capital declined and the means available for private investments were affected. Now investments are not entirely determined by this factor but also by expectations, which at present are also rather gloomy, and by the initial degree of capacity utilization but, nevertheless, it contributed to the decline in the rate of investment.

Another interesting conclusion to be drawn of the table is the gap between the increase of the level of real wages and of real disposable income. Strictly speaking the two series of figures in table 2.7 do not refer to the same groups (all employees versus the modal worker defined at the bottom of the table). However, the differences are very real. They reflect the impact of the strong development of the social security system (cf. section 2.6), the ensuing rise of the premiums to be paid and also the (less important) effect of the increasing direct taxes.

There are substantial differences between the price developments of the different sectors of the economy. This is illustrated by table 2.8 for the four main categories: agriculture, manufacturing industries, building and services (mining has been excluded). It shows that the wage changes do not show very important differences. This is largely due to the system of solidaristic wage formation which will be described in section 2.8.2. There are, however, very considerable differences between the growth rates of labour productivity.

Table 2.8 Prices, wages, labour productivity and labour costs per unit of product for four sectors (average annual increases in %)

	Wage rate			Labour productivity			Labour costs per unit of product			Producer price		
	1953 /62	1963 /70	1971 /75	1953 /62	1963 /70	1971 /75	1953 /62	1963 /70	1971 /75	1953 /62	1963 /70	1971 /75
Agriculture	6.8	8.0	12.0	7.1	8.5	5.6	− 0.3	− 1.5	6.4	2.1	3.4	5.7
Manufacturing industries	7.6	11.7	14.5	4.8	8.0	3.4	2.8	3.7	11.1	0.8	2.3	7.3
Construction	6.1	12.4	13.9	0.4	2.9	1.2	5.7	9.5	12.7	4.9	6.5	12.0
Services	6.5	11.3	14.3	2.5	2.0	1.9	4.0	9.3	12.4	3.2	5.9	9.7
Total	7.2	11.7	14.0	3.9	5.3	3.7	3.3	6.4	10.3	2.3	4.3	8.6

They are highest in agriculture and in the manufacturing industries, much lower in the service sector and almost negligeable in construction. It is well known that the possiblilities of improving labour productivity in the service sector are less extensive than in agriculture and in manufacturing. (See also Driehuis and de Wolff, 1976). The overall increase in labour productivity from the first to the second period is caused by the increased rate of growth of investments which already has been mentioned and which occurred in all four sectors.

The relatively small differences between the growth rates of wages and the important differences between those for labour productivity obviously lead to large deviations between the rates of growth of labour costs per unit of product. These in turn, largely determine the growth rates of prices per sector as can be seen by comparing the third and the fourth set of columns of table 2.8.

It can be seen that unit labour costs rose more rapidly than prices in both periods for all sectors apart from agriculture. This is in accordance with the fact that the wage-earners' share in the first three sectors on the average rose throughout the whole bidecennial period, whereas it declined in agriculture.

Finally, table 2.9 gives some information about the development of import prices and other domestic prices.

Table 2.9 Foreign trade prices and internal prices of investment goods
(average annual increases in %)

	1953	1963	1971	1971	1972	1973	1974	1975	1976	1977
Import prices of:										
raw materials and semi-										
finished products	− 0.8	1.2	8.9	5.0	− 3.2	9.8	46.3*	2.0	7.0	1.9
investment goods	2.0	2.3	7.2	7.4	5.5	5.2	8.6	13.6	8.0	1.9
consumption goods	− 0.7	1.4	4.6	3.0	0.7	3.8	9.3	4.2	4.1	7.7
Total	− 0.3	1.4	8.5	4.4	− 0.7	7.6	34.9	4.1	6.4	2.9
Export prices	− 1.0	1.3	7.4	2.4	0.7	6.5	28.3	4.7	6.2	3.1
Internal price level of										
gross investment in fixed assets										
of enterpr. excl. of dwellings	2.6	3.6	7.2	8.3	5.0	3.1	10.3	11.1	7.7	5.2
Dwellings	4.6	6.7	10.8	13.2	10.5	10.8	12.3	10.0	9.5	9.5
Total	3.4	4.3	8.2	9.3	6.1	5.7	10.9	10.8	8.3	6.6

* of which 74% (34.2 points) due to the increase of oil prices.

Until the end of the sixties the level of raw material prices did not change very much. From 1953 to 1968 it actually fell by some 9 percent and in 1970 it was only 7 percent above the 1953 level.

The share of imports of raw materials and semi-finished products in total imports is very high. In 1953 it was 65.8 percent and it gradually declined to 57.6 in 1973 mainly due to an increasing share of the imports of consumption goods, which rose from 9.2 to 14.8 percent in the same period (the share of investment goods varied between 9 and 10 percent, the remainder is formed by services and income transfers). But in spite of this high share (about 30 percent of G.N.P. throughout the whole period) the net effect of import prices on the internal price level is rather small. This picture changed very markedly after 1968 due to the strong rise of raw material prices, heavily reinforced in 1974 by the trebling of the oil prices. The effects of these developments are discussed more in detail in section 2.8.2 in connection with a description of the wage- and price policy.

It is also clear from table 2.9 that export prices for most of the period moved *pari passu* with import prices and until 1972 these movements were very moderate compared to the rates of changes of the internal prices. However, in 1974, the terms of trade deteriorated very sharply, about 5.5 percent, as export prices could not keep up with the surge of import prices.

Finally, the table shows the development of two very important investment prices, for dwellings and for fixed assets of enterprises (incl. of buildings). The strong rise of the cost of house building, largely due to the low increase in productivity and its sheltered character has already been mentioned in section

The investment in fixed assets of enterprises also contain an important building component, but also makes up a large share of imported goods as a considerable part of equipment comes from abroad. Therefore, its price level rises much less fast than that of the construction of dwellings. Apart from the last two years mentioned in the table this rise even stays below the increase of consumer price.

2.5 The public sector

The public sector of the Netherlands consists of the central government, the provinces, the municipalities and the polder boards. From an economic point of view only the first and the third are important. The expenditures of the other two are very modest. The municipalities also derive their income largely from the central government, partly from a fixed share in the government tax income, partly from subsidies for special purposes. Their own tax income amounts to only some 2 percent of the taxes collected by the central government. In addition to this they receive income from property, public utilities, etc. but at present about 80 percent of their total income comes from governmental transfers. Recently steps have been taken to make the municipalities more independent through an extension of their own tax domain, but the changes so far are not very important.

The expenditures of the total public sector are financed from taxes, earned income and loans. But as far as loans are concerned the municipalities are rather restricted in their possibilities. During the first years after the war they were subject to interest limits imposed by the government. However, this did not prevent a heavy financing of investments with short term loans in 1956 and 1957 when, during a boom period and due to a considerable deficit on the balance of payments, the capital market became very tight and the long-term interest level rose considerably from 3.3 percent to 5.4 percent (which was very high at the time).

The ensuing increase in national liquidity and the inflationary pressure resulting from the boom (which rapidly disappeared due to restrictive policies in 1958) led to a stronger central control on the municipalities through an act passed in 1963. It set an upper limit to the size of their floating debt (25 percent of the normal income of each separately) and it authorized the central government to restrict the total amount of long term loans to be taken up by the municipalities in a given year, if the situation on the capital market made such a step desirable. In very tight situations the government may even completely deny their access to this market. So far this has not happened. But restrictions have been introduced several times and during such periods the Society of the Netherlands' Municipalities is authorized to raise the amount allowed and to distribute it among its members.

During the post-war period the tax-rate, measured by total tax income as a percentage of the net national income, declined from around 30 in the early fifties to a minimum of 23 in 1955 largely due to tariff reductions. From this year onwards it steadily rose to about 32 percent in 1975 because of the continuously growing requirements put to the public sector. Nevertheless, the increase is still modest compared to the development of the social security system which can be considered as part of the public sector in a wider sense and which will be dealt with in a separate section (cf. section 2.6).

The direct expenditures of the public sector (again in the narrow sense) defined as the total net of credits granted (e.g. to house-building), expenditures for participation and debt redemption, show a somewhat different picture. Again as a percentage of the net national income their share fluctuated between 27 and 30 percent until 1966. From then onwards it gradually rose to about 35 percent in 1974 and leaped to 38.2 percent in 1975 as a

Table 2.10 Development of the volume of certain State expenditures (1955 = 100)

Category	1955	1960	1965	1970	1975	share in the 1977-budget (%)
General administration	100	100	130	130	150	8.4
Defense	100	85	90	95	85	11.2
Foreign relations (incl. of foreign aid)	100	120	105	230	520	3.4
Commerce and trade	100	75	195	210	370	2.6
Education, science, culture and recreation	100	195	280	380	465	26.8
Social provisions, health and environmental protection	100	65	80	105	235	22.8
Housing and physical planning	100	310	390	395	555	7.9
Total	100	107	134	174	230	83.1*
Net national income in real terms	100	120	155	205	224	

* Due to incompleteness the figures in this column do not add up too 100 per cent.

consequence of the extensive programmes intended to cope with the high rate of unemployment caused by the recent depression.

Behind these developments are hidden much larger shifts in the expenditures according to function as can be seen from table 2.10 referring to the volume of *some* important expenditures of the central government.

The figures only give a crude indication of the differing trends as it is difficult to compute accurate volume data for the complex aggregates represented in table 2.10. Nevertheless, it shows that for a considerable part of the period the volume of the state expenditures rose less fast than real national income. Only in recent years the relation has been slightly reversed, largely due to the expenditures for social security, etc.

However, there is a considerable difference with respect to the develop-

Table 2.11 Growth rates of the deflator of state expenditure and of the price level of the products of enterprises (average annual increases in %)

	1955/1960	1960/1965	1965/1970	1970/1973	1973/1977
Deflator	4.1	7.7	7.1	10.8	11.0
Price level	2.8	3.9	4.5	7.9	8.7

Finally, table 2.12 gives some information on the development of the output of the whole public sector.

Table 2.12 Volume of consumption and investments of the public sector (index 1955 = 100)

	1955	1960	1965	1970	1975	1977
Consumption						
Wages and salaries	100	106	114	131	147	157
Material consumption	100	98	148	187	193	215
Gross investment	100	134	199	259	221	201
Total	100	108	132	159	166	174
Gross national product	100	121	154	201	232	249

ment in value. The share of wages in government expenditures is higher than in the production of enterprises. Moreover, in the Netherlands' national accounting system the convention has been adopted to measure the output of the public sector by its imputs and, hence, productivity increases, if any, have been neglected. Therefore, the growth rate of the deflator of the state expenditures (net of debt redemption) is considerably higher than that of the product of enterprises as is shown above (see Table 2.11).

2.6 The social security system

In many countries during the post-war period the social security system has been rapidly expanded. Among these the Netherlands rank very highly, if not highest of all. Several important extensions have been introduced and at present a considerable part of the national income is spent on the provisions supplied by the system. It is based on a set of separate laws each regulating a special aspect of the total field. Some of these laws refer to the population as a whole as e.g. laws concerning the insurance of a basic old age pension, the allowances for widows and orphans and the one against incapacity to work. Others have a bearing only on employees as for example the insurance against unemployment, against loss of income due to labour accidents, sickness and against the cost of medical treatment. The system is rather complicated but a few general principles can easily be explained.

For the execution of each law a special fund has been set up fed by premiums and from which payments are made to the persons entitled to receive benefits. For the first group the premiums are levied on the taxable income, for the second group on the wages or salaries earned. In the latter case the premiums are partly paid by the employer and partly by the employee. But from a macro-economic point of view this distinction is not very important as both categories form part of the total labour costs. Finally, in recent years the treasury, at an increasing rate, has been contributing to some of the funds.

Up to a certain 'premium-income limit' the premiums are a constant percentage of the taxable income (or the wages and salaries earned). Above these limits, which are slightly different for different laws, the premiums remain constant in amount. These limits are regularly adapted to the development of the nominal incomes. About 80 percent of all employees (in the private and public sectors together) earn incomes below these limits.

The benefits of the first group are 'geared to prosperity', i.e. they are following the movements of the general index of contracted wages, but in addition to this from time to time other improvements have been introduced. The basic old-age pension has been increased almost tenfold since its introduction in 1953.

The benefits of the second group, as far as income-substituting payments are concerned, are equal to a certain percentage (80 percent) of the wages or salaries actually earned, again subject to certain upper limits.

As a matter of principle the funds have to balance income and expenditures. Due to developments already described and also as a consequence of the soaring costs of medical treatment premiums have risen very heavily. Table 2.13 gives an impression of this development.

Table 2.13 Social security premiums (as a percentage of the income liable to premium payments)

	1953	1963	1973	1974	1975	1976	1977
Insurance for Unemployment	3.9	1.6	1.6	1.6	1.6	1.8	1.6
Accidents, sickness and incapacity to work	5.1	7.7	15.2	16.0	17.3	19.1	18.3
Cost of medical treatment	4.0	4.6	11.5	12.2	11.9	11.7	10.9
Old age pension and allowances to widows and orphans	–	8.1	12.	1.2	11.9	11.9	11.9
Family allowance	5.5	4.9	5.2	5.7	4.7	3.4	3.3
Total	18.5	26.9	45.5	47.7	47.4	47.8	45.9

The figures in table 2.13 obviously do not allow comparison of the total amount of premiums with net national income. This information is given in table 2.14. In 1975 more than 20 percent of the national income was spent on premiums. The table also shows that the total share of the collective sector at present is already well above 50 percent.

Table 2.14 Share of the collective sector in the net national income

	1953	1963	1973	1974	1975	1976	1977
Social security premiums	5.2	10.9	18.3	19.4	20.3	19.9	19.7
Taxes	26.3	25.2	29.8	30.4	30.6	31.1	31.6
Total	31.5	36.1	48.1	49.8	50.9	51.0	51.3

Finallly, table 2.15 indicates the size of the various contributions to the income of the funds as a whole.

Table 2.15 Sources of income of social security funds (mill. of glds)

	1953	1963	1973	1974	1975	1976	1977
Premiums paid by employers (incl. of government)	1131 (85.9)	2212 (39.7)	12720 (41.7)	15246 (41.7)	17244 (40.1)	18910 (38.1)	20510 (38.5)
Premiums paid by employers		2963 (53.2)	15612 (51.2)	18723 (51.2)	21319 (49.5)	24170 (48.6)	26330 (49.4)
Government subsidies	137 (10.4)	259 (4.6)	1805 (5.9)	1922 (5.4)	3833 (8.9)	5850 (11.8)	5730 (10.8)
Interest earned	48 (3.7)	140 (2.5)	378 (1.2)	597 (1.7)	634 (1.5)	730 (1.5)	710 (1.3)
Total	1316 (100)	5574 (100)	30515 (100)	36558 (100)	43030 (100)	49660 (100)	53280 (100)
In % of net national income	6.8	13.1	22.1	23.3	25.5	25.4	25.1

It will be clear that the strong increase of the size of the collective sector, in particular of the contributions to security have had a considerable impact on the economic development and especially on inflation. There has been a continuous effort by both wage earners and employers to pass the increasing collective burden on to each other.

2.7 The labour market

For a long period the Netherlands' population has been increasing rapidly. This development continued for many years after the war. During 1948/-1967 the increase was about 1.2 percent p.a. Afterwards the growth rate went down and averaged 0.8 percent for 1967/1975. The economically active population showed a different pattern. The corresponding figures are 1.0 percent and again 0.8 percent. Consequently, the share of the active population decreased slightly from 38 percent to 36.6 percent. This difference is partly due to changes in the age distribution of the population. The share of the economically active population as a percentage of the age group 15-64 remains at 60 percent during the larger part of the first period and went down to 58 percent afterwards. But there have also been considerable changes in the participation coefficients of the various groups. For men from 15-64 the coefficient declined from about 80 percent around 1950 to about 72 percent at present, largely due to increased scholarity and lowering of the age of retirement. For unmarried women the corresponding percentage rose from around 45 to 48 percent during the sixties to decline to about 40 percent at present. The coefficient for married women on the contrary, traditionally low in comparison with most other Western European countries, rose from some 7 percent to 12 percent. Nevertheless, the total share of 36,6 percent is much lower than in most other countries.

There have also been important migratory movements. After the independance of Indonesia in 1948 a considerable number of Dutchmen repatriated. Recently, a similar movement took place when a sizeable stream of the native population of Surinam decided to migrate to the Netherlands before the planned independance of their country would become effective.

The first wave of immigrants was more than compensated by the emigration of Dutchmen which wanted to try their fortune abroad. This movement was strongly promoted through financial and other support by the government which at that time feared that in the long run it would be difficult to create employment for the increasing population.

The second wave of immigrants was reinforced by the arrival of foreign workers which started already in the sixties due to the tight labour market during the first part of this period.

The net effect of all these developments on the labour market led to an outflow of some 15.000 workers p.a. around 1950. It decreased rather smoothly, changed sign in 1962 and from thereon increased again to 12,000 at present. As a percentage of the labour force it changed from about − 4 percent p.a. to + 2.4 percent p.a.

The composition of the labour force has also undergone considerable changes. The public sector decreased until 1951 mainly due to the gradual abolition of rationing schemes and other economic controls which had been introduced during the reconstruction period. The sectoral composition of employment is shown in table 2.16. From that year onwards a steady growth of about 2.2 percent per annum set in, resulting in a share in the active population which rose from 9.7 percent in 1951 to 14.3 percent in 1977. It reflects the growing importance of the public sector which has already been described in section 2.5. Employment in the private sector was affected by three rather mild recessions which had their troughs in 1952, 1958 and 1967, respectively as an aftermath of the restrictive policy following the Korean war, after the overspending period in the second half of the fifties and the ensuing restrictive measures and, finally, as a consequence of the dip in the growth rate of world trade in 1967. Unemployment rose to 4.8 percent in 1952, 3.0 percent in 1958 and in 1967, after a period of several years of high tension on the labour market, to 2.3 percent.

However, much more important than these cyclical movements is the medium-term development which is much more clearly illustrated by figure 2.2. It shows the registered unemployment together with its seven-years moving average. A period of 15 years of decreasing unemployment ending in a few years of extremely low rates (0.8 to 1 percent) in 1961-1963 was followed by a period of a rising number of unemployed which continued until 1977 and it is still at the high level of 5.2 percent. The phenomenon is still more serious than follows from the graph. In 1966 a law was passed according to which persons partly or wholly unable to perform a normal task could receive an allowance corresponding to their degree of incapacity and the normal pay of the job performed. Although intended to support a category of deprived persons the provisions of the law were also used to facilitate early retirements in economically weak enterprises and to dismiss a category of marginal workers hoarded during the preceding boom. A considerable fraction of the beneficiaries therefore, can be considered as disguised unemployment.

Table 2.16 The Labour Market (× 1000 man years)

	1951/1960	1961/1970	1971/1977	1971	1972	1973	1974	1975	1976	1977
1. Labour supply	4037	4541	4834	4793	4798	4802	4830	4862	4873	4880
2. Employment in:										
Agriculture	524 (13.2%)	386 (8.6%)	304 (6.5%)	320	315	309	304	299	295	289
Industry	1255 (31.7%)	1366 (30.4%)	1159 (24.8%*)	1248	1206	1186	1177	1137	1092	1066
Construction	347 (8.8%)	453 (10.1%)	458 (9.8%)	495	473	472	452	436	438	442
Services	1379 (34.8%)	1757 (39.1%)	2134 (45.6%*)	2077	2088	2111	2137	2154	2174	2197
Government	456 (11.5%)	527 (11.7%)	662 (13.3%)	584	601	607	617	630	650	668
Total	3958 (100%)	4489 (100%)	4678 100%)	4724	4683	4685	4687	4656	4649	4662
3. Persons on social employment projects and additional works	16	6	9	7	7	7	8	10	13	14
4. Unemployed	62	43	147	62	108	110	135	196	211	204

* In 1969 a change in the sectoral registration of employment has taken place. As a consequence employment in the manufacturing industry is lower than before and employment in the services sector higher.

Figure 2.2 Number of unemployed 1948-1979.

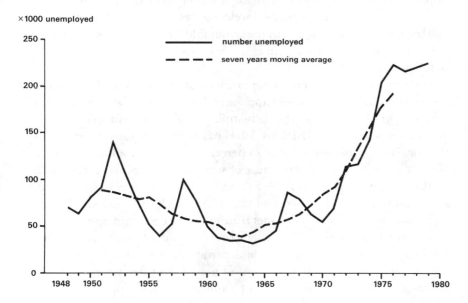

On the subject of employment, which declined after 1971, the following observations can be made. During the early fifties there was, as an aftermath of the war, a scarcity of capital resulting in a certain amount of unemployment due to a lack of sufficient jobs. Wages and prices were kept low, the rate of inflation was modest, resulting in a favourable export position. With a rising investment ratio sufficient capital was built up to increase productivity and at the same time to absorb the growing supply of labour. Unemployment declined and a scarcity of labour gradually developed (Cf. figure 2.1).

In the sixties and especially after the wage explosion of 1963, years of high wage and price increases followed. Due to the capital previously built up, productivity could increase considerably and this higher level was maintained through a strong increase in the level of investments. It was made possible by the prosperous period which followed. But it was also necessary as the increasing labour costs required strong increases in productivity in order to maintain the international competitive position. Investments, therefore, were largely of a capital deepening type and led to accelerated obsolescence of existing captital and, gradually, capital again became scarce. Interest rates rose to 10 percent and the amount of investments, in spite of its high level, was insufficient to absorb the supply of labour. Moreover, a sort of dual labour market developed. The high wage level made entrepreneurs reluctant to hire Dutch labour for unskilled jobs and foreign labour was imported although the trend of unemployment had started to rise. At first this increase was considered as a welcome relief to the strained labour market. Later on it was hidden by the favourable cyclical position of the years 1969-1970. But then it became clear that structural unemployment was building up.

Three types of structural unemployment can be distinguished. One is caused by imbalances between supply and demand in the labour market as reflected in the shift of the U(nemployed)-V(acancy) function (*search structuralism*). A study by Driehuis (1978) has shown that unemployment of this sort is responsible for about 25 percent of total unemployment in the Netherlands in 1975. A second cause of structural unemployment seems to be the shift in the composition of demand. As was shown in section 2.2, autonomous expenditure declined after 1970, which had a negative impact on private investment as well. Other reasons for the decline in private investment were given on p. 17. The unemployment caused by the continuous fall in autonomous expenditure and private investment, can be called *demand structuralism*. These expenditures are two to three times as labour intensive as private consumption or exports. A third type of structural unemployment can be called *cost structuralism*. The most important explanation behind this phenomenon, which seems mainly relevant for the manufacturing sector, is the increasing divergence between labour costs and capital costs, as a result of which, for a given rate of technical progress, it becomes more and more profitable to replace existing equipment by new equipment which uses less labour. Replacement of existing vintages of capital due to economic obsolescence is held to be responsible for a part of unemployment in the Netherlands, although it is extremely difficult to determine to what extent[4]. As a result of all this, potential employment has fallen below the potential labour force after 1970, a situation similar to the fifties, although then the low propensity to invest was mainly responsible, rather than an increasing discrepancy between labour and capital costs.

2.8 Economic policy

This section will start with a description of the goals of economic policy of the post-war period (section 2.8.1) followed by three sub-sections, consecutively dealing with wage and price policy (2.8.2), fiscal policy (2.8.3) and monetary policy (2.8.4).

2.8.1 Goals of economic policy

During the post-war period the goals of the Netherlands' economic policy have gradually changed their character. As has been said already in section 2.1, the policy in the second half of the forties and the first few years of the fifties was aiming at a rapid reconstruction. The government tried to maintain the inherited, rather low, level of real disposable income, to rebuild and extend the basic infrastructure, to stimulate private investments and exports and at the same time to restrict imports as much as possible, in order to improve the balance of payments on current account and to make the country independent from foreign aid and loans.

When this period came to an end in the early fifties, the Social Economic Council (a tri-partite advisory body to the Government, set up in 1950) formulated a set of five general goals for economic policy which were generally adopted and formed the basis for this policy at least until the end of the sixties. They were: full employment, economic growth, a reasonable income distribution, balance of payments equilibrium and price stability. Strictly speaking only the first three were goals in the proper sense of the word, the latter two are more to be considered as constraints. The formulation is rather vague and for some of the goals a more precise norm has been set, albeit that these norms did not remain unchanged over time.

In the definition of full employment allowance was made for a certain amount of frictional unemployment (of the order of 2 percent), but a target for the rate of economic growth has never been specified. It was assumed that steps should be taken to arrive at the highest rate consistent with the other goals. The income distribution again was formulated very imprecisely. Originally, it referred to the distribution of national income between wage earners and others based on a constant 'wage earners share' already mentioned above. In the sixties the international distribution was also taken into account as the decision was made to allocate part of the national income to foreign aid (the 1 percent-target). Still later the emphasis shifted from the distribution between the two broad categories to the income distribution within each of these two. Balance of payments equilibrium was defined as a surplus on current account large enough to enable the contracted repayments of foreign debt and to build up foreign currency reserves sufficiently large to act as a buffer in times of cyclical deficits. In later years when the foreign debt (at an accelerated rate) had been repaid provisions for foreign aid were included. A norm for price stability has never been set. It was assumed that a constant average price level would be most desirable but it was realised that it would be very difficult to obtain this goal and, hence, that here too the lowest possible increase consistent with the other targets and the external circumstances should be aimed at.

Not only did the interpretation of the goals change over time, in recent years the set was also extended. In the first place strong emphasis was put on anti-pollution measures, and more generally, an environment-consering policy is aimed at. Within a few years this goal got a high priority as the conviction rapidly spread that the country, in particular because of its high population density (1000 inh./sq. mile) was very vulnerable to the environmental hazards resulting from increasing economic activity. Other aims which gradually became more important were connected with various aspects of state care, such as education, health, etc. Finally, the 1973-oil crisis raised serious doubts about the possiblility of a continuation of the pattern of economic growth of the preceding years and nowadays more attention is given to the improvement of the quality of life in general within the framework of selective growth, viz. a development aiming at a more economic use of scarce resources (energy and raw materials).

Looking back at the past years one may conclude that with respect to the realisation of a number of goals considerble progress has been made. Economic growth has been very satisfactory leading to a strong rise in prosperity. The income distribution, particularly in the original sense, has not remained constant but shifted in favour of the wage earners. The balance of payments only occasionally did cause some difficulties. But it got high priority and correcting measures usually were rapidly and successfully applied. Even with respect to goals recently adopted already some progress has been made. Based on new legislation strong anti-pollution measures have been taken already leading to a clearly observable improvement of the quality of water and air. The efforts in the fields of education and public health have already been mentioned.

However, there are also less satisfactory results to be mentioned. Unemployment which for the greater part of the period under consideration remained very low, with only a few exceptions, recently rose considerably and not only, as has been explained, because of cyclical factors but also for structural reasons. It poses a challenging problem for future policy, particularly since in the years to come lower growth rates have to be reckoned with. If these expectations are to be fulfilled it will be extremely difficult to strike a satisfactory balance between the still growing demands on the public sector and the social security systems and even a modest target for an increasing real disposable income, especially since a return to greater price stability, which at present seems to be more remote than ever before, still has a high priority.

2.8.2 Wage and price policy

The difference between the different periods mentioned before cannot properly be understood without some reference to the Netherlands' incomes policy. This policy has extensively been discussed in the economic literature, also abroad (e.g. by Windmuller and De Galan (1977) and by Ulman and Flanagan (1971)). Since this subject is more fully dealt with in Chapter Three only the essential elements will be mentioned here.

The policy was introduced immediately after the war. It was already prepared during its latter part when former trade union officials and representatives of employers' organisations started secret deliberations on post-war reconstruction and prepared an organisation to ensure the smooth functioning of the labour market. The outcome was the bipartite Foundation of Labour, which was set up after the conclusion of peace. In it were represented the three main federations of trade unions and also the three employers' organisations. Its ideas agreed well with the policy of the government in exile during the war and soon after the liberation the so called 'Extra-ordinary Decree on Labour Relations' was passed in which the Foundation was recognized as an advisory body and far-reaching powers were assigned to the government to approve, reject, or modify wage contracts.

The executive power was entrusted to the Board of Mediators, an official body set up in 1923 to settle wage disputes but which now was charged with a much more important task. About one third of all industrial workers were organized at the time (it increased slightly since then and is now about 40 percent), but the continuation of prewar legislation gave the Board the power to declare a contract concluded between the parties in a certain branch binding for all workers belonging to it. The rates stipulated in the contract were binding too and it was illegal to pay wages deviating from them in either sense. In addition to the wage policy the Minister of Economic Affairs was authorized to introduce price controls.

This combined wage and price policy went through various phases of development.

i. 1945-1954
During this phase the system worked satisfactorily. The official policy was aiming at a redressing of the balance of payments on current account, which during the first years showed heavy deficits, and at promoting economic growth. Therefore, prices were kept low to stimulate exports. Only cost increases resulting from rising import prices could be passed on in prices

and profit margins had to be kept constant in absolute terms. Wages were raised by uniform 'wage rounds' envisaged to maintain the level of real wages. Deviations from this rule only occurred in order to reduce undesireable differentials (e.g. wages in agriculture were raised to the wage level of unskilled labour in industry).

The spirit of cooperation on which the system was based these years can be illustrated by its results during the Korea crisis. Its consequences strongly set back the improving economic situation. From 1949-1951 import prices rose by some 40 percent and the terms of trade deteriorated by more than 10 percent. As a result the cost of living rose by roughly the same percentage, whereas the balance of payments deteriorated heavily. In order to overcome the difficulties the trade union federations in 1951 agreed to a wage compensation of only 5 percent and, hence, deliberately accepted a reduction of real wages.

ii. 1954-1959

After the Korea crisis the economic situation improved very rapidly and a second phase began when the Social Economic Council recommended increasing the average nominal wage rate *pari passu* to the national income per economically active person. The 'wage-earners share' described before (section 2.4) was computed as a tool to check the realisation of this purpose. Price control remained very strict and wage increases could not be passed into prices (with exceptions for branches with very low rates of return) but had to be absorbed by increased labour productivity. A small amount of differentiation was allowed but usually in most branches wages were pushed upwards to the maximum envisaged.

Moreover, a certain amount of wage drift (1 to 2 percent p.a.) occurred (due to overtime, rank inflation and also to 'black wages' in excess of the rates negotiated) and from 1954-1957 the overall wage level rose about 7 percent per annum. This development was interrupted by the depressions of 1957/58. It was due to national overspending resulting in a balance of payments deficits during 1956 and 1957 and a (probably too strong) restrictive governmental reaction consisting of fiscal and monetary measures coupled with a moderate wage increase in 1958. Unemployment this year quickly rose to a peak of over 4 percent of the labour force. But as foreign demand continued to increase rapidly exports increased too and the depression did not last more than one year. Nevertheless, it still had a strong impact on wage negotiations in 1959, which resulted in an increase of only 2.4 percent.

iii. 1959-1963

The rules for price policy during the second period put a heavier burden on an industry the less its productivity could be increased. Industries unable to bear the charge of increasing wages were only allowed to pass them on provided the wage increases stayed considerably below the overall percentage adopted. This escape did not function very well. Moreover, it was felt that the rigidity of the system prevented prosperous branches from attracting sufficient labour for expansion. The Social Economic Council being asked advice on the matter was divided. But the government in which after 1959 the Labour party was no longer represented favoured the Council's majority voice recommending greater flexibility.

The basic idea of the new policy was to keep the nominal national wage still as much as possible in line with the average increase in labour productivity but to allow branches with a higher average increase in productivity to use about 50 percent of the difference for above average wage increases, whereas the remainder ought to lead to price reductions. In branches with below average productivity the situation should be the opposite. For several reasons the new policy did not work well. It proved very difficult to induce firms with favourable productivity increases to lower their prices. Many disputes resulted from the fact that reliable data on branch productivity trends were hard to obtain. Moreover, the government feared a too liberal interpretation of the rules which might lead to high price increases adversely affecting our competitive position. In the meantime a boom developed, registered unemployment during 1961-1963 fell to 1 percent. Moreover due to fierce trade-union pressure, weekly working hours in almost all branches were reduced from 48 to 44. In order to release the tension in the labour market and to reduce the effect of imported inflation government decided to follow the 1961 revaluation of the DM by 5 percent. These measures, which had a considerable effect on labour costs expressed in foreign currency, made the government still more reluctant to countenance wage increases. As a result the Board of Mediators had to interfere almost continuously in negotiations and many supplementary decrees were issued specifying general rules. It led to frustration but the effect on wage differentiation was very modest.

iv. 1963-1968

The year 1963 marked a turning point in the Netherlands' incomes policy. With hindsight it can now be said that during the preceding years a too cautious policy had been pursued as a result of which Dutch wage and price levels lagged far behind those of its main competitors. After the entry into the Common Market and in view of the prevailing boom conditions the gap could no longer be maintained. In the middle of 1963 the ship-repair yards refused to stick to the rules and decided to pay wages well above those agreed upon. This step caused strong unrest in the labour market, strikes broke out and the trade-union federations which up to that moment had lent support to the incomes policy reacted vigorously as they feared loosing their grip on the rank and file. In the negotiations for 1964 they claimed an overall increase of 10 percent. Peace was restored as this claim was accepted together with the introduction of a minimum wage for adult workers and an increase of the number of paid holidays by two. It was agreed that 5 percent of the wage increase could be passed on in prices, and, the price policy was again strongly reinforced. The final outcome was that in 1964 the general wage level rose by 15 percent and the cost of living by 6.8 percent.

After this episode the old situation could not be restored. Asked for advice the Social Economic Council recommended that it should draw up semi-annual reports on the economic situation with indications of the room available for wage increases bases on quantitative economic forecasts to be made by the Central Planning Bureau[5]. The Foundation of Labour should use the results as an outline for the wage negotiations in the various branches. This novelty starting the fourth phase of the incomes policy was highly unsuccessful. The parties concerned could not agree on quantitative norms for wage increases. Moreover, the Foundation found it difficult to object to negotiated contracts concluded among their member organistion. It was unable to play the role in former days performed by the Board of Mediators.

The central grip on the wage formation was further undermined by the gradual introduction of multi-annual contacts which even contained escalator clauses. Whilst this type of contracts went out of fashion around 1971, price-compensation clauses very soon became a standard component still in use at present. It will be clear that these developments made it rather difficult to check the wage-price spiral which started in 1963, in particular since similar developments occurred abroad which weakened fears for deteriorating the competitive position.

Finally, as a result of a growing desire to leave more room to the negotiating parties to settle their own contracts, in 1968, the Foundation refused to use its influence to moderate contracts and decided to approve them without further consideration. This step meant an almost complete abolition of the traditional wage policy.

v. 1968 until now

During this period the events in the field of incomes policy had a rather turbulent character. Whereas price policy, although varying in content, in general remained very strict, wage policy varied from almost complete freedom to strong governmental interference.

It would take too much space to present a detailed account of all relevant events and, therefore, only a few highlights will be mentioned which, at least in part, may serve to explain the development of wages and prices presented in tables 2.17 and 2.18.

The period as a whole is characterized by a growing polarisation of the social partners due to a complex of factors. The generation which was still aware of the serious post-war problems and, hence, conducive to harmony was gradually fading away and the younger generation had different opinions. Secondly, growing international contracts and ensuing familiarity with less harmonious labour market situations had an effect. But probably the most important factor was the gradual shift in power from the central federations to the separate unions. This necessitated the federations paying more attention to the direct interests of their members and leaving the responsibility for the realisation of more general economic goals to the interplay of government and parliament. This polarisation, which at times even threatened to disrupt the valuable contacts in the Social Economic Council and the Foundation of Labour, took form not only in hard bargaining on direct labour conditions, but also in the growing desire to exert influence on important management conditions (the introduction of profit sharing schemes, wage conditions for higher personnel not covered by general agreements and even the volume and direction of investments). Although progress along these lines in the period under consideration remained rather weak they mark a tendency which will no doubt be reinforced in the years to come.

Although this background is characteristic for the period as a whole, nevertheless two clearly distinct parts may be distinguished, viz. before and after the oil-crisis.

The first period started under favourable conditions. The mild recession of 1967 had a moderating effect on prices (increase 2.4 percent) and wages (increase 8.9 percent). But soon boom conditions developed again and inflationary pressures regained momentum. Several events reïnforced this development. For example the introduction of the V.A.T. on 1st January 1969 led to a price rise of 2.7 percent, almost twice the amount expected from a correct application of the new tariffs. As a result the government

Table 2.17 Wage sum per worker in enterprises (annual increases in %)

	1971	1972	1973	1974	1975	1976	1977
Spill over	1.7	4.3	2.1	2.4	3.4	3.2	1.0
First price compensation			3.3	5.3	3.7	4.3	2.4
Second price compensation	10.0	7.2	2.0	2.1	3.0	1.0	1.8
Initial component			3.5	3.5	3.0	0	2.3
Incidental component	1.5	0.3	2.9	1.5	− 0.2	2.0	1.3
Social security charges	0.8	0.3	2.3	0.9	− 0.1	0.3	− 0.5
to employer							
Lump sum bonuses	− 0.9	0.5	− 0.5	–	–	0.2	− 0.2
Total increase	13.1	12.6	15.6	15.7	12.8	11.0	8.0

Table 2.18 Consumer price index (annual increase in %)

effect of:	1969	1970	1971	1972	1973	1974	1975	1976	1977
1) Unit labour costs		1.3	2.2	2.1	2.5	4.0	4.5	4.4	2.1	
2) Import prices		0.2	1.3	1.2	0.2	2.1	5.7	0.2	1.8	
3) Policy measures										
indirect taxes and excises	1.6	0.1	0.6	0.2	0.7	0.3	0.2	0.8	0.8
adaptations to Common Market policies	0.2 / 2.0	0.2 / 0.3	0.2 / 1.2	0.3 / 1.2	– / 1.5	– / 0.8	– / 1.5	– / 2.4	–
rent increases	0.3	0.2	0.5	0.5	0.7	0.3	0.3	0.9	0.7
Kennedy round	− 0.1	− 0.1	− 0.1	− 0.1	–	–	–	–	–
tariffs of public utilities	–	–	–	0.3	0.1	0.2	1.0	0.7	0.2
4) Price policy	–	–	–	–	2.0	3.5	–		
5) Other factors	2.8	0.7	3.6	4.5	3.2	2.5	4.4	2.8	
Total increase	6.3	4.5	8.1	8.4	8.8	10.	10.5	9.1	

imposed a 6-months' price freeze, but there was no moderating effect on wages, mainly due to the already existing multi-annual contracts in which, moreover, the number of escalator clauses was extended.

In 1970 parliament passed an act proposed by the Minister of Social Affairs replacing the still existing Extraordinary Decree of 1945 by more permanent legislation. The Minister retained the power to interfere in individual contracts which was completely unacceptable to the unions in spite of later explanations that the paragraph would only be applied in very urgent situations. Thereupon the matter was sent for advice to the Social Economic Council and although the paragraph never has applied it certainly contributed to the growing polarisation.

In the same year a wage conflict arose in the Rotterdam harbour which was settled through a lumpsum bonus of f. 400,–. Its effect was quote serious as it rapidly spread throughout the whole working population, civil servants included. This event by itself caused a rise of the general wage level by 2 percent. The total increase for the year led the government at the end of the year to postpone the expiration date of all contracts by 6 months. But when it finished high claims were presented and largely honoured. In spite of the fact that they became effective rather late in the year the total increase remained roughly the same and moreover there was already a considerable overspill into 1972. It will be clear that these increases, by far outstripping productivity levels, also had a strong inflationary impact.

In 1972 the first signs of structural difficulties became apparent. Unemployment rose to 2.8 percent. This, as well as the high wage increases of preceding years, called for moderation, but negotiations were very difficult, mainly as the Industrial League required governmental guarantees for a selective job creating investment policy. Although this condition was not fulfilling, a final settlement was reached but its moderating effect was very small. Claims with respect to governmental policies (investments- and regional labour market policies) were also at stake in 1973. This time a very serious conflict arose leading to a (for Dutch conditions) unprecedented loss of 0.4 percent of annual working days. It was resolved by the middle of the year by granting a complicated package of increased juvenile pay, improved pension schemes, equal pay, a negotiated contractual wage increase half paid in percent and half in cents and, a tiered scheme of price compensation. As also employers' social security premiums went up, total wage costs rose by 15.6 percent and again it was the most important factor in the inflation (8.8 percent).

Such was the situation when the second part of the period started with the trebling of oilprices in the autumn of 1973. But before dealing with its effects it should be remembered that signs of a world wide recessive development became already visible earlier in the year, and world market prices in general were also rising during the whole year. Moreover, it is interesting to note that in spite of the large increases in labour costs (cf. table 2.17) the competitive position of the Netherlands was not strongly effected due to the fact that similar developments occurred elsewhere. Nevertheless, the devaluation of the dollar and the floating exchange rates combined with the strong position of the guilder, due to its favourable balance of payments position (export of natural gas) led to an average appreciation of the guilder which became quite serious in later years (cf. table 2.5).

However these effects were small in comparison to the impact of the upswing of the oilprices. Not only did import prices of raw materials and semi finished products in 1974 rise by 46 percent (of which three quarters due to oil) which led to a deterioration in the terms of trade in the same year of 5 percent but there was also a heavy volume effect. World trade which used to rise by 10 percent p.a. in previous years fell to 4 percent and as a result the growth of the national income came to a halt. Although the oil blockade to which the Netherlands was subject together with the U.S. did not last more than a few weeks it is understandable that the government became alarmed and resorted to drastic measures. On the strength of the 'Authorisation Law' passed in January 1974 it dictated an increase of all wages and salaries by four quarterly steps of f. 15,– each, equivalent to 3 percent of the total wage bill. In addition minimum wages were increased by 6 percent. Due to the depression, wage drift was rather low but the price compensation which was given with a 'floor' of f. 150,– per one percent increase was very high and, therefore, the total increase still remained at the same level as the year before. (15.7 percent). Nevertheless, the settlement must be judged as positive. It brought the wage rate acceleration to an end. Moreover, it was strongly appreciated by the trade unions as their demands were to a considerable extent satisfied. Price controls were also very stringently applied and, in spite of the large increase in labour costs, price rises could be kept at 10 percent. The trough of the depression in the Netherlands was reached in 1975. For the first time since 1958 the national income in real terms decreased, viz. by 1.5 percent. Rates of return became very low and unemployment rose to 5 percent. Under these circumstances both parties in the labour market were convinced of the necessity for moderation, but again difficulties arose not only with respect to the size of the increase, but also with respect to its distribution (cents against percents; skinning 'excess' profits; extension of collective agreements to higher incomes etc.) After long deliberation an initial improvement of 2.5 percent was concluded; again a floor was introduced in the price compensation. The final outcome, viz. 13.3 percent was well below that of the preceding year.

The anti inflationary compaign was not as successful. In spite of a stringent price policy, margins which had been squeezed in previous years had to be increased, which by itself had an effect of 4.4 percent in the total of 10.5 percent[6].

This section on wage policy should not be concluded without a few remarks on the public sector which employs about 13 percent of all workers. It includes the personnel of the central government, the lower authorities and almost the whole educational system. Its wage structure is largely determined by central regulations under the authority of the Minister of the Interior. The annual increases again are broadly uniform throughout the whole system and although they are set in negotiations between the trade unions of civil servants and the Ministry they are principally based on the average increase in the private sector. Since 1961 this has been the officially adopted procedure. However, due to a gradual shift to higher ranks (partly rank inflation) the average for the whole sector rose somewhat more than in the private sector. The most important deviation took place around 1964 when the upper half of the ranking system in three annual instalments received an additional increase which started at the middle with very low percentages up to 30 percent for the highest ranks. It met with vigorous opposition from the unions of civel servants but it was justified by the government as a measure necessary to compete with the private sector for high quality labour which was very scarce at the time due to the strong tension in the labour market. Apart from this episode there is a high correlation between the growth rates of wages in the public and in the private sector, the elasticity of the former with respect to the latter is about 1.08.

Due to the policy described, wage development in the public sector did not play a separate role and, moreover, the country has been saved the trouble sometimes experienced abroad when public wages were kept constant or lagging behind those in the private sector 'to set an example'.

2.8.3 Fiscal policy

During the post-war period the basic principles on which the Netherlands' fiscal policy is based have undergone several changes[7]. Already very soon after the end of the war the classical golden rule of balanced state budgets has been abandoned and been replaced by a stabilizing policy based on Keynesian ideas. The impulse to the economy originating with the state budget should be designed in such a way, that, together with all other impulses acting on the economy, it would just create sufficient demand to absorb unused capacities.

The results of this policy were not very encouraging. After the Korea crisis, which was rapidly overcome due to very strong restrictive measures in 1951, unemployment was very high and at the same time a large surplus of the balance of payments on current account had been built up. Therefore, the conditions for a spending policy were present. However, it started too late and it turned out to be very difficult to adapt it sufficiently smoothly to the upswing which followed. There was a strong tendency to reduce the high tax level and on the other hand many expenditure categories, once started, could not easily be slowed down. Moreover, certain expenditures, for example for infra-structural development, were complementary to private ones. As a consequence of these developments unemployment decreased and the balance of payments' surplus disappeared. It ended with a deficit in 1956, with unemployment slightly over 1 percent and practically no idle capacity in enterprises. Again restrictive measures were taken and another short-lived depression set in. But the government also became aware of the fact that during the second half of the boom the 'balancing' policy had reinforced it instead of dampening it. This led to the adoption of a changed policy, the so called structural budget policy. According to this policy during a period of balanced growth, i.e. growth under conditions of cyclical equilibrium, national savings should be just sufficient to finance all private and public investments together with the necessary capital export (cf. section 2.1). The balance of payments on current account should leave a sufficient surplus to this end. If under these circumstances private savings were higher than investments and capital exports, the public authorities ought to absorb the surplus through borrowing and increasing their expenditures accordingly. When these equilibrium conditions had been fulfilled for a given year the space for next years' fiscal policy could be derived from an estimate of the long-term rate of growth of the economy and the so called progression factor, i.e. the elasticity of tax income (at unchanged tariffs) with respect to the national income. Due to the progressiveness of the tax system this factor was originally estimated at 1.4; later on, due to changes in the income distribution it gradually reduced to 1.16. To the amount obtained a structural budget deficit ought to be added as it was reasonable to assume that even under conditions of balanced growth a savings surplus of the private sector would be available. The budgetary space determined in this way could be used either for increased expenditures or tax reductions or a combination of the two (even increases in expenditure surpassing the budgetary space if compensated by a correspondingly increased tax burden could, of course, be considered). Although it was assumed that the new system would contribute to a more balanced development, the possibility of cyclical disturbances was not excluded. Therefore, the option was left open to surpass the structural space in case of a slack in the economy or to use it only partially under conditions of strain. But still it was felt that the budgetary norm described would yield a better starting point for a sound economic policy than the policy pursued before. The system is still in force as the base for fiscal policy but in the course of time it had to be adapted to changed circumstances. When inflation became more apparent an estimate of the expected rate of inflation was taken into account in calculating the budgetary space. At the same time an estimate was made of that part of the space that would already be taken up by an unchanged volume of expenditures due to expected price increases (in particular the salary increase of civil servants whose pay was coupled to the general wage index). It was also realised that due to real and nominal increases of the national income the tax rate automatically would considerably be raised and certain provisions were made for an adaptation. Another point to be mentioned is the structural deficit. During several years it was kept constant in real terms as it was assumed that the savings surplus of the private sector gradually would decrease in relative terms. However, in 1974 it has been fixed as a percentage of the national income. Finally, it should be mentioned that gradually the need was felt for a more efficient fiscal policy than was possible under the prevailing situation where all changes of the size of the exenditures and of the tax-tariffs had to be authorized by parliament. Therefore, in 1970 a law passed according to which government was given the possibility of changing the tariffs of the most important taxes (referring to some 85 percent of the total) upwards or downwards by maximally 5 percent without previous parliamentary consent. This so called 'swinging' tax has been used twice to counteract cyclical tensions viz. in 1971 and 1972.

After this brief description of the philosophy of the Netherlands' fiscal policy an attempt will be made to evaluate its performance[8]. This is a complicated problem. Obviously, it is impossible to pay attention to all the aspects of this policy. There is great variety of taxes and subsidies and a still greater variety of expenditures and the effect of each on the course of the economy is badly known. Therefore, it will be necessary to develop an overall yardstick but even this cannot be done unambiguously.

One way which often has been used is to compare the total of all 'relevant' public expenditures, i.e. material consumption, investments, salary payments and net transfers (excluding credits and debt repayments) for both the central government and the lower authorities and diminish the change of this total from year $(t+1)$ to year t by tax increases, in so far as they are caused by tariff changes (reductions, obviously, are added). In this line of thought changes in tax income resulting from variations in the basis of agreement are not considered to be pertinent to policy. To this difference are usually added changes in consumer subsidies and deduced increases in public income due to increased tariffs of public utilities. Finally, increases in investments in private building are added. This is done as the building sector is largely governed by public policy measures. For many years all private building was subject to a system of permits to avoid tensions in this market, to a large extent guarantees were given to building societies and later even substantial loans.

As a last step the total change is expressed as a percentage of the GNP of

year t and the outcome is considered as the public impulse to the economy in
year (t + 1).

This method does not pay attention to the effect of built-in stabilizers such
as changes in tax income due to the cyclical development or endogenous
ahanges in the salaries of public servants (only 'volume' changes are taken
into account). This is done deliberately as those changes are considered as
reactions of the 'system', partly due to the policies pursued.

Here preference is given to a simpler method which does not distinguish
between primary policy measures and the effects of built-in stabilizers. It is
based on the changes in the total relevant public expenditures diminished
by the corresponding changes in total tax income to which are added the
increases of public depreciation funds and of the savings of social security
funds (excluding the unemployment fund) as these savings are again largely
determined by public policy.

These changes are again expressed as a percentage of the GNP of the
preceding year in order to obtain the fiscal impulse. Its development for the
period 1951-1975 has been shown in figure 2.3 by the curve FI.

Figure 2.3 Fiscal impulses and capacity targets of economic policy.

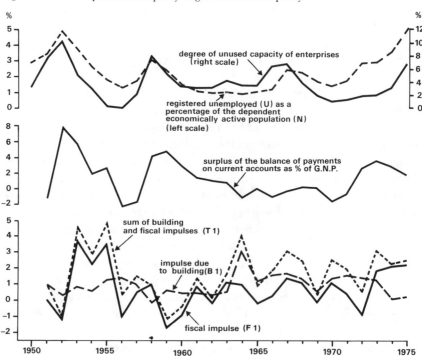

Instead of adding to this impulse the effect of changes in the building activity for private purposes their effects have been reflected in a second impulse computed in a similar way (curve BI). Finally, the two have been added to a 'total' impulse, TI, also illustrated in the graph.

In using these indicators to evaluate the fiscal policy two observations are in order. In the first place a comparison of the two methods (the figures are not given here) for the period for which they are available (1951-1975) shows that there is not a very large difference between the two. This is due to the fact that the endogenous changes in the wage bill of civil servants are largely compensated by the built-in stabilizing influence on tax income. Secondly, it is clear that the evaluation is only possible afterwards. It makes use of information about which the government in shaping its policy at best had good guesses (mainly supplied by the Central Planning Bureau).

In order to form a judgement about the policy as it is carried out two major guide lines for this policy are also presented in figure 2.4. One is the percentage of registered unemployment, the second is the surplus of the balance of payments on current account.

For reasons of completeness, also the degree of unused capacity in enterprises has been added. Strictly speaking, short-term full-employment policy would not be able to reduce the level of unused capacity of one factor if the lowest limit of the other one has already been reached. In 1956 for example unemployment could not be lowered as the available private capital was fully used. On the other hand during the middle sixties the degree of unused capacity of enterprises could not be lowered as unemployment could not be pressed below the extremely low limit of 1 percent. Therefore, both quantities ought to be taken into account. This, however, is rather difficult beforehand as the degree of capital utilisation is only available after some delay. But the similarity of the two, in particular as far as turning points are concerned, is very high. Nevertheless, the examples mentioned do show that they are not entirely identical. This is also brought out by the fact that during the seventies unemployment rose much faster than the degree of unused capacity, clearly pointing to structural unemployment due to capital scarcity which already has been mentioned before.

There is also a large degree of similarity between the variables (U/N) and (E). This is mainly due to the fact that cyclical variations to a much larger extent are reflected in investments than in other national expenditures. As investment goods are to a considerable extent imported there is a tendency for (E) to improve during a recession, at least as long as international cyclical fluctuations are not completely synchronous, so that exports are not reduced but even may be increased.

Now, comparing the impulses with the policy guide lines the very high impulses of the early fifties leap into focus. They have been mentioned already and they contributed to the overspending of 1956. They were reinforced by the increasing building impulses mainly resulting from the growing house building programmes to cope with the prevailing shortages. The effect of the restriction programme designed for 1957 and consisting of a reduction of governmental spending on consumption and investments and increased tax tariffs is entirely overshadowed by the effect of built-in stabilizers (tax income went down by 4 percent in spite of the tariff increases) and by the fact that the municipalities increased their spending financed by short-term loans. The final outcome was an unintended small positive impulse which, however, came on time in connection with the high unemployment in 1958.

The effect on the building activity was rather serious. Programmes were reduced, first to fight overspending, later on to facilitate the revival of the manufacturing industry which was given priority in order to improve exports. The balance of payments very rapidly became positive. Already in 1958 it was healthily positive. But the brunt fell on the building industry. The revival withdrew unskilled labour from this trade and until 1963 it expanded only very moderately. From a cyclical point of view this was favourable as the tension in the labour market which gradually built up after 1958 required a restrictive policy, the more so as the fiscal impulse again rose from negative to (moderate) positive values. But this policy did not contribute much to remedy the housing shortage. Political pressure for more effective measures became very strong, and, therefore, the cabinet which came into office in the middle of 1963 decided to start the heavy building programme referred to already in section 2.1.

With regard to the phase of the business cycle this policy was particularly ill-timed. Its strongest impact fell in 1964 shortly after the 1963-wage explosion which already had given rise to strong inflationary effects. In 1965 both impulses were considerably lower; the fiscal impulse because of reductions in spending, the building impulse because it levelled off after the heavy effort of the preceding year. During the following years 1966-1969 the impulses were correctly timed. They were in line with the mild depression which had its trough in 1967. The next three years were again pro cyclical. Building activity remained at a high level, but the fiscal impulse was lowered. This was caused by an unsuccessful effort to reduce the strong inflationary forces of the year. Its only effect was a contribution to the stagflation. Finally, when the recession after the oil crisis of 1973 set in special programmes were introduced to support the economic activity, in particular to revive investments. Therefore, the impulse was again counter-cyclical. However, at the same time due to saturation of the housing market and a low demand for commercial building the impetus of this activity declined counteracting the effect of the fiscal measures.

Considering the period as a whole, the conclusion can be drawn that fiscal policy was only moderately successful. Although the basic ideas were sound their realisation was often impeded either by measures originating in requirements which stood apart from cyclical consideration or to the lack of foresight combined with the sluggishness of the policy-making machinery leading to ill-timing of the measures envisaged.

2.8.4 *Monetary policy*

As in several other countries the primary responsibility for monetary policy is entrusted to the Central Bank. But the public authorities through their debt management can also exert an important influence on the amount of available liquidity in paricular in the secondary sphere. According to the 1948-Bank law the final authority for the monetary policy rests with the Minister of Finance. If necessary he can give instructions to the president of the Bank. In case of strong disagreement about such instructions the latter has the right of appeal to parliament. However, up to the present moment such conflicts have never occurred. The coordination of the policies of the Bank and Treasury is effected through weekly consultations.

According to the Bank law the Bank is entitled to use different instruments of monetary policy; in addition to the ordinary discount-policy it may resort open market policy, cash reserve policy and even impose quantitative credit restrictions. During the post-war period all these tools have been applied, partly simultaneously, partly consecutively.

It is the basic philosophy of the Bank that the financial conditions of the economy as reflected in the cost of financing – or in other words – the user cost of capital and the availability of funds have a major impact on expenditure and in paricular on investments[9]. This view resulted in the formulation of operational conditions for monetary equilibrium in terms of the liquidity ratio. It also means that monetary policy in the Netherlands attempts to achieve appropriate financial conditions for the economy rather than to rely on monetary actions to control outputs, employment and prices. In this view liquidity is defined as the total of primary and secondary liquidities. Primary liquidities consist of banknotes (outside the bank) and demand deposits. Secondary liquidities include fixed deposits, foreign currency balances, short-term claims on the central government (treasury bills) and on lower

authorities, call loans to public authorities and 'improper' savings deposits
with banks (determined from the turn-over period of such deposits;
secondary liquidity if this period is less than half a year, savings if more than
two years and for periods in between as a percentage gradually declining

Figure 2.4 Development of liquidity

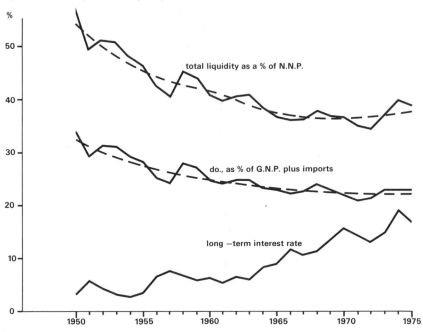

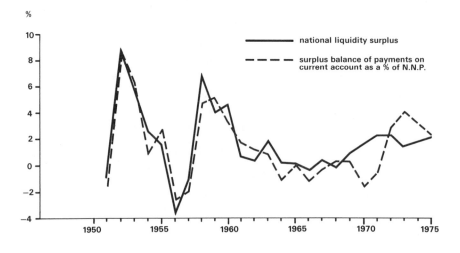

from 100 to 0). Every definition of money is more or less arbitrary. The one described is chosen as it contains categories of near money which according to the philosophy of the Bank 'at short notice and without considerable costs and/or depreciation losses can be changed into money'.

As a yardstick to judge the monetary situation, the total amount of liquidity is usually expressed as a percentage of net national income. Figure 2.4 shows the development of this variable over time (curve A).

It shows a clearly decreasing trend with cyclical fluctuations, largely due to differences in growth rate of denominator and numerator; the total amount of liquidity itself increased almost continuously; there were only two slight decreases in 1951 and 1956.

The idea of using this yardstick rests on the assumption that monetary policy should aim at a supply of liquidities just sufficient to cover the demand arising from the transactions motive and that the net national income is an appropriate indicator for the size of these transactions. The correctness of this assumption can be questioned on various grounds. Time deposits are included in secondary liquidities and savings deposits are not. Hence, shifts from one category to the other due to differential movements may considerably affect total liquidity although its monetary importance may be negligible. For example a considerable part of the increase in the ratio during 1972-1975 is caused by this phenomenon.

Secondly, in an open country like the Netherlands with a very high share of imports, heavy changes of import prices tend to affect the value of imports and, therefore, also of transactions, more heavily than the net national income. This fact could be taken into account by basing the ratio not entirely on the national income, but on this income increased by a fraction, e.g. 60 percent of the value of imports, or by a weighted average in which GNP gets a higher weight than imports. This effect may also be important as is shown in figure 2.4. Whereas curve A, based on the actual definition, shows a considerable increase, curve B based on the so-called national means, i.e. GNP plus value of imports, shows a much more moderate picture.

Also with respect to the liquidity position two periods can be distinguished. Until 1966 the peaks of curve A (or B) coincide exactly with the troughs of the cycles. During a boom period the relative liquidity position gradually deteriorates. When the depression starts and the growth of the national income slows down, the revival is stimulated by a considerable improvement of the balance of payments on current account connected with an increase of the relative liquidity position. These fluctuations are in line with the movements of the long-term interest rate (figure 2.4, curve C). This variable shows an accelerating trend resulting from the fact that the capital market to a growing extent takes inflationary fluctuations in account. But during the period under consideration its deviations from the trend move contrary to the fluctuations of the liquidity situation.

From 1966 onwards this relationship is interrupted. Because of uncertainty in the foreign exchange markets starting with the devaluation of sterling and several other currencies in the autumn of 1967 and the relatively strong position of the guilder considerable amounts of liquidity were entered through the capital account of the balance of payments but in spite of this the interest rate moved almost parallel to the liquidity indicator, mainly due to external influences.

These developments are even more clearly illustrated by figure 2.5 showing the total liquidity creation (as a percentage of the N.N.P.) and its components. It illustrates the fact that during the first period the fluctuations in the liquidity position were largely due to the foreign position. From graph 2.5 it is clear that these fluctuations result from the balance on current account.

Until the second half of the sixties the surplus of the balance of payments on current account and the total national liquidity surplus move almost entirely parallel. Figures 2.4 and 2.5 also show the strong influx of liquidity through the capital account from 1966 onwards.

Turning to policy considerations it should be pointed out above all that at the end of the war liquidities were very high. The amount of banknotes in circulation had considerably been reduced through a purge in 1945, eliminating large stock of money illegally built up during the war. But the banks had high claims on the government mainly in the form of treasury bills resulting from advances to the occupational authorities. For a long time it has been the primary goal of the monetary policy to reduce this abundant liquidity to more normal proportions.

From figure 2.3 it is clear that for a large part of the entire period the central government absorbed liquidities through a larger demand on the capital market than necessary to cover its (total) budgetary deficit. Moreover, it did so largely contrary to the liquidity creation through the balance of payments. It is not clear whether this always was done with the intention to reduce the total liquidity or simply because it is attractive to borrow on an extensive scale when liquidities are easy and, hence, interest rates usually are relatively low. However, it is quite certain that the liquidity absorption in 1956 was intended to contribute to the overspending resulting in the balance of payments deficit of 1956. However it came rather late and reinforced the depression which started the same year.

The policy of the Bank, too, has almost continuously been directed at an

Figure 2.5 Liquidity creation and its components as % of N.N.P.)

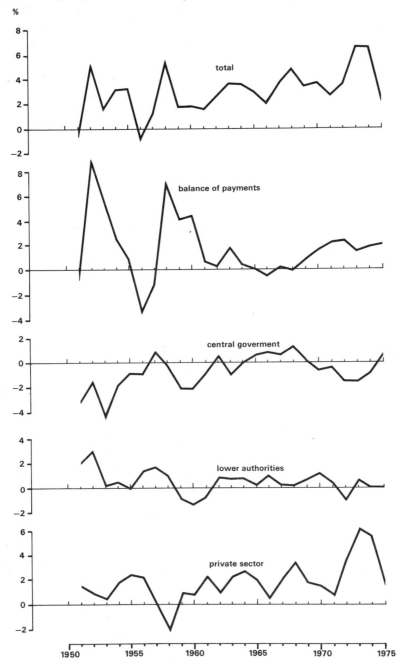

absorption of surplus liquidity and a moderation of the creation of new liquidities. During the first years after the war extensive use was made of qualitative credit controls but these were abolished at the end of 1950 when a more normal situation was achieved. During the next 15 months a general quantitative control was in force, but during the following years the emphasis was on discount policy supported by open market and cash reserve policies. The scope of the open market policy is limited due to the fact that the Bank in its portfolio only keeps treasury bills and no bonds. Moreover its size is limited to 1½ to 2 percent of total liquidity. Nevertheless, by this policy, in combination with cash reserve policy, it was possible to make the discount policy more effective.

A very important step was taken in 1954 when the government placed 1200 mill. gld. treasury certificates (about 10 percent of total liquidity) with a maturity varying from 8 to 12 years with the commercial banks. The cash reserve policy was introduced in the beginning of 1954 at a rate varying from 7 to 10 percent. The important surpluses of the balance of payments at the end of the fifties enabled the banks to lend considerable amounts of money abroad. This portfolio could be used as a buffer to support the liquidity situation at home and this again rendered the cash reserve policy rather ineffective. Therefore, already in 1961 quantitative credit restrictions were introduced. At the end of 1963 the cash reserve policy was abolished. The restrictive policy allows the banks to extend their credits in accordance with a norm based on the situation in the preceding year and an estimate of the growth of the national income. Until 1969 this norm was derived from the estimated growth of the real income. Later on the increasing rate of inflation necessitated the Bank also allowing for a moderate price rise. Credit restrictions have been in force from 1961 to 1972 with interruptions during 1963 and from the middle of 1967 to the beginning of 1969. This policy has no doubt contributed to a tightening of the liquidity situation and may even have contributed to the depression which reached its trough in 1967. The policy was interrupted in the beginning of 1972 when due to the decreasing rates of return and a relaxation of the labour market a continued restrictive policy did not seem to be appropriate. However, when in connection with the oil crisis credits again were rapidly rising, a new phase of reserve policy was started, this time consisting of two percentages: viz. 6 percent for long term deposits and a higher one varying from 8 to 10 for demand deposits.

If one looks at the supply of credits to the private sector it becomes clear that this largely followed the cyclical fluctuations, with perhaps the exception of 1966 and the extra-ordinary demand due to the oil crisis. It is rather difficult to give an exact evaluation of the impact of the monetary policy. It certainly has contributed to the gradual reduction of the liquidity position. But in the early post-war years it was made difficult due to the excessive amounts of liquidity. Later on the free movements of capital interfered and after the floating of the guilder in 1971 and the following 'snake' arrangements the policy had to ensure that the value of the guilder was kept within the adopted limits.

Moreover, neither the restrictive measures nor the reserve policy were watertight. The limits could be and were exceeded albeit at a certain cost. Therefore, the final conclusion seems to be justified that with a few exceptions the volume and price rises of production did not meet with appreciable monetary resistance.

Notes

* This is a revised and abbreviated version of a paper under the title of 'Post-war Economic Developments in The Netherlands, with Special Reference to Inflation', that was submitted to the Brookings Conference on Stabilization Policy, held in Rome May 30 – June 4, 1977. The authors are indebted to F. Daudt and A.A.J. van der Wees for research assistance. Moreover, they benefitted from comments made by M. Fase at the Rome conference as well as from the general discussion of the paper there.

[1] The figures in the tables and graphs have been taken from the National Accounts, Central Economics Plans (bijlagen) and Government Budget Memorandums (miljoenennota).

[2] It is not possible to maintain exactly the same three periods throughout this chapter. One reason is the lack of time series for certain variables in the beginning of the fifties. The other is that the effects of a capital surplus or shortage only make themselves felt after a lag of some years. In a number of cases, therefore, we present figures for the periods 1952%62, 1963/70, 1971/77.

[3] It should be noted that the figure for 1963/70 is based upwards by the exceptionally high growth rates of private consumption in 1969 and 1970.

[4] Since 1974 there has been an extensive academic and political discussion on this subject. See Den Hartog and Tjan (1976) and Driehuis (1979) for more details and for a review of the debate.

[5] An economic braintrust of the government producing i.a. short and medium term forecasts on its own responsibility. See also Abert (1969) and chapter six.

[6] The wage development and wage policy in the seventies is more extensively discussed in Driehuis (1980).

[7] See also Burger (1978).

[8] See also Van den Beld (1963).

[9] For more details see Den Dunnen (1973) and Zijlstra (1979).

References

J.C. Abert, Economic Policy and Planning in the Netherlands, 1950-1965, London, 1969.

C.A. v.d. Beld, Conjunctuurpolitiek in en om de jaren vijftig, Den Haag, 1963.

H. Burger, 'Structural Budget Policy in the Netherlands', *De Economist*, 1978 (3).

W. Driehuis and P. de Wolff, 'A Sectoral Wage-Price Model for the Netherlands Economy', in H. Frisch (ed.) *Inflation in small countries*, Wien, 1976.

W. Driehuis, 'An analysis of the impact of demand and cost factors on employment', *De Economist*, 1979 (2).

W. Driehuis, 'Labour Market Imbalances and Structural Unemployment', *Kyklos*, 1978 (4).

W. Driehuis, 'Enige aspecten van loonontwikkeling en loonbeleid in de jaren zeventig', *ESB*, 20-2-1980.

E. den Dunnen, 'Monetary Policy in the Netherlands', in K. Holbik (ed.) *Monetary Policy in Twelve Industrial Countries*, Federal Reserve Bank of Boston, 1973, pp. 282-328.

H. den Hartog and H.S. Tjan, 'Investment, Wages, Prices and Demand for Labour', *De Economist*, 1976.

G.A. Kessler, 'Monetair Beleid, Stagflatiebestrijding en het Internationale Aanpassingsproces', in Praeadviezen voor de Vereniging voor de Staathuishoudkunde, Leiden, 1978.

L. Ulman and R.J. Flanagan, Wage Restraint: A Study of Incomes Policies in Western Europe, Berkely, 1971.

J. Windmuller and C. de Galan, Arbeidsverhoudingen in Nederland, Utrecht, 1977.

P. de Wolff, 'Incomes Policies' in E. Lundberg (ed.) *Inflation theory and anti-inflation policy*, Hong Kong, 1978.

J. Zijlstra, 'Monetary theory and monetary policy: a Central Banker's View', *De Economist*, 1979 (1).

3. COUNTER-INFLATION POLICY IN THE NETHERLANDS*

C.J. van Eijk

3.1 Introduction

This chapter is devoted to the development of wages and prices in the Netherlands since 1945. Equally, attention will be paid to policies to control and mitigate price and wage rises. During the whole period they have risen; in the beginning moderately, later on – particularly during the first half of the nineteen seventies – much faster. The whole period has been qualified as inflationary. In this chapter the word inflation will be used to indicate a persistent positive rate of change in prices. Consistently, policymakers have tried to moderate inflation. A stable price level has been one of the declared targets of economic policy[1]. For an assessment of counter-inflation policy, insight is required into the determinants of wage and price movements, into the interdependences between these variables and the other targets of economic policy and into the availability of policy instruments to attain these targets.

In a formal way the design of economic policy can be described in the following manner. In the first place recent and expected developments of the target variables are analysed. Secondly the target variables are identified for which actual and desired values are diverging or are expected to diverge in the near future. A target function is specified in which the discrepancies between desired and expected values are weighted according to their relative priorities. Then, a qualitative choice is made of the instruments of economic policy available for changing actual trends. Next the boundary conditions are specified within which the target function is to be maximized. Among these boundary conditions is the model of the economy describing, by means of its reduced form equations, the relationships between targets and instrument variables. Finally the solution of the maximum problem is obtained which consists of the numerical specification of the instrument variables.

This description indicates the structure of this chapter. In the next section the post war development of prices and wages and some other important variables will be described. The importance of price stability will be discussed in section 3. Recent developments in inflation theory, explaining the interdependences between such variables as wages, prices, productivity, excess demand or supply and liquidities, will be set out in section 4. In section 5 attention will be given to the policy instruments, and to the institutional framework of the wage policy because it is rather specific for Dutch economic policy in the post-war period. In section 6 some conclusions are drawn.

3.2 Aspects of inflation in the Netherlands

Data will be provided for the periods: 1950-1956, 1956-1963, 1963-1970, 1970-1977. They have been chosen on the following considerations. In 1949 a devaluation of the guilder marked the end of the first period of reconstruction in which the recovery of the Dutch economy after the second world war was partly financed by means of Marshall aid. In 1950 the aid was reduced significantly. During the next few years recovery progressed though hampered by violent price fluctuations in world markets due to the Korea-crisis. In 1956 the economy showed, for the first time since the war, signs of overheating: a deficit on the balance of payments, probably caused by endogenously generated overspending. In 1957 and 1958 a government-induced reduction created unemployment and improved the balance of payments. Within 2 years however economic activity recovered and showed a more or less steady growth which ended in 1963. In that year the economy was in equilibrium except for a tight labour market. At the end of the year a wage explosion occurred. In the following years wages and prices rose faster than before. The labour market remained tight until 1970, a year in which probably the economy was in equilibrium again: a reasonable low level of unemployment, equilibrium on the balance of payment, a growth rate of 6 percent. However, already in the second half of 1969 import prices began to rise. This event, together with the price rises in 1974, after the war in the Middle East, and the following world recession dominated the development in the nineteen seventies. In table 3.1 data on the growth rates of wages, prices, production per man and liquidities are brought together.

Some aspects of the price movements should be stressed. The first is that prices of domestic expenditure have risen faster than those of exports. This holds for all periods that are distinguished. Several factors may have been responsible. Under the stress of competition productivity may have risen

Table 3.1 Changes in wage rates, prices, production and liquidities

								Prices of										
	Wage rate Private Sector		Consumers' goods		Investment goods		Government Consumption		Government Investment		Domestic expenditure		Exports		Total expenditure		Gross national product (market prices)	
	i	ii	i	ii	i	ii	i	ii	i	ii	i	ii	i	ii	i	ii	i	ii
1950	19		50		47		24		35		47		85		51		42	
		7,2		3,0		5,5		6,3		6,7		2,2		1,9		3,6		4,1
1956	29		60		64		35		52		55		95		63		54	
		6,6		2,8		2,1		5,6		3,4		3,0		− 0,4		2,3		3,3
1963	46		73		74		52		66		68		92		74		68	
		11,0		4,5		4,3		9,3		5,9		5,5		1,1		4,3		5,5
1970	100		100		100		100		100		100		100		100		100	
		12,0		8,4		7,8		10,5		9,7		8,7		6,8		8,0		8,2
1977	231		180		173		209		197		184		161		175		178	

	Imports		Prices of Gross value added private sector (factor costs)		Prices of Gross value added private sector (market prices)		Production per man private sector		Quantity of money		Ratio Quantity of money to the volume of gross nat. prod. (market prices)
	i	ii	i	ii	i	ii	i	ii	i	ii	i
1950	84		46		47		45		26		
		2,5		4,3		3,9		3,7		3,9	− 1,1
1956	96		59		59		56		33		
		− 0,7		2,8		2,8		2,8		6,5	3,0
1963	91		72		72		68		52		
		1,4		4,7		4,7		5,5		9,4	3,6
1970	100		100		100		100		100		
		7,7		7,7		7,7		4,1		12,8	9,4
1977	171		172		172		133		244		

i Index, 1970 = 100.
ii Average rate of change between two dates, per cent per annum.

Sources: Central Economic Plans of the Central Planning Bureau and the National Accounts published by the Central Bureau of Statistics.

faster in export industries than it did in industries producing for the home market. Insofar that increases in domestic costs were higher than in foreign countries, competition has prevented firms from adapting export prices accordingly. As will be shown later this has had consequences for profits. A second aspect worth mentioning is that both prices of government consumption and government investment grew faster than those of other categories of domestic expenditure. By definition government consumption consists of the government wage sum and material consumption. Though the rise in wages of the civil servants is more or less equal to that of private wages, the wage costs per unit of output of the government sector rise faster than in the private sector because by definition productivity increases are equal to zero. A greater part of government investment consists of relatively high-priced products of the building industry than does private investment. This may mean that the rate of growth of the government sector may constitute an independent factor in inflation. Finally, as the burden of indirect taxes did not change very much the price index of national product at market prices did not differ significantly from that of national product at factor costs. The burden of indirect taxes did not form a separate cause of inflation.

Variables which are influenced by inflation, and which are important because they are directly or indirectly considered as targets of economic policy, are the labour income quota and the competitive strength of our exports on foreign markets.

The labour income quota is important as an idicator of one of the aspects of income distribution (the distribution over wage and non-wage income) and, in an indirect way, of the profitability of investment (one of the determinants of investment activity, which determines the future growth of capacity and employment). The Central Planning Bureau defines the labour income quota (L.I.Q.) as the ratio between the wage sum (Np_l^b) and an imputed labour income of entrepreneurs $(N'p^b)$ on the one hand and net value added of the private sector at factor costs (Y_{nf}) on the other hand[2]

$$\text{L.I.Q.} = \frac{(N + N')p^b_l}{Yb_{nf}}$$

In percentages changes:

$$(\text{L.I.Q.}) = p_l^b - p_{ynf}^b - h^b$$

in which p_{ynf}^b is the percentage change in the price of the private sector net value added at factor costs and h^b is the percentage change in net value added per man. In table 2.2 these percentage changes are presented. As officially only the prices of the private sector gross value added at market prices are published the calculations in table 2.2 are done for a labour income quota defined as a percentage of gross value added at market prices.

From these data it can be seen that in the course of time wage rate increases have not been fully compensated by increases in production per man and prices. The above mentioned impossibility of passing on increased labour costs to foreign customers may have been one of the causes. Another element may have been competitive imports from low wage countries.

Another important variable is the competitive power of Dutch exporters on foreign markets, one of the determinants of the volume of exports. As at least part of Dutch exports is traded on competitive markets, and thus export prices will not always differ significantly from those of the competitors, the best measure of the competitive strength of Dutch exports is probably the ratio between Dutch labour costs and those of competitors. The following data on this ratio are available.

Table 3.2 The development of the labour income quota in the private sector.

	$\dot{p}_1^b$	$\dot{h}^b$	$\dot{p}_{ijbm}^b$	L.I.Q. $= \dfrac{\dot{p}_1^b - \dot{h}^b - \dot{p}_{ijbm}^b}{}$	L.I.Q. (Index)	L.I.Q. b)	LIQ c)	LIQ d)	LIQ e)	LIQ f)
							Actual			Forecasts
1950a)				100		55,6	63,5	72,0	55,6	55,6
	7,2	3,7	3,9	− 0,4						
1956a)				97,6		54,1	60,8	68,2	54,3	54,3
1956					100	55,7	62,4	70,0	55,7	55,7
	6,6	2,8	2,8	1,0						
1963				107,3	100	60,0	66,9	75,3	59,8	59,8
	11,0	5,5	4,7	0,8						
1970				105,8	100	63,1	71,3	79,3	63,5	63,2
	12,0	4,1	7,7	0,2						
1977				101,4		63,7	72,2	81,6	64,0	64,1

a) In prices 1958 = 100. For the other years the basis 1970 = 100 is chosen. There are differences in definition between the sources on which the data on these rows are based and those used for the other data.
b) As a percentage of gross value added at market prices.
c) As a percentage of gross value added at factor costs.
d) As a percentage of net value added at factor costs. The C.P.B. uses this definition.
e) The actual value at the beginning of the period is used as basis.
f) The actual value in 1950, resp. 1956 is used as basis.

Sources: Central Economic Plans and National Accounts.

Table 3.3 Labour costs per unit of output in manufacturing industries. (in dollars).

Periods	The Netherlands	Competitors
	% changes	
1956-1963	4.0	2.2
1963-1970	4.5	3.3
1970-1977	13.5	4.9

Sources: Central Economic Plans.

Clearly the competitive strength of the Netherlands has deteriorated. The high percentage changes in the period 1970-1977 are partly due to the depreciation of the dollar.

The world wide price movements in the nineteen seventies have unfavourably influenced the Dutch terms of trade, defined as the ratio between export and import prices, after a long period in which this variable remained constant. In 1978 a small improvement is to be observed[3].

3.3 The importance of price stability for economic policy

Already in one of the first publications of the Social Economic Council[4] price stability was mentioned as one of the five important targets of economic policy. Other targets were full employment, equilibrium on the balance of payments, a high level of investment and a reasonable income distribution. In later reports on economic development in the Netherlands the importance of a stable price level has been stressed repeatedly. According to present standards this target has been reached reasonably well up to 1964. With hindsight, only the final period which we distinguished has been one in which price and wage movements could be called inflationary. In fact, however, in almost all the Central Economic Plans the direction of the C.P.B. showed its anxiety about inflation. The President of the Central Bank did the same in his annual reports.

Why has so much attention been given to price and wage movements during the whole post-war period? The answer is that persistent price increases influence unfavourably other targets of economic policy. Only when in a closed economy price increases are fully anticipated, is no influence on relative prices and real variables to be expected. In that case a policy target as full employment will not be jeopardized. However, price rises are never fully anticipated and the Dutch economy is not closed. In addition certain institutional arrangements cause price changes to influence the volumes of certain economic variables even if they are anticipated. In the Dutch economy, inflation has endangered the targets of external equilibrium, full employment and the desired development of income distribution. A few examples may suffice to illustrate this.

If costs in export industries rise faster than those of competitors on foreign markets, their competitive strength deteriorates. According to the models the Central Planning Bureau uses in its policy analyses the Dutch export volume, depends, among others, on this variable[5]. The deterioration may therefore lower the volume of exports, thus endangering external equilibrium and full employment. Anti-inflation policy, in particular the centrally guided wage policy set up immediately after the war was, among others, meant to maintain the competitive strength on foreign markets and thus to foster external equilibrium and a high level of employment.

Also, in a different way, employment and inflation are related to each other. Though it is often said that a mild inflationary climate is favourable for investment and thus for the growth of production capacity and future employment, persistent and high rates of price and wage increases may endanger capacity formation. At the moment an investment decision is taken the capital intensity of production and the economic life of the capital goods are chosen on the basis of expectations about future wage levels, prices and production per man. If these expectations do not come true – and that will generally be the case in a highly inflationary climate – the economic life of the capital goods may turn out shorter than expected, implying a smaller growth of production capacity than foreseen. This will happen if the wage increases are higher than expected and cannot be passed on to the customers. A second condition is that the capital intensity of the production process cannot be changed *ex post* sufficiently to prevent the quasi rent of machinery becoming zero. Such a development will lead to an unanticipated obsolescence of capital goods and destruction of jobs and may therefore bring about a decrease in employment; at least if sufficient new jobs are not created by means of new investment. If wages rise faster than production per man plus prices, a sufficient level of new investment is not guaranteed. Two reasons can be mentioned. The increased share of labour income may have left a too small a profit income to finance new investment. On the other hand inflation may have created so much uncertainty that investment decisions may be postponed.

Also the targets for the distribution of income over wages and profits can be frustrated by inflation. This already became clear in the previous points. In the period up till 1954 the strictly guided wage policy, leading to only small wage increases, compared with the rise in productivity, and the more rapid increase in prices than expected, resulted in a decreased labour income quote. After 1954 the criteria of the wage policy were changed so as to include the improvement of this quota. As already stated the impossibility of shifting the increase in wage costs, in particular to export prices, has led to an important increase in the labour income quote in later years.

Finally inflation may endanger the steady development of the collective sector, which at least in later years became a target of economic policy. Production in this sector is labour intensive. The price of collective services therefore is closely correlated to the wage rate, and wage rate increases in this sector are not compensated by increases in labour productivity which are by definition equal to zero. Experience has shown that, under certain circumstances, a rise in the burden of taxes and social premiums due to the growth of the collective sector may be shifted by wage earners to the employers by means of wage negotiations directed to maintain a desired growth rate of disposable income[6]. This in turn will stimulate price increases. This will happen when the growth of the collective sector – real or in current prices – is not accepted by the workers as fitting in their preference schemes, notwithstanding the fact that the increase in the production of collective services and in transfers is politically accepted. Thus inflation may be amplified through the growth of the collective sector. A policy directed towards moderating inflation will therefore have to control the growth of the collective sector and may even be forced to lower it, at least for a certain period.

3.4 The theory of inflation

3.4.1 Recent developments

An assessment of counter-inflation policy should be based on inflation theory in an operational and quantified form. In other words in the form of a model. In addition, insight is required into the institutions set up for designing and implementing economic policy. They provide the policy instruments. Particularly important are the institutions required for using endogenous variables as instruments of economic policy, as in the case of the Dutch wage level for several years.

During the past ten or fifteen years inflation theory has changed[7]. New elements have been introduced, and attempts have been made to integrate inflation theory into macro economic models. Important relationships which, according to these models, play a part in generating and maintaining inflation are:
– A relationship between changes in the wage level on the one hand and the growth rate of production per man, expected changes in prices, and variables that characterize the labour market on the other hand. Such relationships are often based on theories describing labour market behaviour with the help of a target function, containing the desired labour income quota as argument, and hypotheses on job search by workers having incomplete information on job opportunities.
– A relationship between changes in the prices of final products on the one hand and the changes in prices of production factors, mark-up factors or a target rate of return, and excess demand on the other hand. The theoretical basis of introducing costs and profit margins is often long term profit maximization. The use of excess demand variables is appropriate in the case of prices formed on competitive markets. A relationship between

profit margins and excess demand, as is sometimes suggested in empirical studies, can be employed in those cases where uncertainty and disequilibrium situations are explicitly considered.

- A relationship between expected and actual price changes, which may be based on various assumptions about the formation of expectations.
- Relationships describing the determinants of excess demand, also those originating in the monetary sector of the economy.

The systematic introduction of expectations in wage rate functions and of monetary factors in demand functions mark the new developments in inflation theory. They are responsible for its increased power to explain the apparently loose relationship between price changes and excess demand in later phases of inflationary processes. Modern inflation theory not only identifies the various inflationary impulses, stemming from price setting behaviour and wage negotiations, but also analyses the way in which these in turn are influenced by price and wage rate increases. It also specifies the conditions under which inflation will be maintained after the impulses have vanished. Thus giving an explanation of what came to be known as stag-flation.

The available operational models for analysing inflation do not contain all the elements formulated by inflation theory. The actual choice of the appropriate elements for describing inflation remains somewhat arbitrary. This is, among other things, due to the fact that the applied econometric methods are not powerful enough to disprove all theories except one. The consequence is that we are left with several competing theories, between which it is impossible to choose on the basis of econometric arguments.

It would go too far to present here an econometric model in which the synthesis mentioned is worked out, even if only partially[8]. In the next subsection a survey is given of the relationships in Dutch operational models that are important for the way in which they describe inflation. Their partial character with respect to inflation will become clear. Only a few aspects of modern inflation theory have in fact been used to analyse the Dutch inflation experience and to design counter-inflation policies.

3.4.2 The factors in Dutch macro economic models that generate inflation

Several operational models have been used for policy design in the Netherlands since the end of the second world war. In the beginning of this period the Central Planning Bureau used simple Keynesian demand models in which prices were related to labour costs per unit of product and the prices of imported raw materials[9]. The wage level was considered an exogenous variable determined by the centrally guided wage policy. No equations for expectations were introduced and no monetary sector was specified. Only foreign price impulses could cause inflation. An analysis of inflation according to the ideas of recent theories was impossible. Policy conclusions from these models had only limited significance.

The same holds for the more sophisticated models for short term analysis that were constructed in the second half of the fifties and sixties[10]. These models differed from the old ones because they had a much more detailed lag structure. Also the tension on the labour market was better defined and incorporated in several equations, as for example, that for changes in the wage level. So, in addition to impulses from abroad, a tight labour market could initiate wage increases which in their turn generated price rises. The monetary sector was reduced to only one equation which described the creation of liquidities. A fully fledged inflation analysis, according to modern standards, could not be set up.

A new generation of policy models in which two important novelties were introduced was constructed after 1974[11]. The first is a set of equations for production capacity. These equations are based on a vintage production function. Production capacity is built up from those vintages of investment goods that are still in use. The lifetime of the capital goods is therefore an important determinant of capacity. It depends on the growth rates of wages, prices and production per man. This part of the new models is important for analysing the way in which inflation influences production capacity. A second important feature is that they describe the influence the collective sector may have on the wage level. The equations of the collective sector define the burden of taxes and social security premiums and this variable is used as an explanatory variable in the wage level equation. In this way the shift of tax and premium increases from wages to profits by means of the annual negotiations on the growth rate of real disposable wages is taken into account. This adds a new possibility of creating inflation. In the course of the nineteen seventies this phenomenon probably contributed to the rise of wages. Other variables in the wage equation are, as usual, the price level of consumer goods, production per man and unemployment. In contrast to the theoretical models mentioned above, not expected but actual price changes, lagged half a year, are used as an explanatory variable. This variable probably describes more accurately the actual mechanism of wage indexation.

The price equations describe, on a macro-economic level, price setting behaviour. Domestic labour costs, import prices and the degree of capacity utilisation, are the important explanatory variables. When determining the labour costs, differences in the growth rate of production per man between sectors is taken into account: in particular the above average increases in productivity in exporting industries.

The model does not contain a monetary sector. The inflationary impulses from such a sector, or the monetary conditions required for inflation cannot be analysed; nor can the feedback mechanisms implied by monetary relationships. The demand functions for consumption, investment in fixed assets and inventories are conventional. The same holds for the export equation. In all these equations and in the equation for imports the degree of capacity utilisation is one of the explanatory variables: exports are limited and imports are stimulated by a high degree of capacit utilisation.

3.4.3 *Some tentative conclusions from the new C.P.B.-model. (VINTAF II)*

The initial causes of inflationary processes are the exogenous variables which determine wages and prices. According to the new generation of C.P.B.-models, these variables are the import prices and certain categories of expenditure that directly, or indirectly through labour market tensions, drive up wages and prices. Directly this can happen through government expenditures – both material consumption and transfers – which contribute to a higher tax or premium burden. Indirectly it occurs through all exogeneous increases of expenditure which lower unemployment and increase the degree of utilisation of capacity. Also decreases in taxes may have such consequences.

The further development of inflation depends on other characteristics of the models. In the first place, the interdependencies between wages and prices are important. Price increases influence wages through indexation clauses in collective wage agreements. Wages influence prices through the labour costs. In an open economy prices and labour costs are not proportional because a part of the total costs is made up of foreign prices that are generally not linked with domestic developments. In addition, all prices are influenced by foreign competition. The wage-price mechanism in the VINTAF II model implies a decreasing inflation when foreign prices remain constant and domestic impulses vanish. So, if after the inflation has been generated the causes of the disturbance vanish, it gradually disappears. Only if, in addition to rises in domestic costs, import prices rise equally fast, will the price rise be maintained when excess demand disappears.

A second aspect, important for the way in which the models describe the further development of an inflationary process, is whether or not excess demand disappears as a consequence of the price rises. In VINTAF II this is difficult to assess definitely. An analysis of the stability characteristics of the model can not be given because of its complexity. Existing excess demand will be diminished if one of the categories of expenditure is fixed in nominal terms, either because of a relationship in current prices or as an exogenous variable. The introduction of the degree of capacity utilisation in some of the expenditure functions may indeed lower the tensions: exports may be reduced because of a high level of capcity utilisation. This effect however may be compensated by a decrease in production capacity if the tension on the labour market presses the wage level above that of productivity thus leading to a decrease in the economic life of capital goods and to scrapping vintages of investment goods still in use. Capacity will be reduced and the degree in utilisation increased.

In principle the models provide the information by means of which economic policy is designed. Of course other information is brought in, in a less systematical way. The fundamental lines of analysis are however those laid down in the models. The picture they give is of course incomplete to the extent the models stylize reality. And that is what they do: Only some important aspects of reality are captured in their equations. Some obvious shortcomings can be mentioned that could be crucial for designing counter-inflation policy. In the first place a regional break down of the information about the economic process is missing, whereas excess demand on labour markets is most apparent in the western provinces of the country. Given an average unemployment percentage, the increase in the wage level will be higher than would have been the case if unemployment would have been spread more evenly over the country. Nevertheless the higher wage level influences prices in the same way in all provinces. A correct forecast of wage increases is therefore crucially dependent on a correct forecast of the regional distribution of unemployment and that does not exist.

Another aspect which could not be taken into account because adequate models were not available is related to the unintended and unobserved consequences of the centrally guided wage policy in the nineteen forties and fifties. It is highly probable that the intentionally low relative wages, sought after because of their healthy influence on the competitive situation on foreign markets, has led to an unintentional high labour intensity of production capacity which, in later years, led to tensions on the labour market and to the wage explosion in 1963 and 1964 which stimulated the inflation of the second half of the nineteen sixties.

Finally, as VINTAF II has no monetary sector the model can not describe how tensions on commodity and labour markets can be influenced by monetary factors. Actually such reactions probably do play a part in the development of inflation. Price rises lower real cash balances which may lead to decreasing expenditure. Also, in earlier phases of inflation, monetary reactions may be created which are worthwhile considering. A tension on commodity markets created by an increase in government expenditure can be reduced by rises of the interest rate due to capital market operations required to finance it. The rise in interest rates may lower investment expenditure. Again, a reaction, contrary to this one, may be due to higher consumption generated by the increase in consumers' holdings of government debt. If the higher government expenditure is financed by means of creation of liquidities this sort of reaction may be avoided. However in that case monetary reserves may be diminished by a deficit on the balance of payments which, through changes in exchange rates, may have similar effects. On the other hand this may increase import prices and thus stimulate inflation.

3.5 The instruments of counter-inflation policy

3.5.1 Categories of instruments

The previous section showed that inflation can be generated and maintained under the following conditions:
- a tight labour market which leads to changes in the wage rate higher than that in production per man;
- expected rises in the price level, which are to be compensated by means of wage rate increases that have the same effect;
- an increase in the burden of taxes and social premiums, which is not accepted by consumers as fitting in their preference schemes and gives rise to wage increases;
- tensions in commodity markets, due to an increase in expenditure above planned production or even production capacity and constitute an upward pressure on prices;
- actual price rises that generate expected price rises;
- wage and price changes that increase the labour income quota and so decrease the rate of growth of capacity in the long run;
- a growth rate of liquidities that finances price and wage increases.

These conditions provide starting points for designing a counter-inflation policy. Such a policy has to take into account targets other than price stability. An efficient counter-inflation policy will therefore use a number of policy instruments. In addition to measures aiming at controlling prices and wages, room should be made for instruments keeping the development of expenditure in line with that of capacity, stimulating productivity, striking the balance between the collective and the private sector in accordance with the wishes of the consumers, preventing actual price and wage rises generating expectations about price rises, and controlling the growth of liquidities. In part these measures can be taken in a form which safeguards the allocating function of the various markets. Generally that holds for measures influencing expenditure. Other measures however will interfere with the working of markets, in particular those that directly influence prices and wages.

It is important to distinguish between these two sets of instruments carefully. The measures that can be applied only when the market mechanisms are eliminated require for their implementation an institutional framework. The other measures can be taken by governments, within certain boundary conditions, without special care. Because in the Netherlands measures that interfere with labour market decisions were important, at least during the forties and the fifties, relatively much attention will be devoted to them in this section. Before doing so a short survey is given of the other measures. It will become clear why in the Netherlands so much weight has been given to direct wage controls.

In the first place indirect measures are meant to influence total demand for final goods and the distribution of this aggregate over its components. Private demand may be influenced by interest rates, tax tariffs and transfer payments. Public expenditure can be influenced by direct government action. It is the government that decides on the magnitude of the collective sector. This decision confronts the government with a difficult choice. The government sector produces services for consumers, takes care of income distribution by means of taxes, transfers and premiums, and has a stabilizing function in the whole economy. As the services the government produces are partly complementary with private consumption, at least in a densly populated country with a high average income, it will be clear that the possibilities for using government expenditure as an instrument in a counter-inflation policy are limited. In addition, when determining the relative magnitude of the collective sector, consumers' preferences should be taken into account in order to prevent the tax and social premiums burden increasing to such an extent that it will be shifted to profit income.

The distribution of private expenditure over consumption and investment, important for the growth rate of production capacity, can only indirectly be influenced by the government. A low rate of interest and fiscal incentives are important instruments.

Several times since the end of the war, the government has taken measures to influence magnitude and distribution of total expenditure. In 1950, for instance, when the Korea crisis endangered the stability of the price level and external equilibrium and in 1966, after the wage explosion of 1963/1964. An important attempt to mitigate the growth rate of the collective sector was started in 1975 when it became clear that the rapid increase during the preceding years was responsible for at least a part of inflation through the shifting of the collective burden. The attempts to limit the growth of this sector to not more than 1 percent of national income has dominated the discussions on economic policy up till now.

From a theoretical point of view, measures to improve the mobility of labour could also constitute important anti-inflation instruments. They increase the degree of utilisation of production capacity when they are effective and thus contribute to diminishing excess demand. On this kind of measure however not much information that is worthwhile is available.

It is not certain that monetary policy in the Netherlands has been directed deliberately towards mitigating inflation. No instance can be mentioned of a monetary policy that indeed limited the creation of liquidities to such an extent that price rises were prevented or lowered. In general, monetary policy followed both real and nominal developments by providing enough liquidities to finance nominal transactions.

The conviction that the instruments mentioned above would not be sufficiently efficient to safeguard full employment, balance of payment equilibrium and stability of the price level in an open economy with a rapidly growing population led policy makers already immediately after the war, to choose instruments that could interfere directly with market forces[12]. A stringent price policy has never been imposed. A centrally guided wage policy though, has from the beginning been a characteristic of the Dutch economy. The idea was that as policy targets are manifold and to some extent contradictory, a number of diversified instruments has to be used to attain them. In an inflationary situation a limitation of expenditure may help prevent the generation of excess demand, however at the cost of unemployment which in turn demands higher expenditure. In these circumstances a limitation of wage rate increases may be more efficient. However, as only wages are to be controlled, undesired developments in income distribution may endanger a wage policy. It has been argued that in a dynamic economy the price mechanism should not be controlled too much in order not to deprive the economy of its allocating device. The fact that a guided wage policy can also frustrate that allocation was only discovered when it was too late.

3.5.2 The institutional framework of the wage policy

As already stated, an institutional framework is required as soon as an endogenous variable, such as the wage level, is used as an instrument of economic policy; an institutional framework that replaces the market forces that otherwise would determine that endogenous variable. It enables the design and implementation of an economic policy in which such a variable is used as an instrument. In this section attention is paid to the institutional framework of the wage policy. Several phases can be distinguished[13].

The first phase runs from 1945 to 1962, the period of the centrally guided wage policy. The following aspects of wage determination were important. On the basis of an analysis of recent and expected economic developments the government gave guidelines about the wage level in the form of instructions to the Board of Government Mediators[14]. They were formulated after consultations with the Foundation of Labour[15], an organisation of representatives of the trade unions and of the associations of employers. In negotiations between trade unions and employers it was decided how wage increases could be implemented at the industry level. Various possibilities were available: general wage rises, premiums, or wage differentiations between groups of workers on the basis of job evaluation. The idea was to get more adequate wage differentials between groups with different education. The draft collective agreements were sent to the Board of Government Mediators for approval. The Board asked the Foundation of Labour for scrutiny and advice. The Foundation asked information from the contracting parties and often a consensus was reached. If not, the Board took the decision. This rather complicated system was used to suggest that in fact workers' and employers' organisations took the decisions, albeit within a framework designed by the government.

In the beginning of this period the main criterium for wage rate increases was the development of the index of the cost of living. Given the rather high rate of increase of labour productivity during the first part of the fifties, this led to a deterioration of the labour income quota. After 1954 this variable became a second indicator for the permitted wage increases. Some of the trade unions asked for a greater differentiation of wage rate increases between industries. In 1956 an attempt to differentiate wages failed. The wage rate increase of 6 percent which was announced as a maximum percentage, meant to be used only by the most prosperous industries, was granted by almost all industries. After 1959 more differentiation in wages was obtained. They were no longer geared only to the average increase in productivity but also to productivity indices specific to the industry itself.

The introduction of this system was accompanied by precise directives, drawn up by the central government, about the way productivity indices had to be calculated and applied. In this way the differentiated wage policy remained centrally guided. Attempts to decentralize the wage policy failed.

The second phase runs from 1963 to 1968. The experiences with the differentiated but centrally guided wage policy led to changes in the institutional framework that destroyed much of the official influence of the government. In particular the trade unions experienced great difficulties in co-operating with employers' organisations in order to implement wage policy. They had to accept the relatively low wage rate increases that were offered officially, while the rank and file knew that in various industries higher results could be obtained, and actually were obtained, in the form of illegal benefits. In the new system the Social Economic Council set up semi-annual economic reports with the help of data provided by the Central Planning Bureau. The government indicated its ideas about optimal wage rate increases. Then, a rather complicated procedure of internal co-ordination between the trade union federations and the individual trade unions, and between the employers' federations and its members took place in order to organize the negotiations on industry level according to the principles worked out at the central level. Also a co-ordination was strived after between workers' and employers' representatives on different levels. Draft contracts were sent to the Board of Government Mediators and the Foundation of Labour for approval by the latter. The Minister of Social Affairs could declare contracts accepted by the Board invalid. If no consensus was obtained the Foundation could ask the Board to take a decision.

This system was meant to bring greater freedom for the contracting parties. That was achieved only partly. The government still maintained the possibility of nullifying the contracts when it considered them a danger for a sound economic development. The government used this weapon several times and also threatened to use it several more. In 1966 for instance, the approval of collective agreements was witheld for a while because the wage rate increases became too high. Only in 1963 a central agreement between trade unions and employers' organisation was obtained. In subsequent years the government itself had to formulate the wage policy, because the social partners could not reach consensus. So the government still had an important influence. Notwithstanding the difficulties the social partners had in reconciling differences on the targets of the wage policy, they insisted on getting greater freedom for real negotiations. In 1967 consensus was reached about a new system and the government accepted it.

This brings us to the third phase: 1968-1973. In this period government influence would, according to the plans, vanish completely. The government would no longer give indications on the desired changes in the wage level. The Foundation of Labour would no longer have the task to approve collective wage agreements. The Board of Government Mediators would have no tasks with respect to the wage policy. The Minister of Social Affairs could nullify those collective agreements which threatened the equilibrium of the economy but should ask advice from a special commission of 'wise men' before doing so. In 1970 this system was incorporated in a new law on the wage policy. The Minister of Social Affairs was given the power of calling for a wage freeze in case of important disturbances in economic development. If he intended to take such a measure he had to ask advice from the Social Economic Council and the Foundation of Labour.

In 1968 the government interfered strongly with the contracts concluded on the basis of free negotiations. The collective agreement in the building industry were declared invalid with respect to agreements about a shorter working week and increases in old age pension premiums. Other contracts received a similar treatment. In 1969, however, a central agreement on the wage policy in 1970 was reached, complete with accurate quantitative indications on the permitted changes in the wage rate. This contradicted the greater freedom for negotiations at lower levels just laid down in the general agreement on the new system. At the end of 1970 the government announced a wage freeze which was implemented in 1971. This led to a strong collusion between trade unions and the government.

In 1971 the Social Economic Council set up new rules for its own role in the wage negotiations on the basis of the new 1970 wage act. The Council would prepare the basis for discussions between the government and the social partners by establishing a report by economic experts: the government appointed members of the Council. During the year discussions between government and employers' and workers' representatives would be organised, not only on issues regarding the development of wages but on all aspects of economic policy. In the Autumn the discussions would be focused on wage and price developments. If possible government and social partners were to agree on a Social Contract with a much broader scope than the central agreement on wages of the preceeding years. The central agreement should become an integral part of a complete economic programme. The government promised not to nullify collective bargaining agreements on general economic considerations. This system still reigns. It has never been possible to conclude a social contract. Often, even the negotiations to reach a central agreement on wages failed.

In 1974 and 1975, after the severe increases in energy prices, the government obtained the power to give binding rules on wages and other remuneration for wage earners, including those for whom collective bargaining agreements do not apply. It could also issue prescriptions about incomes of non-wage earners. At the same time a general freeze on firing personnel was announced. The government had to report the application of its new power to parliament. The purpose of the rules was a socially just distribution of the decrease in real income, implied by the rise of import prices, over all members of the community.

As in 1975 no central agreement was reached, the government announced a wage freeze for 1976. After heated discussions an amendment to the wage act made it possible to control wages in the second half of 1976, after the wage freeze terminated. In 1977 and 1978 the government did not interfere with wage determination. In general trade unions did not ask for high wage increases, probably checked by the high rate of unemployment and a general feeling that only by means of a careful and moderate wage policy could the development of the collective sector, which anyway has to be controlled, be safeguarded.

We should now try to assess the use of the wage rate as are instrument of anti-inflation policy in general terms. The following points may be important.

1. Only for a short period has it been possible to determine the wage rate, in conjunction with other instruments of economic policy, as the solution of an economic policy problem and to make the social partners accept this solution. Perhaps only till 1959 has this type of wage policy functioned. However, even in that period undesired and unintended developments took place. This is not to say that after 1959 no significance at all should be attached to the wage policy as a counter-inflation policy.

2. For an efficient implementation of the wage policy, agreement between the social partners and the government is required on
– the model to be used for policy purposes, i.e. about the relevant relationships between targets and instruments;
– the targets of economic policy;
– the boundary conditions between which targets and instrument variables should be kept.
Probably agreement on these points can only be reached in very special circumstances. In the course of time it became increasingly difficult to convince the rank and file of both trade unions and employers' organisations to accept the conclusions on the desirability of centrally negotiated consensus.

3. It has been pleaded many times that the determination of the wage rate

should be left to the social partners. Such a plea was often accompanied by one of the two following statements:

a The social partners, when negotiating wage rate changes, are able and willing to take into account, the general targets of economic policy, including price stability, and to decide on the growth rate of wages in such a way that these targets are not frustrated.

b It is not the task of employers' and workers' organisations, even on a central level, to help realize the targets of economic policy.

If the first point were correct the sometimes violent resistance against government intervention is understandable. However I am inclined, in line with the second statement, to conclude from Dutch experience that the willingness and the room for manoeuvre, particularly of the trade unions, to take into account other targets than only the welfare of the workers is smaller than is sometimes suggested.

4. The wage policy, that should have been designed simultaneously with other parts of economic policy in order to get an integrated policy programme, has probably been established too much on an *ad hoc* basis. The procedures that were set up to take care of the integration were too weak for that purpose. Often no agreement was reached in circumstances where consensus would have been the only means of guaranteeing the implementation of policy coordinating unanimously formulated targets. Equally, employers' and workers' representatives and the government found it difficult to take into consideration all other aspects of economic policy when designing a wage policy for the short run. Too often the government had to prescribe the permitted wage rate changes. The government could then in principle design wage policy so as to bring it into line with the other aspects of economic policy, however the necessary support by the social partners in implementing it was not then guaranteed. In that sense the attempts to make the wage level a real instrument of economic policy have failed. Nevertheless it cannot be denied that often government interference in the negotiations between employers and trade unions, though contradicting the agreements reached on greater freedom for the social partners, has influenced the level of the wage rate changes and thus mitigated inflation, though the high level of unemployment since 1975 may have contributed too. It is difficult to support this conclusion by means of an econometric analysis – as has been tried for other countries[16] – because wage policy has been used throughout the whole post-war period, including those years in which, according to the rules of the game, the government should have stood aside. It is therefore impossible to compare periods in which the policy was 'on' with periods in which it was 'off'. The description given above, however, contains enough

examples to convey the suggestion of a rather strong, but not systematically designed, influence of government intervention.

3.5.3 Price policy

Though in the Netherlands price policy has not been a strong instrument against inflation it seems justified to make some remarks on its legal basis and its implementation. Price policy before 1961 was based on an old law stemming from 1939 which was meant, among other things, to control the price level during the Second World War. In 1961 a new prices act was issued.

The general targets of the price policy have been to safeguard the allocative function of the price mechanism and to prevent unjustifiable price rises. The policy was implemented, in principle, by means of voluntary co-operation between government and trade and industry, though the government had some powers, based on the prices act, to interfere directly in price setting behaviour. The rules of price policy were designed in the same spirit of co-operation and with the help of the same institutions as were used for wage policy. They consisted of:
- A general permission to pass on changes in external costs as, for instance, changes in import prices.
- A general prohibition on passing on changes in wage costs per unit of product. This rule was based on the idea that wage policy aimed at a restriction of wage rate changes to a level equal to changes in production per man. As only in the period 1959-1963 was this aim explicitly formulated, the government suspended this prohibition on a number of occasions in those years in which this type of wage policy was not pursued.
- A general prohibition on increasing profit margins measured in money units.

In addition, the prices act gave the Government the power to take the following measures by means of price decrees:
- it could prescribe maximum prices for an industry or for individual firms;
- it could oblige firms to announce intended price increases to the Ministry of Economic Affairs;
- it could announce a general prohibition on changing prices for a certain period.

Important was the obligation to announce intended price changes because only when the government knew of the plans to change prices could it try, by persuasion and discussions, to avoid direct intervention. Direct intervention could only be considered as an instrument if social and economic targets were threatened by price rises. It is indicated in the prices act which organisations have to be asked for advice if the government plans to take this kind of measures. In general, price decrees can be issued only for a limited period.

As already said, price policy has not been a strong weapon against inflation. The government has always been anxious to avoid too strong an intervention in the price mechanism in order not to disturb its function as allocating device. Nevertheless the application of the various instruments which the prices act offers, certainly has had a mitigating influence on inflation. In the course of time many price decrees have been issued.

3.6 Summary

In this section the most important results of the preceeding sections will be recapitulated.

a. The Dutch economy has experienced a persistent positive rate of change in prices since the end of the Second World War. This has unfavourably influenced the explicitly formulated targets of economic policy: full employment, equilibrium on the balance of payments, a stable and high level of investment, a reasonable income distribution, and a steady growth of the collective sector. The Dutch government has constantly tried to design and implement a counter-inflation policy.

b. It may be asked whether modern inflation theory can cope with recent experiences and can give indications for the design of counter-inflation policies. The answer is that the synthesis that is developing in the literature in which expectations about prices, and a fully integrated monetary sector are the main ingredients, leads to a better understanding of the generation and development of inflation than earlier theories did. It also indicates that inflation is probably to some extent inevitable in a world in which full employment has an almost absolute priority, the wage level is formed in an institutional market and the social partners, when deciding upon their actions, take into account the reactions of the government.

c. It may be asked whether policy makers in the Netherlands have been able to identify and analyse accurately the character and importance of inflation. Probably this has been the case only to a limited extent justly because the models used for policy design did not contain all important elements of inflation theory. In particular the monetary sector and equations describing the generation of expectations were missing. The shifting of the tax and social premiums burden has only been introduced in the models that have been used since 1975. Secondly forecasts on wages and prices have often suffered from errors. Often price and wage changes were underestimated.

d. It may be asked whether the anti-inflation policy instruments have been effective. The answer must probably be: not sufficiently. When using the wage level as an instrument of economic policy the government has tried to give the social partners, employers and workers, a say in the design of the policy. Given the endogenous character of this variable this is understandable because it could have been expected to lead to a better co-operation of employers' and workers' representatives in the implementation of the policy. However never has a study been set up to find out whether the conditions for success were fulfilled. These conditions are agreement between government, employers and workers about:

. the targets of the policy

.. the relationships between all relevant variables

... the boundary conditions between which the instrument variables had to be chosen.

Secondly the hybrid character of some of the other instruments as government expenditure (on the one hand a part of total expenditure, on the other hand an instrument for stabilizing the economy) and the tax rates (an instrument influencing income distribution and the level of expenditure) makes an explicit determination of the priorities of the various targets a condition for their efficient use. This condition has never been fulfilled.

Notes

* This chapter was written in November 1978 and deals with events up to that date. It is important to note that in 1980 the government took new powers to curb wage increases. At the time of going to press it was too early to be certain over the ramifications of these new initiatives.

[1] See for instance the *Central Economic Plan 1949* page 17. The Hague 1949.

[2] For the first time this concept has been used in the *Central Economic Plan 1966*, The Hague 1966.

[3] See *Central Economic Plan 1978*, The Hague 1978.

[4] *Advies inzake de in de naaste toekomst te voeren loon- en prijspolitiek*, Social Economic Council, The Hague, 1951. The Dutch title can be translated as follows: Advice on wage and price policy in the near future.

The Social Economic Council, one of the institutions created by the Industrial Organisation Act of 1950, is a tripartite advisory body for economic and social policy problems.

[5] See for instance: *Een macro model voor de Nederlandse Economie op middellange termijn, VINTAF II*, (A macro medium term model for the Dutch economy, VINTAF II) Occasional Papers No. 12, Central Planning Bureau, The Hague 1977.

[6] See the wage equation in the model mentioned in footnote 5.

[7] Several publications on inflation theory could be mentioned. (See the references). A recent undergraduate text is: A.J. Hagger, *Inflation: Theory and Policy*. London 1977.

[8] A nice example of such a model is given in J.L. Stein, 'Inside the Monetarist Black Box', in: J.L. Stein, ed. *Monetarism*. Amsterdam 1976.

[9] See for instance *Central Economic Plan 1955.* Central Planning Bureau, The Hague 1955.

[10] See *Central Economic Plan 1971.* Central Planning Bureau, The Hague 1971.

[11] See H. den Hartog, Th. C.M.J. van de Klundert and H.S. Tjan, 'De structurele ontwikkeling van de werkgelegenheid in macro-economisch perspectief', (A macro economic view on the structural development of employment). *Werkloosheid: aard, omvang, structurele oorzaken en beleids-alternatieven*, Preadviezen van de Vereniging voor de Staathuishoudkunde, 1975. See also the publication mentioned in footnote 5.

[12] See J. Tinbergen, 'De betekenis van de loonvoet voor de werkgelegenheid', *De Economist, 1950.* (The significance of wages for employment).

[13] A very good survey of developments in this field until 1967 is given in John P. Windmuller, *Labor Relations in the Netherlands.* Ithaca, New York 1968.

[14] The task of the Government Mediators before the second world war was to prevent or to settle labour disputes. During the war they formed a national board. The Extraordinary Decree on Labour Relations of 1945 gave the Board the authority to issue binding rules on wages.

[15] The Foundation of Labour, set up immediately after the war by representatives of the federations of labour and entrepreneurs, was acknowledged in the Extraordinary Decree on Labour Relations of 1945 as an advisory body for all issues related to social policy.

[16] See for instance M. Parkin and M. Summer, Eds. *Incomes Policy and Inflation*, Manchester 1972. For an attempt to identify the consequences of different forms of wage policy, see W. Driehuis, *Fluctuations and Growth in a Near Full Employment Economy.* Rotterdam, 1972, Chapter 8.

Select Bibliography

In English

Frisch, H. Inflation Theory, 1963-1975: A 'Second Generation' Survey. *Journal of Economic Literature December 1977, p. 1289-1317*.

Hagger, A.J. *Inflation: Theory and Policy*. London, 1977.

Lundberg, E., Ed. *Inflation Theory and anti-inflation Policy*. London, 1977.

Parkin, M. and M.T. Summer, eds. *Incomes Policy and Inflation*. Manchester, 1972.

Stein, J.L. ed. *Monetarism*. Amsterdam 1976.

Verdoorn, P.J. Some long-run dynamic elements of factor price inflation, in: H.C. Bos, H. Linnemann and P. de Wolff, eds., *Economic Structure and Development, Essays in honour of Jan Tinbergen*, Amsterdam 1973.

Windmuller, John P. *Labor Relations in the Netherlands*. New York 1968.

In Dutch

Balk, B.M., G.J. van Driel, C. van Ravenzwaay. Inflatie in Nederland van 1952 tot 1975. *Statistische Onderzoekingen Centraal Bureau voor de Statistiek, 1-4.* 's-Gravenhage 1978. (Statistical data on inflation in the Netherlands.)

Centraal Planbureau, Het jaarmodel 1969, Bijlage A in *Centraal Economisch Plan 1971*, Centraal Planbureau, 's-Gravenhage 1971. (A description of the 1969 model).

Centraal Planbureau, *Een macro model voor de Nederlandse economie op middellange termijn*, (VINTAF II). Occasional Papers no. 12. Centraal Planbureau, 's-Gravenhage 1977. (A description of the model VINTAF II.)

Hartog, H. den, Th. C.M.J. van de Klundert en H.S. Tjan: De structurele ontwikkeling van de Werkgelegenheid in macro economisch perspectief. *Vereniging voor de Staathuishoudkunde, Werkloosheid, Aard, omvang, structurele oorzaken en beleidsalternatieven*, 's-Gravenhage 1975. (A description of the model VINTAF I.)

Jong, J. de, *Een aantal recente ontwikkelingen in het Nederlandse systeem van arbeidsverhoudingen*. (Recent developments in Dutch labour relations.)

Korteweg, P. De Stagflatie van de jaren zeventig: feiten en verklaringen. *Vereniging voor de Staathuishoudkunde, Internationale Stagflatie bij vaste en flexibele wisselkoersen*, 's-Gravenhage 1978. (Stagflation in the seventies, facts and explanations.)

Ridder, P.B. de, Het verband tussen inflatie, afwenteling en arbeidsinkomensquote. *Maandschrift Economie 1976-1977, 126-139*. (The relation between inflation, tax shifting and the labour income quota).

4. THE INFLUENCE OF NATURAL GAS ON THE DUTCH ECONOMY

R.F.M. Lubbers and C. Lemckert

In dealing with the economic problems that existed after World War II, the Dutch have never entertained many illusions over the role that could be played by indigenous mineral resources. There were some limited possibilities for increasing the exploitation of the coal seams in the extreme South and also for recovering salt, marl and gravel on an extremely modest scale. For the rest the Dutch had to find their strengths in other qualities and that they did so successfully is described elsewhere in this volume. This does not alter the fact that exploratory borings for oil and gas, suspended during the war, were revived. Shell and Esso worked together in this in the *Nederlandse Aardolie Maatschappij* (Netherlands' Petroleum Company) henceforth NAM. Success was modest until, barely twenty years ago, productive natural gas reserves were struck under the mainland in the Northern province of Groningen. On the basis of this discovery near the village of Slochteren, it was estimated that 50 billion m³ of natural gas were present. Although the various successful borings in the region of Slochteren all yielded gas of the same composition as the first Slochteren discovery and at the same pressure of 350 atm., it was not until 1963 that it was realised that these borings comprised the same field. This conclusion meant that in 1963 the recoverable quantity of gas was already being estimated at 1,100 billion m³. It is interesting to note that the concessions were granted on May 30th 1963 and that it was only shortly afterwards that the first realistic estimates of the extent of the reserves were made. By 1965 the official estimates had already climbed to around 1,500 billion m³ and two years later they stood at 2,200 billion m³. Roughly speaking it could be said that not until eight years after the first successful boring was a proper insight gained into the extent of the reserves. If, upto 1967, one could say that there was a continuous, very large, underestimation of the natural gas available (after that date was a period in which the expected level of reserves in the Slochteren field increased little), the share that could be considered as proven reserves continued to increase.

From this description it will be clear that, gradually, throughout the sixties, the Dutch authorities realised that, from the standpoint of both energy supply and economic policy, a development of national, even international, importance was being discussed. With subsequent governments this realisation has only increased. The purpose of this chapter is to discuss the economic significance of this gas in greater detail. It will become clear that in the twenty years in which the Netherlands proved to belong to the 'haves' in the energy field, both the policy relating to the gas itself and the economic policy based on that gas have changed. In this period the significance of the gas has been interpreted differently depending upon shifting interpretations of the development of the energy situation and changes in the economic environment. In order to be able properly to evaluate the role of gas in the past as well as to judge the prospects for the future, it is desirable to distinguish between different sub-periods:

a) the 1960's – economic growth and penetration of natural gas
b) 1969-1973 – economic disequilibrium and new scarcity
c) 1973-1976 – socialisation of demand and energy crisis
d) 1976-1985 – public sector restraint and further catching up of gas prices
e) after 1985 – threatened external account and less natural gas.

Within this context greater consideration will be given to the first period because, during these years, gas caused a number of clear structural changes to be brought about which are experienced as economic data in later periods.

4.1 The 1960's – Economic growth and penetration of natural gas

The news of the large natural gas discoveries came in a situation which can briefly be described as follows: in the energy world, competitively priced oil, based on relatively low production costs, had forced coal onto the defensive and nuclear energy was seen as the cheap energy source of the future; ecoomically there was talk of strong growth, full employment, incipient inflation and a competitive business environment. It was against this background that the policy discussion over the optimal use of the natural gas was conducted and decisions taken.

An interesting illustration is offered by the lecture of the then director of the Central Planning Bureau, P. de Wolff.[1] In this lecture, held around 1962/63, the lifespan and rate of exploitation of gas reserves and the contribution to national income were approached primarily as a question of theoretical optimisation. From this lecture we quote the observation that the prevailing oil prices and those of nuclear energy over the next 45 years were considered so competitive and the resistance to conversion to new technical devices so large, that optimalisation of national economic advantage led to the conclusion that rapid depletion of reserves (in 25-40 years) and deep market penetration (thus also implying low prices) were desirable.

In the first major policy document of the government after the gas discoveries – the Aardgas Nota (Natural Gas Note) of the Minister of Economic Affairs, de Pous[2] – similar elements came to the fore (active market penetration, a lifespan of one generation, a subsidy for gas prices for industrialisation in the North). Shortly thereafter a new incoming government picked up the drastic consequences of the closure of coal-mines.

4.1.1 Conversion of the Dutch economy to natural gas

Once the decision had been taken in the mid-sixties to make natural gas as available as possible to the Dutch economy, the process of market penetration proceded very quickly. This appears very clearly in Figure 4.1 which presents the final use of energy per energy form. In an extremely short space of time a large mains network covering the entire country was lain and

Figure 4.1 Total final energy used in the Netherlands, by energy form, 1950–1980 (in million tonne oil–equivalent)

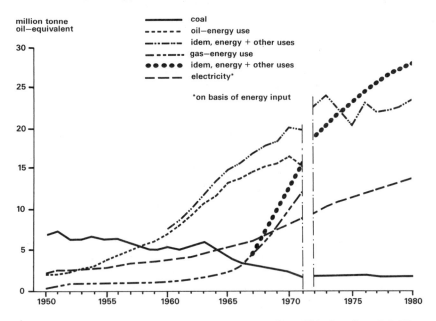

Source: Ministerie van Economische Zaken

gas heating and cooking apparatus converted. This affected particularly the private sector.

In households, in particular, this led not only to a change over to natural gas but also to much higher energy consumption. Central heating in houses advanced extremely rapidly and, with it, the practice of heating all the rooms in what were not, generally speaking, well insulated houses. In addition to housing, there was, of course, space heating in offices and industrial buildings. Following the application of natural gas for big industrial boilers for the generation of steam, there was also a strong increase in its application in electrical power stations. Finally natural gas provided a raw material in the chemical industry.

4.1.2 Gas sales policy

The first device for the selling of gas was, as mentioned above, the penetration of the domestic market. The most important element in this was the choice of a low price, and in this way the Dutch economy also received support. In the interests of structural-industrial and regional targets, in addition to the generally low price, a certain quantity of gas at an extra low price was reserved for special projects. This operation was not particularly successful; the employment-creation effects were small and later it transpired that it was extremely costly, once energy prices had climbed steeply.

Alongside the above-mentioned special reserve there was a not unimportant application of gas in the chemical sector against somewhat reduced prices, although these were linked to the general energy price level.

In the second half of the sixties people had been so impressed by the enormous size of reserves that they began to look for sales in the form of a number of export contracts. The Dutch parliament continually kept pressure on the government to conclude this sort of contract. Now, in the light of the scarcity in the seventies, this all seems extremely curious. However it must be emphasised that in the sixties people were still confronted by low oil prices and there were few prophets who predicted any change in the situation. In addition, in accordance with expectations, nuclear energy was coming slowly but surely to the deployment stage and it was estimated that each rise in energy prices would trigger an enormous expansion in nuclear energy. In short, it was assumed that in the future natural gas would yield relatively less.

Just as in the domestic market penetration, price was used as the primary instrument in the export contracts. Some of the contracts were stipulated in fixed price terms and some linked to current oil prices. The latter was, at the time, not always considered advantageous – a contrast to the seventies. In explaining this sales urgency in the second half of the sixties one must point to the underestimation in the growth of the domestic use of natural gas.

In the end, export contracts were concluded for approximately 1,000 billion m³ of gas. Deliveries were to be spread over a large number of years and to run down gradually in the 1990's.

4.1.3 Coal-mine closures

In 1963 the Minister of Economic Affairs, den Uyl, published the decision to begin the closure of the coal-mines in South Limburg. In 1963 coal mining employed virtually 50,000 men. by 1968 this number had been halved and at the end of 1973 this had been further reduced to the last 5,000 jobs. In considering this gigantic operation it must be remembered that already in the second half of the fifties, coal mining had been thrown onto the defensive by the enormous rise in oil usage. In many respects the use of oil was both cheaper and more attractive. Moreover competition was increasingly felt from cheaper coal supplies from abroad. For whichever reason, when linked with a rise in welfare and thus wage costs, our coal-mining industry incurred increasing trading losses. This phenomenon was also apparent in other western European countries, including many which could not profit from natural gas. An incidental point was that there would be steadily fewer people available willing to do unattractive work in the mines. The heroic associations with that occupation stood in an increasingly unfavourable light

Table 4.1

Gross investment in gas extraction and distribution compared with that in the total energy sector (as a percentage of total business investment excluding residential construction).

	1951/55	56/60	61/65	66/70	71/72
	average percentage per period				
gas sector	1,5	2,0	3,5	5,1	6,3
energy sector (total)	14,1	12,1	12,3	14,9	16,6
	average level per year				
energy sector (million guilders) (1970 prices)	0,8	1,0	1,5	2,5	3,1

Source: C.P.B., Centraal economisch plan, 1974, p. 150.

against the enormous increase in welfare and improvement in working conditions which characterised the post-war decades.

The closure of the mines in the Netherlands occurred as a very well planned operation. It did indeed have strong negative implications for the economy – an enormous direct loss in employment, a significant negative effect in the region via the 'multiplier effect' and, finally, negative implications for those firms throughout the land supplying the stream of investment goods which the mines still required. As we have already observed, there prevailed a climate of optimism over the possibilities of redeploying the labour and capital released by the operation. This optimism fitted easily into the picture of the sixties, outlined briefly above, characterised by a strong growth in production and an expansion in the number of jobs.

4.1.4 Macro-economic aspects

The economic implications of natural gas in the sixties can be summed up by the Dutch expression 'you have to spend money to make money'. Naturally it required investment on a large scale in the energy sector to build up a suitable infrastructure (pipe-line network, machine conversion, well heads, compressors). Table 4.1 gives an indication of the acceleration in this investment activity.

In industry, too, potential purchasers had to make the switch to natural gas and, in the process expanded many of their activities. In addition ancillary gas industries (artificial fertilisers, metallurgy, etc.) were established. The strong response of industry to the change in relative energy prices is apparent in Figure 4.2.

In short, there was a strong proclivity for investment by businesses resulting in a continuous stream exceeding the sum of one billion guilders a year. Many of the investment goods, e.g. the gas network, were imported from abroad as was a large share of the necessary labour force. The balance of payments, therefore, experienced negative pressures from the occurrence of natural gas. In terms of newly created jobs, the introduction of natural gas was not particularly interesting, the more so because it led to the expansion in the relatively labour extensive sector. Against the background of the tension existing in the labour market (unemployment had been under one per cent for years on the trot) this was not much of a problem.

Although, initially, the sixties were characterised economically by the incurrence of the necessary expense, between 1966 and 1970 gas production for domestic sales began to rise nicely. Weitenberg calculated that as early as

Figure 4.2 Substitution of oil by gas in industry

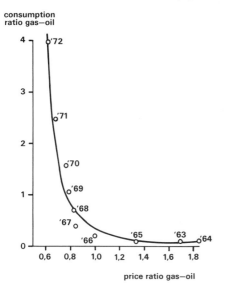

Source: C.P.B., Centraal Economisch Plan, 1974, p. 151

the period 1966-68 the growth of macro-economic productivity was 0.4 per cent per annum higher than it would otherwise have been[3]. Another item of invisible income can be added to this welfare-effect because the preponderantly domestic consumers received a consumption surplus (using any alternative source of energy they would have been worse off). Finally there were social benefits which were realised (see, for example, Figure 4.3 in which the positive correlation between gas production and air quality is apparent).

4.1.5 Final considerations

To round off this section, some comments about the economic background in general. The keyword is expansion. Even without natural gas the economy was booming. Important in this were the liberalisation of trade within the EEC, the growth of world trade and also the stimulating effect of low oil prices. The Netherlands was able to exploit these factors through its position in the Rhine delta (trade, refineries, chemical plants, etc.). These developments are considered at greater length elsewhere in this book. Looking at results, it is perhaps useful to point out that this total configuration of economic growth within a tight labour market could precipitate large wage

**Figure 4.3 The development of natural gas production and
an indicator of air quality**

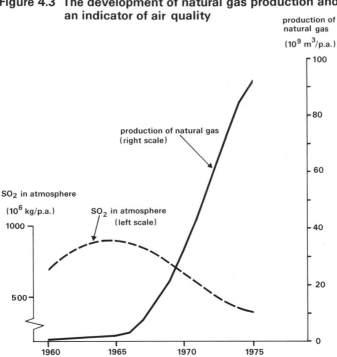

claims and, indeed, from 1964 this led to an increase in labour's share of national income. This general increase in welfare established a climate for the provision of many kinds of public services (largely social) which in the longer run could be of significance to the government budget. In this process, natural gas appears to have played only a subsidiary role.

4.2 1969-1973 Economic disequilibrium and new scarcity

If the sixties presented an economic picture of relative stability or of stable expansion, the end of the decade announced more or less easily recognisable changes which were of importance for the interaction between economic circumstances and developments in energy.

Firstly, there was evidence of a growing hard core of unemployment, independent of cyclical movements. This structural unemployment made its appearance in the very period in which the decision to curtail coal mining was being implemented. With hindsight we have to accept that the decision to close the mines fitted into the pattern of optimism in the sixties over the possibilities for redeploying the labour and capital released, but the actual implementation of the decision largely coincided with the appearance of stagnation in employment opportunities. As far as the miners themselves were concerned, the promise remained that they were to be guaranteed a satisfactory income, either through early retirement or through re-employment in other industries. A special commission, the so-called Hellemans Commission, continued to implement this policy until deep into the seventies. From the standpoint of employment opportunities in South Limburg, however, the policy must be considered a failure. This came about as a result of what is called the second generation effect. Because so many old miners opted for early retirement – the normal pensionable age was already relatively low – employment had to be found for the second generation. This problem, together with the problem of derived unemployment is still substantial. In respect to employment creation to compensate for job losses in mining, one can point to the successful rebuilding of the *Staatsmijnen* (State mines) enterprise under the predominantly chemical firm D.S.M. In 1978

Table 4.2

Government support to South-Limburg (million guilders).

	65/69	70/73	74	75	76	77	65/77
	average per annum						cummulative total
Support to the mining industry	91	162	150	125	107	140	1625
Specific costs of a regional policy of which:	32	73	195	250	180	493	1560
Support to industry							(475)
Investment premium regulation							(331)
Employment creation programmes							(450)
Infrastructural improvements							(218)

Table 4.3

Composition of production in the enterprise sector and its relative changes, 1963-1973 (expressed as a percentage of total production in the enterprise sector).

	Composition 1963	Change attributed to prices	volume	Composition 1973
Agriculture	10,0	− 2,5	− 0,8	6,7
Manufacturing	39,3	− 7,4	5,4	37,3
(residential construction excl.)				
of which:				
Gas extraction	0,5	− 1,1	2,8	2,2
Public utilities	2,7	− 2,1	2,2	2,8
Residential Construction	7,7	3,2	− 1,9	9,0
Services	43,0	6,7	− 2,7	47,0
Total Production in the enterprise sector	100			100

Source: C.P.B., *De Nederlandse economie in 1980*, p. 135.

D.S.M. employed approximately 16,000 workers in South Limburg. Alongside this, there was the establishment of the DAF car plant which now employs approximately 4,000 workers; a number significantly lower than originally anticipated.

In an agreement with the private mines made at the time it was intended that the newly released capital should preferably be reinvested in South Limburg. This agreement has not so far appeared to have been very successful, not least because the firms concerned saw little opportunity for establishing other profitable activities in the area. Although the negative effects of the coal mine closures on the development of national income were relatively small – mining was a loss-making activity – total budgetary costs for social and economic settlements in the region over the years have been not inconsiderable.

In this respect the figures in Table 4.2 are illuminating – showing the amounts paid out under the so-called mine-articles (subsidies for the miner's pension funds, individual and general support measures and measures for further adaptation). At the same time an estimate is given for the specific costs of regional policy in South Limburg (for example investment premiums, support for individual firms, expenditures on economic infrastructure, work creation programmes, etc.). Other clearly stimulating factors as the establishment of a medical school at Maastricht, a new NATO Headquarters (Afcent) and gas profits, insofar as they accrued to D.S.M., are not even included.

A second important disequilibriating factor in the economy, compared with the previous period, was the acceleration in the tempo of inflation. It is not the place here to analyse the problem of Dutch inflation – that is done in Chapter 3. It can be mentioned, however, that the causes of inflation must be sought in the labour factor, showing escalating gross wage claims (and not shrinking net wage claims!) to absorb collective burdens. This materialized more particularly, in the 'soft' sectors such as the service sector (e.g. health). By contrast the 'hard' capital intensive sectors as 'other mining' and 'public utilities' probably exercised a restraining influence on inflationary pressures. This appears clearly in Table 4.3.

Inflationary pressures also originated in the world economy. A strong recovery in demand by the large industrial countries led to a noticeable rise in the price of industrial and agrarian raw materials. As a result discussion began over the finiteness of natural resources which, combined with some interesting theorising over the external effects of industrial activity, led to a change in the climate of opinion[4]. In the Netherlands this also embraced discussion over the value of natural gas.

As a result agreement was reached between the government and the oil companies to attempt to bring the domestic price of gas to the level of oil prices and to achieve some economy in its use. This policy of higher pricing found a counterpart in a renegotiation of the sharing of the gas revenues between the oil companies and the Dutch treasury. When, in the beginning of the sixties, the then minister, de Pous, set up a framework for the exploitation of the natural gas and for the sharing of revenues, the model chosen was a mixture of private initiative and government intervention. At the time the exploitation concessions were given to NAM, on the condition that the exploitation be shared in a ratio 60:40 between NAM and the then Staatsmijnen. In addition the State would receive a royalty of 10 per cent of the net revenue. Next the *Gasunie* was established which was granted a monopoly in the distribution and sale of Slochteren gas. In the Gasunie the two oil companies each took a 25 per cent share, Staatsmijnen 40 per cent and the State 10 per cent. The Gasunie was only to take a moderate return on invested capital so that the largest share of the profits could be taken by the combination of oil companies (NAM) and DSM. Under this scheme, inclusive of profits tax, 70 per cent of net revenues flowed into the Treasury and 30 per cent to Shell and Esso. It was on this ratio that Minister Langman re-opened discussion in 1971/72. It was agreed that in the event of a rise in price per m³ above a certain indexed threshold (approximately 5 cents) the extra revenue would be shared 85:15. This applied only to domestic sales.

In addition to the implications of natural gas for unemployment and inflation already discussed, we must point to the not unimportant income-effect which resulted from the active marketing policy, now also involving foreign markets. This involved what could be called a volume-effect; as already stated, prices were still modest. Weitenberg calculated that 0.7 per cent per annum of the annual rise in macro-economic labour productivity was the consequence of gas[5]. Gas also began slowly to assume importance for the balance of payments. On the foreign exchange markets, which clearly became more volatile after the Smithsonian agreement, the position of the guilder hardened. Although initially the effective appreciation of the guilder can be attributed to factors other than its own strength, it was gradually helped along by the unmistakable role which gas played in raising the economic potency of the Netherlands. A final word over the gas contribution to the government budget – this was still modest because of the still low level of revenues.

4.3 1973-1976 Socialisation of demand and energy crisis

Just as in the third act of a classical drama, the action in this third episode takes a definate turn through outside events. The oil crisis of 1973 radically altered the picture and forced the adoption of a new energy policy, embodied in the so-called Energienota of 1974[6]. The economic picture as a whole also changed radically and this called for important shifts in policy.

4.3.1 Pricing policy

It became clear all too quickly that it was not the boycotts or the other quantitative restrictions on the flow of crude oil but the sharp increase in its price and its implications which had to be considered a political fact of the first order. If only on grounds of its calorific content it was obvious that the value of the gas had increased considerably. Meanwhile it had also become clear that the price charged for a specific volume of gas could be higher than for a volume of oil with the same calorific content. Steadily more arguments came in for this excess value or premium – clean air, an advantage of gas, yielded a social price on the basis of the polluter-pays principle; there was security of supply; high interest rates and scarcity of space made oil storage steadily more difficult; comfort and precise regulations were increasingly rated more highly. The trend towards the concept of market-conformity prices (oil parity plus a premium) coincided with government policy to use the price instrument to deal with energy problems in the long-term. Put another way the allocative role of the price mechanism was to be used to avoid energy waste, to get insulation off the ground, to make district heating pay its way, to encourage new supplies from existing and yet to be discovered energy sources, etc.

For the Netherlands this implied a firm grip on energy prices. This led to a further re-opening of discussions over revenue sharing and over foreign sales. As a result of these negotiations, the share of revenue from Groningen gas above a certain level was fixed at 95:5 in favour of the State. An Act of Parliament was passed to implement the policy of bringing prices upto market levels which also gave increased powers to the Minister of Economic Affairs (known as the Law on Minimum Prices). Originally ministerial competence had been restricted to protecting the public against the abuse of monopoly power (by the Gasunie) in forcing up prices. Under the new act he received powers to order minimum – not maximum – prices both for domestic sales and for gas delivered abroad. Thus renegotiations began between the Gasunie and foreign purchasers – the new law functioning as a cudgel held in reserve. This policy of altering gas prices was reasonably successful though more so with domestic sales than with export contracts. The reason for this was that with foreign sales one had to contend with long-term contracts and foreign buyers appealed over the impossibility of passing on the higher costs so quickly to their customers. Moreover because of the earlier policy of actively looking to penetrate export markets, gas was not always sold on premium markets. In this respect the renegotiation of the Italian contract was notorious. It had been expressed entirely in fixed prices and it was only re-opened with the greatest difficulty. Although it was not easy to express the concept 'market value' for gas exported in concrete terms, the judgement seems justified that the new act made possible the obtaining of better terms via renegotiation or other means. Even today the issue is far from dead.

4.3.2 Selective marketing policy

In addition to the price instrument, a marketing policy[7], in a more definite sense, was developed. As far as exports were concerned this was extremely straightforward. Even before the crisis, Minister Langman had compelled a quantity of natural gas found in the North Sea by the American company

Placid and sold to Germany to be returned to the Netherlands (under pressure from the EEC only half was to be returned) and had ordered that no new export contracts be concluded. This policy was continued. Domestically priority was given to the household sector whilst, on the other hand, burning of gas for electricity generation and the like, was precluded from any extension of contracts. In this way it was hoped to use the available reserves of gas as sparingly as possible for as long a period as possible. At the beginning of the exploitation period Minister de Pous had spoken of a desired timescale for exhaustion of reserves of 30 years. Now, ten years later, after the oil crisis this idea of a lifespan of at least one generation became questionable, a slower depletion was thought desirable.

4.3.3 A strategic reserve

The oil crisis had made clear how vulnerable economies could be as far as energy supplies were concerned. Thus the beginnings of the idea for a strategic reserve were introduced into Dutch thinking on natural gas. In practice this contained two elements. The first, already mentioned, was the policy of preserving natural gas for as long as possible within the Netherlands for essential purposes. The second, more immediate element was to hold a strategic reserve in transport and production capacity so that a number of installations (in electricity generating and industry), which would again use coal and oil in normal circumstances, could, if necessary, switch back to natural gas. This provision for dual-firing was cheap because the normal pattern of gas use by households, dominated by central heating, followed a strong seasonal pattern. Naturally capacity in transport and production had to be sufficient to cope with peak demand on the coldest winter's day, so for the rest of the year reserve capacity was in fact available.

4.3.4 New extraction and purchases

Alongside the policy of conserving natural gas it was felt that it would be sensible to proceed as energetically as possible with the exploitation of small natural gas occurrences as well as turning to purchases of natural gas from abroad. This was feasible because Norwegian gas, via pipeline, and Algerian gas, in liquified form, could be supplied. The primary intention of this policy was to spread Dutch reserves over as long a period as possible. There was an obvious strategic reason for this but there was also an important economic consideration. The potential natural gas surplus on the balance of payments per year had become so gigantic because of the enormous price rise that it was better for the economy to spread these over a larger number of years. When one considers that Groningen gas is naturally much cheaper to obtain than North Sea gas, to say nothing of the purchase price of Norwegian and *a fortiori* Algerian gas, it is obvious that this policy had the effect of deferring income in large amounts to the future.

There were also technical arguments for this policy. The Groningen field appeared eminently suitable for absorbing seasonal fluctuations in demand, a quality which will become increasingly important later this century (with an increasing proportion of demand for central heating). There is a further argument: on the one hand, gas from different sources has different calorific values but, on the other hand, a single calorific value is preferable for gas-using appliances, so it will be self-evident that mixing the gas while Groningen reserves are still relatively plentiful will yield a single overall average value. Moreover, in this way, more certainty can be given that small reserves, that might otherwise have been unprofitable to exploit in the future, could now be integrated into the whole network.

At this time, because of the completely new energy price situation, it was natural to investigate the possibilities of re-opening the coal mines (in 1974 it had been decided to close the last two remaining mines). In the so-called 'Martens Report', made on the request of the government, various calculations appeared all of which yielded an impressive series of losses. As a result it was decided not to undertake a follow-up study into whether the necessary labour force would be available. It might be helpful to know, by way of support for this position, that calculations made on the two remaining mines, 'Beatrix' and 'Emma/Hendrik', which yielded a cumulative negative cashflow by 1994 of anything between f. 7.1 billion and f. 13.8 billion, depending on the assumptions made. Thus the coal mines in the Netherlands will not be re-opened in the foreseeable future. The technically recoverable reserves, calculated to a depth of 1,200 metres at 710 million tonnes, will remain underground, unless unconventional techniques, as underground gassification, become technically and economically feasible.

4.3.5 Natural gas income

The contribution of natural gas to the value-added in Dutch production rose strongly in this period; the production volume of gas rose further (chiefly because of obligations under the export contracts) and the price effects were considerable. For the same reasons the cash flow to the government budget was also substantial though, in addition, the 95:5 share-out agreement described above considerably increased the government take. The develop-

ment of the gas surplus is found in Figure 4.5 page 107. The domestic price
of gas rose sharply which explains a large part of the rise in the cost of living.
In this context one should remember, however, that account had been taken
of this in incomes policies and that had Dutch citizens and industry been
dependent upon imported oil, the price rise would have been even greater.

4.3.6 Some macro-economic comments

In this period the interrelationship between energy and economic developments became even clearer than hitherto. The economic consequences of
the oil crisis were profound – that much is apparent. At the time it was difficult to estimate the intensity and duration of the depression resulting from
the deflationary impact of the oil price rise – the reports from that time of
international agencies as the IMF, OECD, EEC testify to this fact. The
general opinion anticipated a relatively short depression during which
countries, such as the Netherlands, with a relatively favourable energy
balance were expected to maintain purchasing power largely through
budgetary expenditure. Because of the short-term character of such
measures and the desired speed of implementation, the stimulus was apt to
be of a consumptious nature. In this respect the gas income allowed the
government to increase its own expenditure without translating this into
high tax increases. The government's own predisposition was in this
direction. Alongside the counter cyclical argument there was the consideration that under pressure from the stagnating economy, the social insurance
structure built up in the sixties began to carry greater burdens which partly
had to be absorbed by the budget. In Figure 4.4 it is apparent that there was a
considerable increase in income transfers within the budget. Thus in this
period the influence on total demand exerted by public authorities as such,
or at least on behalf of needy groups in society via public regulations, was a
striking feature. That is why the emphasis on the needs of collectivities rather
than individuals – the so-called socialisation of demand – is mentioned in
the title of this paragraph.

Because, later, it appeared that the world depression was more serious
and longer lasting than had earlier been generally anticipated and that the
rise in domestic demand, reinforced by government expenditure, had not
been followed by a expansion in export orders, an unhealthy situation had
arisen with respect to the Dutch competitive position which required serious
consideration. Here, the *Economische Structuur nota* was important.

**Figure 4.4 Government expenditure as a percentage of
Net National Income at market prices**

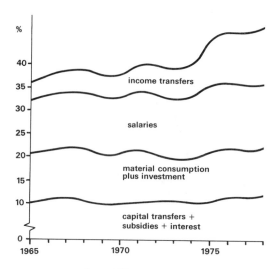

Source: C.P.B., Centraal Economisch Plan, 1978, p. 103

4.3.7 The 'Economische structuur nota'

Two years after the onset of the oil crisis note on selective growth, often called
the 'structuur nota', attempted to give shape to a new economic policy in
light of the deteriorating unemployment situation[8]. The 'structuur nota'
underlined the need to drastically reduce the level of inflation, which had
reached 10 per cent, and to expand profits to encourage investment. The still
flowing tide of gas guilders made it possible to improve the position of
business whilst maintaining the purchasing power of the population. Since
the government had to cope at the same time with the effects of the appreciation of the guilder, the struggle against inflation assumed 'great' importance
if the competitive position of Dutch business were to be improved. Although,
year in, year out, Dutch inflation had lain several percentage points above
inflation in other industrialised countries, especially West Germany, linked
in the 'snake' mechanism to the Deutschmark, the guilder had continued to
appreciate against other currencies. This was not surprising given the
fact that the Netherlands had a strong balance of payments position because
gas yielded export earnings as well as reducing the need for oil imports. In a
way these surpluses were misleading because the reduction in domestic investment also implied a reduction in the considerable share of investment goods
usually imported from abroad. Here we meet a symptom of what has been

called the 'Dutch disease'. This arose from a double phenomenon. On the one hand there was the optimistic bias in the views on the economic situation because of the natural gas. On the other hand there was a very real problem of relative costs through a relative over-valuation of the guilder. Because there was a certain assymetry between the weighted appreciation of the guilder on markets where the Dutch acted as supplier and those where they were the buyer, the competitive disadvantages were greater than the cost advantages. Again the answer to this was to attempt to slow down the rate of inflation, to revive the profitability of businesses and to give investment premiums to offset these disadvantages.

4.3.8 Final considerations

Thus it can be said that natural gas played a completely different role in events in the turbulent years 1973-1978 than in the preceding period. Now it was the revenues that played a major role. Because of the gas revenues it proved possible to finance fairly extensive public expenditure and because of the gas surplus on the balance of payments there was no external check on this policy.

During the seventies a great deal of thought was given to the best use of the gas revenues. One possibility was not to spend the income at all. This alternative presented difficulties both because a government cannot help but be inclined to dispose of money available and because the situation of stagnation and recession demanded an expansionary policy. Looking back it cannot be said that the government contributed to an increase in net savings in the economy. The impressive flow of purchasing power into the Dutch economy by the government spending its guilders enabled Dutch business and Dutch citizens to acquire capital abroad. The preference for foreign investment was related to the appreciating guilder and to the relatively high cost of investment at home. In fact, direct investment by Dutch business abroad increased substantially with the result that, in all probability, foreign holdings of Dutch enterprise will be larger at the end of the seventies than at the beginning. In assessing the contribution of natural gas to the Dutch economy, this effect should not be neglected. Although the international distortions in economic and capital relationships make it difficult to clearly identify the size of Dutch foreign capital, it is not impossible that part of this 'reserve' may prove to be repatriated at some point in the future.

Now one must point to the second possible alternative, namely spending the revenue in productive investment in the Netherlands. Very little has been done in this direction – partly because of the political choice in favour of more expenditure on consumption, partly because of political doubts over whether the government itself should act as an investor and partly because cost relationships left few profitable openings. It appears that at the beginning of the gas period the then Minister of Economic Affairs, de Pous, was urged by his colleague Zijlstra to keep gas income apart for the very purpose of undertaking productive initiatives. This was prevented by a veto from the then Minister of Finance: options for political initiatives and their financing should be weighted within the overall framework of the government budget. This argument has remained decisive. In fairness it should be added that this same government, perhaps through the gas revenue, was responsible for constructing an excellent material and social infrastructure upon the basis of which the Dutch economy has become one of the most productive per worker.

4.4 1976-1985 Public sector restraint and further catching up of gas prices

In the second half of the life of the previous cabinet it became clear that, despite promising signals that counter-inflation policy had begun to bite, a change in direction was required to resolve a number of inherent weaknesses in the economy[9]. In this respect attention was focused on the diminished 'competitive force of the economy' and the resultant short-comings in Dutch export performance. Only the reprieve of the f. 14 billion[10] contribution made by natural gas prevented balance of payments problems. The political discussion concentrated, among other things, on the balance between the public and private sectors. The first steps were taken to get the strong increase in the claims of the public sector and the associated fiscal burdens under control. This was intended to ease the tax burden on enterprise especially the heavy collectivist elements in labour costs, to stimulate production and to establish conditions for reviving the investment incentive in order to improve the sombre outlook for employment opportunities.

The Act on the investment account stemming from the 'structuur nota' and the greatly enhanced fiscal facilities for investment, represented an attempt to make part of the available purchasing power available for investment purposes, against the trend in cost-relationships. This involved a sum of approximately f. 3.5 billion per annum. It is extremely difficult to establish how far the success of this initiative may be attributed to the use of gas revenue. All in all it appeared that there were relatively few opportunities for making gas revenues available for investment in an economy such as the

Netherlands which was already well provided with a decent material infra-structure and productive equipment.

The extemely difficult process of curbing public demand, involving the realisation of the goals set out in *Bestek '81* (Blueprint '81), the economic programme of the present government, has been endangered in the course of this period by new external events. In particular the political troubles in Iran gave way to new very serious shocks in the world energy market and demonstrated that OPEC's role in energy provision and energy pricing was again decisive. The world had to absorb oil price rises of a similar magnitude as those of the energy crisis of 1973/74. The inherent worsening of the Netherlands terms of trade, at least in the short run, destroyed the fine tuned equilibrium in the Blueprint-proposals and forced the Government to resort to legislatory measures especially regarding wages. The damaging first order effects of the higher oil bill however contributed to a stronger determination of government, broadly supported by parliament, to improve the prices and price mechanisms for natural gas. The sitting Minister of Economic Affairs, Van Aardenne, intervened in the contract the municipal gas companies have with Gasunie and forced them to accept higher prices for small end users. Moreover he is engaged in visits to his colleagues abroad in order to reveal his worries on export prices for natural gas which are lagging behind and not fully geared to oil prices. This remarkable action, since gas prices primarily are private matters between private gas companies, must be seen in the light of the light of the drastic changes on the international energy markets in 1979-80 and it should be remembered that after the 1973-74 energy crisis the Minister of Economic Affairs had aquired special powers under the so-called Law on Minimum Prices, adopted in 1974 (See above p 99).

A final phenomenon is the revival in parliament of the discussion of the question whether under current circumstances the profits received by Shell and Esso for natural gas activities should not be curtailed (i.e. via a revision of the previously mentioned share-out agreements).

All these developments – higher oil prices, fuller indexation, shorter time lags and perhaps revised government takes – affect and will affect gas turn-over and the balance of payments.

First, some words about the information presented in Figure 4.5 which will be used to illustrate these points. For the projections into the future, the trustworthiness of the figures is tentative. There is very little public material with which to work. Figure 4.5 can be regarded as satisfactory as an indication of the trends but no more than that.

The graphs on the left describe three developments in absolute terms; those on the right, in relative terms. For estimating the economic signific-

Figure 4.5 Significance of probable future natural gas development, 1979−2000

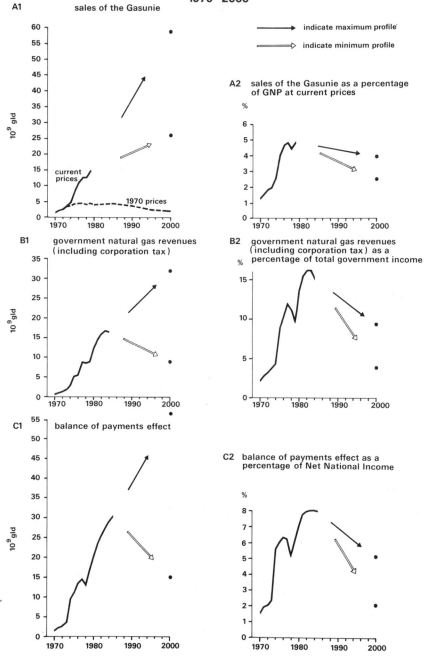

A1 sales of the Gasunie

A2 sales of the Gasunie as a percentage of GNP at current prices

B1 government natural gas revenues (including corporation tax)

B2 government natural gas revenues (including corporation tax) as a percentage of total government income

C1 balance of payments effect

C2 balance of payments effect as a percentage of Net National Income

indicate maximum profile

indicate minimum profile

ance of these developments, the latter are of more importance but both will receive consideration.

Graph Al makes it clear that reaching the turning point in volume terms (i.e. in 1970 prices) certainly does not imply that the revenue from gas has reached its peak[11]. In the sphere of prices the process of upward adjustment is not yet complete (this applies to export prices as well as prices charged to market-gardeners, small users, etc.). At the same time it can be assumed that the general energy price level will continue to rise, a process which will apply equally to gas. How this trend will develop is difficult to quantify. In addition, as a result of sales policy, the small-user share of the market, in which a higher price can be charged, is growing. Herefore we have used the sales estimates for the year 2000 which appear in a recent '*Plan van Gasafzet*' (Gas Marketing Plan).

Bearing in mind the gigantic uncertainties in these matters especially over such a long period we would nevertheless like to give a rough impression by giving maximum and minimum indications of the outcome in the year 2000, a year in which use of domestic gas has fallen back to about 25 per cent of the present volume. The arrows underline our uncertainty on the profile of the curves to those points. To clarify the minimum and maximum positions: the minimum picture assumes moderate inflation, constant real oil prices, unchanged government take, high distribution margin for municipalities, relatively high gas extraction and import costs, relatively little Groningen gas. The maximum profile assumes more inflation, moderately rising energy prices in real terms, increased government take, a reasonable distribution margin, more profitable import and production activities.

From Graph Bl it is clear that the strong upward trend in gas revenues will continue, at least in the period 1976-85. Also in the years thereafter a very serious decline, at least in absolute terms, may not even materialize at all.

The development of the balance of payments effect defined as the sum of net export yield and import substitution[10], in graph C1 presents initially a picture of a further increase, as a result of upward price adjustments, followed by an uncertain development which rests heavily on the assumptions chosen for the import: domestic production ratio and the development of crude oil prices.

In relative terms the importance of the quantities considered seems unlikely to decline before 1985 and even then sometimes only at a gradual rate. Commenting on the gradually declining sales: GNP ratio (graph A2), one has to add that unlike the seventies, the ratio no longer gives an accurate reflection of its contribution to national economic activity. Whilst in the seventies, when a large proportion of gas sales stemmed from domestic production, and thus the value-added remained within the Dutch economy, this contribution to GNP will decline as the role of imported gas increases. Graph B2 in our opinion indicates strikingly that in the current period, '76-'85, the budgetary significance of natural gas is greater than ever before and presumably than it ever will be again. It means that responsibility to spend the gas revenues in an economic optimally effective way assumes major importance. Also the continuing high contribution of natural gas to the balance of payments until '85 (graph C2) is remarkable. The downturn thereafter very unhappily coincides with other unfavourable developments on the energy account. These will be dealt with in section 4.5.

4.5 After '85. Threatened external dangers and less natural gas

We wish to restrict our discussion on this period to some observations on the relationship between natural gas and the economy.

Notwithstanding the fact that a positive price effect will probably continue, the policy relating to the sales volume and composition will mean

Figure 4.6 Production and consumption of primary energy in the Netherlands

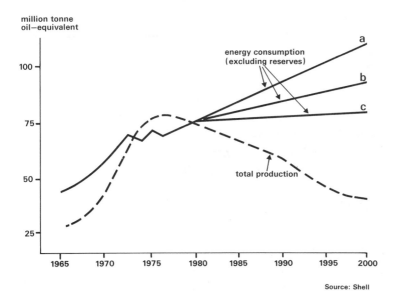

Source: Shell

that both gas revenue and the contribution to the balance of payment will play a smaller economic role. Independent of the balance of payment effect which is directly related to price developments in the gas sector itself, the current account balance will further seriously deteriorate because of a rising demand for energy resulting in growing import dependence (three alternative scenarios are presented in Figure 4.6). Financing the government budget, bearing in mind the falling supply of savings via the current account, will then become a serious economic bottleneck. With some justification, Duisenberg has recently emphasised this point[13]. Moreover, the contribution of the gas sector to national production will slump, resulting, *ceteris paribus*, in a series of considerable yearly losses of welfare. This could lead to enormous inflationary pressure since, in general, no-one will be willing to accept this. These external dangers are thrown into greater relief when it is remembered that trying to replace that share of national income derived from gas by other activities will almost inevitably aggrevate the already acute balance of payments problem (the cumulative import ratio of gas extraction and distribution is almost certainly lower than that of any substituting activity). It falls outside the scope of this chapter to go any deeper into this – the uncertainties implied in this kind of long-term forecasting are too great. What is clear, however, is that in a number of respects the means for aleviating the problem are at hand. The conditions can be created for keeping the deterioration in the energy balance as small as possible[13] (by a vigorous policy of energy saving). Our conclusion from Figure 4.5, however, is that it would be very short-sighted to wait until problems of this kind are experienced in their full impact. The chances of coping successfully with the problems ahead lie here and now.

4.6 Summary and conclusion

Natural gas was, soon after its discovery, identified as a factor of major importance. From the beginning authorities have tried to optimise its role over the course of time. Of course policy makers did not have perfect foresight. Neither have we, but afterwards we can observe that some of the appraisals to support the policy – thought optimal – of quick and deep penetration in the market at relatively low prices have proved incorrect. Most striking were the quicker pace of economic growth and consequently the coming of environmental problems and the prospect of scarce energy. Moreover the growing wariness of nuclear energy as a promising option in the short run became manifest. These new views have led to a gradual modification of the chosen marketing concept, 'time preference' is shifted towards the future, gas is reallocated to premium markets and the elimination of energy waste is strongly promoted.

When we considered – as was the aim of this chapter – these energy matters in their interdependence with the economic well being of the Netherlands it proved meaningful to distinguish between various periods. In the *sixties* the stimulus to investment caused by the introduction of natural gas attracts attention, a new capital intensive sector arose and the economic structure became gas intensive. By the end of the sixties the Netherlands inhabitants first – foreign customers somewhat later – started to pick fruits from their new energy source in terms of income per capita as well as in the shape of an invisible consumer surplus. The period *'69-'73* can be characterised as a period of economic disequilibrium especially in the field of prices (heavy inflation) and employment (structural unemployment). It can be said natural gas mitigated the problems of the first kind but in the area of employment natural gas played a more dubious role. The gas sector hardly absorbed any labour but showed a very substantial rise in productivity, which in the Netherlands' income-policy context meant that this productivity gain in a sector with little labour led to wage claims and labour costs in the other much weaker and much more densely populated sectors. The coal mine closure however has been the most disappointing side effect of the introduction of natural gas. Though unintentionally this measure has meant a very unwelcome reinforcement of unemployment, especially in the southern part of the country. In *'73-'76* availability problems of energy lead to an emphasis on a pricing policy for natural gas that aimed at a new much higher level (premium value). Gas revenues dramatically increased and gave a significant contribution to the government budget; on the other hand the government budget was used to cope with deflationary consequences of the oil crisis.

So much for past developments: three periods that left behind distinct impressions dominated however by two observations: natural gas gave to the Netherlands much higher per capita consumption, especially – but not only – on the lower income ranks via minimum wages and social benefits. The introduction of natural gas however has been detrimental to the full employment objective partly because natural gas and derived activities could not compensate for the loss of jobs in coal mining and partly via indirect effects, i.e. negative exchange rate effects.

At present, let's say *the period '76-'85*, natural gas offers hopeful perspectives for an economy entangled in a painful but necessary process of adaption, especially in the sphere of public expenditure. Against the back-

ground of new waves of energy price increases attention has be focussed
again, and for good reason, upon imperfections in the natural gas pricing
mechanism such as the long time lags, and even absence altogether, of full
indexation to oil prices. These imperfections are to be removed, preferably
by a process of serious and urgent negotiations, both of a private and a
public nature.

Simultaniously a new wave of world energy prices, in absolute terms
comparable to that of the first energy crisis 73/74, emerges. Both these
factors will push up the natural gas contribution to the government budget
to a record level of some 15 percent of total government income by the end
of the period. In fact the circumstances in this period offer further opportunities to employ these revenues for structural reinforcement of the
economy (the energy system included) before – in the last period considered,
the period after '85 – domestic production of natural gas diminishes and the
total energy account on the balance of payments worsens. If by that time the
Netherlands has not reorganised economically, nasty political conflicts
occassioned by severe attacks on per capita income must be anticipated.

All in all one has to admit the interaction between the gas sector and the
Netherlands economy is only one aspect of political reality. Nevertheless its
relevance in the *fourth* period distinguished, roughly correspendending with
the period of the sitting cabinet and the one to come, is striking. Discipline in
social-economic discussions and energy conservation exerted by all concerned, government, political parties and social partners, are now crucial
and certainly will pay off in terms of long run welfare.

End notes

[1] De Wolff (1964).
[2] Ministerie van Econ. Zaken, *Aardgasnota* (1961/62).
[3] Weitenberg (1975).
[4] Mishan (1967), Heuting (1974).
[5] Weitenberg (1975).
[6] Ministerie van Econ. Zaken, *Energienota* (1974/75).
[7] N.V. Ned. Gasunie, *Marketing Plan* (1979).
[8] C.P.B. (1976), Lubbers (1976).
[9] Stevers (1971).
[10] For import substitution domestic gas consumption is calculated at crude oil parity.
[11] N.V. Ned. Gasunie, *Annual Report* (1978), O.E.C.D. (1978).
[12] Duisenberg (1978).
[13] Lubbers (1977), Ministerie van Econ. Zaken, *Nota Energiebeleid* (1979/80), Tieleman (1979).

References and select bibliography

C.P.B., *De Nederlandse economie in 1980*, 's-Gravenhage, 1976.

Duisenberg, W.F., *De overheidsfinanciën . . . vol gas?* Inleiding voor de landelijke economistendag, 24-10-1978.

Heuting R., *Nieuwe schaarste en economische groei*, Amsterdam/Brussel, 1974.

I.E.A./O.E.C.D. *Energy Policies and Programmes of International Energy Agency Countries, 1978 Review*, Paris, 1979.

Lubbers R.F.M., 'Kernenergie' *Economisch-Statistische Berichten*, 4-5-1977.

Lubbers R.F.M., 'Opmerkingen over het actuele economische beleid n.a.v. de Nota Selectieve Groei' *Economisch-Statistische Berichten*, 8-12-1976.

Ministerie van Economische Zaken, *Aardgasnota*, Tweede Kamerstuk No. 6767 (zitting 1961-62).

Ministerie van Economische Zaken, *Energienota*, Tweede Kamerstuk 13/122 Nos. 1 + 2 (zitting 1974-75).

Ministerie van Economische Zaken, *Nota Energiebeleid. Deel 1*, Tweede Kamerstuk 15/802 Nos 1 + 2 (zitting 1979-80).

Ministerie van Economische Zaken, *Nota inzake de Selectieve Groei* (Economische Structuurnota) Tweede Kamerstuk 13/955 Nos. 1-3 (zitting 1975-76).

Mishan E.J., *The Costs of Economic Growth*, London, 1967.

N.V. Nederlandse Gasunie, *Annual Report*, Groningen 1978.

N.V. Nederlandse Gasunie, *Marketing Plan, 1979,* Groningen, 1979.

O.E.C.D., *Economic Survey of the Netherlands* (especially chapter and appendix on natural gas), Paris, 1978.

Stevers T.A., *Openbare Financiën en ekonomie*, Leiden, 1971.

Tieleman W.H.J., 'Realistisch Energiebeleid' *Economisch-Statistische Berichten*, 7-3-1979.

Weitenberg J., 'De betekenis van het aardgas voor onze economie', *Politiek perspectief*, July/August, 1975, pp. 77-88. (CBP Reprint Series No. 151).

De Wolff P.J., 'Economische aspekten van het aardgas' *Akademiedagen* D, XVI, 1964. (CBP Reprint Series No. 91).

5 SECTORAL AND REGIONAL IMBALANCES IN THE DUTCH ECONOMY

G.A. van der Knaap

5.1 Introduction

In the past century we have witnessed a continuous change in the sectoral composition of the national economy. This development is shown in fig. 5.1, which reveals two periods of particularly rapid change. In the first period (1910-1930) most of the declining job opportunities in the agricultural sector were absorbed by the growth in both the secondary and tertiary sector. In the second period (1945-1970) the compensating growth occurred mainly in the secondary sector.

Table 5.1 Employment by sector and period

Nation	Agriculture (primary)			Industry (secundary)			Services (tertiary)		
	1950	1960	1970	1950	1960	1970	1950	1960	1970
United Kingdom	5.3	4.0	2.8	49.2	47.7	45.0	45.3	48.2	51.2
Ireland	40.3	36.4	26.4	24.6	24.6	31.0	35.0	38.9	42.4
Denmark	25.6	18.0	11.1	33.5	37.0	36.8	40.7	44.8	52.0
Germany (F.R.)	23.0	14.1	7.4	43.0	47.7	48.0	33.9	38.1	44.4
France	30.9	22.1	13.7	34.5	38.6	39.6	34.5	39.2	46.
Italy	43.9	30.7	18.7	30.9	39.5	43.8	25.0	29.7	37.4
Belgium	11.8	7.9	4.8	50.6	47.6	44.7	37.5	44.3	50.3
Luxembourg	24.0	15.4	7.9	40.4	44.0	43.7	35.5	40.4	48.2
The Netherlands	17.6	10.7	8.1	36.1	42.4	43.8	46.1	46.7	48.0
Community	24.3	16.5	9.9	39.8	43.6	44.1	35.7	39.8	45.9

Source: Labourforce estimates and projections 1950-2000 of the International Labour Office, Geneva, (1977).

This process of change and adaptation is common to most other West-European countries. When we compare the composition of the Dutch economy with those of the members of the European Common Market, it appears from table 5.1 that there is not much change in the relative position of the Netherlands. Already in 1950 the United Kingdom, Belgium and the Netherlands have the smallest proportion employed in agriculture. The percentage employed in the service sector is the highest amongst the common market countries in 1950. This situation changes over the 1950-1970 period, when we can observe that in the United Kingdom, Belgium and Denmark already over 50 percent of the working population is employed in the tertiary sector.

Fig. 5.1 The development of the occupational structure by group of economic activity

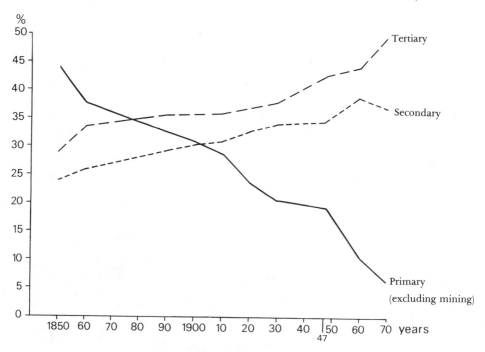

The nature of this process of change was formulated by Fisher (1939) and Clark (1940) in the late 1930's, and is usually referred to as the sector theory. In this theory the dynamics of change are conceived as occurring from without the region. The development sequence starts from an agricultural subsistence economy and leads through intra-regional specialization in primary activities and inter-regional trade with accompanying investments in transport facilities, to the introduction and growth of secondary (mainly industrial) activities. The latter are most likely to develop in places with the best access to markets and material sources in varying combinations, according to the locational pull related to the requirements for the type of production involved. Another basic element of sector theory is that there exists an excess population with a high fertility rate in the agricultural areas which can flow to the developing secondary activities. Such a development will finally lead towards a relocation and re-orientation of the population within a country.

So much for the theory; in practice this development sequence is by no means automatic and is not always completed within the same region, a phenomenon which may lead some areas towards increasing agriculturalization coupled with a lack of job opportunities. As there is no perfect mobility of labour, regions such as these will be burdened by an increasingly large number of unemployed, especially when population growth rates are high. Several types of corrective action, such as a deliberate industrialization-cum-urbanization policy, an infrastructure investment policy and a population policy, can be suggested already at this stage. But, before we start a discussion on these policy options and their instruments, we have to consider the spatial structure in which they might be applied and, in particular, some relevant aspects of the Dutch space economy.

5.2 The spatial structure of the Dutch economy

When the spatial distribution of the three sectors of the economy is mapped relative to the national sector composition, areas of regional specialization emerge. The coefficient of localization expresses this ratio and when this coefficient is larger than one, an above average share is indicated (see fig. 5.2). On this basis it becomes possible to divide the country in three types of regions: (1) the North, in which agricultural activities are relatively dominant in contrast with (2) the South, which has both a larger than average share in industry and agriculture, and (3) the city-rich West in which the service sector is predominant. This division of the country also corresponds roughly with the spatial pattern of income inequalities (see Bartels, 1976) and can be a relevant division for regional policy as one of the objectives is to reduce regional inequalities.

Closely associated with this regional classification is the way in which the various regional economies interact with each other, because this may give us some understanding of (1) the ways in which growth is transmitted from one regional subsystem to another, and (2) the sensitivity of a regional economy to general, i.e. national, policy measures. Analysis of a number of inter-provincial interactions for 1970 reveal a close correspondence be-

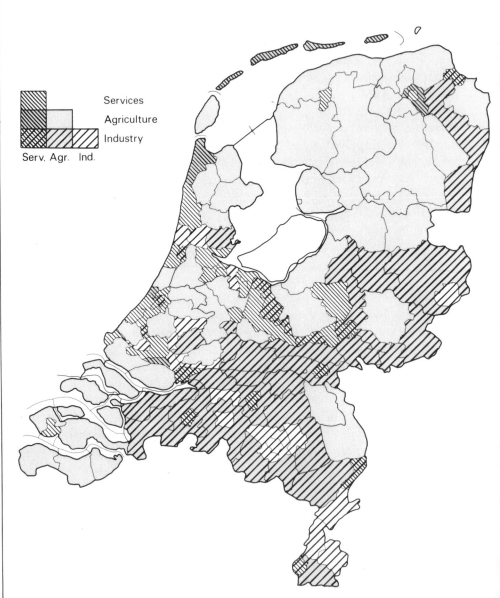

Fig. 5.2 The areas of regional specialization by Economic Geographic Region

Services
Agriculture
Industry

Serv. Agr.   Ind.

Only sectors with a location quotient larger than one are represented.   *Source:* C.B.S. census 1960

tween, for example, railway passenger flows, truck haulage movements and population migration flows (Van der Knaap and Lesuis, 1976). On the basis of this result one can profitably use a regionalization based on migration flows for the analysis of other types of interactions. Thus the migration subsystems which are shown in fig. 5.3 are relevant units for the study of regional and sectoral differences in the Netherlands. The three subsystems which emerge support the broad classification presented on the basis of the coefficient of localization.

When considering the regional structure presented above, it is not directly evident that it can be used as a framework for the study of the post-war period, because the spatial stability of the system is, of course, a pre-requisite for such an analysis. In the literature it is strongly suggested, often with little evidence, that regional systems only change very slowly, but in the case of the Netherlands this hypothesis has been verified by studying the changes in inter-provincial migration flows (Van der Knaap and Sleegers, 1978). In this study migration systems were compared on an annual basis for the period 1948–1976 and it was clear that the three subsystems were stable over the whole period.

This observed spatio-temporal stability at the level of the three subsystems can be considered as an important element in evaluating Dutch regional economic policy, because this policy did not take into account specific regional interdependencies, such as shown in fig. 5.3. The spatial level at which the various policy instruments are operative thus becomes a matter of concern: were the instruments used on a sub-national level, but not at the level of the subsystems, or were they set out in a different context? As will become apparent from the discussion in the next sections, regional policy in the immediate post-1945 period was not explicitly spatial, but was instead organized sectorally to solve problems at some specific locations. However, over the whole period we can observe an increasing integration of economic sectoral planning and physical planning.

5.3 The evolution of regional and economic policy since 1945

One urgent task facing the government in the early post-war years was to ameliorate the problems arising from structural unemployment caused by changes in agriculture and the decline of the peat industry. A policy, which may be characterized as an employment policy, to deal with these problems became effective in 1952, but the emphasis soon shifted from the abatement of agricultural unemployment towards an industrially orientated

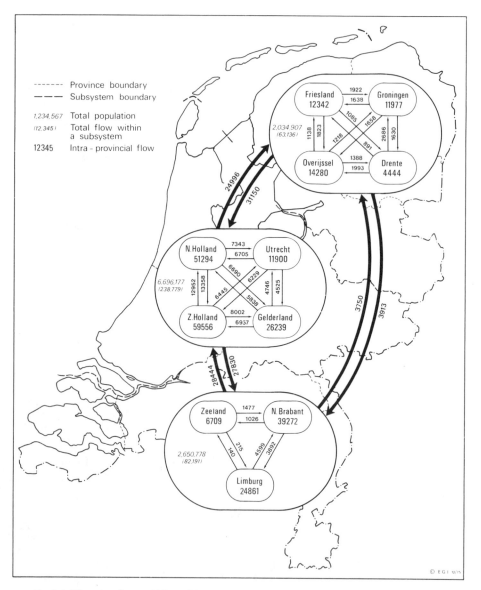

Fig. 5.3 Migration flows within and between subsystems

policy. One reason for this change was the relative decline in demand for coal in Western Europe after 1956, a decline which had far-reaching consequences for Dutch mining. Also, in the mid-1960's the textile industries were facing problems, not only because of competition with chemical fibres, but also because of rationalization, re-orientation of the market and increasing labour costs. And after 1963 another important factor was the easing of a lengthy period of wage restraint (see Abert, 1969); this led to a wage explosion which accelerated the shift from labour-intensive to capital-intensive forms of production.

Viewing the years since 1945 as a whole, we are able to identify four different stages in the evolution of regional policy (see also Pinder, 1976):
1. *1952-1958;* the abatement of structural unemployment. In this period two sets of instruments operated, namely a removal subsidy for individual migrants and an improvement subsidy in 42 selected centres to create a more favourable industrial environment (see fig. 5.4a). During this period we can observe the beginning of a growth centre policy, which was, of course, conceptually linked with similar developments in most other problem areas of Western Europe.
2. *1958-1968;* in this period the broad regional nature of the problem was recognized and the industrialization of large problem areas became an explicit goal. Indeed, the Second National Physical Plan (1966) explicitly incorporated a decentralization/relocation policy, and was conceptually comparable with French regional planning approaches, in which the idea of counter poles (métropole d'équilibre) was formulated (Hansen, 1968). In the Dutch context Groningen was thought to be such a counter pole, but it must be stressed that this city was not alone in offering industrialization incentives. As before, the number of development centres was large, and there was, in fact, an attempt to concentrate on a limited number offering additional investment grants for industry (fig. 5.4b).

During the second part of this period, 1965-1968, the problems confronting mining and the textile industry became apparent, partly as a result of a minor recession. As the policy up to 1968 was already formulated, complete immediate revision was impossible, but the size of the districts covered by the assistance programme was increased and a distinction was made between problem areas (characterized by long-term structural problems) and restructuring or depressed areas (characterized by an unfavourable economic structure, dominated by one type of industrial structure). Equally important, however, was the extension of the policy through the introduction of an investment subsidy in 1967. This signalled a change in policy supporting primarily labour-intensive industries to the assistance of capital-intensive activities in the designated areas.
3. *1968-1972;* in this third period of regional economic planning the number of specially selected centres decreased and there was a shift towards a concentration on the larger centres in the problem areas. The total area in

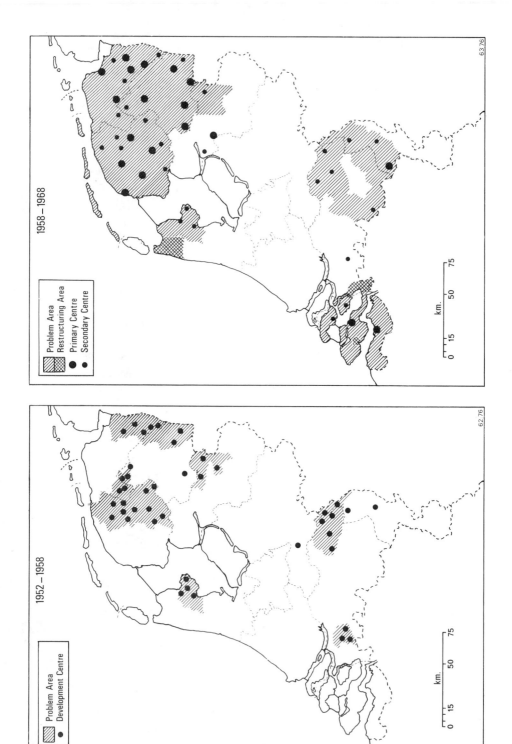

1958 – 1968

Problem Area
Restructuring Area
Primary Centre
Secondary Centre

km.

0   15   50   75

63.76

1952 – 1958

Problem Area
Development Centre

km.

0   15   50   75

62.76

Fig. 5.4 Four stages in the evolution of Dutch regional policy

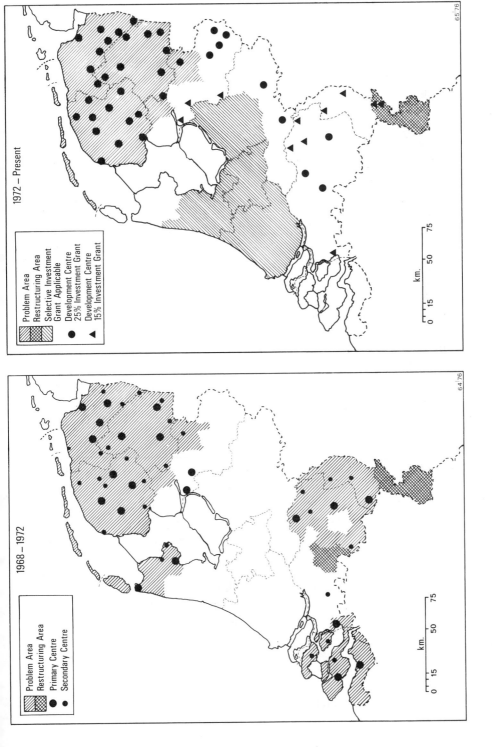

Fig. 5.4 Four stages in the evolution of Dutch regional policy

which special support was given was extended to incorporate the coal-mining area (Southern Limburg) and the area suffering most by the change in the textile industry (Tilburg); both areas were called restructuring areas (see fig. 5.4c). The second major textile region was located in the eastern part of the province of Overijssel, which did not become designated as a restructuring area but in which the industry was directly assisted by the sector structure policy.

To facilitate the change not only the investment subsidy and special tax relief measures were extended to more categories of investment but also to incorporate those parts of the service industry which stimulated regional growth. The national government had also taken an increasingly active part in the decentralization of industry and services by locating DAF-cars in Born in Limburg. This industry is 50 percent state-owned and in 1976 was renamed VOLVO-cars when it became part of this Swedish company. The other decision was to decentralize some government activities from The Hague to the North and South. Examples of this are parts of the Central Bureau of Statistics, the Government Pension Fund to Heerlen in Limburg, parts of the National Giro offices and of the head-office of the P.T.T. to Leeuwarden and Groningen respectively, the two northern provincial capitals.

4. *1972-1980;* an important concept in the previous periods of regional policy was the decentralization of activities from the West. Until 1972 this part of the policy was not very successful. To achieve this goal the policy which contained both infrastructure and investment subsidies as instru-ments was expanded in 1974 by the introduction of the selective investment rule. This new instrument could be used to stimulate industry to locate outside the West, as it was now possible to have a tax penalty on investment within the area (see fig. 5.4d). The selectivity of this instrument operates in such a way that for each location/investment decision permission has to be sought and it was then decided whether or not this permission was granted and whether or not, in the case of a positive decision, a special tax levy was appropriate.

Another element in the policy to relieve the pressure in the West was a complete change in migration policy. Although in the first period there were stimuli to move to the West, the situation became completely reversed following a general migration regulation of 1971 by the Ministery of Social Affairs and a specific migration regulation for the North. The first set of measures are aimed at the support of the unemployed or those becoming unemployed to locate outside the Randstad, if there is no suitable work avail-able in the short term. The second set of measures are aimed specifically to stimulate a permanent relocation of workers from the Randstad with special skills in demand in the North.

This second set of measures also brings out another element in the regional policy in which now, for the first time, a distinction has been made between two problem areas, the North and the South. It was recognized that the structural elements in the regional policy were not sensitive to specific combinations of regional problems which vary by region and, with the continuing expansion of the regions falling inside the categories of assistance, a more discriminating approach was called for. This differentiation by location was also extended in the instruments, such as the investment subsidy which ranges from 15 percent in the case of expansion of existing plants to 25 percent for the location of new plants.

The increase of the subsidy led, however, to a conflict with the European Committee for regional policy as the Netherlands is part of the economic core of the European Community. The national governments which are assisting problem areas within their own territory, but which are also located within the economic core, are not allowed to give investment subsidies above 20 percent net. This was agreed in Brussels when discussing the general problem of regional inequalities within the E.E.C. between member countries. However, the post-1973 economic depression has led to the increase of regional inequalities on a European scale, while a truly coordinated European regional policy does not exist. (The common agricultural policy cannot be considered in this context as a regional policy but is much more a sector structure policy with strong regional implications.)

5.4 Changes in the regional structure

At the national level the general trend was a decrease in agricultural employment and an increase in industrial employment. This trend continued after 1945 and we can observe structural changes in both sectors. As the situation in agriculture is extremely complex, both on a national and European scale, we shall concentrate here on the industrial component as this has received the most attention in the regional policy since 1945. Within the industry we can observe three major trends (see Jansen en De Smidt, 1974):

i.   a change from labour-intensive to capital-intensive industry
ii. an increasing scale of production and increases in firm size
iii. a growth in the number of basic industries, petro-chemical or carbo-chemical based, often having a seaboard location.

The interesting question now is the degree in which these changes in industry are reflected in the changing regional structure of the economy and the regional policy over the period. When we consider the policy as discussed in the previous section, we are able to recognize the four types of government intervention discussed by Stillwell (1972): (1) expenditure policy, (2) price policy, (3) the creation of a set of controls, and (4) a policy aimed at the reduction of factor immobility. This kind of intervention is of a rather indirect nature, as it is not directly associated with a set of regional problems specific to a particular region. A second consideration is that policies tend to be following, rather than leading, the direction of change and because of this feature they have a tendency to reinforce the existing regional structure.

In 1950 there was already a strong industrial structure in the West and it is within this region that the three major trends in industry mentioned above became noticeable. The consequence of growth was a selective spread from the West to the North and South of mainly labour-intensive industries employing unskilled labour. This spread, considered as a spatial process, does not necessarily imply a relocation of a plant, but characterizes also the relative shift in the industrial composition of the national economy. This created within the region the possibility of the expansion of capital-intensive industries using highly trained labour with special skills. The combination of a large number of small industries into a fewer number of firms created a situation where there is a relative large number of dependent branch plants amongst the industry which is dispersed from the West. It is those plants which may be closed down first during an economic recession, such as that experienced since 1973.

The general trend in the West is a relative decrease in the employment in industry and a growth in the South and North until the end of the 1960's. People leaving industry moved generally towards the service sector, where the major growth in the job opportunities took place. Thus, we can observe during the 1960's a decentralization of the capital-intensive industry towards the perifery and a growth of the service sector in the West as the second stage (see fig. 5.5). A third stage in this process would be the decentralization of service activities which have low information or communication contact requirements for their own operation. The communication factor is stressed by Pred (1972) amongst other authors, as one of the most important elements in the operation of an urban environment and this factor is gaining in importance in the post-industrial period towards which some of the main cities in the West are heading. It must be stressed, however that the decentralization of offices outside the West is not a spontaneous development, as the action is taken by the government and the offices

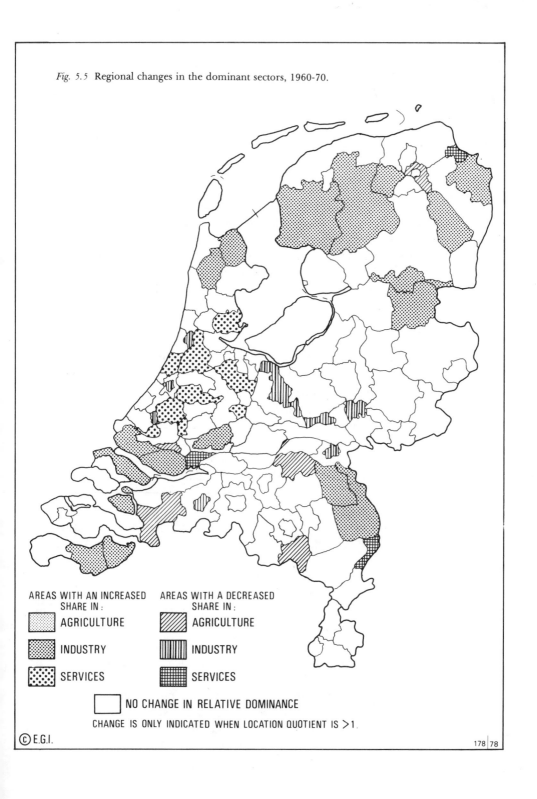

Fig. 5.5 Regional changes in the dominant sectors, 1960-70.

AREAS WITH AN INCREASED
SHARE IN :

AGRICULTURE

INDUSTRY

SERVICES

AREAS WITH A DECREASED
SHARE IN :

AGRICULTURE

INDUSTRY

SERVICES

NO CHANGE IN RELATIVE DOMINANCE

CHANGE IS ONLY INDICATED WHEN LOCATION QUOTIENT IS >1.

© E.G.I.

178 78

are governmental agencies with a low contact requirement with other institutions. The first few steps in this direction were set much more to relieve the city of The Hague from some of its growth problems during the 1960's than a deliberate attempt to beat the trend. The relocated offices, however, remained within the direct sphere of influence of the West (for example, one postal giro office moved to Arnhem and the motor-tax office was decentralized to Apeldoorn). The next step in this process was the first in the more peripheral areas, but concentrated on the main urban centres of Leeuwarden, Groningen, Heerlen and Maastricht (in which a new university was founded) in an attempt to create 'counter magnets'. One must note, however, that a parallel response from the private sector has been minimal. As a regional economic policy cannot be considered without taking into account the urban and population policy, we shall deal with this briefly in the next section.

5.5 The main elements of urban and population policy

The urban and population policies of the past 25 years can be characterized by two major events: (1) the change from physical land-use planning to socio-economic urban planning was accompanied by a changing scale of spatial perception, and (2) the change in the demographic trends during the 1960's called for a reconsideration of the proposed policies. Over the period there have been published three governmental reports on physical planning. The first was published in 1960, the second in 1966' and the third report appeared over the period 1973 to 1977, not as one single report but as a set of discussion documents, reflecting also the idea of planning as a continuous process of change. In the first report the idea of the West of the country as one large metropolitan area (Randstad Holland) was officially formulated. Although this concept may be supported on the visual inspection of maps and air photographs, it is not realistic when one uses the functional characteristics as criteria. Steigenga (1972) describes the 'Randstad' as having an urban structure in which there is no hierarchy but an equality of structure amongst the cities which are considered to be a part of it.

In the second report reference is still made to the idea of the 'Randstad' but this rim-city is divided into two wings, a northern wing running from Alkmaar to Arnhem and a shorter southern wing from Leiden to Gorinchem. In this report the idea of a city region is formulated for the first time. The general problem is considered as the decentralization of jobs and people not mainly from the West, but also in view of the population forecast for 2000

Table 5.2 Population projections for 2000 – by two age-groups

Projection published in	Population in the year of forecast	Total population forecast	0-34 years	35 years and above
1965	12,377,000	20,976,500	12,848,600	8,127,900
1967	12,661,000	17,895,200	9,766,900	8,128,300
1971	13,269,000	17,058,200	9,241,900	7,816,300
1973 A	13,491,000	16,055,200	8,188,200	7,867,000
B		15,402,100	7,535,100	7,867,000

Source: Staatscommissie Bevolkingsvraagstukken (1977), p. 48.

(see table 5.2). The 1965 forecast estimated a total population of about 21 million people compared with the 12.4 million in 1965. The solution was sought in the creation of counter magnets outside the West and a concentrated dispersal in a larger number of centres to prevent a filling-up of the open space, not only of the so-called 'Green Heart', but also in other more densely populated areas of country. The changes in the forecasts for 2000 which have been made in subsequent years are not caused by a change in the forecasting methodology used, although it did change, but are due to a sharp decline in birth rates which dropped from 20.9 0/00 in 1965 to 13.0 0/00 in 1975. This change in fertility behaviour has considerable implications for the size of the future population. As the present birth rate implies a net replacement factor of 0.84, the consequence in the long term will not only be a stable population but, if it does not change, it will ultimately result in a declining population. This problem, however, is not unique for the Netherlands but could be observed in many countries of North-west Europe and even outside Europe. In the German Federal Republic, for instance, the birth rate is already at 10 0/00, which is creating severe headaches for the politicians who are responsible for spatial policy. The changes in birth rates can also be observed on a regional level but, although one may note a general declining rate, the changing pattern of inter-provincial migration has a more direct effect on regional population growth in the short run.

Some of the ideas mentioned above have become basic elements in the third report, such as the idea of the city region (see fig. 5.6). A city region, from a spatial point of view, is a region in which the labour market and the housing market are in balance. The objective is to decrease the journey to work. The other element in the third report is the decision to have a number of smaller growth centres within the vicinity of the main centres in the West, as well as a few large centres located outside the West, such as Groningen,

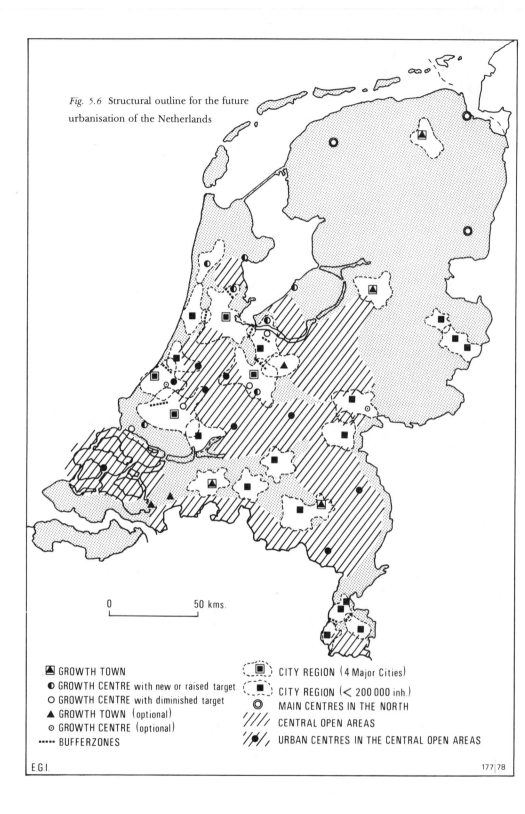

Fig. 5.6 Structural outline for the future
urbanisation of the Netherlands

0   50 kms.

▣ GROWTH TOWN
◑ GROWTH CENTRE with new or raised target
○ GROWTH CENTRE with diminished target
▲ GROWTH TOWN (optional)
◉ GROWTH CENTRE (optional)
▪▪▪▪ BUFFERZONES

▣ CITY REGION (4 Major Cities)
▪ CITY REGION (< 200 000 inh.)
◎ MAIN CENTRES IN THE NORTH
//// CENTRAL OPEN AREAS
//●// URBAN CENTRES IN THE CENTRAL OPEN AREAS

E.G.I.

Zwolle and Breda and Helmond. Both types of locational decisions reflect the idea of concentrated dispersal. The indication of Zwolle can be partly explained by the wish to create a development axis instead of having an isolated growth pole in the North (Groningen). Population growth can be achieved at certain centres because the national government controls most of the housing production by (1) the regional allocation of a share in the annual production and (2) a mechanism for granting building permission. The allocation of production undoubtedly affects the main urban centres which have been losing population at an accelerated rate since 1967; by steering growth into adjacent localities. Another important consideration is the consequences of such a policy for the organization of the urban/regional system as a self-organizing system, given the fact that under the changing demographic regime this policy is decreasingly focused on the allocation of the growth and more on the reallocation of the total population within this system. The relationships between regional-economic and urban policy are by no means clear and we will make an attempt in the next section to make some integrating comments.

5.6 Urban and regional economic policy in retrospect

The main goal of regional-economic policy is to decrease regional socio-economic imbalances. The policy focuses on instruments which influence production and employment structures in a region (Nota, 1977). The instruments as such remain global and rather indirect, as the policy is conceptualized from a national point of view. Although the instruments, e.g. infrastructure improvement, grants and subsidies, have been refined over the period, it remains very difficult to assess their impact in a quantitative manner. Both Van Duyn (1975) and De Smidt (1977) agree that there is a difference in development potential in the Dutch regions, which has not been exploited in the conceptualization of the regional problems. The main result of the policy is an improvement and reinforcement of the existing structure, but not a change in the relationships. The regional problem cannot be formulated as being only a different level of economic development, whether this is expressed in the contrasts from the early 1950's, agriculture versus industry, or in that of the 1970's higher order service activities versus industry, but should also be expressed in differences in developmental potential.

These differences were discussed in previous sections in which also the interregional interdependence was stressed, using the migration subsystem as an example to illustrate the interdependent structure of the various subsystems. This regional structure was only considered from a general point of view. Growth centre or growth pole policy was becoming extremely popular in the policy approach during the 1960's. The basic problem of this policy, the realization of self-sustained growth, has not been solved. This problem in combination with the failure to understand the spatial nature of the transmittance of growth has created a growing lack of confidence in its success. In addition to this the welfare expectations implied by it in the regions concerned have not been met.

When we follow the change in emphasis from a regional towards an urban policy it is also possible to describe the Dutch urban system within this context (see Van der Knaap, 1978). In the urban system the cities in the West are part of an urban subsystem with a service oriented industrial basis. This subsystem operates as a hinge for the interrelationships between the northern and southern subsystem and it dominates these two subsystems at the same time. The northern subsystem can be characterized as agricultural-service oriented, while the southern subsystem has an agricultural-industrial basis. The nature of the regional interdependencies have not been recognized and used, neither in the economic policy nor in the population policy context. Understanding of these inter- and intra-regional relationships, from an urban-system point of view, may explain possible growth path in the regional economies as well as the process of population distribution and change through migration.

This last comment is gaining in importance when we recall the discussion on the indication of development nuclei within the regional policy and the growth centres indicated in the third report on physical planning, in combination with population distribution goals on a regional basis. A comparison of these two policies indicates that there is still a wide discrepancy between the two. This may be a matter of time as we also could observe a change in the formulation at the level of the conceptualization of the problem from a single structural approach towards a regional-functional approach and from a macro-geographic scale towards the concept of city regions. The step in which these two concepts become integrated and interpreted in an interdependent way should not be too far ahead.

References

Abert, J.G., *Economic Policy and Planning in the Netherlands, 1950-65*, New Haven, 1969.
Bartels, C.P.A., *Economic Aspects of regional welfare*, Martinus Nijhoff, Studies in Applied Regional Science, Vol. 9 (1978).
Clark, C., *The conditions of economic progress*, London, 1940.
Van Duijn, J.J., De doelmatigheid van het regionaal-economisch beleid in Nederland in de jaren zestig, *Tijdschrift voor Economische en Sociale Geografie*, Vol. 66, (1975), pp. 258-271.
Fisher, G.B., Production primary, secondary and tertiary, *Economic Record*, Vol. 15 (1939), pp. 24-28.
Hansen, N.M., *French regional planning*, Bloomington, Indiana, 1968.
Jansen, A.C.M. en M. de Smidt, *Industrie en Ruimte*, Assen, 1974.
Van der Knaap, G.A., *A spatial analysis of the evolution of an urban system: the case of the Netherlands*, Rotterdam, Erasmus University, dissertation, 1978.
Van der Knaap, G.A. and P.J.J. Lesuis, *The integrated analysis of spatial systems: a problem area*, The Institure of Economic Research, Discussionpaper Series No. 7601/G, 1976.
Van der Knaap, G.A. en W.F. Sleegers, *Onderzoek naar de structuur van interregionale migratiestromen*, Rotterdam, Economisch-Geografisch Instituut, Erasmus Universiteit, 1978.
Nota, *Nota Regionaal Sociaal-Economisch Beleid 1977 t/m 1980,* Den Haag, 1977.
Pinder, D.A., *The Netherlands*, London, 1976.
Pred, A., *City systems in advanced economies*, London, 1972.
Second National Physical Plan, *Tweede Nota voor de Ruimtelijke Ordening*, Den Haag, 1966.
De Smidt, M., N. Abcouwer en F. Vonk, Bezinning op het regionaal beleid, *Stedebouw en Volkshuisvesting*, No. 9 (1977), pp. 413-424.
Steigenga, W., Randstad Holland, concept in evolution, *Tijdschrift voor Economische en Sociale Geografie*, Vol. 53 (1972), No. 3, pp. 149-161.
Stillwell, F.J.B., *Regional Economic Policy*, London, 1972.

Selected Bibliography

a. Some general readings on regional economic approaches:

Bourne, L.S,m *Urban systems, strategies for regulation; a comparison of policies in Britain, Sweden, Australia and Canada,* Oxford, 1975.
Chisholm, M., Regional policies in an era of slow population growth and higher unemployment, *Regional Studies (1976)*, pp. 201-213.
Friedman, J. and W. Alonso, *Regional Policy, readings in theory and applications,* Harvard, Massachusetts, 1975.
Hansen, N.M., *Public policy and regional economic develôpment, the experience of nine western countries,* Cambridge, Massachusetts, 1975.
Holland, S., *Capital versus the Region*, London, 1976.
McLoughlin, J.B., *Urban and regional planning, a systems approach,* London, 1969.

b. Further readings on the Netherlands:

Hauer, J., G.A. van der Knaap and M. de Smidt, Changes in the industrial geography of the Netherlands during the sixties, *Tijdschrift voor Economische en Sociale Geografie*, Vol. 62 (1971), pp. 139-146.
Nota over de ontwikkeling van de Haagse agglomeratie en de afremming van de groei van de kantorensector, Den Haag, 1972.
Ottens, H.F.L., (1976), *Het groene hart binnen de Randstad*, Assen, 1976.

134 G.A. van der Knaap

Planning and Development in the Netherlands, *Physical planning in the Netherlands*, Vol. 9, No. 2, Assen, 1977.
Reinink, G.J., *Industriële bedrijfsmigratie in Nederland in de jaren 1950-62, een onderzoek naar vestigingsplaatsfactoren*, SISWO, Amsterdam, 1970.
Ruimtelijke Ordening en Geografie, KNAG, Leiden, 1966.
Sociaal Economische Raad, *Rapport inzake de sektorstruktuurpolitiek*, 's-Gravenhage, 1969
De Smidt, M, J.G. Borchert en G.J.J. Egbers, *Ruimtelijk beleid in Nederland*, Roermond, 1974.
Staatscommissie Bevolkingsvraagstukken, *Bevolking en Welzijn*, 's-Gravenhage, 1977.
Tijdschrift voor Economische en Sociale Geografie, Vol. 3 (1972), *Special Issue on the Netherlands*, at the occasion of the 22nd International Geographical Congress, pp. 124-225.
Vanhove, N.D., *De doelmatigheid van het regionaal-economisch beleid in Nederland*, dissertatie, Rotterdam; Gent/Hilversum, 1962.

6 THE NETHERLANDS CENTRAL PLANNING BUREAU

R.T. Griffiths

6.1 Introduction

Throughout Western Europe since 1950 the role of government in the economy has become increasingly pervasive. A number of factors have contributed to this development, among which one can point to the increasing share of the collective sector in national income, the increasing openness of national economies, the increasingly interventionist nature of counter-cyclical policy and the assumption of responsibility by governments for areas not previously considered its preserve. At the same time the tools available to government for successful policy-making have become increasingly sophisticated. On the one hand theoretical advances in economics and econometrics have identified and quantified more and more complex sets of interrelationships whilst, on the other hand, improvements in statistical techniques have provided more up to date data upon which decisions are based. These twin trends have resulted in a better understanding of the past and a more accurate appreciation of the present. It was natural, then, that governments should seek to employ these techniques to help appraise them of the probable future consequences of a particular course of action. The result was the birth of indicative planning and economic forecasting. It is important to clarify this concept of planning and particularly to differentiate it from its better-known counterpart in socialist countries. The concept of planning in the West is more in the nature of prediction as opposed to prescription; of forecasts rather than obligations.

In almost all Western European countries, economic forecasting has become an indispensible part of government policy formation. A few examples may suffice to illustrate this. Among the larger European economies the system of planning is perhaps nowhere more institutionalised than in France where since 1947 a series of five year plans have outlined economic forecasts and targets for the economy. The plans are formulated after an extensive process of consultation, supplemented since 1970 by the use of econometric models, and aspects of government policy are supposedly geared towards the attainment of the goals prescribed therein. An ill-fated attempt at emulating French-style medium-term planning was made by the United Kingdom in 1965 but the much heralded plan was wrecked on the rocks of one of the recurrent sterling crisis the following year. Less conspicious but more permanent in the U.K. was the introduction of an econometric model for public expenditure by the Treasury in 1961. Even in Germany, where the free-enterprise enshrined in *Sozialemarktwirtschaft* doctrines would normally eschew such interference, financial planning has been practised since 1969[1].

However there is probably hardly any country in Europe where the application of macro-economic models plays such an important role in the preparation of economic policy as in the Netherlands. Whereas in the United Kingdom, for example, the appearance of Treasury forecasts merit only transient attention in the financial pages of the quality press, in the Netherlands they occupy a central position in press discussion and in parliamentary debate. Even in France, where planning is so much a part of public consciousness, the implementation of government policy seems to pay scant regard to planners targets. The annual budgetary process is rarely compatible with the global forecasts made by the Plan and on a number of occasions, the Plans have been entirely set aside by *ad hoc* contingency programmes[2]. What this chapter will examine are the reasons behind the predominance of macro-economic forecasting in the Dutch political process. Is its permanence and dominance because the planners at the Central Planning Bureau are so much more successful at forecasting than their counterparts elsewhere or because the forecasts of the C.P.B. fulfill a political function fulfilled by other agencies in other countries?

6.2 The Origins of the Central Planning Bureau

The development of the planning idea in Western Europe can be traced back to two developments which occurred in the depression years of the 1930's – the industrialisation of the Soviet Union command economy under the regime of Five Year Plans and the advances in liberal economic theory under the influence of Wigforss in Sweden and Keynes in the United Kingdom. Confronted by the numbing atrophy of classical economics in finding a solution to the persistent crisis these policy alternatives made a deep impression on socialist parties in particular. In 1935 the Belgian socialists (*Parti Ouvrier Belge*) published the de Man Plan and in the Netherlands the

Labour Plan (*Plan van den Arbeid*) appeared under the auspices of the
S.D.A.P. (Social-Democratic Workers Party). These socialist programmes
had in common the extension of public ownership, large public works
schemes and greater government intervention in economic management.

Ir. H. Vos, the director of the bureau charged with drafting the Labour
Plan stressed the need for 'a good national plan, fitting in an international
framework' but at the same time he stressed its political role as 'the
democratic way to socialist production methods'[3]. The Plan itself, or
planning in general, was viewed as the corner-stone of a new policy of
socialist dirigism. At approximately the same time potential improvements
in the methodology of planning were being pioneered by another of the
Plan's authors, Professor Jan Tinbergen, who succeeded in 1936 in
constructing the first crude econometric model of the Dutch economy[4].
However the failure of the socialists to achieve any participation in government until 1939 and the almost immediate onset of War, inevitably put paid
to the implementation of socialist proposals.

In the immediate post-war cabinet, socialists held virtually all the
economic portfolios and in September 1945 the new Minister of Trade and
Industry, Vos asked his friend and colleague, Professor Tinbergen to set up a
Central Planning Bureau which was to produce an outline recovery plan.
However it was not exactly clear what the responsibilities of the new bureau
were to be. The initial draft of the Act to give the C.P.B. statutory basis
presented to Parliament in March 1946 gave the bureau itself responsibility
for drafting 'a national welfare plan.' In comparison with its later evolution
this early draft gave the C.P.B. a considerable degree of autonomy even
though its role was as an advisor to government. Given the strong personal
links with the authors of the 1935 Labour Plan and the initial intention for
the Plan to be used as an agent for the structural reform of the economy and
society, it was not impossible that the C.P.B. may have evolved into an
overtly sectional political instrument.

In June 1946 there occurred a change in the complexion of the cabinet
and in November these were reflected in changes in government proposals
concerning the C.P.B. The ultimate responsibility for the Plan was firmly
vested in the government itself, the very name of the Plan was altered to a
'central economic plan' and time after time in the subsequent debate, it was
stressed that the C.P.B. was to be 'exclusively a technical aid' for government policy and business life. Vos' successor as Minister of Economic
Affairs, Dr. Huymans strove at great lengths to distance himself from the
term 'a guided economy' and great efforts were made to neutralise and
depoliticise planning as a concept. The socialist Drs. Nederhorst declared

that 'Planning is a technique which may be combined with different social systems' and that socialists did not claim a monopoly on planning. Whilst a number of socialists expressed unease at what they saw as a dilution of the planning principle, these concessions not only guaranteed the continued existence of the C.P.B. beyond the immediate recovery period but saw the law permanently establishing the C.P.B. pass through the Second Chamber without having to be put to the vote. In April 1947 the law giving the C.P.B. its statutory foundation finally gained the royal consent.

Article 3 (i) of the Act stipulated 'The task of the Central Plan Bureau is to carry out all activities relating to the preparation of a Central Economic Plan, which at regular times shall be lain down by the government for the benefit of the co-ordination of the government's policy in the economic, social and financial fields, as well as the submission of recommendations on general questions which may arise with respect to the realisation of the Plan.' Article 3 (ii) amplified this by describing the Plan as 'a balanced system of forecasts and directives in relation to the economy of the Netherlands.' Just how the C.P.B. and the Plans it was to prepare fitted into the policy-making process is discussed in the next section.

6.3 The C.P.B. and the Policy-Making Process

The primary function of the C.P.B. lies in preparing technical advice to assist the government in the policy-making process. In its earliest and most institutionalised form this consists of advising the cabinet in the preparation of the annual budget and it is to this end that the annual Central Economic Plan (henceforth C.E.P.) is published. In the course of the year the C.P.B. regularly formulates analyses of current trends and tentative forecasts to assist in the direction of policy but the show-piece of the entire exercise lies in the preparation of the C.E.P. itself, work on which begins in September, once the budget has been agreed. A first draft is submitted informally to the Ministries for comment and, in particular, for clarification of the implications of budget decisions. On the basis of these reactions a second draft is presented for confidential discussion by members of the Central Planning Commission – a statutory advisory/supervisory body of the C.P.B. whose membership, appointed by the Minister of Economic Affairs, includes representatives from the civil service, trade unions, employers organisations, scientific experts, etc. Once again, advice from this body contributes towards modifying the draft. It is also at this stage that consultations are made with industry to obtain information on sales trends, investement plans, etc. which are not easily built into an econometric model. The third draft is then submitted to the Council for Economic Affairs – an important cabinet sub-committee comprising all ministers with economic portfolios. A final version, embodying any final recommendations, is then submitted for government approval and publication in the early months of the New Year[6].

In its formal presentation it is clear that the forecasts are based on government policy and not vice-versa, but it is equally clear that in the process of consultation leading upto the budget, the information supplied by the C.P.B. plays an important role. The C.E.P. represents projected developments for the economy in the following year bases on known government policy. However it frequently contains analysis anticipating possible deviations in the forecasts in the form of 'datum alternatives' should the economy be blown off-course by developments outside government control and, occassionally, 'policy alternatives' where a real choice is left open at policy level (e.g. in 1960 the C.E.P. calculated the effects of revaluing the guilder by different amounts in the event of a Deutschmark revaluation).

The role of the C.P.B. in the policy-making process was extended when in 1961 Parliament requested the publication of preliminary forecasts to coincide with the debate on budgetary measures in order to facilitate better informed discussion. These *Macro-Economische Verkenningen* (henceforth M.E.V.) or macro-economic estimates are very much in the nature of tentative predictions.

The publications of M.E.V.'s was to bring the C.P.B. more to the centre of the policy-making process in another area – that of wage formulation. This lay in the coincidence of the publication date of the M.E.V.'s in September with the start of wage negotiations in the autumn of every year. In 1963 the attempt of the government to de-escalate controls in the wage arena led to a new institutional structure for wage bargaining. In this new procedure the Social Economic Council (a 45 member tripartite body representing equally trade union federations, employers associations and government appointed independent experts) set the scene for negotiations with the publication of its own economic prognosis – heavily dependent on the M.E.V.'s. These, together with official government commentary, provide the foundation for actual negotiations in the Foundation of Labour (a voluntary bi-partite group representing unions and employers) and the Government Board of Mediators. Although the precise format of the negotiation procedure was to alter later, the C.P.B. has continued to play an important role in informing discussions[7].

In 1963 the activities of the C.P.B. were further extended when it was entrusted with the preparation of medium-term forecasts. This development was in recognition of the fact that changes in the world economy to which the Netherlands had to adapt itself required perspectives longer than the one year horizon offered by the C.E.P. itself. To date three of these medium-term forecasts have been published covering the periods 1966-1970, 1968-1973 and 1976-1980. The last of these exercises in medium-term planning, and the subsequent reworkings of the forecasts, made in the wake of problems caused by the energy crisis, the wage explosion and the subsequent slowdown in the world economy has made for a greater impact in policy formation than either of its predecessors. It is a subject which we shall consider in greater detail later in the chapter.

Thusfar we have limited our attention to those areas in which the work of the C.P.B. is systematically used in the policy-making process. It is impossible in a chapter of this length to do full justice to the complete range of its activities in other areas. Among its many other fields of activity the C.P.B. engages in preparing *ad hoc* reports for individual ministries in regional policy, education, etc. and is represented in many multinational organisations[8].

The foregoing analysis has illustrated the important role occupied by the C.P.B. in the policy-making process in the Netherlands but how successfully it fulfills this role depends largely on the accuracy of the advice it is able to offer. It is this question which we will examine in the next section.

6.4 The Forecasting Performance of the C.P.B.

Before undertaking an analysis of the forecasting performance of the C.P.B. it will be useful first to examine the planning process itself in broad outline. Any econometric model represents a number of equations of interdependencies between the economic quantities or *variables* included therein. A number of these variables are obtained from outside the model and are termed *exogenous variables.* These are of two kinds. *External exogenous variables* represent those factors influencing the economy which originate from outside the country itself including trends in world trade (reweighted for its impact on the Netherlands), prices of Dutch imports, competitors' export price levels and the effective exchange rate of the guilder. Quantities for these variables are derived partly from other country's forecasts and partly from the C.P.B.'s own models designed for the purpose. Those exogenous variables originating internally are those factors determined by government policy and are known as *instrument variables*. These factors include trends in public sector expenditure, investment in dwellings, liquidity creation and, sporadically, the rise in per capita wage levels.

All the other variables are derived from the definitional and reaction equations contained in the model itself and are known as *endogenous variables*. Here again it is useful to distinguish two categories. Of most direct interest to the government are *target variables*, those goals which it wishes to influence by policy measures. These target variables include the balance of payments, unemployment, the price level of consumption and the level of enterprise investment (the latter as a determinant of the long term rate of growth). The remaining variables are rather unhelpfully classified officially as 'irrelevant' even though they, too, respond to both external and policy variables and, in turn, affect the performance of the target variables. For example, even when wages are not considered an instrument variable, movements in wage levels have direct implications for all the target variables. It is more helpful, then, to term these *intermediate variables*.

When the planning process begins the expected changes in external variables are fed into the model and forecasts are made on the basis of an unchanged policy. The results thus obtained are then compared with the goals of government policy. Should this comparison prove unsatisfactory, further forecasts are made assuming changes in the instrument variables and the implications of these for the target variables are then analysed. On the basis of these alternative forecasts the government is free to choose the policy alternative which provides the best compromise between target attainment and the political costs which each alternative implies. Obviously the final choice is far more complex and difficult to make than this brief outline suggests but it does reveal how planning can assist effective policy-making. However, in the last analysis, the utility of planning in this particular context depends very much on the accuracy of the forecasts themselves.

6.4.1 Annual Plans

Errors in forecasting stem largely from three sources: errors in estimating base year data, errors in forecasting exogenous variables and deficiencies in the model itself. This first source of error arises because the plans are prepared and published before the finalised data from the previous year becomes available. Clearly if a particular forecast is expressed in absolute terms an error in base year data can substantially alter the result. Similarly errors in estimating the results of exogenous variables, will distort the outcomes of the endogenous variables derived from the model. Base year errors in estimating the realised percentage changes in the endogenous variables themselves, however, will usually only have a marginal impact on subsequent forecasts[10]. With the increasing sophistication of data collection and collation, this source of error has diminished in importance over time but has yet to be eliminated altogether. Errors are still made in the estimation of the important category of exogenous variables. For example the C.E.P. for 1976 was made on the basis that in 1975 the weighted volume of world trade had fallen by four per cent and that the value of public consumption of goods had risen by 22 per cent. In the subsequent plans these realisation figures had been revised to two per cent and 15 per cent respectively. Similar revisions were made in estimated base year developments upon which the C.E.P. for 1977 were made in the volume of world trade initially estimated to have grown by 12 per cent but subsequently revised to 14 per cent, the value of public consumption of goods revised from 12.5 per cent growth to 15 per cent and the value of public investment revised from 2.5 per cent growth to 5.5 per cent. The base year errors are important not only because they are made in respect of variables which represent a large component of national

Table 6.1 Accuracy of C.E.P.'s Annual Forecasts for Selected External Exogenous Variables 1971-1978
(percentage change on previous year)

	Weighted Volume of World Trade		Import Price (guilders)		Competitor's Export Price Level (guilders)	
	F	R	F	R	F	R
1971	6.0	7.0	1.0	4.4	1.5	1.6
1972	6.0	9.5	−0.5	−0.6	0	0
1973	10.0	11.3	3.5	7.4	2.5	5.3
1974	2.0-4.0	4.1	±25.0	35.0	8-11	20.0
1975	0	−2.1	3.0	4.1	5.0	7.2
1976	6.0	14.0	5.0	6.5	5.0	5.5
1977	7.0	4.0[a]	4.0	3.0[a]	3.0	1.5[a]
1978	5.0	5.0[a]	0	−2.0[a]	0.5	0.5[a]
U_i (1971-75)		0.26		0.31		0.37

F = Forecast change
R = Realisation

Source: F and R; C.P.B. Central Economisch Plan, 1971 *et seq.* U_i; H.C. Elte et al, 'De Kwaliteit van de voorspellingen van het Centraal Planbureau: Een analyse van de verschillen tussen voorwaardelijke voorspellingen in realisaties 1953-1975', *Economisch-Statistische Berichten* 30.8.78, 874.
a) These realisation figures may well be subject to reestimation.

income but also because these exogenous variables are the crucial factors in determining the model's outcome.

The second source of error lies in the difficulties in forecasting the exogenous variables. This is particularly acute in the case of the external variables. Dr. V. Lutz's analysis of French indicative planning highlights its failure in this particular direction[11] and one can only reflect how much wider are the ramifications for the Dutch economy, with virtually half of its GNP originating abroad, of a failure to estimate levels of world trade or prices correctly. A number of investigations have been made into the accuracy of the Dutch annual plans[12] which have revealed the continuing vulnerability of forecasts for this set of variables. A survey covering the period 1953-1975 reveals that, standardising by sub-period, a gradual improvement has taken place in the accuracy of forecasts between each of the periods 1953-1962, 1963-1970 and 1971-1975, though throughout the period all forecasts were characterised by a persistent tendency towards underestimation[13]. Yet despite recent improvements in accuracy significant errors continue to be made as can be seen in Table 6.1.

The period after 1971 is a convenient one for analytical purposes. In the first place the uncertainties of the international economy and the problems which they posed for national governments, make the period a testing ground for the utility of planning as a tool for policy formulation. In order to be able to make a comparison between the accuracy of different sets of forecasts a calculation has been made for a coefficient of error known as the standardised root-maan square error with the symbol U_i[14]. It relates the prediction errors by variables to their normal state of change. Thus a value of U_i (1971-1975) of 0.26 for the weighted volume of world trade means that the forecasts were wrong to the extent of 26 per cent of the normal rate of change in the period. A value of $U_i = 0$ would mean that all the predictions were perfect. There is no upper bound for values of U_i but when $U_i = 1$ the errors are, on average, as large as the normal rates of change.

In each of the three periods 1953-1962, 1963-1970 and 1971-1975 the forecasting performance of the group of instrument variables comprising public investment and consumption, investment in dwellings and liquidity creation was worse in each period than errors in any other group of variables (i.e. external, target and intermediate)[15]. This is at first sight extremely surprising since the C.E.P.'s cover the same period as the government budgetary year and are prepared in full knowledge of what the budgetary measures are to be. A number of factors have contributed to this poor forecasting record. One reason is that the Dutch national budget is an authorisation rather than a performance budget and as a result the government's control over expenditure is relatively lax. This is compounded by the looseness of the government's accounting procedures since, as we have seen, the base year data for public investment and consumption is particularly untrustworthy. Another reason is that should the government need recourse to mid-course policy changes, this again will influence the end-year performance of the instrument variables but should such mid-course corrections prove necessary this must in itself be considered a serious indictment of the Plan's failure to fulfill its educative and predictive function[16]. The forecasting error in the liquidity ratio lies entirely with the central Bank whose own forecast is incorporated, uncorrected, into the C.E.P.'s. This variable is extremely prone to impulses from abroad, *ad hoc* changes in monetary policy and liquidity creation in the private sector.

Table 6.2 Accuracy of C.E.P.'s Annual Forecasts for Instrument Variables 1971-1978

	Value of Public Cons. of Goods		Value of Public Investment		Volume of Inv. in Dwellings in Enterprise		Per Capita Wage Earnings		Liquidity Ratio	
				percentage change on previous year					(yr. end)	
1971	F	R	F	R	F	R	F	R	F	R
1971	a)	a)	a)	a)	6.5	8.5	12.0	13.0	34.0	33.5
1972	a)	a)	a)	a)	−1.0	14.0	12.0	12.5	35.0	32.6
1973	8.0	9.5	17.5	−0.5	−5.0	2.0	13.5	15.5	32.0	34.7
1974	20.0	18.5	16.0	5.5	−6.0	−13.0	14.5	15.5	35.5	38.0
1975	22.5	24.5	18.0	22.0	−9.5	−7.0	12.5	13.0	38.0	36.1
1976	18.0	14.5	7.0	7.0	0	2.5	8.5-9.0	11.0	38.0	40.0
1977	7.0	10.0[b]	4.5	0.5[b]	12.5	16.0[b]	7.5	8.0[b]	39.0	37.4[b]
1978	4.5	9.5[b]	6.5	2.0[b]	2.5	2.5[b]	7.0	7-7.5[b]	38.0	36.2[b]
U_i (1971-75)						0.83		0.09		1.01

F = Forecast change
R = Realisation

Source: F and R; C.P.B. Centraal Economisch Plan, 1971 *et seq.*
U_i; H.C. Elte et al, 'De Kwaliteit van de voorspellingen van het Centraal Planbureau: Een analyse van de verschillen tussen voorwaardelijke voorspellingen en realisaties 1953-1975', *Economisch-Statistische Berichten*, 30.8.78, 874.

a) These figures are expressed in volume rather than value terms
b) These realisation figures may well be subject to re-estimation

Although since 1963 the government has attempted to reduce its own influence in the process of wage formulation during the 1970's it has intermittantly had recourse to a formal wages policy[17] and in the C.E.P.'s of 1971, 1974, 1975, 1976 and 1978 the rise in per capita wages has been treated as an exogenous variable. Moreover from Table 5.2 it is clear that the forecasts have consistently underestimated the rate of growth of this variable. Now, the forecasting of wages presents a rather unique problem since, as we have already seen, the C.P.B.'s own forecasts are part of the initial phases of the wage formulation process. Thus the realisation is partly conditioned by the 'announcement effect' of the forecast itself. In other words the very publication by the C.P.B. of a forecast is likely to ensure that it will be surpassed. This is partly because the Unions are aware that in the period 1949-1963, apart from the years 1961-1963, every single C.E.P. underestimated the increase in business production and, with it then, the scope for granting increases in earnings[18]. A further problem is that the figure published by the C.P.B. as an average increase in earnings are likely to be treated by negotiators as a minimum figure. It is not clear whether the government has attempted to take this announcement effect into account (i.e. by publishing a lower figure than the actual forecast) but it is curious in this respect that the wages forecast for 1978 were treated as an exogenous variable despite the fact that there was no formal wages policy in that year.

The third source of forecasting error which we have identified lies in the sophistication of the model itself, because no matter how accurate the input data might be, the results will be poor if the model fails to recognise certain interrelationships or inaccurately estimates certain reaction coefficients. The first model, known as Model 1955, after the year in which it was first published, consisted of 27 linear equations including 11 reaction equations. The model was deficient in a number of respects: the coefficients were crudely derived from basic statistical time series and there was an almost complete absence of time-lags. Subsequent improvements were made in Model 1961 and Model 1963 which increased the number of equations, extended the sampling period for calculating coefficients and improved the sophistication of such calculation, introduced a curvi-linear function for unemployment and made much more allowance for lagged effects[19]. In 1969 work was started on a new model, the 69-C Model, which was first employed in 1971. It is this model, which until recently, has been the backbone of the C.P.B.'s annual forecasts. In 1974, for the first time, the results of a new quarterly model were first published enabling a more accurate prediction of turning points in the economy to be made[20] and in 1976 it entirely superceded the previous model. Work is now in progress integrating the current quarterly model with the medium-term C.S. cyclical model. The 69-C Model consists of 13 reaction equations and 29 definition equations made

up of almost 100 variables. The 13 reaction equations were made up of four
concerning categories of expenditure (family consumption, private investment, stock formation and exports), two for supply factors (labour and
imports), one each for unemployment and monetary developments and five
for wages and prices. These are supplemented by three equations for foreign
trade in services, one for the size of unemployment payments and four for
taxation. The main differences in content between the 69-C Model and its
predecessors are the replacement of the unemployment equation by one for
labour supply, the explicit introduction of the concept of surplus capacity
and the use of real wage costs as one of the explanatory variables in the
labour demand equation. In addition the data for the reaction coefficients
was further updated and the econometric techniques employed even more
refined[21].

Table 6.3 Accuracy of C.E.P.'s Annual Forecasts for Target Variables 1971-1978

	Unemployment		Price Index of Private Consumption		Balance of Payments		Gross Business Investment	
000's	000's		% change on prev. yr.		bln. guilders		% change on prev. yr.	
	F	R	F	R	F	R	F	R
1971	65	69	6.0	8.0	−1.25	0.9	7.0	−0.5
1972	110-120	115	6.5	8.5	1.0	3.7	−6.0	−6.5
1973	110	117	7.5	9.0	2.5	6.3	8.5	12.0
1974	130-135	143	11.5	10.0	2.0-2.5	5.5	2.0	0.5
1975	185-190	206	9.5	10.5	5.0	4.4	0	−7.5
1976	220	211	8.5-9.0	9.0	7.0	7.5	−6.5	−3.5
1977	210-215	204[a]	6.5	7.0[a]	5.5	1.0[a]	8.0	15.5[a]
1978	230	206[a]	4.5	4.5[a]	2.5	−2.5[a]	3.0	6.0[a]
U_i (1971-75)	0.29		0.18		0.98		0.61	

F = Forecast change
R = Realisation

Source: F and R; C.P.B. Centraal Economisch Plan, 1971 *et seq.*

U_i; H.C. Elte et al, 'De Kwaliteit van de Voorspellingen van het Centraal Planbureau: Een analyse van de verschillen tussen voorwaardelijke voorspellingen en realisaties 1953-1975', *Economisch-Statistisch Berichten,* 30.8.78., 874.

a) These realisation figures may well be subject to re-estimation.

The forecasts and realisation for the target variables are summarised in Table 6.3. It is noticeable that the accuracy of the forecasts for unemployment and prices is far higher than those for the balance of payments and levels of business investment. The errors in predictions for the balance of payments can probably be traced back to the vulnerability of the planners in forecasting external exogenous variables. The disparity between prediction and actuality in the trend of gross business investment is almost entirely model-determined. In spite of the complexity of the equations, taking into account the lagged growth rate of production, unlagged surplus capacity, gross disposable profits and liquidities, and despite the 'qualitative' dimension of forecasting in the form of last minute consultation with enterprise, the forecasting of this variable is a black point of the Model's performance[22].

The errors made in forecasting endogenous variables stem both from errors in the exogenous variables and from imperfections in the model. One way of separating these sources of error is to apply the model to a historical period for which the results of the exogenous variables will then be model-derived. Such as exercise has been performed with the 69-C Model for the period 1962-1971 and a number of the C.P.B.'s critics have also tested their alternative models against the same historical period. The coefficients of error of the C.P.B. model and the alternative models are summarised in Table 6.4[23].

The most comprehensive analysis of the 69-C Model itself was made by Bemer and Miltenberg. They first calculated the outcomes of the original model in the period 1962-71 using the known results for the values of the exogenous variables and the lagged variables in the equations. The model was then modified in the course of a number of experiments with striking improvements in accuracy. They concluded that the simplification of the model by removing from the behavioural equations those variables with only a marginal impact on the outcome greatly improved its predictive performance. In particular, the new transformation variable for the supply of labour had serious implications for the accuracy of the model. Moreover the accuracy of the 69-C Model deteriorated seriously from the year 1966 onwards[24] and since the information for the reaction coefficients was drawn from the periods 1923-1938 and 1949-1966, the implication is clearly that these no longer reflect the change after the sampling period.

Among the interrelationships not adequately reflected in the 69–C Model, it has been argued, was the role of monetary factors in the economy. The *Naief Monetair Model* formulated by Bomhoff and Ooms deviated from the 69-C Model in two fundamental respects. Although it still used a

Table 6.4 Coefficient of Error (U_i) of the 69-C and Alternative Forecasting Models Applied to the Period 1962-1971

	i 69-C Model	ii Bemer & Milten- burg Experi- ment I	iii Naief Monetair	iv Grecon A	v Grecon B
Target variables					
Price Private Consumption	0.51	0.35	0.23	0.50	0.51
Unemployment	2.62	1.14	1.00	1.50	1.08
Gross Business Investment	1.40	0.81	0.70	1.27	1.02
Balance of Payments	3.59	1.18	1.48		
Intermediate Variables					
Volume Consumption	0.41	0.37	0.28	0.50	0.29
Price Investment Goods	0.28	0.26	0.22	0.21	0.32
Stock Formation	1.13	0.56	1.00	0.90	0.81
Volume of Imports	0.44	0.27	0.31	0.63	0.43
Employment	0.85	0.42	0.52	0.24	0.46
Production of Enterprise	0.18	0.18	0.13	0.42	0.34
Wages	0.23	0.22	0.21	0.50	0.24

Sources: i and ii, R. Bemer and A.J.M. van Miltenburg, *Enkele experimenten met het jaarmodel 1969*, Onderzoek Verslag, No.1 Technische Hogeschool, Delft, August 1974.
iii, E.J. Bomhoff and J. Ooms, 'Een Naief-Monetair model van de Nederlandse economie', *Economisch-Statistische Berichten*, 23.6.76., 592.
iv, M.A. Kooyman et al, 'Het GRECON-model 77-A voor de Nederlandse economie', *Economisch-Statistische Berichten*, 30.3.77., 311.
v, E.J. Bomhoff and J. Ooms, 'Het Grecon-model 77-B nader bekeken', *Economisch-Statistische Berichten*, 29.6.77., 626.

number of C.P.B. equations, the exercise in simplification was taken a step further than in the Bemer-van Miltenberg experiment (not only were all non-significant variables expunged but all reaction coefficients were rounded off to values of 0.25, 0.50 and 1). In addition the price equations were modified drastically to take account of monetary impulses and the primary monetary definition M1 replaced M3. To maintain comparability with the 69-C Model no attempt was made to extend the sampling period beyond 1966. When applied to the period 1962-1971, the forecasting performance of the Naief-Monetair Model was significantly better in all respects than the 69-C Model and furthermore, it was claimed by the authors (though the data was not published) that there was no deterioration in performance after 1966[25].

A third experiment in model-building stemmed from a group of economists at Groningen who formulated the so-called Grecon Model[26]. This is in essence a much simplified version of the C.P.B. 1963 model using a sampling period for coefficients of 1952-1973 in the Grecon A version and 1952-1975 in the Grecon B model. Moreover the monetary equation is omitted altogether. Unlike the other experiments which were designed for *exante* model analysis, the authors of the Grecon model have attempted to use it for *ex post* forecasting and they have attracted criticism both on the grounds of limitations in its use for policy-making[27] and on the grounds of theoretical shortcomings[28]. Nonetheless, the Grecon forecasts were more accurate over the period 1962-1971 than the 69-C forecasts though they, in turn, were bettered in every case by either the Bemer-van Miltenburg model or the Naief-Monetair model.

Although there still remain important differences between the alternative models and although the fact that they combine various innovations makes it difficult to quantify the effects of individual changes, they do suggest directions in which the forecasting performance of the C.P.B. might be improved. In the first instance they suggest that the C.P.B.'s planning models are unnecessarily complicated and that the inclusion of marginal variables weakens rather than strengthens predictive success. Secondly, it seems probable that greater recognition of the role of monetary factors in the economy would provide a closer approximation to economic realities.

Thusfar the analysis has concentrated on the C.P.B.'s accuracy in predicting the magnitude of change largely because it is the area most amenable to analysis but equally important is the ability of forecasts to predict the direction of change and particularly to identify turning-points in the economy. In this respect the fortunes of the annual plans have been mixed. Two well-documented examples point in different directions. In 1955 a turning-point error in the estimation of unemployment contributed to ill-conceived policy changes and subsequent economic difficulties[29] whereas in 1961 the C.P.B. scored a spectacular success in preparing the government for the consequences of a possible revaluation of the Deutschmark[30]. A study of the forecasting ability of the 69-C Model for the years 1971-1975 covering 22 exogenous and endogenous variables has revealed that an acceleration in a variable's performance was correctly identified in 84.6 per cent of cases and turning-points in 58.6 per cent of cases. The fact that the accuracy of these observations taken together represented an improvement over the relatively tranquil years between 1963 and 1970 must be reassuring to the planners but whether these results were that much better than could have been achieved by intelligent prognosis is a matter of conjecture[31].

6.4.2 Medium Term Plans

The violent fluctuations which characterised the international economy in
the 1970's posed a serious challenge for the economic planners and government alike. Not only did they present acute problems of short-term
economic management but they fundamentally altered the environment
within which the economies of Western Europe had to function. Adjustment
to the structural problems which flowed in the aftermath of the inflationary
boom of 1971-1973 and the subsequent deceleration in growth rates in the
wake of the oil crisis required perspectives longer than 12 to 18 months
offered by the M.E.V.'s and C.E.P.'s. In consequence medium-term forecasting began to play a larger part in policy formulation.

The formal plans drafted by the C.P.B. marked the beginning of an ongoing exercise in recalculation and updating of forecasts which was
continued in government blue and white papers and reports of the Central
Economic Council (an advisory body to the Ministry of Economic Affairs)
drawing on the expertise of the C.P.B. planners. The environment against
which the plans were formulated was one of unacceptable levels of inflation,
slowing growth rates, rising unemployment, deteriorating levels of investment, an eroding share of world markets, gradual exhaustion of natural gas
reserves and an inexorable rise in public expenditure. In February 1976 the
C.P.B., at the request of the den Uyl cabinet, published its first forecasts for
the economy covering the period upto 1980 which portrayed a sombre
outlook for the future if no corrective action was taken. If the government
continued to absorb an ever increasing share of G.N.P. it foresaw the persist-
ence of high inflation levels, sluggish industrial investment and a further rise
in unemployment (see Table 6.5 column ii).

As a policy alternative it considered the consequences of restricting the
growth of the government's share of national income to one per cent per
annum, to allow for increased outlay in existing social/welfare policies and
to leave some room for new initiatives to be taken. This alternative, known as
the one per cent Norm, would have some positive implications for the level
of investment and inflation but unemployment would stick at 210,000,
though this represented an improvement on the initial forecast (see Table 6.5
column iii). By June 1976, when the government published a blue paper
'Selective Groei' (Selective Growth) it was clear that the C.P.B. had had second
thoughts on the implications of the one percent Norm for the economy and
had revised downwards its forecasts for the annual average growth rate of
enterprise investment from three per cent to between 1.5 and two per cent and
had revised upwards its inflation forecast from seven per cent per annum to

Table 6.5 Medium Term Forecasts for the Dutch Economy 1976-1982
(per cent per annum change unless otherwise stated)

	i	ii	iii	iv	v	vi
Date of Publication		Feb 1976	Feb 1976	Sept 1976	June 1977	June 1978
Name of Publication		MEV '80	MEV '80	Ned. Ec. '80	C.E.C. Nota I	C.E.C. Nota II
Time-Span of Forecast	1970-75	1976-80	1976-80	1976-80	1976-81	1978-82
Policy Assumption	Trend	Simple Extra-polation	1% Norm	1% Norm + Additional Measures		
EXOGENOUS VARIABLES						
Weighted Vol. World Trade	5.9	7.5-8.0	7.5-8.0	7.5-8.0	7.0	6.0
Import Price Level (guilders)	9.2	5.0	5.0	5.0	5.25	4.5
Competitors Export Price (guilders)	6.0	5.0	5.0	5.0	4.75	4.5
Value Public Cons. of Goods	12.5	10.5	9.0	8.0		
Value Public Investment	7.4	8.5	7.0	6.5		
Volume Public Cons. of Goods	6.0 1974-78a)				5.0	4.5
Volume Public Investment	0.1 1974-78a)				−0.5	0
Volume Investment in Dwellings	0.7	0.5	0.5	0.5	3.0	1.0
TARGET VARIABLES						
Unemployment [b)	206	260	210	150	270	255-280
Price Index Private Consumption	9.1	8.5	7.0	7.0	6.5	4.0-4.5
Balance of Payments [c)	1.9	3.6	3.9	2.9	2.6	1.5-2.0
Gross Business Investment	−0.7	1.5	3.0	4.0	5.5	3.5
INTERMEDIATE VARIABLES						
Per Capita Wage Earnings	14.1	11.5	9.0-9.5	8.5	9.0	7.0
Real Disposable Income (modal worker)	2.5	−0.5	1.0	1.0-1.5	1.5	1.5
Volume Private Consumption	3.2	3.5	3.5	4.0	2.5	2.5
Volume Goods Exports	6.9	6.0	7.5	8.0	7.0	6.5
Volume Production by Enterprise	2.9	3.5	4.0	4.5	3.5	3.5
Real Labour Costs	5.4	3.5	2.5-3.0	2.0	4.0	3.5
Labour Productivity in Enterprise	3.5	4.0	4.0	4.0	3.5	3.0-3.5
Volume Gross National Product	2.9	3.0	3.8	4.0	3.5	3.0
Borrowing Requirement of Govt. (accrual basis) [c)	5.1	3.0	4.0	5.0	4.5	4.5

a) These figures are obtained from C.E.C. Nota II (see Source vi)
b) These figures are estimates for the final year of the period covered expressed in thousands
c) These figures are estimates for the final year of the period covered expressed as a percentage of national income in that year

Source: i and iv   C.P.B. *De Nederlandse economie in 1980*, 's-Gravenhage, 1976, 122.
          ii and iii   C.P.B. *Een macro-economische verkenning van de Nederlandse economie in 1980*, 's-Gravenhage, 1976, 24.
                v   C.E.C. *Een macro-economische verkenning van de periode 1976-81*, Bijlage bij de brief van de minister president dd 23-6-1977 nr 261353, 19.
               vi   C.E.C. *Macro-economische verkenning op middellange termijn 1978-1982*, published in *Bestek '81*, 's-Gravenhage, 1978, 74.

nine per cent[32]. Moreover it was equally clear that the government had decided
to adopt a more vigorous policy to combat unemployment, modifying the one
per cent Norm to permit additional measures of wage subsidies and investment incentives worth 3,500 million guilders over two years. The implications of this policy were forecast as being almost universally favourable

especially on the, revised, investment forecast and on unemployment, which would fall to 150,000 by 1980. The implications of these policies were more comprehensively worked out in the C.P.B.'s plan *'De Nederlandse economie in 1980'* published in September (see Table 6.5 column iv).

The next development took place in an extremely sensitive political situation. In March 1977 the socialist-led den Uyl coalition had fallen and the May elections proved inconclusive. The complex process of cabinet formation had already begun when in June the Central Economic Council (C.E.C.) published its updated forecast for the economy to 1981. Based on a new C.P.B. model, the publication of C.E.C. Nota I was a political bombshell especially for the socialists. With unchanged policies unemployment would rise to 270,000 and a public sector deficit of 4.5 per cent of national income left little room for manoeuvre (see Table 6.5 column v). On the basis of these calculations the Christian Democratic Alliance proposed cuts in government expenditure beyond those envisaged by the one per cent Norm and restrictions in the growth of real incomes. The socialists requested a re-forecasting exercise using the old model. This gave an unemployment forecast of 225,000 but a reduced government deficit of 3.5 percent of national income which allowed the socialists room to suggest further measures to stimulate the economy. The choice of C.P.B. model had now become a political question[33].

In January 1978 a new C.D.A.-V.V.D. conservative coalition led by van Agt was formed and it requested a new set of forecasts covering its four year period of office. In June C.E.C. Nota II was published, again using the new C.P.B. model, covering the period to 1982. Assuming a slower growth in world trade and a deterioration in the terms of trade, it envisaged a slower growth in the economy and thus less scope than previously for growth in government expenditure (see Table 6.5 column vi). These forecasts formed the basis for a government white paper *'Bestek '81'* (Blueprint '81) in which the government undertook to reduce umemployment to 150,000 by 1981 and to bring inflation levels down to West German levels by cutting back government expenditure from 210 milliard guilders in 1981 to 200 milliard and by restricting growth of real incomes. In place of the one percent Norm, Bestek '81 signalled the government's intention of stabilising the share of the collective sector in national income – in effect a 0 percent norm[34].

The worsening prognoses for the economy in successive plans quite clearly played a major part in shaping the evolution of government policy. It is worth considering briefly why such changes occur. One reason is that each subsequent forecast is made using new inputs for the exogenous variables in the form of more reliable figures for the recent past, a clearer impression of the development of the effects of government policy and re-estimation of likely trends in the international economy. Alterations in forecasts using the same model derive from a combination of these factors. Plans may also vary because of the introduction of a new model as occurred in the critical period in the middle of 1977. The earlier versions were based on a model which integrated an unpublished Cylical-Structural medium-term forecasting model with a macro-economic model for the analysis of employment – VINTAF I which has been published[35], a combination referred to as c.s.-VIN. This was superceded by the VINTAF II model which revised a number of specifications in the original model and expanded it by making the supply of labour an endogenous variable and introduced an equation for the social insurance sector[36]. The C.P.B. have argued that the change in forecast in

Table 6.6 Alternative Model Forecasts for the Period 1976-81 Using the C.S.-VIN and VINTAF II Models
(percent per annum change unless otherwise stated)

	C.S.-VIN	VINTAF II
TARGET VARIABLES		
Unemployment (000 man years)[a]	255	250
Price Index Private Consumption	7.5	6.5
Balance of Payments (000 million guilders)[a]	1.25	1.9
Gross Business Investment	6.5	5.75
INTERMEDIATE VARIABLES		
Per Capita Wage Earnings	10.25	9.25
Real Disposable Income (modal worker)	1.5	1.5
Volume Private Consumption	3.75	3.0
Volume Goods Export	7.75	6.75
Volume Production by Enterprise	4.25	3.5
Real Labour Costs	3.75	3.75
Labour Productivity in Enterprise	3.75	3.5
Borrowing Requirement by Govt. (transaction basis) (% nat. inc.)[a]	3.5	5.5

a) Level in 1981

Source: W. Driehuis and A. van der Zwan, 'De voorbereiding van het economisch beleid Kritisch bezien II', *Economisch-Statistische Berichten*, 7-9-77, 860.

1977 could partly be clarified by the fact that the cyclical upswing anticipated in 1975 had failed to materialise and this new information had been incorporated in C.E.C. Nota I[37]. The alternative model calculations using c.s.-VIN and VINTAF II for the period 1976-81 allow some estimation of the 'model effect' on the new predictions (see Table 6.6)[38].

It is noticeable that both estimates predict a deteriorating unemployment situation. The other changes, it was argued by the C.P.B. represented not merely model change but model improvement. In particular, it was admitted 'the c.s.-VIN model generates implausible projections upto 1981 on the point of the progress of investment. From the purely theoretical standpoint there also exist objections against this need. The small influence of foreign competition on internal price formation and the very large influence of real labour costs on business investment present the greatest questions'[39]. However, after a simulation exercise with the VINTAF II model over the period 1960-1973 its authors concluded, despite some residual problems, that 'the VINTAF II model offers an in every way acceptable macro-economic analysis of the Dutch economy in the 60's and 70's'[40].

The satisfaction of the C.P.B. with its model was far from universally shared. Ever since it was first published the VINTAF model has evoked a continuous stream of criticism which the improvements introduced into VINTAF II have done little to allay. The central assumption of the VINTAF models is that the structural unemployment in the Netherlands is determined by the acceleration in real wage rates. Following the model, the development of work opportunities is the result of the number of jobs created by investment in new equipment and the number of jobs lost through the obsolescence of existing equipment. There is no room in this chapter to consider the criticisms of the model in detail. In Chapter Three Professor van Eijk has criticised VINTAF II for failure to disaggregate unemployment on a regional basis and for a failure to consider monetary impulses satisfactorily[41]. In an extensive attack on VINTAF II Professor Driehuis and Van der Zwan considered a number of earlier criticisms as well as adding some new ones of their own. At the risk of gross oversimplification these may be enumerated as follows: the estimation of the maximum technical lifespan of machinery is unrealistic, the lifespan and capital intensity of new investment have been wrongly estimated, the use of constant capital: output ratio is unrealistic, the model results are highly sensitive to small alterations in the coefficients used, the conditions under which capital is scrapped are oversimplified, the failure to disaggregate the model into sectors ignores the different work creation effects of different forms of investment and (again) that the absence of a monetary bloc is unrealistic[42]. The integrity of the

VINTAF models was vigorously defended in an equally extensive reply by the C.P.B. which, whilst accepting some criticism, rejected others out of hand[43]. Yet the authors were forced to admit that VINTAF II was not yet an ideal model and that the C.P.B. was working to improve it in a number of directions where criticism was felt to be valid – the construction of a monetary bloc, refinement of the social-insurance bloc in the model, revision of the labour supply equation, a more improved approximation of investment behaviour and the introduction of the concept of capacity utilisation into the equations for captial obsolescence[44].

The discussion on the relative merits of c.s.-VIN and VINTAF II is not just a highly technical argument between econometrists but strikes at the very root of economic policy-making. The acceptance of both the den Uyl and van Agt cabinets of the dire forecasts for the economy based on the C.P.B. models has been central to the formulation of government policy. Yet the question remains as to how trustworthy the C.P.B.'s models are as a foundation for policy-making. If the forecasts of the now discredited c.s.-VIN model were misleading, what guarantee is there that those of VINTAF II, with its admitted deficiencies are any more reliable? When taken together with the question-marks over the annual forecasting models, it is not surprising that attention should have turned to a consideration of the role of the Planning Bureau in the entire policy-making process.

6.5 Conclusion

The analysis in this chapter makes clear that the C.P.B.'s annual and medium-term forecasting performance is far from perfect. Given the advances in econometric techniques elsewhere and that the openness of the Dutch economy makes it more vulnerable to change than economies with a smaller share of G.N.P. in the foreign sector, it is doubtful whether Windmuller's claim that 'the Bureau's forecasts have turned out to be generally more accurate than those made by similar bodies in other European countries'[45] any longer holds true. Thus the considerable influence of the C.P.B. in the formal policy-making process cannot simply be attributed to the unique level of refinement of its models.

In a way, however, whether the C.P.B. forecasts well is not as important as the general acceptance of the belief that it does. Windmuller's confidence is indicative of such acceptance. Elsewhere it has been observed that 'in the past an air of unimpeachibility has hung round the use of econometric models in our country' – a position attributed to the international scientific reputation of successive directors of the C.P.B. and its monopoly position in econometric modelling[46]. Hessel emphasises the importance of this consensus as a factor in explaining the influence of the C.P.B. in policy-making: 'During the years of its existence, the C.P.B. has won the good will and confidence of both employers organisations and trade unions by its objectivity and capability. To make programming workable in a society, this kind of confidence is needed; otherwise any detail of the plan and any implicit assumption could become disputable'[47]. The position of the C.P.B. as a neutral technical advisor to government with an enviable, if unfounded, reputation for reliability performs an important functional role in providing government with external legitimisation for its policies. For example in 1970 the then secretary of the Dutch Federation of Trade Unions complained that the forecasts provided by the C.P.B. had enabled the government to exercise an (over)strong influence on any tripartite wage negotiations. 'In this situation,' he stated, 'the government had the first and the last work'[48]. In the recent debate over medium term policy, the government and various subcommittees may have had good reason to believe that wages were too high, profits too low, the public sector too large, the market sector too small without recourse to a model. In the words of one of its members 'to come to such a conclusion the C.E.C. (Commission of Economic Experts, subcommittee of the Social-Economic Council) did not find the VINTAF II model directly necessary'[49]. Yet it would be difficult to deny that the quantification of the effects of both a no-change policy and the successive policy formulations into the future lent government policy an authority it would not otherwise have had. Moreover the question has been asked rhetorically whether the government and quasi-governmental bodies would have accepted the models so unquestioningly had it not conformed with their intuitive analysis of the economy[50].

Although, as an advisory body, the C.P.B. is not a powerful agency constitutionally, it performs an important function in the policy-making process by helping to achieve agreement around the assumptions upon which decisions are made and by lending external legitimisation to policy decisions. Thus the forecasts of the C.P.B. serve a similar function in the decision-making structure as do the pronouncements of the Bundesbank in the Federal Republic of Germany. In the same way it could be argued that the problem in the United Kingdom is not too little forecasting but too much and that government has failed to build a consensus around any agency that might have served a similar function.

Herein lies the irony of the current situation in the Netherlands. The questioning of the accuracy of the C.E.P.'s, the proliferation of alternative annual models and the controversy still raging over the VINTAF models may well, in the long run, contribute to improvements in predictive performance but in undermining the foundations of confidence these developments may diminish the utility of the C.P.B. in the co-ordination of economic policy – a case of better forecasting but more difficult planning.

End notes

* I would like to thank Mr. Karstens of the Central Planning Bureau and Drs. B. Bemer for their help in providing information for this chapter.
[1] A useful recent summary of planning procedures in France, The Netherlands, Norway, Federal Republic of Germany and United Kingdom is A.W.R. Hawthorne, *Economic Planning in Five Western European Economies; an Overview.* A study prepared for the use of the Joint Economic Committee, Congress of the United States. Washington, 1976.
[2] In 1963 the Ministry of Finance introduced a stabilisation plan which took precedent over the official Plan. A similar, more recent example, is afforded by the Barre austerity programme.
[3] Quoted in E. van Cleeff 'De Voorgeschiedenis van het Centraal Planbureau', *25 jaar Centraal Planbureau*, p. 11 C.P.B. Monografie, No. 12, The Hague, 1970.
[4] J. Tinbergen, 'Kan hier te lande, al dan niet via Overheidsingrijpen, een verbetering van de binnenlandse conjunctuur intreden, ook zonder verbetering van onze exportpositie?' *Prae-advies aan de Vereniging voor Staathuishoudkunde en Statistiek*, 1936.
[5] Van Cleef, 'De voorgeschiedenis van het Centraal Planbureau', pp. 12-18. The quotations not contained in this chapter are derived from the relevant parliamentary papers.
[6] P. de Wolff, 'Central Economic Planning in the Netherlands', pp. 11-12 in I.E.A. *Planning and Markets: Modern Trends in Various Economic Systems,* J.G. Abert, *Economic Policy and Planning in the Netherlands, 1950-1965,* pp. 117-122, Yale, 1969.
[7] See Chapter 3, pp. 76-79 for an uptodate summary of developments. See also J.P. Windmuller, *Labor Relations in the Netherlands*, pp. 297-313, New York, 1969.
[8] C.A. van den Beld, 'Het Centraal Planbureau als bedrijf', *25 jaar Centraal Planbureau*, pp. 54-60.
[9] De Wolff, 'Central Economic Planning', pp. 4-5.
[10] This point can be demonstrated quite simply mathematically. Suppose a particular variable in base year minus one is 100 units and it is estimated to have grown by 10 percent in the course of the year in which the Plan is being prepared (i.e. it is valued at 110 units). As a result of new information fed into the model the value of the variable is forecast to grow by a further 10 percent of 11 units. Now if the estimate for the base year is revised downwards and the growth recorded as 5 percent (i.e. it is valued at 105 units), a forecast growth rate of 10 percent will only yield an increase of 10.5 units or, expressed differently, an anticipated increase of 11 units should have been expressed as 10 percent. The degree of misestimation therefore has to be of a very large magnitude before it significantly affects the following years' forecast; far longer than is usually made in practice.
[11] V. Lutz, *Central Planning in a Market Economy. An Analysis of French Theory and Practice*, London, 1969.
[12] *Een vergelijking van de ramingen van het Centraal Planbureau met de feitelijke economische ontwikkeling, 1949-1953*, C.P.B. Monografie, No. 4, The Hague, 1955. *Forecasts and Realisation: The Forecasts of the Netherlands Central Planning Bureau, 1953-1963*, C.P.B. Monografie, No. 10, The Hague, 1965. H.C. Elte, R.F. Hochheimer, W. Kuipers, C.L. Worms, 'De Kwaliteit van de voorspellingen van het Centraal Planbureau: Een analyse van de verschillen tussen voorwaardelijke voorspellingen

en realisaties 1953-1975', *Economisch-Statistische Berichten*, 30-8-1978.

[13] H.C. Elte et al, 'De Kwaliteit van de voorspellingen', 874.

[14] In calculating a numerical measure for predicative accuracy, the symbol R_i used to indicate the realisation (the observed percentage change over the year) and F_i t for the forecast rate of change. The forecasting error is:

$$U_i t = F_i t - R_i t$$

Now it makes sense to standardise the error to take into account the normal intensity of change since, for example, a prediction error of 2 percent per annum when the average rate of change in the variable is 2 percent is much worse than the same prediction error when the average rate of change is 10 percent per annum. The average rate of change in realised values is:

$$SR_i = \sqrt{\frac{1}{n} - \Sigma \, R_i t^2}$$

The standardised error of forecast for the variable i in year t is:

$$U_i t = \frac{U_i mt}{SR_i}$$

To obtain the standardised error of forecast for variable i over a given number of years n, the following formula is used:

$$U_i = \sqrt{\frac{1}{n} - \Sigma \, (U_i t)^2}$$

Forecasts and Realisation, 16, 17; Elte et al, 'De Kwaliteit van de voorspellingen', 879.

[15] Elte et al, 'De Kwaliteit van de voorspellingen', 874.

[16] A survey of the C.E.P.'s between 1953 and 1963 has shown that the mid-course corrections made in that period had only a marginal impact on the outcome of the model. *Forecasts and Realisation*, 19, 58.

[17] See Chapter Two, pp. 39-46 and Chapter Three pp. 76-79.

[18] H. ter Heide, 'Centraal Planbureau en Vakbeweging', *25 jaar Centraal Planbureau*, 47-50.

[19] Van den Beld, 'Het Centraal Planbureau als bedrijf', 64-65, Abert, *Economic Policy and Planning*, 179-229.

[20] It is impossible to say how this quarterly model relates to the 69-C model since, at time of publication, the details have not been printed.

[21] *Centraal Economisch Plan*, 1971, 181-201 for the Plan itself. A simplified account of the structure of the 69-C model is to be found in B.H. Hasselman, J.J. Post and C.A. van den Beld, 'The Fix-Point Estimation Model and a Revision of the 69-C Annual Model', *Modelling for Government and Business. Essays in Honor of Prof. Dr. P.J. Vendoorn*, 82-86, The Hague, 1977.

[22] In an interesting experiment the C.P.B. recalculated its forecasts for 1969 on the assumption that all the exogenous variables had been perfectly realised. The original prediction for investment was altered as a result from a 6 percent to a 6.7 percent increase. In fact it had risen by a mere 0.5 percent, *Centraal Economisch Plan*, 1970, 177-178.

[23] The list of variables for comparison has been determined by the lowest common denominator, i.e those for which results are published for the Grecon models. It must be emphasised that these are exercises in pure model calculations whilst the published plans themselves temper or

modify the model results with information from other sources. As a result the coefficient of error of the actual plans in the period 1963-1970 are better in many cases than the model outcomes of the 69-C model and even the alternative models despite the fact that the plans had to predict exogenous variables whereas the model exercises were able to feed the actual results into their calculations. For example, the coefficients of error for the target variables in the actual plans between 1963-70 were unemployment 0.51, enterprise investment 0.66, consumption price index 0.18 and balance of payments 1.43. Elte et al, 'De Kwaliteit van de voorspellingen', 874. The fact that these results do not cover exactly the same years as covered in the model experiments is of only marginal consequence. *Ibid.*, 879, footnote 21.

[24] R. Bemer and A.J.M. van Miltenberg, *Enkele experimenten met het jaarmodel 1969*, Technische Hogeschool Delft, Vakgroep Economie, Onderzoek Verslag, No. 1, August 1974.

[25] E.J. Bomhoff and J. Ooms, 'Een Naief-Monetain model van de Nederlandse economie', 588-593, *Economisch-Statistische Berichten*, 23-6-1976.

[26] M.A. Kooyman, B. Bos, R.H. Ketellapper and W. Voorhoeve, 'Het Grecon model 77-A voor de Nederlandse economie', 309-311, *Economisch-Statistische Berichten*, 30-3-1977, 'De Grecon voorspellingen voor 1978', 325-327, *Economisch-Statistische Berichten*, 5-4-1978.

[27] B. Bemer and A.J.M. van Miltenburg, 'Grecon 77-A als symptoom van een ontwikkeling', 599-601, *Economisch-Statistische Berichten*, 22-6-1977. The authors criticise the Grecon forecasting catagories for being insufficiently differentiated to distinguish instrument variables. They also, slightly unfairly, compare the Grecon forecasting accuracy 1962-71 with the 69-C model 1960-69 thereby removing the two worst forecasting years of the 69-C model from the reckoning. It should also be noted that the Grecon model uses the C.P.B.'s forecasts for exogenous variables and therefore, as a model, sidesteps the most difficult part of the entire forecasting exercise.

[28] E.J. Bomhoff and J. Ooms, 'Het Grecon model 77-B nader bekeken', 623-627, *Economisch-Statistische Berichten*, 29-6-1977. Not surprisingly the omission of the monetary equation altogether was like a red rag to a bull for the monetarist and it was on these grounds that the most serious criticisms were levelled.

[29] *Forecasts and Realisation*, pp. 49-52.

[30] De Wolff, 'Central Economic Planning in the Netherlands', pp. 15-17.

[31] Elte et al, 'De Kwaliteit van de voorspellingen', 877.

[32] R.T. Griffiths, 'Techniques of Macroeconomic Management in the Netherlands', *Government, Business and Labour in European Capitalism*, (ed. R.T. Griffiths), London, 1977, pp. 146-148. There is an obvious error in this chapter where it states that the 69-C model was first used in 1969.

[33] R.B. Andeweg, K. Dittrich and T. van der Tak, *Kabinetsformatie 1977*, Leiden 1978, 42-47.

[34] *Bestek '81. Hoofdlijnen van het financiële en sociaal-economische beleid voor de middellange termijn*, The Hague, 1978.

[35] H. den Hartog and H.S. Tjan, *Investeringen, lonen, prijzen en arbeidsplaatsen. Een jaargangen- model met vaste coefficienten voor Nederland*, C.P.B. Occasional Paper No. 8, The Hague, 1974. H. den Hartog, T. van de Klundert and H.S. Tjan, 'De structurele ontwikkeling van de werkge- legenheid in macro-economisch perspectief', *Preadvies voor de Vereniging voor de Staathuishoud- kunde*, The Hague, 1975, (C.P.B. Reprint Series No. 152).

[36] *Een Macro-model voor de Nederlandse Economie op Middellange Termijn (VINTAF II)*, C.P.B. Occasional Paper No. 12, The Hague, 1977.

[37]* H. den Hartog and J. Weitenberg, 'Econometrische Modellen en economische politiek (II)', *Economisch-Statistische Berichten*, 21/28-12-77, 1271-1272.

[38] The results of the model calculation for VINTAF II differ from those published in C.E.C. Nota I because the latter has taken into account the effects of restrictive government finance.

[39]* Den Hartog and Weitenberg, 'Econometrische modellen (II)', 1270.

[40] *Een Macro-model voor de Nederlandse Economie*, 20-25.

[41] See Chapter Three, pp. 71-73.

[42]* W. Driehuis and A. van der Zwan, 'De voorbereiding van het economisch beleid kritisch

bezien II', *Economisch-Statistische Berichten*, 7-9-77, 856-861.

[43]* H. den Hartog and J. Weitenberg, 'Econometrische modellen en economische politiek (I)', *Economisch-Statistische Berichten*, 14-12-77, 1236-1243.

[44]* Den Hartog and Weitenberg, 'Econometrische modellen (II)', 1273.

[45] J.P. Windmuller, *Labor Relations in the Netherlands*, 1303, New York, 1969. This claim was based on a survey of the 1950's in S. Wellisz, 'Economic Planning in the Netherlands, France and Italy', *Journal of Political Economy*, Vol. 68, 1960, 265.

[46]* Driehuis and van der Zwaan, 'De voorbereiding van het economisch beleid II', 835.

[47] W. Hessel, 'Quantitative Planning of Economic Policy in the Netherlands', in B.G. Hickman (ed.), *Quantitative Planning of Economic Policy*, 165.

[48] Ter Heide, 'Centraal Planbureau en Vakbeweging', 47-48.

[49] B.D.J. Schouten, 'Hoe komen we eigenlijk aan meer winst'. *Economisch-Statistische Berichten*, 16-11-77, 1128-1130.

[50]* Driehuis and van der Zwaan, 'De voorbereiding van het economisch beleid II', 835.

* Since this chapter was written, these articles, together with others relevant to the debate on the preparation of economic policy, have been reprinted in W. Driehuis and A. van der Zwan (eds), *De voorbereiding van het economisch beleid Kritisch bezien*, Leiden/Antwerp, 1978.

Select Bibliography

In English

Abert, J.G., *Economic Policy and Planning in the Netherlands, 1950-1965*, Yale, 1969.

Beld, C.A. van der, 'Short-term Planning Experience in the Netherlands', *Quantitative Planning of Economic Policy*, ed. B.G. Hickman, Washington, 1965.

Blanken, M., *Force of Order and Methods. An American View into Dutch directed Society*, The Hague, 1976.

C.P.B., *Forecasts and Realization. The forecasts by the Netherlands Central Planning Bureau 1953-1963* (CPB Monograph no. 10), The Hague, 1965.

Hasselman, B.H., Post, J.J. and Beld, C.A. van den, 'The Fix-Point Estimation Model and a Revision of the 69-C Annual Model', *Modelling for Government and Business. Essays in Honour of prof. dr. P.S. Verdoorn*, The Hague, 1977.

Hessel, W., 'Quantitative Planning of Economic Planning in the Netherlands', *Quantitative Planning of Economic Policy*, ed. B.G. Hickman, Washington, 1965.

Verdoorn, P.J., 'The Short-term model of the Central Planning Bureau and its forecasting performance 1953-1963', United Nations, *Construction and Practical Application of Macro-Economic Models for Purposes of Economic Planning (Programming) and Policy Making*, 1968.

Wolff, P. de, 'Central Economic Planning in the Netherlands', IEA, *Planning and Markets: Modern Trends in Various Economic Systems*, ed J.T. Dunlop & N.P. Fedorenko, New York, 1969.

In Dutch

Bencer, R. and Miltenburg, A.J.M. van, *Enkele experimenten met het jaarmodel 1969*, onderzoeksverslag Nol, Vakgroep Economie, T.H. Delft, 1974.

Bestek '81. Hoofdlijnen van het financiële en sociaal-economische beleid voor de middellange termijn, Tweede Kamer-stuk, 15 081, nrs. 1 en 2 (zitting 1977-78).

C.P.B., *Een macro-model voor de Nederlandse economie op middellange termijn: VINTAF II* (CPB Occasional Paper no. 12), The Hague, 1977.

C.P.B., *Een vergelijking van de ramingen van het Centraal Plan Bureau met de feitelijke economische ontwikkeling, 1949-1953*, (CPB Monograph no. 4), The Hague, 1955.

C.P.B., *25 jaar Centraal Plan Bureau* (CPB Monograph no. 12), The Hague, 1970.

Driehuis, W. and Zwan, A. (eds.), *De voorbereiding van het economisch beleid kritisch bezien*, Leiden/Antwerpen, 1978.

Elte, H.C., Hochheimer, R.F., Kuipers, W. and Worms, C.L., 'De kwaliteit van de voorspellingen van het Centraal Plan Bureau, een analyse van de verschillen tussen voorwaardelijke voorspellingen en realisaties 1953-1973', *Ekonomisch Statistische Berichten*, jrg. 63, no. 3169, 30-8-1978.

Selectieve Groei. Economische structuurnota, Tweede Kamer-stuk, 13 955, nrs. 1-3 (zitting 1975-76).

7 INTEREST GROUPS IN DUTCH DOMESTIC POLITICS

J. de Beus and H. van den Doel

7.1 Introduction

7.1.1 The image of power

Dutchmen may not lead 'the imagination to power', but they do have an image of power. They are in the habit of ascribing an almost ubiquitous power to interest groups which take established positions in the political system and are permanently and conspicuously present. During the general debate on the government budget in the parliamentary session 1978 Mr. Terlouw, a radical-liberal MP, was very concerned that the functioning of the mechanism of parliamentary democracy was being disturbed through the interest groups:

> (. . .) We raise objections to the fact that politicians let themselves be taken by surprise. Cabinet and parliament do not dare to express their own judgements any longer, without taking cover at all sides, without continuously throwing frightened gazes at the interest organizations. (. . .) we wonder with uneasiness if in fact we have perhaps arrived in a corporate state already. In parliamentary democracy the political decision-making rests primarily with government and parliament. Is this still true, now that the co-operation of interest organizations has become so dominating and the number of advisory boards so overwhelming?[1]

In the crucial phase of preparation of this 1979 budget, the first one of the centre-right Van Agt-cabinet that came into power in December 20 1977, the Minister for Social Affairs Mr. Albeda pointed to the chairmen of both the biggest employers' association and the biggest workers' association as the most powerful men of the nation, who were able to make government's social and economic policy or to break it. Similarly, political commentators argued that the Dutch trade union movement formed the 'social base' of the new government that has set out a programme for stabilization of taxes and social security contributions and a reduction of public expenditure. Moreover the jurist Couwenberg[2] declaimed in 1977:

> It will appear more and more that, without the co-operation of the trade union
> movement one cannot govern effectively any longer. This could indicate that
> parliamentary democracy becomes a façade, behind which a factual develop-
> ment towards a trade-union-state comes about, that is, a state in which not the
> liberal-democratically organized state authority but the organized workers'
> class strikes the key-note in the most important field of governmental policy,
> namely social and economic policy.

In an essay on the future of the Dutch welfare state the political scientist
Daudt[3] asserts that interest groups are exposing political decision-making to
pressure by means of the arousal of expectations and the pursuit of partial
interests to such an extent, that a majority of the citizens are bound to
conceive the supply of collective goods by the state as compulsory consumption. Election results would be manipulated by interest groups, competing
for transfers. Political parties would be willing instruments of these groups
owing to their application of the vote-trading strategy.

Daudt's argument, that resembles the ideas of Brittan (1977) in England
about the internal contradictions and malicious economic consequences of
modern political democracy, dates back partly to ideas of prominent Dutch
economists as Drees and Hartog[4]. Already in 1955 it was Drees who considered the activity of interest groups as one of the factors that cause upward
pressure upon government expenditures, otherwise combined with a factor
as the budgetary behaviour of specialized, and with certain sector-interests
affiliated, politicians. Hartog pointed out that the practice of pressure
groups is to pick and steal collective privileges and shift off the collective
financial burden. He even concluded that pressure groups were the biggest
enemies of maximization of social welfare.

Outside the setting of partisan politics and social science, interest groups
also have a reputation of power. In the year 1972 sixty percent of Dutch citizens thought that the trade unions had too much say in important decisions.
Only ministers, the Lower House and big business attained higher scores. 49
percent of the persons interviewed mentioned the employer organizations, a
percentage that was only matched by the political parties. Interest group
power was perceived not just as big, but also as too big. Not less than 23
percent and 27 percent of the respondents thought that the influence of the
employee organizations and the employer organizations, respectively, was
too extensive[5]. A study undertaken in the 1970's[6] shows that more than 50
percent of the Dutch senior civil servants regarded the continual clash of
particularistic interst groups as a danger for the general welfare of the

country. These senior officials regarded employer organizations as less influential than trade unions and more influential than farm organizations. However, as far as their personal evaluation was concerned, only 14 percent of the senior civil servants were opposed to connections between departments and interest groups. Professor Karsten, one of the Dutch captains of industry, holds the view that the employer and employee organizations in the Netherlands have less power than the state, but are, on the other hand, more powerful than the media action groups, political parties and churches. In the long run the power of employer organizations and corporations would shrink and trade union power would grow[7].

In short, the interest groups in the Netherlands possess the unshakable and useful *image* of being powerful and too powerful. The question is, of course, if this reputation is also underpinned by the results of social-scientific research. In a well-known study of economic power by Mokken and Stokman (1975) little weight is given to the power of interest groups. The process of interest promotion by interest groups is in merely one sector of public policy exceptionally thoroughly investigated (see the dissertation of Leune (1976) on the influence of teachers' associations in the making of education policy[8]). Leaving aside the action groups[9], the extensive field of research on interest groups and their influence seems somewhat neglected, certainly when compared with neighbouring countries and the United States. This impression also emerges from the special bibliography of Von Beyme[10]. In some surveys of Scholten (1971), Rosenthal c.s. (1977) and Braam (1978) the same, rather obsolete, publications are regularly reported. For the time being therefore, variety of opinions mentioned above is unfortunately accompanied with a scarcity of empirical material.

Within the Dutch political arena a kaleidoscope of interest groups is operating, of which the exact number is unknown since the Dutch counterpart of the American lobby-index is wanting[11]. Examples are the *Katholieke Nederlandse Boeren- en Tuindersbond* (farmers), the *Vereniging van Dienstplichtige Militairen* (soldiers), the *Koninklijke Nederlandse Maatschappij tot bevordering der Geneeskunst* (surgeons) and the *Nederlandse Vereniging van Gemeenten* (municipalities), but also the gamut of action- and protest groups (particularly in environmental issues), that came into existence in the 1960's.

In this chapter we choose from sheer necessity – the foregoing considered – a partial approach. We will occupy ourselves with the central, that is on the national level, active *employer and employee organizations*. We do not provide specimen of a power-study, but examine in outline:
- the functioning of these interest groups in the Dutch arrangement of political institutions (par. 7.2);

- some important economic effects of the activity of these interest groups in a so-called negotiations democracy (par. 7.3);
- the significance of our argument for the political philosophical vision on the position of interest groups in a modern political order (par. 7.4).

In the remaining part of this introduction we will discuss some concepts and models, which are relevant to our subject.

7.1.2 Concepts

For our purpose the phenomenon of interest groups can be broadly defined. Interest groups are organized groups that pursue collective objectives – attempting to influence parts of public policy without assuming political and constitutional responsibility for public policy.

Just like Olson (1965) we conceive of groups as sets of individuals with a common goal, that is as individuals who share one and the same individual goal. A group, composed of the persons $x_1, \ldots, x_i, \ldots, x_n$, has an interest in y if y is wanted or demanded by the group. Therefore, a particular collective interest (goal or object) can never be objectively postulated, but is inferred from the subjective preferences of group members. Interest groups want or demand something, for instance y, from political decision-making. Group members ((self-) elected spokesmen included) usually justify such a claim to y by means of ideology. This justification can be weighed by an outsider, for instance a political philosopher (Held (1973)).

An organization exists, when the relations between group members have a distinct formal structure, which is purposefully created by group members themselves. Interest promotion by influencing the state never concerns integral public policy[12]. One could further trace to what extent leaders and ordinary members of interest groups regard the influencing of political decision-making as the main product or by-product, and to what extent the scope of influence fluctuates in a certain period. In our opinion, it is no longer valid to accept Key's (1952) much used criterion for an interest group. He stressed the difference between interest groups and political parties (viz. the nomination of candidates for state organs). In the Netherlands the trade unions have put forward candidates for a long time, while, on the other hand, political parties act as interest groups by getting publicity in a one-issue-oriented style[13] (see, for a different conceptual framework, Richardson and Jordan (1979)).

We prefer, moreover, the concept of *interest group* to the concept of *pressure group*, that became vogue during the interwar years in American journalism and political science (Odegard a.o.). Pressure is a far too vague indication of a long series of possible techniques of influencing (personal persuasion, intimidation, strike, etc.). Salisbury (1975) has made a list of types of interest promotion, among which are different forms of lobbying, representation and mobilization. Thereafter, many researchers[14] have emphasized that nowadays representation in political institutions has become the dominating type of interest promotion, in place of the old arsenal of 'pressure politics' (but see [15]).

Above we have used the terms (political) influence and power rather loosely. *Influence* can come about through an exchange of information between persons who in fact pursue the same object. *Power* is a specific form of influence, to wit that form which is supported by the possibility of enforcing negative sanctions. The leadership of an interest group may, for instance, threat to stop co-operation (tax-paying, supporting the governmental policy, and so on). The quasi-monopoly of information and expertise is frequently mentioned as the primary source of interest group power[16].

Power can have economic and political aspects, according to the sanctions which are enforced. Power has an *economic* aspect, when sanctions are founded on scarcity-relations. If subject A is entirely committed, for the realization of his goals, to scarce means, which are exclusively controlled by subject B, then B can wield power over A. Power has a *political* aspect, when sanctions are based on the use of political means: the abstinence of support, the use of physical violence, etc[17].

Interest groups address themselves to *political decision-making*, that is the making of binding decisions, which allocate values for society as a whole.

7.1.3 *Models of socio-economic decision-making*

The relations between the central government, the employer and the employee organizations can not only be studied by means of various scientific approaches to the relationship between state, society and social change (Alford (1975), Schmitter (1977) and Berki (1979)), but can also be described in a stylized manner in different models of the process of socio-economic decision-making. We shall concisely discuss three such models, namely the neo-corporatist model (sociologists), the 'consociational' model (political scientists) and the model of negotiations democracy – or concerted action – (economists).

The spell of the pluralist approach in the interest group literature has been broken in the 1970's by a number of authors, who are concerned with the growing interaction between polity and economy. They try to give the concept of corporatism a scientifically workable content. Classical corporatism is often conceived as a social order, based on the principles of status and functional representation of occupation groups (for example, fascism in the Mediterranean area and South-America). At present, however, the term stands for a particular group of doctrines and for a system of interest promotion by groups:

> Corporatism can be defined as a system of interest representation in which the constituent units are organized into a limited number of singular, compulsory, noncompetitive, hierarchically ordered and functionally differentiated categories, recognized or licensed (if not created) by the state and granted a deliberate representation monopoly within their respective categories in exchange for observing certain controls on their selection of leaders and articulation of demands and supports (Schmitter (1974)).

Afterwards, this modern description of corporatism is elaborated and partly revised by Schmitter (1977) himself. Following in Schmitter's path, Lehmbruch and Panitch[18] make mention of liberal corporatism or *neo-corporatism*, in order to stress that:
– this system of interest promotion is compatible with parliamentary democracy, a multi-party-system, a market sector and individual propterty rights;
– the formation of interest-groups, their entry into the political arena, their mutual relations and their internal organization are not *ex ante* arranged by the public authorities, but *ex post* ratified by them.

In recent literature on neo-corporatism[19] the Netherlands is treated as a striking example of neo-corporatism. One could discover a creeping transition to neo-corporatism:

> (. . .) it began with local and sectoral level, jointly managed social insurance schemes (1913); then moved to abortive attempts at establishing Conciliation Boards (1919; 1923); to sectoral consultative bodies (1933); to public extensions of cartel decisions (1935) and labour-management agreements (1937), obligatorily covering nonmembers and nonparticipants; to sectoral licensing board on investment (1938); to the re-establishment of a nationally coordinated wage determination board (1945); to indicative national planning (1945); then back to the establishment of specialized Product and Industrial Boards along with an overall coordination agency the Social and Economic Council (1950) and finally, to the creation of a national level, joint coordination council for social insurance (1959) – right back where they started in 1913 (Schmitter (1974); see Kraemer (1966)).

In the model of neo-corporatism incomes policy, based on the cooperation of the central government with the central employer and employee organizations, is treated as a cornerstone of the neo-corporatist construction and the pièce de résistance of the neo-corporatist doctrines. The model is partially tested by Wilensky (1976) with respect to several welfare states, including The Netherlands.

From neo-corporatism to the *consociational democracy* it is only one step. The resemblance between both these models is the existence of so-called elites in the organizations concerned (interest groups, political parties, government agencies). These elites strive for the formation of consensus and accept together, that essential interests of separate population groups should not be affected. The Dutch political scientists Daalder and Lijphart[20] have concentrated their studies on consociational democracy, defined as:

> (. . .) a certain pattern of political life in which political elites of distant social groups succeed in establishing a viable pluralistic state by a process of mutual forbearance and accomodation (Daalder);
> (. . .) government by elite cartel designed to turn democracy with a fragmented political culture into a stable democracy (Lijphart).

According to Lijphart (1977) different groups, which are themselves minorities and are guided by an elite, form big government coalitions, have veto-power in the decision-making procedures, are proportionally represented in the organs of the public sector, and, last but not least, enjoy internal autonomy. The consociational model is fruitfully applied to the study of the history of the Dutch political system[21] and the evolution of the Dutch industrial relations[22] (see Wheaton (1979)).

Finally the *negotiations democracy* (Van den Doel (1979))[23]. Here, negotiations take place between persons and organs on a similar hierarchical level in order to obtain an outcome that is accepted by all the parties involved. A characteristic of the negotiations democracy is the circumstance that these parties are free to leave negotiations (freedom of exit) and are not committed to the ultimate outcome of them (non-commitment). The negotiations democracy is operative in that type of economy, for example the Dutch, described variously as 'concerted economy', 'mixed economic order' and 'oriented market economy'. Decision-making on important fields of economic policy, for instance labour conditions, is based on the voluntary co-operation and the non-committing agreement between the central government on the one hand and the central employer and employee organizations on the other. If negotiations between these parties result in an agreement, if any (the stabilization-agreements in Finland, the social contract in Great Britain, the National Pay Agreements in Ireland, the 'central agreements' in the Netherlands), *then this agreement cannot be binding.* The interest groups themselves do not, *de facto*, have any authority to force member-organizations or individual employers and workers to abide by decisions which have been taken. As far as the Dutch 'central agreement' is concerned, its legal standing is as yet not determined. When single member-organizations, or even associations which are not affiliated with the central organizations, do not accept the results of negotiating, then the possible consequences are not the concern of public law nor can the central organizations use sanctions against dissidents effectively (Van Veen (1976) and Windmuller and De Galan (II) (1977)). In the next two paragraphs we will discuss the Dutch case of negotiations democracy further.

Which model provides the best analytical devices? In each of the three model-worlds specific problems are formulated. In the neo-corporatist world the student occupies himself with the determining factors in the rise of neo-corporatism and draws attention to the position of the trade union movement. In the consociational world the relation between the political culture and the stability of the democracy is analysed. However, we are interested in the connection between the structure of socio-economic decision-making and the *economic efficiency* of macro-economic decisions[24].

Add to this that the model of neo-corporatism is still debated and needs elaboration, while authors who use the consociational model attribute normative meaning to their model[25]. We want, on the contrary, to distinguish, in principle, between the description of socio-economic decision-making (par. 7.2.), the examination of the effects of decision-making (par. 7.3.) and the philosophical argument (par. 7.4.).

The model of negotiations democracy is less a product of casuistry of social and political cultures and structures in a number of Western countries than the other two models. The negotiations democracy is an *ideal type* of social decision-making, which one observes in impure forms in many Western economies. The advantage of selecting this model is, perhaps, that one can benefit from the growing theoretical understanding of the economics of public choice.

7.2 Organized employers and employees: an outline

7.2.1 Some data

There are two central employer organizations in the Netherlands, namely the Union of Dutch Enterprises (VNO) and the Dutch Christian Employers' Union (NCW). At present about 10.000 employers are affiliated with the

VNO, all of them leaders of enterprises with more than twenty employees. The NCW brings together more than 4.000 employers. It is estimated that 90 percent of the bigger enterprises are affiliated with both the employer organizations. These enterprises include together 90 percent in private industry (excluding agriculture and retail)[26].

The employee front is concentrated in two organizations, namely the Federation Dutch Trade-union movement (FNV) and the Christian Dutch Trade-union (CNV). The FNV, an amalgamation of Roman-Catholic and social-democrat trade unions, is by the biggest employee organization. As it is current in the employers' world, it is also true of the central employee organizations that officially not the individual workers are regarded as members, but the unions in the separate branches. The FNV is the master organization of fifteen big trade unions and the CNV of eight[27]. In 1977 the organization rate, that is the membership of the unions as a percentage of the dependent labour force, was 39 percent. This is a moderate figure in comparison with foreign countries. A remarkable increase of the organization rate came about recently in Great Britain as a consequence of the worsening economic conditions, the intensified union militance, the increasing market concentration and the closed shop (Taylor (1978)), but failed to develop in the Netherlands. The organization rate of women is low (in 1975 about 14 percent). The organization rate of men is substantially higher (in 1975 about 48 percent). Further, the rate is higher in the two urbanized provinces in the West and varies strongly in different branches (with the printing industry at the top in 1971 with 64,6 percent and trade and banking at the tail with respectively 9,5 percent and 10,4 percent in the same year).

The decision-making process within the trade union movement is centralized. Headey (1970) ascertained by means of a centralization index that the decision-power in the Dutch trade union movement is extremely centralized. Only Austria and Israel attained a higher score. Just as Wilensky (1976) we could not find comparable data about Dutch employers. Yet it is often said in our country that the authority of salaried officials and the cohesion of organization are somewhat scantier in employers' associations than in employees' associations.

Representatives of the interest groups participate in peak-bargaining at the national level about labour conditions and government policies. Through numerous institutions, among which are the Social Economic Council, the Dutch Labour Organization and the Dutch Industrial Reconstruction Society, the interest groups are fully integrated in the complete process of preparation, determination and implementation of the social and economic policies of the Dutch central government. We do not intend in the following parts of this paragraph to write a survey of post-war evolution of these institutions, the peculiarity of which drew the attention of many foreign observers[28]. Nor do we give a detailed view of the functioning of interest groups in different phases of the policy process itself. Instead we give a sketch of the penetration of the central employer and employee organizations in Dutch domestic politics (par. 7.2.2.) and the actual functioning of the system of negotiations democracy (par. 7.2.3.).

7.2.2 Penetration

Following De Jong's (1959) footsteps, Scholten defined the phenomenon of *penetration* as the entering of representatives or sympathizers of interest groups into the political decision-centres, directly or indirectly[29]. To these political decision-centres are the government, the bureaucratic apparatus, the representative bodies and, if required, the political parties. Direct penetration is the occupying of official positions in these centres by persons who have, some way or another, ties with interest groups. Classical examples of this are sector ministers and sector specialists in the Lower House, who are drawn from agricultural organizations (the so-called Green Front). Indirect penetration is the entering of the process of political decision-making beyond official positions. An example of this are the regular meetings of interest group delegations and parliamentary parties.

Direct penetration was much induced after 1945 by the Industrial Organization Act (1950). The Act is based on the principle that parties involved in certain sectors of society should have maximum freedom to arrange their own affairs and should have authority, guaranteed by public law, to do this. The Act introduced the product and enterprise councils. A product council is a vertical organization that covers all enterprises in an 'industrial column' (from raw material to finished article, for instance the dairy industry). An enterprise council is a horizontal organization, that covers all enterprises with a similar function (for instance agriculture). The boards of management of these organizations, which have corporate competence, consist completely or partly of representative employer and employee organizations, commissioned by the Crown (that is the Cabinet and the Queen). Another illustration of direct penetration occurs in those organs which are concerned with implementation of social security arrangements. Representatives of the employer and the employee side participate in the management of the Councils of Labour, the Social Security Bank and the industrial associations, all of them institutions with corporate responsibilities. Empirical material on the extent and significance of direct penetration of interest groups in successive cabinets, in public bureaucracy and in political parties is scarce.

The relations between interest groups and parliament, especially the Lower House, was studied, among others, by Kooiman (1976)[30]. The MP's keep in touch with interest groups by means of hearings, double-functions and personal contacts. From two inquiries and one secondary analysis it emerged that, in the opinion of MP's, interest groups were not the most important source of information. The government, academic institutes and libraries were respectively more important. Yet 86 percent of the MP's interviewed thought that interest groups have much influence on parliament. But influence of farmers, employers and middle classes was estimated to be larger than that of trade unions.

The most characteristic example of *indirect* penetration does not relate to parliament but to the executive power. In this century, which is labelled by some as the golden age of corporatism, a legal, gradual – but after 1945 accelerated – growth of the so-called *external consultative boards* came about in the Netherlands. These boards are established for an undetermined period and they are charged to advise the central government, to admiinister to regulate. On these boards are, exclusively or partly, non-official members[31]. In 1976, the Dutch Scientific Council for Public Policy counted 368 consultative boards, of which 42 percent was established in the years 1965-1975. The boards, that cover every department, are closely connected with social organizations, among which the interest groups, which are called by the typically Dutch collective noun 'het particuliere initiatief' (the private initiative). Some figures may illustrate this connection. Thirty six percent of the boards consist completely of persons, who represent social organizations. Twenty six organizations (from a total number of 801) sit on more than 15 boards. These 26 organizations are mainly employers' – and employees' associations from industry, agriculture and trade.

The most relevant of the consultative boards for our subject is the *Social Economic Council* (SER), installed by the Industrial Organization Act (1950). The SER advises the government, either on its request or on its own initiative, on national social-economic matters[32]. The SER is a tripartite body: 15 members are appointed by the Crown, 15 members are recruited from central employer organizations (designated by the Crown) and 15 members represent corresponding employee organizations. The SER is regarded as the most crucial connective link between the central government and organized industrial life. Mokken and Stokman (1975) registered by means of network analysis the double-functions which arise when a top-functionary in one organ (for instance the management board of a trade-union) also holds a top-function in another organ, in this case, the SER. Their research, undertaken in 1965, showed that 39 representatives of the employers and 54 representatives of the employees both hold the same amount of double-functions. The spreading of these functions over three departments, towards which SER-members are primarily oriented (Economic Affairs, Social Affairs and Education and Science with respectively 36 percent, 23 percent and 13 percent of the double-functions) is likewise equal. Only in the organs of the Department of Economic Affairs are employer organizations more represented than employee organizations[33].

As with every application of the position method in power-studies, network analysis does not provide the student with any information about the power that political subjects (in this case, the penetrated interest groups) actually owe to their positions by using them. This aspect of penetration can be studied with the decision method, as Scholten (1968) and Braam (1973) have demonstrated.

Scholten analysed the status of the (generally unanimous) SER-advice in nine cases. The SER has no statutory power to make any department follow its advice. What status in the political decision-making process does this advice have, then, and what does this status tell us about the power of interest groups, represented in the SER? In five cases, viz. the advice about the Agriculture Act (1957), the price of milk (1956), the Prices Act (1961), the wages in 1955 and the social-economic policy in the years 1959 and 1960, the advice was, at best, one of the influence factors. The advice had no appreciable consequence for political decision-making, although the politicians regarded the information, contained in the advice, as relevant. In two cases, the SER-advice clearly acted as an influence factor. The content of the advice, but also its application and the moment of publication were together proper instruments for some political decision-makers to strengthen their position against others (a minister who gets support, a parliamentary majority that puts pressure on the cabinet, politicians who escape from an impasse). Only in two cases, viz. the advice about spending (1956) and, on several occasions, about the level of sick-fund premiums, was the SER-advice a power factor. The advice about spending (1956) turned out to be decisive: it brought about a change of opinion in parliament and cabinet. In a detailed report Scholten[34] makes clear that not only the arguments of the SER were persuasive (in a period when politicians had not developed their vision on the economic situation sufficiently), but also the advice was a successful instrument of the employee and employer organizations. These organizations made their co-operation with cabinet's policies conditional on following the advice. The advice about premiums was simply not regarded as a political issue by the political parties: in these matters the SER had *de facto* statutory power. One may infer from Scholten's case-studies that SER-participation adds to the political power of interest groups.

Braam (1973) examined the influence of coalitions of business firms. A coalition comes about when separate business firms make influence-attempts with the government at the same time, when they do this together, or when an interest organization makes influence-attempts on behalf of a number of business firms. In Braam's field of investigation, the sector of hydraulic works (waterways, bridges, etc.), he registered 37 coalitions of business firms (mostly ship yards), that had made influence-attempts, which were settled by the government (in this case, the Ministry of Public Works). Braam's criterion of testing influence is the degree of 'success': a coalition is more influential to the extent to which its influence-attempts are more successful. Of these 37 coalitions, 15 apparently undertook collective action by means of an interest organization (an action committee, the Chamber of Commerce, etc.) and 22 performed without an interest organisation. It emerged that, from the 15 coalitions, eleven were successful, while from the 22 coalitions, only twelve were successful. Braam found a positive correlation between the extent to which business firms are integrated in interest organizations and the influence of these firms. This correlation still existed, when other influence factors (among which the growth of the firm) were kept constant. Braam showed that the growth of business firms and their integration in interest organizations were independent influence factors which made political influencing successful and concluded that his research did not affirm Wright Mill's vision of the existence of merely one power elite, but corroborated the pluralist idea of the existence of different elites in a negotiations structure[35].

According to many Holland-watchers (politicians, journalists, essayists) penetration has meanwhile reached alarming proportions. They warn against an overshadowing fifth power; they criticize the invisibility and the ungovernability of a twilight state, that emerges when the boundary-lines of the public sector and the private sector become blurred; they hold the closed policy-circuits responsible for excluding non-organized interests, and they worry about the increasing incapacity of the overloaded welfare state to control the welfare society.

7.2.3 Interest groups in a negotiations democracy

In a negotiations democracy final decision-making about the *benefits* of publicly supplied goods, services and income-transfers takes place in the democratic household (the parliament), while the market decides about the *costs* of this supply. The coordination of both decisions takes place through non-committing negotiations. The government makes proposals to numerous interest groups in society (especially employer and employee organizations), which then go and negotiate with the government and with each other about a package of collective and semi-collective goods and services, about the distribution of the financial burden and about the income-transfers. These negotiations, however, do not lead to an all-embracing contract.

Partly, the coordination takes place in a *fragmentary* manner. The government conducts negotiations with social institutes for subsidies, with employer organizations for prices and taxes and with employee organizations for wages and taxes. The employer and employee organizations negotiate with each other for wages. Partly, the co-ordination does *not* take place at all. For, negotiations democracy does not have a method to arrange disputes. When disagreements are taken away, this appears at the utmost from a joint statement of intentions or from joint standpoints. Ultimately, every organ or interest group decides autonomously about its own behaviour without being coerced in any way.

This process, that we have decided very briefly, has been studied theoretically, that is by means of the theory of games, by Van den Doel (1975; 1979) (see par. 7.3) and, later, by Johansen (1979) and practically, as for the performance of interest groups in the field of industrial relations, industrial reconstruction policy and education policy, by Windmuller and De Galan (1977), Teulings a.o. (1978) and Leune (1976).

7.3 Economic effects of negotiations democracy

7.3.1 The Prisoners' Dilemma Game

In this paragraph the effects of the negotiations democracy will be treated. In the first part we will simulate these effects by means of a game-theoretical model. In the second part we will compare these simulated effects with Dutch empirical evidence. We begin, therefore, with a game-theoretical simulation.

In a game-theoretical simulation the goals of the subjects, their ways of acting and the results which they attain are logically connected with one another. The subjects, whose behaviour is studied, are called *players.* The way in which a player will act in a certain situation is called a *strategy.* The results of strategy are defined as the *outcome,* and this outcome is evaluated on the basis of the *utility,* or the *satisfaction,* that the players derive from it.

Van den Doel[36] has simulated the effects of negotiations democracy by means of a two-person game, which is known as the Prisoners' Dilemma. This name is borrowed from a game situation, invented by the American mathematician A.W. Tucker, in which two prisoners have committed a joint crime, that, however, has not yet been proved. Tucker supposes here, that:
- refusal to confess leads to detention under remand of 1 year, after which both the prisoners will be released;
- unilateral refusal to confess leads to immediate release of the prisoner who proves the guilt of the other (that is, the one who speaks), but to life-long imprisonment (in this case 30 years) for the prisoner who keeps silence;
- bilateral confession leads to an imprisonment of 15 years for both.

The *outcome* of this game ranges, therefore, from immediate release (0 years) to lifelong imprisonment (30 years). It goes without saying, that both of the prisoners prefer an imprisonment as short as possible and most of all each wants to be released immediately. This hypothetical ordering of preferences is presented in *table* 1.

Table 7.1 Hypothetical ordering of preferences by a prisoner

Preference ordering	Does the prisoner confess himself?	Does the other prisoner confess?	years of imprisonment
1	Yes	No	0
2	No	No	1
3	Yes	Yes	15
4	No	Yes	30

It appears that each prisoner ordered preference as follows:
1. His most preferred outcome is that the other keeps silent while he himself confesses. For in that case his satisfaction is greatest: he is immediately released.
2. His second preference is that both keep silent and are released from prison for lack of evidence. In that case he needs to stay in prison for just 1 year.

3. His third preference is that neither of them keep their mouths shut, that is that both confess. In that case he stays in prison for 15 years.

4. His least preferred outcome is that only he himself keeps his mouth shut while the other uses this opportunity by confessing unilaterally and throw the blame on him. In that case he has to stay in prison for 30 years.

When both the prisoners cannot threaten each other with sanctions (for instance expulsion from the criminal underworld, thrashing or strangling inside the prison), then it can be predicted that both confess and furnish the proof of each other's guilt. Dror[37] drew the funny conclusion: 'As a result, both rational prisoners will spend fifteen years in prison thinking about the limitations of pure rationality'. The Prisoners' Dilemma, however, does not demonstrate that 'extrarational decision-making processes are demonstrably better than pure rationality', as Dror thinks, but merely that *individual rationality in the case, in which individuals cannot influence each other's decision, does not lead to collective rationality.*

The problem, that is illuminated by the Prisoners' Dilemma, can be formulated still stronger. Both the prisoners have a common interest in agreeing upon a *co-operative* strategy. That is the strategy which leads to an imprisonment of 1 year for each person. This co-operative strategy does not, however, lead to an *equilibrium.* For the non-co-operative strategy is *dominating* because each player will be wanting to choose this one, regardless the strategy of his opponent. If the strategy of his opponent is co-operative, then he will choose a non-co-operative strategy in order to be able to realize preference no. 1, instead of no. 2. If the strategy of his opponent is non-co-operative, then he also will choose a non-co-operative strategy in order to realize preference no. 3 instead of no. 4. The result is, that both of them choose a non-co-operative strategy, in spite of their common interest and the resulting outcome that is bad for both of them (viz. 15 years imprisonment for each).

The Prisoners' Dilemma is a game which produces benefits and costs. Co-operation produces benefits: one needs to stay in prison for just one year. But co-operation also involves costs: one has to stay in prison for a year indeed. Recapitulating, the essential features of a Prisoners' Dilemma are:

1. the prisoners cannot strike each other with sanctions in case one of them breaks the co-operation;

2. the prisoners have a common interest in co-operation; in other words, there are collective goods at stake, from which both derive benefits;

3. the prisoners do not have a common interest in paying the costs of the co-operation;

4. each prisoner puts his self-interest before the interest of his fellow-prisoner.

7.3.2 The negotiations democracy as a Prisoners' Dilemma Game

In numerous publications Van den Doel[38] argued that the Prisoners' Dilemma is an accurate model of an important aspect of a 'concerted economy' (that is a negotiations democracy). He sees several resemblances:

First, a negotiations democracy is also marked by the absence of sanctions. We have defined the features of a negotiations democracy in par. 7.1.3 as freedom of exit and non-commitment. This means that every group or each individual can leave the negotiations or can ignore the results of these negotiations without being struck by sanctions of others.

Secondly, in a negotiations democracy the individuals have also a common interest. This interest concerns e.g. the supply of social goods; the maintenance or expansion of social security; the struggle against recession and unemployment.

Thirdly, the individuals have no common interest in paying the costs, which have to be made for the realization of the aforementioned macro-economic goals.

Fourthly, in a negotiations democracy the individuals usually put their self-interest before the self-interest of other individuals and the interest of their own group before the interest of other groups.

In the application of the Prisoners' Dilemma Game to a negotiations democracy, Van den Doel takes the line that the individuals, both employers and employees, strive after an active and effective employment policy as a social good. Purely for argument's sake, he assumes here that the employers and employees agree that present-day unemployment results from a shortage of capital. Such unemployment must be combated with extra investments in either the private or the public sector of the economy. As the employees have announced that they want to maintain the existing level of transfer incomes, the extra investments will have to be financed to a large

Table 7.2 An individual's hypothetical preference ordering

Preference ordering	Does the individual pay for employment himself?	Do others pay for the employment	What is the effect on the relative income position of the individual?	Does employment recover?
1	No	Yes	Better	Yes
2	Yes	Yes	Unchanged	Yes
3	No	No	Unchanged	No
4	Yes	No	Worse	No

extent by reducing the rate of growth of earned incomes. But, as for everyone's share in this reduction, the employers and employees are divided among themselves. For they hold different opinions on the distribution of income: each individual and each group strive after a change in the distribution in its own favour. In table 7.2 the goals in the fields of employment and income distribution are combined.

Apparently, every individual worker and employer arranged his preferences as follows:

1. his most preferred outcome is to create employment at another's expense; this will improve his relative income position and employment will recover;

2. his second preference is to create employment at everyones's (including his own) expense; this means his relative income position will be unchanged and employment will recover;

3. his third preference is that no employment is created so that no one (including himself) need pay anything; his relative income thus remains unchanged, but employment does not recover;

4. his lowest preferred outcome is when employment is created but he alone pays for it while others sponge on his generosity; this worsens his relative income position, but because a sacrifice by a single individual is as a drop in the ocean, employment does not recover.

In a political order in which binding decisions can be taken, the eventual choice will concentrate on the real alternative 2 (everyone shares in the costs) or 3 (nobody pays). The parasitical alternatives 1 and 4, in which some share in the costs and others do not, may be excluded in principle. In this example, the individuals will vote for priority 2 so that employment will recover. In the negotiations democracy, however which is not able to take binding decisions, all four alternatives are possible. An individual worker or employer is uncertain about the decisions of others. As long as he cannot bind the other workers and employers (that is punish them with negative sanctions) he will be afraid that as soon as he has decided to make a sacrifice in order to improve employment, he will have chosen priority 4 which means that the others will not share in the costs so that his relative income position will worsen without his achieving the desired result in increased employment. So long as the other employers and workers are unable to bind him (that is to punish him by applying sanctions) he will be tempted to choose his highest priority by which others will pay for the creation of employment so that his relative income position will improve. The fact that the decision-making process is unable to bind the participants means that the individual is caught up in a dilemma: he does want employment to be created, but out of the desire to avoid payment and the fear that others will succeed in doing the same, he will refrain from contributing. As all individual workers and employers argue this way, no one will make a sacrifice. In a political order in which politicians have the power to forbid the parasitical alternatives, the second priority will be chosen and implemented. But in trade unions and employers organisations, which cannot do much more than hold discussions which commit no one, the third and not the first or second priority will be chosen. In this model, the employers' and employees aims of combating unemployment and redistribution of incomes will never be realised.

7.3.3 Testing the Prisoners' Dilemma Game-hypothesis

In this chapter we will not systematically discuss the way out from this dilemma. The way out that Van den Doel proposed, the criticism levelled against that and the alternatives then suggested are extensively described in Van den Doel (1979). We shall, however, go further into the subject by investigating empirically if his simulation can predict the effects of negotiations democracy correctly.

The hypothesis of Van den Doel (1979) also implies *in a strong form* that those collective goals, which are pursued by all individuals, will not at all be realized in a pure negotiations democracy, since the individuals will not pay the price for the realization of those goals, not because they would grudge this price, but because they would be caught in the Prisoners' Dilemma trap. *In a weak form* the hypothesis of Van den Doel implies that in 'concerted economies' collective goals of the citizens indeed will be realized in some degree, but not on the scale wanted by the citizens themselves. Putting it differently: the citizens in a 'concerted economy' will pay a certain price in the form of income restraint, but this restraint will be less than the citizens themselves regard as necessary, on behalf of the realization of their collective goal (full employment; social goods; social security; etc.).

Both the strong and the weak hypotheses are testable and refutable predictions. The strong hypothesis, however, corresponds more with a pure negotiations democracy in *Ideal*-typical form, while the weak hypothesis is more relevant to *Real*-typical economies in the West, in which the features of negotiations democracy are combined with other decision-making methods. Therefore we confine ourselves to the weak hypothesis.

For testing the (weak) hypothesis two problems have to be solved. The first problem concerns the period, for which the test is undertaken. The second problem concerns the manner of identifying the goals of the citizens.

We fix the mentioned period at the years 1971-1977. In the year 1977 the negotiations democracy in the Netherlands becomes a main component of social-decision-making (compare Ter Heide (1976) and Van Doorn a.o. (1976)). In that year the civil resistance under the leadership of the trade-union movement against the enforcement of the *Wage Formation Act* (on the basis of which concluded Collective Labour Contracts, the so-called CAO's, can be declared non-binding) was crowned with a victory and a new consensus came into existence in organized industrial life: that macro-economic decisions should henceforth be taken by way of 'concerted action'. This consensus exists to this day. We end the period, however, with 1977, because this is the last year for which reliable data can be collected.

In principle, the goals of the individuals can be found in three ways:
1. by studying the factual decisions of the individuals with respect to their wages and prices;
2. by interviewing the individuals;
3. by analyzing the policy-goals of the governments, chosen by the individuals.

The first method is unsuited to our purpose, for the hypothesis is, that the factual decisions of the individuals concerning their wages and prices *deviate from* their own goals. The establishment of such a deviation is, in principle, only possible when the goals are not founded on the basis of the factual decisions, but on the basis of method 2 or 3. In the next paragraph the following analysis will be undertaken. The goals of the individuals with respect to wages and prices will be examined on the basis of inquiries and on the basis of the programmes of the governments chosen by the individuals. Then these goals will be compared with the factual development of wages and prices in the period 1971-1977 in the Netherlands.

7.3.4 *The goals of the individuals (inquiries)*

The ideas of the *citizens* in the first half of the test period are examined by the Dutch Institute for Public Opinion and Market Research[39]. In late December 1971, 35 percent of those interviewed regarded housing policy as the primary governmental task. Wage and price control gained the second highest score (19 percent) and environmental policy the third (16 percent). Nearly one year later, 38 percent of the respondents regarded wage and price control as the primary governmental task; housing policy was now second (33 percent) and the struggle against unemployment third (22 percent). In 1973 the priority order was somewhat different again. Then, 34 percent considered wage and price control the primary governmental task, followed by environmental policy (19 percent) and housing policy (16 percent). The great break came in 1975, when 95 percent of the respondents regarded the struggle against unemployment as the primary governmental task. In 1976 struggle against unemployment was mentioned by 88 percent as the primary governmental task, fighting against inflation by 84 percent and housing policy (city renovation) by 79 percent. One could argue that these figures merely reflect a shift of economic and social problems (namely under the influence of unemployment and stagnation of the growth of collective goods). More important, therefore, is the question what the citizens thought of the wage and price movement itself.

In 1972, 66 percent of the respondents accepted a governments' proposal to stabilize real incomes in the year 1973. In 1974, according to a first inquiry, 49 percent were willing to accept no increase or even a decrease in real income.

Again there is a change in 1975. Now half of the people interviewed were willing to renounce a nominal income improvement (viz. a compensation for rising prices) for the sake of fighting unemployment. The number of supporters of a *permanent* zero-growth of real incomes increased in that year by 9 percent to 65 percent. In 1977, 65 percent made it more or less clear that they were willing to renounce even a maintenance of purchase power on behalf of a reduction of labour-time, an aim then championed by the trade-union movement[40].

One can find the most complete insight into citizens' attitudes in two inquiries of the Dutch broadcasting corporations the NCRV (1976) and the AVRO (1977). In the NCRV-inquiry those interviewed were first of all confronted with a pair of 'solutions'. The 'leftist' solution implied:

> Better no further increase of wages *in order that* the government can spend more on social and collective provisions, such as expenditure for the permanently ill and handicapped; expenditure for the supply of employment; for good houses and for a better environment.

The 'rightist' solution was:

> Better a decrease of public expenditure for social and collective provisions, such as expenditure for the permanently ill and handicapped; expenditure for the supply of employment; for good houses and for a better environment *in order that* wages can increase.

54 percent of the respondents chose the 'leftist' solution and 29 percent the 'rightist' solution. Among members of trade-union an even higher percentage chose the 'leftist' solution. 58 percent of the total number of respondents

were willing to accept a zero growth of real incomes for five years on behalf of the preservation of the collective sector (31 percent was not willing). The AVRO-inquiry put two ideas about the struggle against unemployment to those interviewed. The *first idea* takes the line that unemployment must be fought by increasing the co-partnership of the workers and the trade-union movement with respect to investments, by expanding the public sector, by putting – for that reason – higher pressure on private incomes and by better distributing the existing number of jobs. The *second idea* takes the line that unemployment must be fought by improving the climate for enterprises, by having more confidence in the private sector, by contracting the public sector, by cutting subsidies, and by leaving more room for profits and private prosperity. Sixty-one percent preferred the first idea, while only 38 percent chose the second idea.

7.3.5 The goals of the individuals (governmental programmes)

Both in 1971 and in 1972 general elections were held in the Netherlands. One can find the standpoints about wage and price movement in the programmes (platforms) of the biggest political parties. In their *priority-program 1971-1975* the three Christian-Democrat parties (KVP, ARP and CHU) advocated a half percent increase of the tax-burden each year, in order to finance their policy proposals. The increase of real incomes should therefore, under this policy, remain restricted to 2 percent. In *Outlines of a Government's Program* (1971) the leftist parties (PvdA, D'66 and PPR) wanted a total increase of the tax-burden by 2.5 percent in the period 1971-1975 (combined with an average annual economic growth of 4 percent). The average annual increase of real disposable incomes was therefore allowed to amount to merely 2.25 percent. In their programme *Turning-point '72* (1972) these parties have again brought their goals up to date. For the period 1972-1976 they wanted an average annual increase of the tax-burden by 0.6 percent and an annual increase of savings by 0.5 percent. They pointed out the need for wage restraint, combined with levelling down and control of higher incomes. In 1971 and 1972 all parties stressed thus the relevance of restraining wages and prices for the sake of fighting inflation and expanding the collective sector.

These election programmes inevitably took effect in the programmes of the distinct cabinets. In 1971 the cabinet-Biesheuvel came in, which strove to restrict nominal wage increases in 1973 to 9 percent and price increases to 5 percent. The point of view of the government implied a zero growth of real incomes, apart from a increase of the 'incidental' wage-component (annual increments, bonusses, promotions and the like). The ministers justified this attitude, which was at that time unusually rigorous, with reference to inflationary price and wage developments, which were rather strong in international perspective and which would have a negative effect on public investments, profits, employment and national production growth.

In May 1973 the centre-left Den Uyl-cabinet came in, which based its policies on leftist and Christian Democrat programmes. In the years after 1973, however, economic conditions have worsened in the Netherlands. While in the period 1948-1973 a rate of growth of 4.9 percent was realized, the average annual rate of growth of net national income was only 1.4 percent in the period 1973-1977. The Dutch Bank calculated that unemployment rose from 2.7 percent to 5.3 percent in the years 1973-1977. All this did not fail to have its effect on the position of the government. In the course of 1975 the Den Uyl-cabinet decided to revise the complete government programme. Policy-makers were impressed by the economic wisdom, that became conventional at that time, viz. the idea that unemployment is caused by the increase in real labour costs (that is the ratio of the gross wage rate and the production price) which, in its turn, results of collective burdens, that yearly increased, by 1.4 percent of net national income. In the *Note on Policy-making in the matter of Collective Provisions and Employment* (June 1976) the cabinet adopted this principal argument and formulated the norm that the annual increase of the collective burdens in the period 1976-1980 should not amount to more than 1 percent of net national income. Starting from a computed economic growth of 3.75 percent and a planned reduction of unemployment in the direction of 150,000 man-years in 1980, a drastic reduction of the growth of the government budget and social security spending should be realized. Even if this operation would turn out to be successful, the amount that would be available for the improvement of family incomes, would be extremely scanty, certainly when compared with the 1960's. Within the framework of this new economic policy the government proclaimed that real income improvement of modal employees in 1977 would amount to a mere 1.5 percent. Further, the Den Uyl-cabinet considered necessary a nominal wage increase and a price increase no more than 8.25 percent and 6.5 percent respectively.

The five political parties, which formed part of the coalition-cabinet Den Uyl, reluctantly found consensus about reducing the expansion of the collective sector (especially of outlays, which do not directly generate employment) and restricting wage-increases. Thus, also real incomes of modal employees would not be allowed to exceed zero-growth until 1981. During the election campaign in 1977 all big Dutch political parties took the

stand that in the next government period no resources would be available
for increasing personal disposable income, in spite of different ideologies
and economic analyses[41]. The convergence of standpoints became most
clear when, during the long cabinet formation of 1977, two governmental
agreements were signed. Both the 'liberal' agreement of the Christian-
Democrats and the leftists and the 'conservative' agreement of the Christian-
Democrats and the bourgeois-liberals provided over-all real income restraint in order to ensure full employment and maintenance of social provisions. The first of these agreements, which turned out to be a purely formal
one since a centre-left cabinet was not formed, pleaded zero-growth of the
incomes of modal employees (and upwards a differentiated levelling) and a
restriction of the wage drift to 0.5 percent. The second agreement, which was
the basis of the Van Agt-cabinet, chose a restriction of the wage drift to 1.5
percent and a zero-growth of all incomes under the f. 50,000 level.

7.3.6 The realization of individual goals

Both the methods used in par. 7.3.4 and 7.3.5 provide the same result. The
goals of the individuals relate to a 'selective' economic growth, that is an
economic growth under certain constraints concerning environmental
control and spatial planning. This economic growth does not need to be
expressed in a growth of disposable incomes, but has to be used primarily
for a maintenance of public spending, social security and employment.

Let us now look at the actual performance of the negotiations democracy,
in the light of the aforementioned factors. In the years 1971-1979 the average
increase of real incomes of modal employees amounted to 2.4 percent, which
exceeded the wildest expectations of political parties and trade-unions (and,
implicitly, employers' associations). Nominal wages increased in the same
period, also according to the Dutch Bank, by an average of 12.6 percent.

Surely the general conclusion is justified, that the annual rise of nominal
wages has been about 5 percent bigger than that desired by the vast majority
of the Dutch citizens, while the annual rise of real incomes of modal
employees was definitely 2 percent higher than the zero-growth, which the
citizens had already accepted in the beginning of the test-period.

The tension between the object of governments, chosen by the citizens,
and the factual wage rise can yet be demonstrated in another manner. Each
year on the third Tuesday of September the annual budget is presented,
which is accompanied by a wage computation by the Central Planning
Bureau. This wage computation, however, is not simply a forecast of the

factual wage development in the next year, but is determined by the Central Planning Bureau in concert with the government. In practice, the computed figure is a mix of the policy goal of the government, a forecast of the labour market tension and a capitulation for expected trade-union-power[42].

More exactly defined, this wage computation consists of the following components:

1. the *compensation* for price rises and the rise of collective burdens (taxes, social security contributions), which is regarded as unavoidable;

2. the so-called '*initial*' rise of contract wages, viz. the rise of contract wages that exceeds the compensation for raised prices and raised collective burdens;

3. the so-called '*incidental*' rise of earned wages, that is the rise of wages, that is not affected by annual wage-bargaining (age related payments, bonusses, promotions, etc.).

In table 7.3, which is published for the first time in this form, the differences between the computations, influenced by the government, and the factual wage development is described, for the components 2 and 3. The conclusion is as follows: although the computations do not represent pure policy-goals of the government and are partly based on concessions to existing reality, in which both market forces and trade-union power are strong, there is in the whole test-period an average annual difference of 1.8 percent wage rise, as far as this rise exceeds compensation for price rises and rise of collective burdens. Contrary to what has been contended by the biggest Dutch trade-union (FNV), the largest part of this difference is not formed by the 'incidental' wage rise, with which collective contracts have nothing to do, but by the 'initial' wage rise, which is for the greater part determined by collective labour contracts.

Table 7.3 furnishes one possible illustration of the fact that negotiations democracy is not solving economic problems by the road that participants in the negotiations want themselves. It makes no difference if the goals of citizens are measured on the basis of inquiries or on the basis of programmes of political parties and governments, chosen by these citizens. Notwithstanding this, in all cases there is a yawning abyss between the goals of the vast majority of citizens with respect to wage rise, on the one hand, and factual wage rise, on the other hand. A negotiations democracy is not capable of paying the price for collective goods and joint goals, which are appreciated by most of the citizens, that is for which most of them are willing to pay that price. On the basis of this we conclude that the negotiations democracy is *inefficient*, not with regard to the private goals of both the authors of this chapter, but from the view-point of the goals of the consumers themselves, as identified by means of our empirical investigation.

Table 7.3 Computation and realization of some components of annual proportional wage rise in Dutch negotiations democracy (1971-1979)

Year	Computed initial wage rise (1)	Realized initial wage rise (2)	Difference (2) − (1) (3)	Computed incidental wage rise (4)	Realized incidental wage rise (5)	Difference (5) − (4) (6)
1971	1.9	3.1	+ 1.2	2.2	1.5	− 0.7
1972	0.1	4.9	+ 5.0	2.0	0.3	− 1.7
1973	1.6	3.5	+ 1.9	1.0	2.9	+ 1.9
1974	1.7	4.0	+ 2.3	1.0	1.5	+ 0.5
1975	1.4	3.2	+ 1.8	1.0	0.2	− 1.2
1976	0.1	0.3	+ 0.2	0.5	2.0	+ 1.5
1977	2.0	2.2	+ 0.2	1.0	1.0	
1978	0.0	1.1	+ 1.1	1.5	1.7	+ 0.2
1979	0.0	1.2	+ 1.2	1.3	1.3	0.0
average			+ 1.7			+ 0.1

Comments

The data are provided by the Dutch Department of Economic Affairs. In macro-economic terminology these data relate to 'exogenously' (so, not 'endogenously') wage computations. In the initial wage rise are included: the effects of minima in price compensation and increases of holiday-allowance. The data about 1979 are preliminary. Further, the conputations are based on the following assumptions:

1971 – there is stringency on the labour market and no corrections will be made to wage developments
1972 – no wage restraint is assumed
1973 – a wage restraint is assumed, viz. by 1.3 percent 'initial' and by 0.5 percent 'incidental'
1974 – the line of restricting inflation and restraining in the nominal sphere is taken
1975   the line of maintaining price policy and a very scanty 'initial' rise is taken
1976 – the line of non-full price compensation and retardation of the rate of wage increase is taken: a very scanty 'incidental' rise, no 'initial' rise and no extra rise of minimum wages
1977 – minimum computation
1978 – the line of wage restraint is taken: no 'initial' rise (by request of the government) and a somewhat higher 'incidental' rise
1979 – no 'initial' rise is assumed and a minimum computation of 'incidental' rise.

7.4 The significance of economic efficiency for political philosophy

7.4.1 Interest groups and efficiency

We have seen that in Dutch domestic politics in the years 1971-1977 some manifestations of economic efficiency (ineffective struggle against inflation and unemployment, gap between a general willingness to restrain incomes and actual wage and price-behaviour) sharply came to light. This inefficiency could be ascribed to the fact that in the institutions of the Dutch negotiations democracy no binding collective decisions about social-economic issues are taken, which brings about large-scale Prisoners' Dilemma's. If one wants to escape from this inefficiency in the future, then one shall have to eliminate the Prisoners' Dilemma itself. Before developing this argument further, however, we will consider the views of other authors, who also showed their interest in the *effects* of the performance of interest groups. Notably Wilensky (1975, 1976) and Olson (1965, 1978) have written exemplary and original studies about the subject.

Wilensky paid attention to the *welfare backlash*, which he defined as a national resistance of the public to taxes, public expenditure, social policy and public bureaucracy in the welfare state. He formulated the hypothesis that the welfare backlash is dampened because of a neo-corporatist structure, in which penetrated peak-organizations of employers and employees negotiate with the central government for social contracts. The reasons for this dampening are threefold. First, a large, strongly organized working class, that participates in the administration of welfare schemes, will foster pro-welfare state ideologies and will oppose the cuts of social security spending. Secondly, the social contract partners prefer diversified financing of welfare services, especially by means of indirect taxes and social security contributions of employers and employees. This method of financing is less visible for the tax-payers and arouses less resistance than direct taxing. Thirdly, neo-corporatist bargaining creates a consensus with regard to fiscal, monetary and social policies that strengthen the welfare state. Not only did Wilensky logically specify his hypotheses, he also offered an empirical test. He showed that the welfare backlash was blocked in neo-corporatist countries, among which were Austria, France, Scandinavia and the Netherlands.

Wilensky did not draw any political philosophical inference on the position of interest groups in the modern political order. But he did defend the welfare state against attacks of conservatives and radicals out of '(. . .) sympathy for the underprivileged, aged, unemployed, handicapped and other minorities' (Wilensky (1975), preface). Gough (1979), who tried to give a synthesis of Wilensky's conclusions and a marxist theory of public finance, likewise emphasized that penetrated interest groups may contribute to the survival of the welfare state in a protracted period of economic crisis by following the neo-corporatist 'strategy'.

Olson developed by means of his economic theory of groups a vision of the relation between the performance of common-interest organizations

and the *retardation of economic growth* in order to explain growth-differences between rich countries. The economic theory of groups explains that interest groups will limit the entry into the industries and the occupations which they control. Olson gave some examples of this practice (for instance a cartel that blocks the discussion of an invention or a trade-union that struggles against labour-saving automation). He arrived at the generalizing conclusion that entry barriers, thrown up by the interest groups, have negative consequences with respect to the technical innovation and the free allocation of resources in (blocked) markets. From this he deduced the hypothesis that the accumulation of narrowly based common-interest organizations will have a substantial adverse effect on the rate of growth of national economies. This effect will be less substantial if, and only if, the interst groups are so large and so encompassing that they will take into account the effects of their performance at the national level. From this three sorts of contentions follow:
− totalitarian countries which do not acknowledge the freedom of association will realize a relatively higher rate of growth than democratic countries;
− countries with a participatory tradition and a protracted social stability will grow relatively slower;
− countries with encompassing and centrally organized interest groups will experience relatively less growth-retardation.
On the basis of data about 48 American federal states from the period 1965-1974 Olson succeeded in rigorously testing these several hypotheses. They were roughly corroborated.

Olson pointed out the significance of his argument for political philosophy. There is, he asserted, a so-called internal contradiction in the evolution of Western economies between the pursuit of democratic stability, on the one hand, and the pursuit for full economic potential, on the other. Olson foresaw a drive to reform the interest group system, to the extent that Western economies suffer more serious inefficiency, caused by the institutional sclerosis of the interest group system.

In our view the *legitimacy* of interest groups in the political order (justifying arguments about interest groups of practitioners of social science included) is closely connected with the insights into the *efficacy* of interest groups. Assume that it is irrefutably established that the performance of interest groups frustrates the struggle against inflation and unemployment (par. 7.3), buttresses the edifice of the welfare state (Wilensky) and causes the stagnation of economic growth (Olson), then the legitimacy of interest groups will also become the focus of public debate (supposing the public opinion is informed about the effects of interest group performance and evaluates them negatively).

7.4.2 *Interest groups and legitimacy*

It was once again pointed out by Anderson (1977) that the legitimacy of interest groups has of old been scanty in countries with a representative democracy. The citizenry often considered pressure-actions of interest groups suspicious and distrusted the closeness of the intercourse between professional politicians, top civil servants and leaders of pressure groups. In the classical doctrines of the public interest and the majority rule, the phenomenon of interest groups was neglected. These groups could perhaps have power or influence, but in the eyes of the public and the practitioners of academic science their position in the process of political decision-making missed sufficient justification.

The increase of the number of interest groups and their penetration in the state apparatus after 1945 brought only a partial change in this situation. With good reason the advocates of the neo-corporatist model drew the conclusion that in countries like the United States (the New Deal), the Netherlands (the Special Decree Industrial Relations (1945) and the Industrial Organization Act (1950)) and Great Britain (the founding of the welfare state and the planning machinery (Taylor (1978); Smith (1979)), the emergence of negotiations structures did not come about independently from an undecisive and hostile government, but was rather actively stimulated by the politicians. The big political parties expected from the 'ingrowing' of interest groups more administrative convenience and more social stability. A justification of the massive entry into all sorts of tripartite organs in terms of a normative theory of democracy (and correlated criteria) not seldom failed to turn up.

The philosophical defence of the new system, for the first time comprehensively described in Shonfield's *Modern Capitalism* (1965), was not, however, delayed very long and came pre-eminently from political science, in which group theory and power-studies provided the building stones of the philosophical structure of *pluralism*. Pluralist authors emphasized the position of interest groups in the modern political process. In their vision these groups signified a new and promising form of political participation for self-confident citizens, apart from the traditional participation in elections. They formed, as it were, a buffer between the individual and the state, that is a dam against unwanted centralization of bureaucratic decision-power. Further, an unfettered competition of a multitude of interest groups was the touchstone of the free, open, permissive and emancipatory character of the post-war society. Moreover, the interest promotion of these groups would lighten the task of responsible politicians to determine the public interest considerably.

Pluralism developed successfully into an ideology, which Lowi (1969) called so strikingly the doctrine of *interest group liberalism.* This success was especially owed to one argument. Namely the argument that the political arena could function as efficiently as a perfectly competitive market, provided that the formation of interest groups would progress smoothly and spontaneously, the entry of and the competition between interest groups would be free and the relations between governments and interest groups would be transparent for everyone. Just this argument has been refuted by our findings above (par. 7.3). Even if all these conditions could be fulfilled – which is considered impossible by Schattschneider (1960) and Olson (1965) –, Prisoners' Dilemma's would come about which impede economic efficiency.

7.4.3 Interest groups and the future

Our findings seem to support the critique of the philosophy of pluralism, dating back from the 1960s. Touching lightly on the present critique, it is obvious, that, first, the central political philosophical question concerns the position, that is the rights and obligations, that interest groups should have in the *constitution* of a modern political order (the system of economic planning included), and, secondly, the solution of indicated problems of the negotiations democracy is sought in *structural* reforms, rather than cultural change.

Neo-marxists regard neo-corporatism as a system, in which the place of labour remains subordinate to the place of capital. The interest group system is a last attempt of the ruling class in capitalism to integrate the workers' movement (Panitch (1976, 1977); Grouch (1977)). They find a solution in the direction of a radical reform of the capitalist economy and the bourgeois state, but this solution is not elaborated since marxist political theory of old neglects any philosophy of constitutional decision-making and post-revolutionary social order, as a historically obsolete subject matter. The *neo-conservatives* regard the 'para-government' of interest groups as a dangerous perversion of the democracy-ideal. An economic and political order, in which majority rule is in force, is very sensitive to the claims of organized minorities (for instance with respect to the policies of 'socially just' redistribution and supply of collective goods). Hayek (1979), who recapitulated this vision and formulated it once more[43], pleads the restoration of the rule of law, the introduction of constitutional safeguards against the arbitrariness of democratic politicians and the de-centralization and de-concentration of the public sector. The *neo-liberals* think, with Lowi as the spokesman, that interest group liberalism makes the principle of the separation between the public sector and the private sector inapplicable, renders inoperative – or undermines – the monopoly of legitimate use of coercion by the government and makes effective public planning impossible. Lowi's organizational way-out at that time (1969) was the introduction of juridicial democracy, which stood for a strengthening and regimentation of public administration.

In the current debate on economic policy (especially incomes and employment policies) in the Netherlands the position of interest groups in the future are also discussed. Van den Doel, De Galan and Tinbergen (1976) and Driehuis and Van den Doel (1979) take standpoints, which are similar to those of Lowi and date back to the monumental studies of Mannheim. They point out the necessity of a restructuring of socio-economic decision-making in the direction of a *democratically planned economy*. They launch the idea of democratic imperative planning of economic affairs. The most important decisions about the size of the collective sector, private investment and incomes should be taken in the organs of the representative democracy. The decision-making about the financing of plans (for instance concerning the volume and composition of the total wages sum) takes place in parliament and should be binding.

This brings us back to the Prisoners' Dilemma's in negotiations democracy. Generally the practitioner of political economy does not embark on the issue of which choices should be made by citizens, for instance between economic efficiency and property rights of interest groups. Especially the game-theoretical literature can only describe which ways out from the Prisoners' Dilemma are possible (Nurmi (1977), De Beus (1978), Collard (1978), Van de Doel (1979). It is up to the citizens to determine which way out shall be feasible. For instance, the Prisoners' Dilemma-preference-structure (par. 7.3.1) could crumble consequent to turns in the social culture, for instance in the direction of a stronger altruism of individuals and collectives. As long as such a turn does not come about in Dutch domestic politics, the only remaining way out in the future is political centralization and coercion.

This way out, which is widely acknowledged in the liberal philosophy of state, does not have to be incompatible with political democracy. The restructuring of socio-economic decision-making, that is proposed by the Dutch economists mentioned above, could be authorized by the electorate by means of general elections. The restructuring could be ratified by parliament. And, last but not least, the most important decisions about wages and prices would be taken by parliament, instead of by central employer and employee organizations, and, therefore, would no longer be subject to the laws of the negotiations democracy but to the laws of political party competition in the representative democracy. However such a restructuring of socio-economic decision-making is determined in detail, beyond any doubt, it would signify a *step back by the interest groups*. Its feasibility requires a complete revision of public ideology, that is nothing less than a cultural revolution, that, perhaps, could determine if democracy, in any form, will outlive its critique.

Notes

[1] Official Lower House Reports, session 1978-1978, fifth meeting (5-10-78), p. 291.

[2] S.W. Couwenberg, *Inaugural address*, Rotterdam february 17, 1977. See also W.H.J. Reynaerts, Vakbeweging en parlementaire democratie, *Beleid en Maatschappij*, V (1978), no. 5, pp. 118-123.

[3] H. Daudt, De politieke toekomst van de verzorgingsstaat, in: J.A.A. van Doorn and C.J.M. Schuyt (eds.), *De stagnerende verzorgingsstaat*, Meppel, 1978, pp. 189-219; See also H. Daudt and E. van der Wolk (eds.), *Bedreigde democratie?*, Amsterdam, 1978.

[4] W. Drees Jr, *On the level of government expenditures in the Netherlands*, Leiden, 1955, pp. 61-66; F. Hartog, *Toegepaste welvaartseconomie*, Leiden, 1963, 1973, pp. 163-168.

[5] *De Nederlandse Kiezer '73*, Alphen a.d. Rijn, 1073, pp. 48-51.

[6] S. Eldersveld a.o., Elite perceptions of the political process in the Netherlands, looked at in comparative perspective, in: M. Dogan (ed.), *The mandarins of Western Europe*, New York, 1975, pp. 144-150.

[7] C.F. Karsten, Machtsverhoudingen in Nederland, *Intermediair*, 14 (1978), no. 38, September 22, pp. 19-25.

[8] J.M.G. Leune, *Onderwijsbeleid onder druk*, Groningen, 1976. Less recent is A.D. Robinson, *Dutch organized agriculture in international politics*, 's-Gravenhage, 1961.

[9] Workshop V.U.-department of Political Science, Invloed van demonstranten op de standpunten van de Tweede Kamerleden, *Acta Politica*, VI 1971, no. 4, pp. 417-440. W.A. Beck, *Basisdemokratie*, Utrecht, 1973; H.M. Jolles, *De poreuze demokratie*, Alphen a.d. Rijn, 1974; C.E. van der Maessen, *Participatie en democratie*, Amsterdam, 1974; G.P.A. Braam a.o., *Collectieve acties*, Meppel, 1976.

[10] K. von Beyme, *Interessengruppen in der Demokratie*, München, 1969, 1974.

[11] This index is made on behalf of the American Congress. In his study of the interest group-system Schattschneider was one of the first, who used it: E.E. Schattschneider, *The semi-sovereign people*, New York, 1960.

[12] R.H. Salisbury, Interest groups, in: F.J. Greenstein and N. Polsby (eds.), *Handbook of Political Science*, vol. 4, Reading (Mass.), 1975, p. 175.

[13] In the former Roman-Catholic People's Party, now integrated in the Christian Democrat Party (CDA), it was prescribed by the rules that a certain number of positions on the candidate lists were available for representatives of interest groups. The relationship between interest groups and the biggest political party in the Netherlands, the Labour Party (PVDA), is discussed in S.B. Wolinetz, The Dutch Labour Party: a social democratic party in transition, in: W.E.

Paterson and A.H. Thomas (eds.), *Social democratic parties in Western Europe*, London, 1978, p. 346, p. 352 and p. 358.

[14] For instance several authors in P.C. Schmitter (ed.), Corporatism and policy-making in contemporary Western Europe, *Comparative Political Studies*, 10 (1977), no. 1., and in J.E.S. Hayward and R.N. Berki (eds.), *State and society in contemporary Europe*, Oxford, 1979.

[15] J.A.A. van Doorn, Pressiegroepen: correctie of corruptie?, in: J.A.A. van Doorn, *Organisatie en maatschappij*, 1966, 1971, p. 44 and further G.H. Scholten, *De sociaal-economische raad en de ministeriële verantwoordelijkheid*, Meppel, 1968, p. 39; G.P.A. Braam, Invloed van pressiegroepen en actiegroepen, in: A. Hoogerwerf (ed.), *Overheidsbeleid*, Alphen a.d. Rijn, 1978, p. 219 and beyond.

[16] P. Bernholz, Einige Bemerkungen zur Theorie des Einflusses der Verbände auf die politische Willensbildung in der Demokratie, *Kyklos*, 22 (1969), pp. 276-288; P. Bernholz, Die Machtkonkurrenz der Verbände im Rahmen des politischen Entscheidungssystems, in: H.K. Schneider and Ch. Watrin (eds.), *Markt und ökonomische Gesetz*, Schriften des Vereins für Sozialpolitik, 74 (1973), pp. 859-881; P. Bernholz, On the reasons of the influence of interest groups on political decision-making, *Zeitschrift für Wirtschafts-und Sozial-Wissenschaften, 94 (1974)*, pp. 45-63; P. Bernholz, Dominant interest groups and powerless parties, *Kyklos*, 30 (1977), pp. 411-420; W. Dettling (ed.), *Macht der Verbände-Ohnmacht der Demokratie?*, München, 1976.

[17] Our definitions are borrowed from H. van den Doel, Gelijkheid en ongelijkheid in het economische systeem, in: H. van den Doel and A. Hoogerwerf (eds.), *Gelijkheid en ongelijkheid in Nederland*, Alphen a.d. Rijn, 1975, pp. 59-63 and from H. van den Doel, *De basis van ekonomische macht*, Amsterdam, 1976 (lecture notes).

[18] G. Lehmbruch, Liberal corporatism and party government, in: P.C. Schmitter (1977) (see note 14.), pp. 91-125; L. Panitch, The development of corporatism in liberal democracies, in: P.C. Schmitter (1977 (see note 14.), pp. 61-90.

[19] P.C. Schmitter, Still the century of corporatism?, in: F.B. Pike and T. Stritch (eds.), *The new corporatism*, London, 1974, pp. 11-112; P.C. Schmitter (1977) (see note 14.); W. Grant, Corporatism and pressure groups, in: D. Kavanagh and R. Rose (eds.), New Trends in British politics, London, 1977, pp. 167-183; C. Grouch (eds.), The state, capital and liberal democracy, in: C. Grouch (eds.), *State and economy in contemporary capitalism*, London, 1979, pp. 13-54; T. Smith, *The politics of the corporate economy*, Oxford, 1979; Classical corporatism in the Netherlands is discussed in J.F. de Jongh, *De organen der sociaal-ecnomische ordening*, Amsterdam, 1945, 1946.

[20] H. Daalder, On building consociational consensus: the case of the Netherlands and Switzerland, in: K.D. MacRae (ed.), *Consociational democracy*, New York, 1974, p. 107; A Lijphart, Consociational democracy, in: K.D. MacRae (1974), p. 79.

[21] A. Lijphart, *Verzuiling, pacificatie en kentering in de Nederlandse politiek*, Amsterdam, 1968, 1976.

[22] A. Peper (ed.), *De Nederlandse arbeidsverhoudingen: continuïteit en verandering*, Rotterdam, 1973.

[23] H. van den Doel, *Democracy and welfare economics*, Cambridge, 1979, pp. 47-72.

[24] The historical background of some of these different stated problems is discussed in B. Barry, *Economists, sociologists and democracy*, London, 1970.

[25] U. Rosenthal, *Political order*, Meppel, 1978, pp. 254-256.

[26] J.P. Windmuller and C. de Galan, *Arbeidsverhoudingen in Nederland*, Utrecht/Antwerpen, 1970, 1972, part 1, pp. 151-158 and part 2, pp. 158-160.

[27] G.J.M. Conen, Ontwikkeling en samenstel ledental vakorganisaties, in: T. Akkermans (ed.), *Facetten van vakbondsbeleid*, Alphen a.d. Rijn, 1977, pp. 22-57; J.P. Windmuller and C. de Galan (1977) (see note 27.), part 2, pp. 144-158.

[28] M. van den Vall, *De vakbeweging in de welvaartsstaat*, Meppel, 1963; J.·Barbash, *Trade unions and national economic policy*, Baltimore, 1972; W. Singh, *Policy development; a study of the Social and Economic Council of the Netherlands*, Rotterdam, 1972; W. Albeda, Recent trends in collective bargaining in the Netherlands, ILO-report, *Collective bargaining in industrialized market economies*, Geneva, 1974, pp. 315-336; W. Albeda, *Arbeidsverhoudingen in Nederland*, Alphen a.d. Rijn, 1975; A. Peper, The Netherlands: from an ordered harmonic to a bargaining relationship, in: S. Barkin (ed.), *Worker militancy and its consequences 1965-1975*, New York, 1975, pp. 118-153.

[29] G.H. Scholten, Pressiegroepen, in: A. Hoogerwerf (ed.), *Verkenningen in de Nederlandse politiek*, Alphen a.d. Rijn, 1971, pp. 212-223; G.H. Scholten in U. Rosenthal, M.C.P.M. van Schendelen and G.H. Scholten, *Openbaar bestuur*, Alphen a.d. Rijn, 1977, p. 324.

[30] J. Kooiman, *Over de Tweede Kamer gesproken*, 's-Gravenhage, 1976. See also H. Daalder and G. Irwin, Interests and institutions in the Netherlands, in: *Annuals of the American Academy of political and social sciences*, vol. 413 (1974), pp. 58-71 and W. Albeda, Parlementarisme of corporatisme?, in: *Civis Mundi*, 14 (1975), no. 2, pp. 66-69. In the article of Daalder and Irwin the influence of interest groups, as perceived by politicians and the public, is examined.

[31] Wetenschappelijke Raad voor het Regeringsbeleid, *Overzicht externe adviesorganen van de centrale overheid* (rapport no. 11), 's-Gravenhage, 1976; Wetenschappelijke Raad voor het Regeringsbeleid, *Externe adviesorganen van de centrale overheid* (rapport no. 12), 's-Gravenhage, 1977.

[32] See Singh (1972) (note 29.).

[33] H.M. Helmers, R.J. Mokken, R.C. Plijter and F.N. Stokman, *Graven naar macht*, Amsterdam, 1975, pp. 347-376.

[34] G.H. Scholten (1968) (see note 15.), pp. 334-384.

[35] G.P.A. Braam, *Invloed van bedrijven op de overheid*, Meppel, 1973, pp. 177-178 and pp. 259-272.

[36] See note 24.

[37] Y. Dror, *Public policymaking reexamined*, Scranton, 1968, p. 152.

[38] H. van den Doel, Ekonomie en demokratie in het staatsbestuur, *Inaugural Address*, Nijmegen, 1973, pp. 11-12. H. van den Doel, *Demokratie en welvaartstheorie*, Alphen a.d. Rijn, 1975, pp. 58-60. H. van den Doel, *Democracy and welfare economics*, Cambridge, 1979, pp. 53-56 and pp. 58-60.

[39] Most of the data, presented in this paragraph, are based on reports, regularly published by the NIPO.

[40] NIPO-report, february 26, 1977. The exact percentage was 65.5.

[41] J.G.A. van Mierlo, Twee voorstellen voor de werkgelegenheid, *Beleid en Maatschappij*, IV (1977), no. 6, pp. 357-369.

[42] In the Miljoenennota 1980 the Minister of Finance uses the term 'policy's starting point' instead of the term 'exogenously wage computation'. See *Miljoenennota 1980*, p. 17.

[43] Some readers will insist that our description of Hayek's position is inappropriate. In *The constitution of liberty* (1960) Hayek rejects conservatism and calls himself a Whig. His colleagues of the Mont Pelerin Society agree with this argument (see F. Machlup (ed.), *Essays on Hayek*, London, 1977. It is also notable that Lowi derived his idea of the judicial democracy from Hayek's social and legal philosophy. Finally, it is striking that both Mannheim and Hayek (bien étonnés de se trouver ensemble) reject the system of corporatism, as has been pointed out by Smith (1979) (see note 19.).

Select Bibliography

R.R. Alford, Paradigms of relations between state and society, in: L.N. Lindberg a.o., *Stress and contradiction in modern capitalism*, Lexington (Mass.), 1975, pp. 145-160.

C.W. Anderson, Political design and the representation of interests, in: P.C. Schmitter (ed.), Corporatism and policy-making in contemporary Western Europe, *Comparative Political Studies*, 10 (1977), no. 1., pp. 127-152.

R.N. Berki, State and society: an antithesis of modern political thought, in: J.E.S. Hayward and R.N. Berki, *State and society in contemporary Europe*, Oxford, 1979, pp. 1-20.

J.W. de Beus, De onafwendbaarheid van een geleide loonpolitiek, *Economisch Statistische Berichten*, I and II, February 8 and 15 1978, pp. 132-137 and pp. 828-831.

S. Brittan, *The economic consequences of democracy*, London, 1977.

D. Collard, *Altruism and economy*, Oxford, 1978.

H. van den Doel, C. De Galan and J. Tinbergen, Pleidooi voor een geleide loonpolitiek, I and II, *Economisch Statistische Berichten*, march 17 and september 1, 1976, pp. 264-268 and pp. 828-831.

H. van den Doel, *Demokratie en welvaartstheorie*, Alphen a.d. Rijn, 1978.

H. van den Doel, *Democracy and welfare economics*, Cambridge, 1979.

K. van Doorn a.o., *De beheerste vakbeweging*, Amsterdam, 1976.

W. Driehuis and H. van den Doel, Werkloosheid en economische orde, in: *Werkgelegenheid: recht of beleid?*, Geschriften van de Vereniging voor Arbeidsrecht, Alphen a.d. Rijn, 1979, pp. 83-129.

I. Gough, *The political economy of the welfare state*, London and Basing stoke, 1979.

F.A. Hayek, The political order of a free people, vol. 2 from *Law, legislation and liberty*, London, 1979.

B.W. Headey, Trade unions and national wage policies, *The Journal of Politics*, 32 (1970), pp. 407-439.

H. Ter Heide, *Overleg en strijd*, Leiden, 1976.

V. Held, *The public interest and the individual interests*, New York, 1970.

L. Johansen, The bargaining society and the inefficiency of bargaining, *Kyklos*, 32 (1979), pp. 497-522.

J.J. de Jong a.o., *Pressiegroepen*, Utrecht, 1959.

V.O. Key Jr., *Politics, parties and pressure groups*, New York, 1952.

P.E. Kraemer, *The societal state*, Meppel, 1966.

A. Lijphart, *Democracy in plural societies*, New Haven and London, 1977.

T.J. Lowi, *The end of liberalism*, New York, 1969.

H. Nurmi, Ways out of the prisoner's dilemma, *Quality and Quantity*, 11 (1977), no. 2., pp. 135-165.

M. Olson, *The logic of collective action*, Cambridge (Mass.), 1965, 1971.

M. Olson, *The political economy of comparative growth rate*, University of Maryland, 1978 (paper).

J.J. Richardson and A.G. Jordan, *Governing under pressure*, Oxford 1979.

P.C. Schmitter, Models of interest intermediation and models of societal change in Western Europe, in: P.C. Schmitter (1977) (see note 2.), pp. 7-38.

R. Taylor, *The fifth estate*, London, 1978.

A.W.M. Teulings (ed.), *Herstructurering van de industrie*, Alphen a.d. Rijn, 1978.

N. van Veen, *Overheidsingrijpen in collectieve arbeidsovereenkomsten*, Deventer, 1976.

H.L. Wilensky, *The welfare state and equality*, Berkeley, 1975.

H.L. Wilensky, *The 'new' corporatism, centralization and the welfare state*, Beverly Hills, 1976.

M. Wheaton, Political parties and government decision-making, in J.E.S. Hayward and R.N. Berki (1979) (see note 3.)

8 PATTERNS OF VOTING BEHAVIOUR IN THE NETHERLANDS

G.A. Irwin

Had a chapter on patterns of voting behaviour in the Netherlands been written as recently as 1967 it could have been considerably shorter than this one. It would have given basic information on the electoral system, described the dominant parties, stressed how these parties were related to particular segments within the population, and noted the considerable stability with which these segments has supported the corresponding party. This is also done in this chapter, but that is only the beginning of the story. The year 1967 proved to be a watershed, and the decade which followed brought fundamental changes in the Dutch system. Some minor changes were made in the electoral system itself, as dramatic changes were taking place in the voting patterns of the electorate. Although it is perhaps too soon to say whether this has been a period of 'realignment', it was most certainly one of 'dealignment'. A description and analysis of this dealignment complete the current discussion.

8.1 The traditional Party System

The Dutch party system is anchored in two dominant social cleavages current in the 19th century. The older of these cleavages was the religious one, dating back to the Spanish occupation of the 16th century. In the wars to expel the Spanish overlords, nationalism and protestantism became intertwined. With the final expulsion of the Spanish and the reconquering of the southern provinces, protestantism had become the established religion of the north. Catholicism was never officially forbidden as a personal faith, but Catholics were relegated to second class citizenship (as were adherents of certain dissident Protestant sects, not to mention Jews). Catholics were forbidden to hold public office and were forced to hold their religious services in secret. The reconquered provinces of Brabant and Limburg were governed virtually as colonies, with heavy taxes and other measures keeping the inhabitants bound in traditional ways.

Themselves the product of rebellion within the Church, Protestant denominations have themselves seldom been spared from internal division, and the dominant Dutch Reformed Church has proved no exception. Basic questions of orthodoxy vs. latitudinarianism and centralism vs. local autonomy of church structure led to two major divisions in the 19th century. Groups favouring orthodoxy and local autonomy twice broke away (in 1834 and in 1886), eventually combining to form the 'Gereformeerde' Churches (1892). These orthodox Calvinists were the object of varying degrees of church, social, and judicial discrimination until late in the 19th century[1].

The national census of 1899 showed that 48.4 percent of the population identified themselves as belonging to the Dutch Reformed Church; 35.1 percent were Roman Catholics; and 7.1 percent belonged to the various Gereformeerde groups. Only 7.2 percent belonged to other groups and 2.2 percent reported no religious identification.

Despite the somewhat backward economic position of most Catholics and orthodox Calvinists, one must see the social class cleavage as more of a cross-cutting than a reinforcing cleavage. The Industrial Revolution was relatively slow in reaching the Netherlands, yet a pre-industrial class structure was existent. In the cities and towns a commercial and merchant elite, known as 'regents', dominated political and social life. The lack of a powerful aristocracy had facilitated their rise to power by the 16th century and the absence of a strong central government had left their position untouched until the Napoleon period. In rural areas, certain farmers had larger holdings and held a dominant position.

Beneath this dominant commercial class, one must distinguish between two groups. On the one hand, there was the so-called 'middenstand' or independent middle-class of small shopkeepers, artisans, fishermen, inland shippers, and independent farmers. At the bottom of the social ladder was the class of workers and paupers. With the coming of industrialization, an industrial proletariate began to emerge.

These religious and social differences were to provide the basis for the emerging political parties. Into the second half of the 19th century, property, sex, and other restrictions excluded large portions of the population from voting. The history of this latter half of the century is one of continued and increasing demands for greater and fuller participation for those excluded, and movements were begun for the 'emancipation' of these socially and politically deprived groups. The first group to organize effectively were the orthodox Calvinists, under the leadership of the clergyman Abraham Kuyper. In the time span of a single generation, Kuyper organized a daily newspaper, an Anti-School Law League, a separate church organisation, the Free University in Amsterdam, and the first national political party[2]. This Anti-Revolutionary Party was founded on the principle of 'Against the Revolution, the Gospels', that is, in opposition to the secularising influences seen as arising out of the liberal philosophy of the French Revolution.

With the arrival of more liberal ideas in the Netherlands, the political emancipation of the Catholics became possible. Constitutional revision and new legislation (1853) made the re-establishment of the church hierarchy possible and paved the way toward more equal participation. This road was not easy and the establishment of a movement which would encompass all Catholics, regardless of social class, was slow in coming. Eventually a single, dominant Catholic Party emerged which received the votes of virtually all those identifying with the Catholic Church.

The third group seeking greater participation within the political system was the new industrial working class. Socialism arrived later than in England, France, and Germany, and encountered considerable competition from the two groups just mentioned. The mobilisation of religiously oriented workers into the religious parties deprived the socialist movement of considerable potential support, so that even after the introduction of universal manhood suffrage, socialists usually received only 20 to 24 percent of the vote. This was far less than the working class percentage of the population.

In addition to these three emancipatory movements with their associated political parties, two additional parties must be mentioned. The predominant political grouping in the Parliament during the middle portion of the 19th century were the Liberals. Under the leadership of Johan Rudolf Thorbecke, the constitution had been reformed, which among other measures clarified the role of the monarch versus the ministers and Parliament and guaranteed the freedom of religion. It was only after this period that the first organised Liberal party was founded in 1885. It was never a mass party, and with the introduction of universal suffrage, its portion of the vote and thereby its influence declined substantially.

The final major party to be mentioned is the Christian-Historical Union, which was founded after a split within the Anti-Revolutionary Party. In 1892 all of the political parties had been divided internally by a proposed law which would have substantially expanded suffrage. Within the Anti-Revolutionary parliamentary party this led to the withdrawal of the more conservative group and to the eventual establishment of the Christian-Historical Union. This new party also received support from many Dutch Reformed adherents who felt that the influence of the orthodox Calvinists within the Anti-Revolutionary Party was too great.

To summarise, by the time of the introduction of universal suffrage, five parties dominated the Dutch political scene. They continued to do so with relatively little change until 1967, even re-emerging relatively unchanged (although in some cases with different names) after the period of German occupation. These parties were quite clearly dependent upon specific segments of the population for support. Survey results are not available until the 1950's (see Table 8.2 below), but the electoral base of these parties was quite clear. The Catholic party received the vote of virtually all of the Catholic population, as did the Anti-Revolutionary Party among the Gereformeerden. The other Protestant party, the Christian-Historicals, were far less successful in obtaining the votes of members of the Dutch reformed Church. Middle and upper class members of this church also supported the Liberal Party, while Protestant and non-religious workers formed the basis for the Socialist party.

Despite the fact that the Dutch electoral system facilitates the establishment of parties and many small parties have competed in elections between 1918 and 1963, these five parties never received less than 83.9 percent of the vote and reached a height of 91.6 percent in 1959[3]. Relying upon the stable support of their appropriate segments of the population, gains and losses at elections were minimal. In 1948, 1952, and 1956 only 4, 5, and 7 of the 100 seats in Parliament changed hands, and even after expansion of the Parliament to 150 seats, the number changing after the elections of 1959, and 1963 was only 8, and 9 respectively.

8.2 The electoral system

Before turning to an examination of the changes which have occurred in voting behaviour since 1967, it is important to examine various specific features of the Dutch electoral system. Long before the important work by Rae[4], politicians and political scientists were aware of the potentially important consequences of electoral laws. These can certainly be seen in the Netherlands, and it is useful here to summarise the electoral system and the various changes it has undergone. Certain impacts of these electoral laws will be mentioned here, and others will become evident in the discussion of electoral change which follows[5].

The constitutional compromise of 1917[6] brought three major changes in the electoral system[7]: 1) universal male suffrage was introduced (and was followed two years later by female suffrage), 2) proportional representation replaced the two-ballot district system[8]. As voting was now universally available, results could only be truly proportional if all individuals exercised this right, 3) compulsory attendance at the polls was legislated in order to insure this true proportionality.

As we have seen above, the multi-party system of the Netherlands preceded this introduction of proportional representation and universal suffrage. One of the arguments in favour of PR was the fact that it would allow for more equitable representation of existing groups. Although, in perhaps typically Dutch fashion, the discussion preceding these electoral changes was carried on in terms of principle, the potential political effects of the changes surely did not escape the parties involved. The Catholics stood to gain substantially, as they generally amassed considerable surpluses in the homogeneous districts of the South. The Liberals feared the introduction of universal suffrage, but noted that proportional representation might save them from complete oblivion. The Socialists expected to profit from universal suffrage and were less concerned, although somewhat divided, on PR. The Protestant parties had learned that they could be big winners under the district system but could also lose[9]. Three elements of the electoral system are particularly relevant for consideration here.

1. Although there are formally 18 electoral districts in the Netherlands, these have only a minor impact upon the final composition of Parliament. Parties may compete in any number of districts and may submit either the same or different lists of candidates in the various districts. However, for the purpose of determining the number of seats accruing to the various parties the votes in all districts are combined. After the number of seats, based upon these national totals has been determined for each party, these seats are distributed proportionally among the districts according to the number of votes received. This distribution determines the number of candidates elected from each district. Within each district the proper number from the top of the list are declared elected. For those candidates who appear at the top of the list in more than one district and would thus be elected more than once, the assignment of the districts in which such an individual is finally declared to be elected is determined by lot. According to this procedure the existence of electoral districts may influence which individual candidates are elected, but has no effect upon the number of seats which a party receives.

2. Access to the ballot was made extremely simple; a party need obtain only 25 signatures within a district in order to be placed on the ballot. The number of lists competing at elections was thus quite high, averaging approximately 40 in the period between 1918 and 1933.

In an effort to limit this number somewhat, after 1933 parties were required to make a deposit which is forfeited unless the party obtains three-fourths of the electoral quotient (= the number of valid votes divided by the number of seats in the Second Chamber). The requirement of a deposit drastically reduced the number of parties competing at the elections to an average of less than 14 between 1937 and 1967. At present the deposit is set at 1000 guilders in each district, so that with 450 signatures and 18,000 guilders, a party can take part in all districts[10].

The threshold required for representation in Parliament is equal to the electoral quotient. For each multiple of this quotient, a seat is received. As the actual distribution of votes will not be such that all seats can be distributed in this manner, the so-called 'remainder' seats are divided according to the d'Hondt largest average system. Since 1938 only those parties which have achieved the electoral threshold are considered for these remaining seats.

The actual minimum figure required for election has varied somewhat over the years, but has never exceeded 1 percent. With the expansion of the Second Chamber in 1951 from 100 to 150 seats, this natural quotient was lowered to 0,67 percent. In actual numbers, this now means approximately 50,000 votes in an electorate of 9 million[11].

3. The third aspect of the electoral system which should be mentioned briefly is the physical make-up of the ballot. The system is strictly a list system. Parties list the candidates, of which a maximum of 30 may be named on the ballot in each district. (For most parties this number is considerably more than can be expected to be elected across all districts). Beside each candidate's name is a circle; the voter may fill in only one of these circles and must do so with a red pencil. There is no circle at the top of the ballot for the party, as for example in Belgium. In fact, only since 1956 has the electoral law provided that the names of the parties be placed on the ballot above the list of candidate names; previously the voter had to either know the name of the candidate for whom he intended to vote or recall the number of his favourite party.

Most voters cast their ballot for the first name on the party list. If votes are given to candidates placed lower on the list, these accrue to the party for the tallying. Candidates are declared elected according to their position on the list, and these 'preference' votes can alter this position only if the candidate himself receives one-half of the number of votes needed by his party for gaining one seat, and only then if the number of votes he received is larger than the number which have accrued to candidates above him after the transfer of votes from the top-candidates. Election by 'preference' votes is extremely rare, and is actively discouraged by the parties[12].

More recently, some changes in the electoral system have been important for both the voters and the parties. Perhaps the most striking was the abolition in 1970 of compulsory attendance at the polls. This compulsion was seen as no longer consistent with democratic principles of freedom[13]. The impact of this change was greater than anticipated, and at the provincial elections of 1970 only 68.1 percent of the electorate cast a ballot. Turnout has been higher for parliamentary elections (79.0 percent, 83.5 percent and 87.5 percent for 1971, 1972, and 1977 respectively), but remains lower than the roughly 95 percent which had been usual previously.

Although turnout declined in virtually all relevant sociological groups, the magnitude of decline was greater among the young, those with lower education, urban dwellers, females, and Catholics. Those with less interest in politics and those revealing some degree of alienation from the political system also began to turn out less frequently[14]. Chief among the losers because of the drop in turnout were probably the Catholic Party and Democrats '66, while the Anti-Revolutionary Party may have gained relatively since its supporters continued to turn out strongly.

A second change in the electoral system has been the reduction twice of the minimum voters age – from 23 to 21 in 1967 and to 18 prior to the 1972 election. Although younger voters are less likely to turn out than older voters, this infusion of new voters has undoubtedly had some effects. As will be shown in more detail below, younger voters have shown greater preferences for leftist and newer parties, and these parties have profited accordingly. However, as younger voters are also less stable in their preferences, love affairs have often been short and parties have lost the youth vote as quickly as it was gained.

A third change is of more importance to the parties than to the individual voter. Beginning with the parliamentary elections of 1977, parties are allowed to link their lists. For the allocation of seats, these parties ar counted as a single list. Because the system for allocating seats (the d'Hondt largest average system) favours larger parties, such coalitions are encouraged. However, since the distribution of seats within the coalition is calculated according to the largest remainder method, small members of the coalition are favoured[15]. In the first election utilizing this new system, one of the small parties of a left coalition (the Radicals) gained three seats in Parliament with fewer actual votes than the Communists who gained only two seats.

8.3 Patterns of change

We have seen above that the social and political system combined to produce considerable stability in voting behaviour during the half century from 1917 until 1967. This does not mean, of course, that there was no change whatsoever, nor that change was unimportant. Short term forces occasionally produced changes in party strength, and in such a stable system even small changes took on major importance. As there are virtually no survey data available for this 1917-1967 period, it is impossible to know just how large the percentage of actual 'switchers' between elections really was. One study from 1951 estimated this percentage to be approximately 20 percent[16], which would be considerably higher than estimates based upon aggregate changes. Apparently, the votes of many switches cancelled each other out, producing rather less aggregate change.

In figure 8.1, one can see the nature of this aggregate change for the postwar period. One obvious instance of short-term change is the height of 32.7 percent achieved by the Socialists in 1956, which to a great extent can be attributed to the popularity of the prime minister Willem Drees. Yet the general pattern of stability is clear; aggregate changes between elections of three to four percent are the exception.

Although there were some earlier signs of change before 1967, it is at this election that it became evident that something lasting was taking place. In that year one first sees evidence of the dramatic slide which was to almost halve the Catholic Party vote in a ten-year period. Although the Christian-Historicals were always much smaller, a similar fate befell this party. The year 1967 has so far proven to be the low point in post-war support for the Socialists. Yet despite the dramatic losses by the two religious parties, only in 1977 were the gains of the Socialists really substantial. The Liberals have done better proportionally; although starting their climb only in 1972, they had almost doubled their vote by 1977.

Between 1967 and 1972 the losses by the two religious parties were not compensated by gains for the Socialists and Liberals, so that the percentage of the vote for the five dominant parties declined sharply. Their combined percentage of the vote dropped from an all time height of 91.6 percent in 1959 to only 73.0 percent in 1972. Taking up the slack were numerous new parties. As early as 1959 a Pacifist-Socialist Party had gained two seats in Parliament. In 1963 a new Calvinist party gained a seat, and a new Peasant's Party threw a scare into the existing parties by gaining three seats. In 1966 another new party, Democrats '66, was formed with the express purpose of 'exploding' the existing party structure and shocked the political world by

Figure 8.1 Electoral support for major parties (1946-1977)

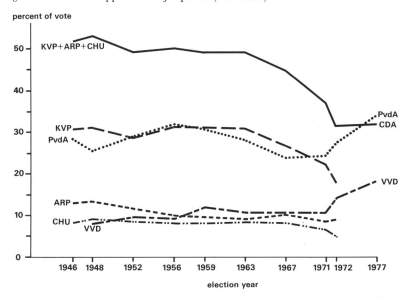

gaining 7 seats at the elections only a few months later. In 1969 a group from the left wing of the Catholic Party parliamentary caucus left the party to form the Radical Party. This party eventually received the support of progressive Calvinists, and achieved its greatest success in 1972 by obtaining 7 seats. In opposition to the growing influence of the New Left within the Labour Party, a group of supporters broke off to form Democratic Socialists '70. This party gained 8 seats at the 1971 elections and became the first party other than the Big Five to enter a cabinet. By 1977 all of these parties had suffered major losses (although D'66 managed to recover for these elections) and the Big Five had recovered to take 83.7 percent of the total vote.

These aggregate voting changes leave us with three basic questions to be asked concerning the individual voting behaviour of the electorate:

1. What were the sources of the considerable losses suffered by the Catholics and Christian-Historicals?

2. Why did the Socialists (and the Liberals) profit so little (or late) from these religious losses?

3. From where did the support for the new parties come, and why did it dry up so quickly?

As we are dealing with a single electorate, the answers to these questions will be intertwined, yet are deserving of individual attention.

Table 8.1 Comparison of vote preferences by religious groups, 1954 and 1977

	1954[a]					1977[b]			
	Roman Catholic	Dutch Reformed	Gerefor- meerd	No Preference		Roman Catholic	Dutch Reformed	Gerefor- meerd	No Preference
Catholic Peoples P.	87	1	–	1	CDA	54	31	70	8
Anti-Revolutionary P.	–	13	82	2					
Christian Historical	–	27	2	1					
Labor (Socialist)	7	41	4	72		24	35	6	57
VVD (Liberal)	1	14	2	13		12	20	7	16
Communist	–	1	–	10		1	–	–	2
Other	5	3	10	1		9	14	17	17
	100%	100%	100%	100%		100%	100%	100%	100%.

a. Source: *De Nederlandse Kiezer*, These figures have been recalculated and include only those answering a question concerning party preference.

b. Source: *Dutch National Election Study*, 1977.

8.3.1 Deconfessionalisation

As we have just seen, beginning in 1967 two of the three religious parties, the Catholic Party and the Christian-Historicals began a rather severe downward spiral. Internal pressure built up to do something to stop this trend, and among other solutions the idea of a federation of the three religious parties was revived[17]. First the parties began to cooperate at the local level and within Parliament, and eventually a single list of candidates at the elections in 1977. Therefore, in the analysis presented below it will occasionally be necessary to combine the votes of the three parties in order to make comparisons with the vote for this new Christian Democratic Appeal. The nature of the decline in votes observed in figure 8.1 is seen more clearly in Table 8.1. It is difficult to make comparisons, since the data collections were not always similar. For older surveys data have often been lost so that percentages must be recalculated from previously published sources. Nevertheless, despite certain limitations, overall trends in support for those parties and the process of 'deconfessionalisation' are unmistakeable.

In neither of the years considered were the religious parties able to obtain more than a handful of votes from individuals with no religious identification. In this sense, although the Christian Democratic Appeal may have hoped to become a more general centre party in 1977, it remained a party attractive only to religious voters. Yet the number of religious identifiers who cast their vote for this party in 1977 was far less than the percentages who cast votes for one of the three major religious parties in 1954.

Daalder[18] has offered several possible sources for the declining hold of these parties on their potential supporters. Most are directly related to the general 'disarray' of the religious subcultures. Emancipation was essentially completed, so that segmentation was now more the honouring of traditional differences than a current ideological struggle. Changes in attitude were to be found among the religious leaders, with growing concern for problems of the world outside the immediate subculture. Dissension among the leadership led to disorientation and indifference among the followers. New means of communication, especially television, weakened the monopoly of information which had previously been held by the churches, schools, newspapers, and the family. Within the subcultures, organisational structures began to break apart. Newspapers, for example, abandoned their traditional signatures and some religious organisations began to federate. This latter was particularly true for the Catholic subculture.

The sources of change tell us something about what was happening within the religious subcultures, but less about who and to whom this was happening. In particular, three hypotheses must be examined:

Hypothesis 1. Individuals dropped their religious identifications and accordingly ceased to vote for a religious party.

Hypothesis 2. Individuals retained their religious identifications, but no longer associated their personal religious feelings with the necessity of casting a vote for a religious party.

Hypothesis 3. No individuals changed, but the composition of the group was altered. As older religious voters died they were replaced by younger voters who were not socialised into the older patterns of choice, and, even when religious, were less likely to translate this identification into political terms.

The first of these hypotheses indicates the possibility of a process of the breakdown of religion ('ontkerkelijking'), whereas the second is more directly related to specific political processes ('deconfessionalisation'). The third hypothesis suggests the possibility that these processes were restricted to or dominant among younger cohorts, and this vast difference between age groups accounts for the overall change. Given the magnitude of the aggregate change it is unlikely that one of the hypotheses can account for all change; all will probably contribute to the explanation. Yet it is important that we distinguish between the three possibilities and attempt to determine the relative importance of each explanation.

With regard to the first hypothesis, for example, we might expect that the number of religious identifiers had decreased dramatically over the last decade. That the explanation for the decline is more complicated than this can be quickly demonstrated from the figures in Table 8.2. The various national censuses do indeed show that the percentage of the population stating no religious preference has increased by more than five percent over the period 1960 to 1971. However, examination of the other columns reveals that the percentage of Catholics increased slightly until 1960 and remained steady until 1971. Thus a decreasing number of Catholics cannot account for the decline in Catholic vote. The number of Gereformeerden has also remained remarkably steady over the years, but this group has also been relatively consistent in its support for religious political parties. It is among the Dutch Reformed that one finds the losses which turn up as gains in the 'No preference' column. However, this trend began at the beginning of the century, and although it has accelerated over the more recent decades, it has hardly been of sufficient magnitude to account for the extent of change in religious voting.

Table 8.2 Religious preference

	Roman Catholic	Dutch Reformed	Gereformeerd	Other	No religious preference
1899	35,1	48,4	7,1	7,2	2,2
1909	35,0	44,2	8,4	7,4	5,0
1920	35,6	41,2	8,3	7,1	7,8
1930	36,4	34,5	8,1	6,6	14,4
1947	38,5	31,0	7,0	6,4	17,1
1960	40,4	28,3	6,9	6,1	18,3
1971	40,4	23,5	7,2	5,3	23,6

Source: Central Bureau of Statistics.

If the number of religious identifiers did not decrease substantially during the period under consideration, then something else must have happened to these individuals. One possibility is that religious identification became increasingly less important and that many individuals became 'Catholic' or 'Reformed' in name only. Indications of such change can be seen in the declines in church attendance which have occurred during the period. In a religious survey taken in 1966 86 percent of the Catholics, 50 percent of the Reformed and 95 percent of the Gereformeerden reported that they attended church regularly (82 percent of Catholics, 34 percent of Reformed, and 81 percent of Gereformeerden stated they had attended the previous Sunday)[19]. In the 1977 Dutch Election Study the percentage of Catholics reporting 'weekly' attendance had fallen to 40 and to 22 percent for Reformed. Only the Gereformeerden remain relatively high with 76 percent claiming weekly attendance. Even if we add the 1977 percentages reporting attendance at least once a month, the figures are only 62 percent for Catholics, 41 percent for Reformed, and 90 percent for Gereformeerd. There are over this period substantial rises in the percentages reporting they 'never' attend. These figures only document what church officials have long noted, namely that church attendance had declined drastically.

Whether individuals first began to attend church less and then changed their vote preference or whether the two went hand in hand is difficult to determine from the available data. In table 8.3 religious identifiers are divided into a group reporting weekly church attendance and those indicating less than weekly attendance. Those in the group attending less than weekly are still far more likely to vote for the Christian Democratic Appeal than are those reporting no identification. Catholic non-attenders still give a plurality to this party and the few Gereformeerden who attend infrequently vote in a majority for religious parties. Yet the differences with the church attenders are quite impressive. Among all denominations the percentages of church attenders supporting the religious parties exceeds 75 percent. When these figures are compared to comparable figures

Table 8.3 Vote choice by religious preference and church attendance

	Attended church weekly			Attend church less than weekly			No religious preference
	Cath.	Dutch Ref.	Ger.	Cath.	Dutch Ref.	Ger.	
Party							
Christen-Dem.	75	64	78	40	21	50	8
Other religious parties	0	17	17	–	–	4	0
Labour	12	9	3	34	44	14	58
Liberal	8	9	1	15	24	25	16
Democrats '66	5	–	–	6	8	–	10
Other	–	1	1	6	4	7	9
	100%	100%	100%	101%	101%	100%	101%
Number	183	59	90	254	194	28	412

Source: 1977 Dutch National Election Study.

from 1954 or other years before 1967, one finds that the changes among church-going people have been minimal. In short, the churches have been losing hold on their followers (except for Gereformeerden) and the related political parties on their voters.

Examination of the figures in Table 8.3 have moved us into consideration of the second hypothesis. We have now established that church attendance has decreased and that those who attend less frequently are more likely to vote for other parties. However, we still have not answered directly the question whether these are changes in individuals or whether they are the result of changes in the make-up of the electorate. In the first case, one would expect to find specific individuals who once had been regular in church attendance and religious party support, but who had now consciously broken away. In the second case, we would find that few individuals had changed, but that younger voters entering adulthood and the electorate for the first time had rejected things religious, both in terms of church attendance and in their voting patterns. As they replace older voters, aggregate voting change occurs.

In order to answer this question directly, one would need information concerning the same individuals over the time period involved. Unfortunately, such 'panel studies' are rather limited for the period involved, so that we must rely upon a less direct, but useful method. By examining an age group at a particular point in time and the same group again at a later period, we can learn a great deal about the change occurring within this age 'cohort'. If we make the assumption that the chances of survival are equal for the adherents of each political party, then change within a cohort must be individual change. Again the information for the pre-1967 period is very limited and exists only in the form of published reports. These values must be recalculated on the basis of these reports and compared to the current figures. Differences in the technical aspects of the surveys involved caution us against placing too much emphasis on the precise figures. The general trends, however, do cast some light on the question posed.

In Table 8.4, two sets of cohorts are examined. The first is a comparison of religious voting for four age groups as reported for 1954[20]. In 1977 the groups had aged 23 years, and the voting preferences for these cohorts are presented. An election study after the crucial election of 1967 reported the voting patterns for fairly detailed groupings by age[21]. The preferences for these age groups ten years later are also presented for comparison.

The first column of this table indicates that few differences in support for religious parties were found across age groups in 1954. Only the 50-65 group is slightly below the average, while all the other groups were above 50

Table 8.4 Age cohort analysis of religious voting (% preferences for major religious parties)

Age in 1954 Age in 1977	Preference 1954[a] Three major parties	Vote[c] 1977 CDA	Age in 1967 Age in 1977	Vote[b] 1967	Vote[c] 1977
23-34	53		21-24	44	
46-57		39	31-34		26
35-50	53		25-30	45	
58-73		45	35-40		36
50-65	48		31-35	42	
73+		38	41-45		40
over 65	54		36-50	47	
			46-60		38
			51-65	49	
			61-75		46
			over 65	55	
			over 75		42

a Source: *De Nederlandse Kiezer* (Staatsdrukkerij: 's-Gravenhage, 1956)
b Source: *De Nederlandse Kiezer in 1967* (Elsevier: Amsterdam, 1967)
c Source: 1977 Dutch National Election Study

percent in their preference for the religious parties. The average for these groups is a bit higher than the actual vote figures for the elections of 1952 and 1956 but suffice as a base line against which to measure the subsequent change. By 1967, this change had begun and the three religious parties dropped below 50 percent of the vote for the first time (see figure 8.1). From looking at the 1967 figures in the third column of Table 8.4, it would seem that this was indeed the result of individual decisions to change. Although one cannot construct directly comparable age cohorts, one does see that again the differences across age groups is minimal. Only the over 65 group is now above the 50 percent figure. The remaining groups vary only between 42 percent and 49 percent, and although the older groups are a bit higher in religious voting, these differences are far from substantial. Returning to column two and the earlier age cohorts, we find percentages still lower than in the third column. Two of the three figures are now less than 40 percent, and the differences across the cohorts is still negligible. It is only among those under 30 in 1967 (see column 4) that change appears substantial and rapid. In ten years, the drop in the very youngest group is estimated at 18 percent and in the next youngest at 9 percent. (No explanation is available for the drop in the very oldest group, which may be due to real change or to violation of our assumption of non-selective survival.)

With the figures on church attendance above and these from the analysis of age cohorts, we are now in a position to give a partial answer to the questions posed in the first two hypotheses. Apparently some individuals did alter their voting behaviour. They either did so after loosening ties with the church or together with their break from the church. Among those who were eligible to vote before approximately 1960 this change has been gradual, though steady. From a figure of somewhat above 50 percent for the major religious parties, support has eroded to approximately 40 percent[22]. For those who became eligible to vote between 1960 and 1967, change has been more rapid. More than the older groups, these groups deserted the Christian-Democratic cause rapidly after 1967. Yet, all of this change is insufficient to account for the almost 20 percent drop in the total religious vote. The fact that the youngest age group in 1967 changed so rapidly suggests that we must look to those age groups entering the electorate since 1967 for further evidence to account for the total aggregate electoral change.

8.3.2 *Younger Voters*

In the above tables we have seen that even as late as 1967, those young voters casting their first ballots differed little from their elders. This fact helped to keep the total balance of forces so unchanged for half a century. Since 1967 this pattern has not been extended, and younger voters have differed substantially from those who had gone before. Daalder has compiled information on the voting behaviour of younger voters during the 1960's and 70's. These figures are reproduced in Table 8.5. It has not always been possible to produce similar age groupings, and occasionally different sources for the same year differ somewhat, but once again the trend is obvious.

Because this information will be relevant to questions to be examined below, the figures for the age groups are given for all of the political parties. For the moment we are concerned only with the column relating to the religious parties (KVP, ARP, CHU) individually and together. The figures for 1961 and 1963 again reveal patterns similar to those for the electorate as a whole. In 1967 the voting age was lowered to 21 so that the youth vote was expanded. Although religious voting for that year is still estimated as rather high, the Catholic Party seems to have been losing support. The gap between 1967 and 1971 is considerable. Support for the Catholic Party declined dramatically among new voters; the two surveys disagree somewhat concerning the decline for the Christian-Historicals. The following year elections were held

Table 8.5 Political preferences of youngest age cohorts, 1961-1977*

Year	Age group	% unknown	CPN	PSP	PvdA	PPR	D'66	Total left	KVP	ARP	CHU	Total three religious parties	VVD	DS'70	others
1961 (not eligible to vote)	18-25	18	1	2	26	–	–	*29*	42	11	6	*59*	11	–	1
1961	18-35	12	1	2	28	–	–	*31.5*	40	9	7	*56.5*	11	–	1
1963	23-37	7	1	4	27	–	–	*32*	38	10	8	*56*	10	–	2
1967	21-22	11	2	1	10	–	22	*36*	30	9	9	*50*	13	–	1
1971a	21-25	21.5	5	3	18.5	5	13	*46*	13	9	8	*30*	11	12	1
1971b	21-22	–	4	8	20	4	15	*31*	17	7	3	*27*	8	8	6
1972a	18-22	14	3	6	28	13	6	*56*	12	8	2	*22*	12	2	?
1972b	18-22	–	6	6	24	15	7	*38*	9	7	2	*18*	17	4	3
										CDA					
1977a	18-24	13		2	37	4	7	*51*	30			*30*	14		3
1977b	18-24	–	2	4	35	5	9	*55*	23			*23*	17	21	2

Source: H. Daalder, *Politisering en Lijdelijkheid in de Nederlandse Politiek* (Van Gorcum: Assen, 1974); updated in 'Party System and Changing Parties in the Netherlands: A first outline' (mimeo).

* Percentages under the parties are competed for those actually expressing a preference, and should be totalled across rows. The percentage expressing no preference is listed under '% unknown'.

again and the age required for voting was again lowered, this time to 18. By then the hold on the youngest groups by the Christian-Historicals had clearly been broken and that of the Catholics continued to decline. In 1972 the Catholic Party obtained almost 18 percent of the total vote, but only approximately half that amount among the newest voters. Although the lowering of the voting age was certainly not the sole source of problems for these two parties, it clearly did not help either.

In 1977 the three religious parties combined to present a single list of candidates. In this effort to revive their popularity they seem to have been at least temporarily successful among the newest voters. Although the size of this revival depends somewhat upon which figures are accepted, 1977 surveys indicate support for the Christian Democratic Appeal than for the individual parties a little more than four years earlier.

Before turning on to other questions concerning the voting behaviour of the electorate, it is useful to note again the stability of the vote for the Anti-Revolutionary Party. Alone among the three religious parties it has held a fairly constant percentage of the vote throughout the 1970's. Examination of the figures in Table 8.5 indicate that it was equally successful in socialising the young members of the orthodox Calvinist ('Gereformeerden') denominations into voting along traditional lines. The greater homogeneity of these groups and the sustained influence upon the members stands in contrast to the patterns for the other Dutch denominations.

We are now able to summarise the evidence available with respect to the three hypotheses posed. As expected the total change in religious voting was the result of three distinguishable forces. The churches began to lose influence some time during the 1960's. Among the Dutch Reformed group this accelerated an existing decline in the numbers identifying with the church, and for Catholics this is seen in declining attendance at mass. Declining identification with the church was often accompanied by a break with the related political party. This decline began some time during the 1960's and continued gradually throughout the 1970's. The change among younger groups was greater and more rapid. Moreover, still younger groups which were just entering the electorate were never socialised into the old patterns. They attended church less frequently[23] and have never supported religious parties to the extent of the older voters. Thus their influence into the electorate, at a more rapid rate because of the lowering of the voting age, helped to change the shape of the total electorate to the detriment of the religious parties.

8.3.3 Polarisation

With the vote of the Catholics and orthodox Calvinists monopolized by their repective political parties, the Socialists and Liberals have been left to fight over the votes of those with no religious identification, smaller non-fundamentalist Protestant seats, and those Dutch Reformed with somewhat looser ties to the church. Overt attempts at breaking this monopoly were never very successful, and post-1967 success can be attributed more to the loosened grip of the religious parties. As the decline of the two religious parties set in, the Socialists and Liberals found themselves joined in a common strategy of attempting to win over those voters who were leaving the confessional fold. This has led to a heightened polarisation of Dutch politics.

The Socialists and Liberals have never been as successful in securing the votes of their potential support groups as the Catholics and Calvinists had been. Lijphart has reported figures for 1956 indicating the percentage of the secular working class and secular middle class supporting the Labour and Liberal parties. These figures and roughly comparable figures for 1977 are given in Table 8.6.

Perhaps the most surprising aspect of the comparative figures in this table is the stability over the years. Whereas the religious parties showed considerable stability until 1967 and then declined, the percentages for the

Table 8.6 Vote preference of those with no religious affiliation by social class

1956[x]	KVP	ARP	CHU	Labor	Liberal	Other
Secular working class	4	6	7	68	5	10
Secular middle class	3	4	12	44	32	6
1977[xx]		CDA				
Secular working class		12		68	5	17
Secular middle class		19		36	29	16

x. Source: A. Lijphart, 'The Netherlands' Continuity and Class in Voting Behavior', in R. Rose (ed.) *Electoral Behavior*, A Comparative Handbook (Free Press: New York, 1974), p. 246.
xx. Source: R.B. Andeweg, "Factoren die het stemgedrag mede bepalen', in G.A. Irwin, J. Verhoef, and C.J. Wiebrens, *De Nederlandse Kiezer '77*, (VAM: Voorschoten, 1977), p. 162.

Socialists and the Liberals remain very similar over the entire period. (This does not mean that they would have been exactly the same for all of the intervening elections.) Approximately two-thirds of the secular working class supports the Labour Party and a little less than one-third of the secular middle class supports the Liberal Party. As was seen in figure 8.1, these parties did begin to improve their positions in 1971 and 1972, yet these percentages for only the secular voters would indicate that the increase in total number of votes for these two parties occurred because this group of secular voters was itself increasing. Apparently more important were the inroads being made among those voters who were loosening ties with the church. In Table 8.3 we have seen that among those attending church less than weekly, 34 percent of the Catholics and 44 percent of the Duch Reformed supported Labour in 1977, whereas 24 percent of the Duch Reformed and 24 percent of the Gereformeerden supported the Liberals.

There is, in fact, a time-lag between the point at which the confessional losses began and the Socialist and Liberal gains started. In 1977, as the confessional downward trend was halted, the Socialist and Liberal gains were greatest. Dittrich has put forth an hypothesis suggesting that these are not mere coincidences[24]. In his view, given traditional differences and animosities it was difficult for a previously confessional voter to move immediately to one of the secular parties. Instead he often made his move in two steps, either by sitting out one election and not voting or voting first for one of the new, minor parties. Other research has shown that the Catholic turnout in the provincial elections immediately following the absolution of compulsory attendance at the pools was particularly low[25]. Following this thesis, by 1977 most voters would have completed this two-step switch or would have made this switch directly as the secular option became more acceptable. This would help to account for the gains made by the Socialists in 1977.

8.3.4 New Parties

The suggestion of a two-step switch involving the small, new parties leads us to the examination of the third question posed at the beginning of this analysis. Beginning in 1967 several new parties burst upon the scene and scored (by Dutch standards) phenomenal success. Certainly they threw considerable fear into the politicians of the older parties. Yet in 1977 only D'66 would have survived had not the Dutch system of proportional representation been so kind to small parties. Only D'66 obtained more than 5 percent of the total vote and only D'66 and the Radicals obtained more than 1 percent of the vote. Four others remained in Parliament with only a single member. Even the Communists and the Political Reformed Party, who have both been represented in Parliament since 1918, were hard hit.

Others have examined the period from 1967 until approximately 1975 in greater detail than can be considered here[26]. These were years of turmoil in a large number of countries and the Netherlands were no exception. Significant changes were found both within politics and society in general, with many voters breaking away from traditional patterns, and a 'silent re-volution' occurring among the young[27]. In the Netherlands there was considerable frustration with the existing political party system, and that frustration found expression in a number of new parties.

Especially the younger voters, who had not yet established regular and consistent patterns of voting were attracted to the new parties. The extent of this attraction can be seen by again examining Table 8.5. In 1967 22 percent of the youngest voters supported the new D'66. In 1971 D'66 was still relatively popular with younger voters, but was also joined by Democrats Socialists '70. In 1972 both of these were already out of favour with the youngest voters who now turned to the Radicals. Needless to say, these parties hardly had the time or opportunity to build up a stable body of voters.

In 1977 the youngest voters once again had voting preferences which were not so very different from those of their elders. They tended to vote for religious parties a bit less often than the older groups and support smaller, leftist parties a bit more. Yet these differences were far less substantial than they had been for the groups entering the electorate just a few years earlier. This may have been due partially to a combination of short-term forces.

There was no new party to capture the fancy of the floating vote, so that the new Christian Democratic combination may have profited somewhat. On the left, the Socialists managed to rally enough votes from previous supporters of small leftist parties, previous non-voters, and young voters to offset their losses to the right and score the largest victory (in terms of absolute number of seats gained) in Dutch parliamentary history[28]. Personalities of the leading candidates loomed large in the elections as did the emphasis on the movement toward a three-party system.

8.4 Conclusion

The most obvious question with which to conclude is whether the 1977 election began the reversal of a trend or whether it was merely an intermission. It may be that the religious federation has reached a core of support upon which it can now rely for some time. It was generally viewed to be the biggest winner at the 1978 provincial elections, which are often viewed as a barometer for national trends. Whether it will be able to develop into a centre party capable of attracting non-religious voters still remains in doubt. It must, however, first solve certain internal differences brought on by the attempt to fuse three previously autonomous parties.

Perhaps the electorate is now frustrated with a constant influx of new parties, none of which were ever quite able to penetrate and break the domination of the older parties. For the moment the Labour Party has gathered the left under one banner, with D'66 supplying 'An Acceptable Alternative' (their 1977 election slogan).

Little has been said here of the attempts of the Liberals to become something of a 'catch-all' party appealing to all those who are willing to work. The participation of the Liberals in the Cabinet formed at the end of 1977 (see Chapter 9) has given them the opportunity to broaden their exposure, especially of other party leaders than their leader Hans Wiegel. However, this participation has so far not been rewarded. The party incurred losses at both the provincial and municipal elections of 1978, and continues to suffer in the polls.

One element which so far remains unchanged are those aspects of the Dutch electoral system which helped facilitate both the change and the stability. That is the system of proportional representation which so accurately registers both minor changes and small interests will continue to do so in the future, and provide the voters with ample opportunity to express their varied and changing (?) preferences.

[1] H. Daalder, The Netherlands: 'Opposition in a Segmented Society' in R.A. Dahl (ed.) *Political Oppositions in Western Democracies* (New Haven, Conn., 1966); and I. Lipschits, *De protestants-christelijke stroming tot 1940* (Deventer, 1977), pp. 19-23.

[2] Daalder, *op. cit.*, p. 200.

[3] H. Daalder, 'De kleine politieke partijen – een voorlopige poging tot inventarisatie', *Acta Politica*, Vol. 1, no. 1/4 (1965–66), pp. 172-196.

[4] D. Rae, *The Political Consequences of Electoral Laws* (Revised edition), (New Haven and London, 1971).

[5] In all of the subsequent discussion of the electoral system, only elections for the Second Chamber of Parliament will be considered. Members of the First Chamber are elected by the provincial legislatures; this process will not be dealt with here.

[6] In addition to the changes in the electoral system, this compromise settled the 'school question'. Religious schools were granted equality with public schools and were henceforth subsidised from public funds. For a short description of this compromise, see A. Lijphart, *The Politics of Accommodation* (2nd edition), Berkeley and Los Angeles, 1975).

[7] For discussions of the pre-1917 electoral system, see H. Daalder, 'Extreme Proportional Representation: The Dutch Experience', in S.E. Finer (ed.), *Adversary Politics and Electoral Reform* (London, 1975); A. Lijphart, 'Extreme Proportional Representation, Multipartism, and Electoral Reform in the Netherlands', (paper prepared for presentation at the 'Journées d'études sur les modes de scrutin européens', University of Paris II, January 7-8, 1977); and J. Verhoef, 'Kiesstelsels en politieke samenwerking in Nederland, 1888-1917', *Acta Politica*, Vol. 6, 1971.

[8] The two-ballot system resembled the current French presidential election procedure. A candidate receiving an absolute majority on the first ballot was declared elected. If no candidate received such a majority, the top two candidates went over to the second round. For this second round parties often made electoral pacts, and it was possible for one of the top two candidates to withdraw in favour of a candidate who had originally received fewer votes. With only two candidates, an absolute majority was received by one of the candidates in the second round.

[9] Daalder, 'De kleine partijen . . .'.

[10] For precise figures for each election, see Daalder, 'De kleine partijen . . .

[11] See Daalder, 'De kleine partijen . . .' for precise figures, and Lijphart, *loc. cit.* for effects of electoral quotients.

[12] See Daalder, 'De kleine partijen . . .'.

[13] For a summary of the discussion surrounding the abolishment of compulsory attendances at the polls, see G.A. Irwin, 'Political Attitudes and Compulsory Voting in the Netherlands', paper prepared at the Midwest Political Science Association Convention, April 1972.

[14] G.A. Irwin, 'Compulsory Voting Legislation: Impact on Voter Turnout in the Netherlands', *Comparative Political Studies*, vol. 7, 1974, pp. 292-315.

[15] See D. Rae, *loc. cit.*

[16] Dr. Wiardi Beckman Stichting, *Verkiezingen in Nederland*, April 1951, p. 77.

[17] S.B. Wolinetz, *Party-Re-alignment in the Netherlands* (unpublished Ph. D. dissertation, Yale University, 1973), and S.B. Wolinetz, 'Dutch Politics in the 1970's: Re-alignment at a Standstill?', *Current History*, Vol. 70, no. 415, April 1976.

[18] H. Daalder, 'The Netherlands', in S. Henig and J. Pinder (eds.), *European Political Parties*, 2nd edition (forthcoming).

[19] *God in Nederland* (Amsterdam, 1967), pp. 158-171.

[20] *De Nederlandse Kiezer: Een onderzoek naar zijn gedragingen en opvattingen* ('s-Gravenhage, 1956).

[21] *De Nederlandse Kiezers in 1967* (Amsterdam/Brussel, 1967).

[22] Figures reported in K. Dittrich, 'De gevolgen van de veranderingen in partijvoorkeur van de Nederlandse kiezers sinds 1966 voor KVP en PvdA', (M.A. thesis, Leiden University), 1975, indicate that the support for religious parties among these age cohorts may actually have been lower than this 40% figure during the early 1970's.

[23] W.E. Miller and Ph. C. Stouthard, 'Confessional Attachment and Electoral Behavior in the

Netherlands', *European Journal of Political Research*, Vol. 3, September 1975, pp. 219-258. This article gives considerable additional insights into the process of deconfessionalisation.
[24] Dittrich, *loc. cit.*
[25] G.A. Irwin, 'Compulsory Voting Legislation. . .'.
[26] H. Daalder, *Politisering en Lijdelijkheid in de Nederlandse Politiek* (Assen, 1974); J.Th.J. van den Berg and H.A.A. Molleman, *Crisis in de Nederlandse Politiek* (Alphen aan den Rijn, 1974); Lijphart, *The Politics of Accommodation* . . .; Wolinetz, *Party-Re-alignment* . . .
[27] R. Inglehart, *The Silent Revolution* (Princeton, New Jersey, 1977).
[28] H. Daudt, 'Winst en Verlies van de Partijen', in G.A. Irwin, J. Verhoef, C.J. Wiebrens (eds.), *De Nederlandse Kiezer '77* (Voorschoten, 1977).

Bibliography

English language titles

Daalder, H., 'The Netherlands: Opposition in a Segmented Society', in: R.A. Dahl (ed.), *Political Oppositions in Western Democracies* (New Haven, 1966).
Daalder, H., 'Extreme Proportional Representation: The Dutch Experience', in: S.E. Finer (ed.), *Adversary Politics and Electoral Reform* (London, 1975).
Daalder, H., 'The Netherlands', in: S. Henig and J. Pinder (eds.), *European Political Parties*, 2nd edition (forthcoming).
Irwin, G.A., 'Compulsory Voting Legislation: Impact on Voter Turnout in the Netherlands', *Comparative Political Studies*, vol. 7, 1974, pp. 292-315.
Irwin, G.A. and J.J.A. Thomassen, 'Issue Consensus in a Multi-Party System: Voters and Leaders in the Netherlands', *Acta Politica*, Vol. X, no. 4, 1975, pp. 389-420.
Jennings, M. Kent, 'Partisan Commitment and Electoral Behavior in the Netherlands', *Acta Politica*, Vol. 7, no. 4, 1972, pp. 445-470.
Lijphart, A., 'Extreme Proportional Representation, Multipartism, and Electoral Reform in the Netherlands', (paper prepared for presentation at 'Journées d'études sur les modes de scrutin européens', University of Paris II, January 7-8, 1977).
Lijphart, A., 'The Netherlands: Continuity and Change in Voting Behavior', in: R. Rose (ed.), *Electoral Behavior; A Comparative Handbook* (New York, 1974).
Lijphart, A., *The Politics of Accommodation: Pluralism and Democracy* (Berkeley, 1968).
Markus, Gregory B. and M. Kent Jennings, 'Responsible Voting in The Dutch Electorate' (paper presented at the convention of the American Political Science Association, September 1977).
Miller, Warren E. and Philip C. Stouthard, 'Confessional Attachment and Electoral Behavior in the Netherlands', *European Journal of Political Science*, Vol. 3, no. 3, 1975, pp. 219-258.
Thomassen, J.J.A., 'Party Identification as a Cross-National Concept: its Meaning in the Netherlands', in: I. Budge, I. Crewe and D. Farlie (eds.), *Party Identification and Beyond: Representations of Voting and Party Competition* (London, 1976).
Wolinetz, S.B., *Party Re-Alignment in the Netherlands* (Ph. D. dissertation, Yale University, 1973).

Dutch language titles

Bronner, A.E. and R. de Hoog, *Politieke Voorkeur: oordelen en beslissen* (Ph. D. dissertation: University of Amsterdam, 1978), with English summary.

Daalder, H., 'De kleine politieke partijen – een voorlopige poging tot inventarisatie', *Acta Politica*, Vol. 1, no. 1/4, 1965-66), pp. 172-196.

Daalder, H., *Politisering en Lijdelijkheid in de Nederlandse Politiek* (Assen, 1974).

Daudt, H. and J. de Lange, 'Constante kiezers, wisselaars en thuisblijvers bij de gemeenteraadsverkiezingen', *Acta Politica*, Vol. 6, no. 4, 1971, pp. 441-464.

Dittrich, K.L.L.M., 'De gevolgen van de veranderingen in partijvoorkeur van de Nederlandse kiezers sinds 1966 voor KVP en PvdA', (M.A. Thesis: Leiden University, 1975).

Irwin, G.A., J. Verhoef and C.J. Wiebrens (eds), *De Nederlandse Kiezer '77*, (Voorschoten, 1977).

Kiezen in 1967: Eindverslag van het Nationaal Verkiezingsonderzoek 1967 (Amsterdam: Vrije Universiteit, 1977), mimeographed.

De Nederlandse Kiezer: Een onderzoek naar zijn gedragingen en opvattingen ('s-Gravenhage, 1956).

Thomassen, J.J.A., *Kiezer en Gekozene in een Representatieve Demokratie* (Alphen aan den Rijn, 1975).

Werkgroep Nationaal Kiezersonderzoek 1971, *De Nederlandse Kiezer '71* (Meppel, 1972).

Werkgroep Nationaal Verkiezingsonderzoek 1972, *De Nederlandse Kiezer '72* (Alphen aan den Rijn, 1973).

Werkgroep Nationaal Verkiezingsonderzoek 1972/73, *De Nederlandse Kiezer '73* (Alphen aan den Rijn, 1974).

Dr. Wiardi Beckman Stichting, *Verkiezingen in Nederland*, mimeo, April, 1951.

Verhoef, J., 'Kiesstelsels en politieke samenwerking in Nederland', *Acta Politica*, Vol. 6, no. 3, 1971, pp. 261-269.

9 GOVERNMENT FORMATION IN THE NETHERLANDS*

R.B. Andeweg, Th. van der Tak and K. Dittrich

9.1 Introduction

In parliamentary multi-party systems in which no party acquires a majority on its own, the most usual way to govern is by coalition. Dutch politics is characterised by such a coalition imperative, and hence the interregnums during which these coalition-governments are forged – such as the record 207 days required for the formation of the Van Agt-coalition in 1977 – are often moments of great political importance. In the first place, contrary to the situation in a two-party system, the Dutch electorate cannot express its disgruntlement with past policies succinctly by voting the incumbents out and the opposition in. Instead, the election outcome normally leaves several options open for the politicians to choose from during the cabinet-formation interregnum. In the second place, two-party electoral contests gauge precisely the political situation of the moment, leaving no doubt as to who is in power. In the Dutch multi-party system, however, the cabinet-formation serves as the instrument by which the recent political power relationships are interpreted. Finally and perhaps most importantly, the cabinet formation is a policy instrument. In a multi-party system there is no majority-party platform that becomes a government programme instantly following election day[1]. In Holland long negotiations are necessary during which detailed compromises are painstakingly hammered out in order to create a single policy statement out of several party platforms. Once agreement has been reached it is virtually impossible to make amendments without risking a rift in the coalition. Thus, in the words of former Catholic leader Romme, 'Parliament can influence government policy only before, not during the "ride"'[2].

Having stressed the importance of cabinet formations as a political thermometer and in policy-making, let us re-emphasize that it is primarily an intra-elite affair, a fact sometimes obnoxious to democratic-minded observers.

9.2 Description

9.2.1 Procedures

If it has not already done so, the sitting government submits its resignation to the Queen on election day. It is customarily asked to stay on as a caretaker government until a new cabinet can be formed. Although, as a rule, such a *demissionaire regering* does not introduce important new legislation or take controversial actions, it is far from being a completely lame-duck government; pending legislation is routinely brought to an end, subsidies are handed out, and appointments are made.

The head of state of a country with a coalition government has generally considerable discretionary power in the cabinet-formation process[3]. This is true for the Dutch monarch, even though the constitutional provision that 'The King appoints and dismisses Ministers at his pleasure' is a dead letter[4]. In fact there are no written legal rules that apply to the formation of a new government. Soon after the elections the Queen invites a number of political leaders to her palace for a first round of consultations and to 'advise' her concerning the most logical and feasible coalition. Tradition dictates the order in which these advisers visit the Queen: the chairman of the First Chamber of Parliament (the Senate), the chairman of the Second Chamber, the acting chairman of the Council of State – a body of seasoned advisers with some judicial tasks, formally presided over by the Queen herself – and the leader of each of the parliamentary parties (not the party-chairman as in Belgium) in order of party size. If in the course of the interregnum more rounds of consultations become necessary, generally only the representatives of the parties involved are invited. The parliamentary parties' leaders present written recommendations to the Queen. Recently they have been allowed to publish these, but what is actually said during the consultations remains a well-guarded secret. Only very rarely do 'leaks' violate this 'Secret of Soestdijk', so called after the former Royal residence.

After these consultations, under normal circumstances, the Queen would appoint a *formateur* (usually the parliamentary leader of the largest party)[5] to form a new cabinet, in which he would in most cases be Prime Minister. However, since World War II, due to the often complicated inter-party relationships, no *formateur* has succeeded in forming a cabinet on the first attempt. The Queen therefore has often resorted to initially appointing an *informateur*[6]. As his title implies, his duty is to inform the Queen as to the viability of various options left open by the election outcome and to advise her on whom to appoint as *formateur*. As we shall see later, *informateurs* are sometimes assigned the task of overcoming a deadlock in the negotiations. The main attractiveness of the office of *informateur* lies in the fact that whereas a *formateur* can fail, an *informateur* cannot; information can always be obtained, whereas a cabinet cannot always be formed. Thus the political risks involved in being *informateur* are far less than those inherent in the position of *formateur*.

In negotiations with the leaders of the parliamentary parties having coalition potential, the *(in)formateur)* (or *(in)formateurs*; sometimes two are appointed in order to accommodate antagonistic parties), attempts to narrow down the range of possible coalitions to the most feasible one. Once the parties that will share government responsibility are agreed upon, the negotiations focus on the formulation of a government programme and on the distribution of Ministerial and State-Secretarial posts among the coalition partners. Customarily, the programme is first on the agenda and its contents may vary from a rough outline of the principles of the new government's policy to an elaborate enumeration of detailed plans and drafts for new laws.

When a programme is drafted, and the seats are apportioned, an *informateur* usually makes way for a *formateur* if he has not done so earlier on. The final task for the *formateur* is to staff his cabinet with Ministers and State-Secretaries who are acceptable both to him and the coalition partners. After that the new cabinet may be sworn in at the Royal Palace.

However, at any of the stages just described, the parties may be unable to reach a compromise. Usually, a 'fresh' *informateur* is called upon to 'glue' the rifts and to 'put the train back on track', as the jargon has it. In 1977 this proved to be necessary several times when negotiations between the Socialists (PvdA) and Christian Democrats (CDA) stalled on plans for a new excess-profit sharing law, on the legalisation of abortion, and on the distribution of Ministerial posts. If the parties remain intransigent, however, the whole process must be started again from scratch. After 163 days of negotiations in the summer of 1977, the PvdA and CDA had finally reached agreement on a very elaborate programme, the distribution of posts, and on most of the candidates for these posts, but could not reach agreement on the final appointments. Ultimately, negotiations between the parties collapsed and were begun anew between the CDA and the liberal-conservative VVD. After 207 days of interregnum, involving nine *(in)formateurs* the 1977 cabinet formation finally ended with the acceptance of the CDA-VVD coalition headed by the Christian-Democrat Dries Van Agt.

The government-formation process described above is an extrapolation from the formations in recent years; every individual cabinet formation has its own peculiarities. The traditions and customs that determine the procedure are continuously evolving and can be set aside completely whenever political expedience requires[7].

We might add that despite the room left for idiosyncracies and new developments, the general procedure is surprisingly similar to that used in some other coalition-governed countries such as Belgium, Denmark, Finland, Norway and Sweden[8].

9.2.2 Cabinet-Parliament Relations

Once a new cabinet is sworn in, the interregnum is over[9]. Dutch cabinets are almost invariably majority governments. However, the nature of the relationship between the government and the coalition partners may vary.

The Constitution provides that an individual may not be simultaneously a Minister and member of either the Second or First Chamber of Parliament[10]. This reflects an established tradition of separating government and parliament and explains why the term 'government' and 'cabinet' are used indiscriminately in Dutch political parlance. The Christian Democrats are particularly inclined to emphasize this 'dualism' between government and parliament, whereas the Social Democrats, for example, take a more 'monistic' posture, that comes close to the British system of government-parliament relations.

The degree of support parliamentary parties give to governments in which they take part may also vary. The main difference is between so called 'parliamentary' and 'extra-parliamentary' cabinets. A government is called 'parliamentary' when party leaders and the *formateur* have made very definite agreements about the government programme. Unless they have agreed to 'free issues', parties supporting a parliamentary cabinet are more or less obliged to vote for the government's legislative proposals. When a cabinet is named 'extra-parliamentary', this does not mean that it is a minority government, but rather that there are no explicit agreements between the cabinet and the parliamentary parties about the support for the government's policies; the parties will judge the government on the basis of its actions.

It is not always crystal-clear when a government is a 'parliamentary' one and when it is 'extra-parliamentary'. Indeed, sometimes it can be both. For instance, the 1973-1977 Den Uyl cabinet was a 'parliamentary government' in the eyes of the leftist coalition-partners, while the KVP and ARP regarded it as 'extra-parliamentary'. When, during the 1977 interregnum, both CDA and VVD agreed to support a new Van Agt-cabinet, a small number of

Christian-Democratic MPs voted against the proposed governmental pro-gramme. Instead they announced that they would await the cabinet's concrete policies. Constitutional questions were thus raised as to whether these dissidents were depriving the new government of its razor-thin (77 seats out of 150) majority in parliament. Since these dissidents never actually voted against the government, the issue of the difference between 'parlia-mentary' and 'extra-parliamentary' proved to be moot[11]. Besides, Dutch governments usually enjoy some support from parties outside the coalition as well. On most issues, for example, the small right-wing religious parties will vote for a centre-right government, providing an extra six votes for the present Van Agt coalition.

9.2.3 The Parties

Not all the political parties represented in Parliament are taken into consideration by the architects of government coalitions. In the literature one encounters terms such as coalition- or government potential and *Koalitionsfähigkeit* to identify the relevant parties. De Swaan operationalises coalition potential as having at least 2½ percent of the parliamentary seats – a criterion which he admits to be rather arbitrary[12]. Sartori, on the other hand, asserts that a party can only be shown to have coalition potential when it has actually entered a coalition government[13]. Unfortunately, this touchstone is postdictive (that is, it can only be established *ex post facto*), but it has the ad-vantage of being less arbitrary.

According to Sartori's denotation, the relevant parties for Dutch govern-ment formations up to 1971 were the Catholic Peoples' Party (KVP), the (calvinist) Anti Revolutionary Party (ARP), the (Dutch Reformed) Christian Historical Union (CHU) – these three religious parties now federated into the Christian Democratic Appeal (CDA) –, the Labour Party (PvdA), and the Liberal-Conservatives (VVD), or their pre-war predecessors.

None of these five major parties has ever come close to a majority in Parliament so that coalition government has always been mandatory. The KVP was for a long time and almost without interruption the largest party, and since World War I no government has ever been formed without it. Since the religious parties have to accommodate voters from different social strata belonging to the same church, they almost naturally take a centre position on economic issues. Until 1967, although the three religious parties controlled at least half of the seats in the Second Chamber, they generally have preferred not to govern on their own. The numerical dominance of the religious parties has been strengthened by the fact that PvdA and VVD, which can be positioned left and right of the religious parties respectively, refuse to co-operate with one another in government coalitions. The VVD first publicly precluded a coalition in which the Social Democrats would also take part in 1959, and the PvdA soon reciprocated this gesture.

9.3 Explanations

9.3.1 A Game-Theoretical Explanation

Two bodies of theory may be used to help explain how governments are formed in the Netherlands – coalition-theory and the theory of consociational democracy.

Having confronted game-theoretical coalition theories with actual cabinet formations in a number of countries De Swaan reports that 'on the whole, the theories that have shown good overall test results achieve very good results for the Netherlands'[14]. The best predictor turned out to be 'closed minimal range theory'. This theory holds that, when we order the political parties on a policy scale from left to right, majority coalitions will consist of parties that are adjacent on that scale. (Such a coalition is 'closed', which is to be preferred over a situation in which an opposition party is positioned ideologically between coalition partners, because such a party can play the coalition partners to either side off against each other.) 'Closed minimal range theory' further stipulates that, of all 'closed' majority coalitions possible, the one that spans the shortest distance on the left-right policy scale ('minimal range') will be formed. (This is advantageous because such a 'minimal range' coalition will be ideologically most homogeneous, reducing the chances of intra-coalition conflict.) Using this definition 12 of the 20 majority cabinets that governed the Netherlands between 1918 and 1972 can be classified as 'closed minimal range'[15].

It is interesting to note that 'classical' coalition theories that predict coalitions to be 'minimal winning' perform badly in forecasting the results of Dutch government formations. A 'minimal winning' coalition is one in which no party is included that is not necessary to obtain a parliamentary majority. It would not be rational to add 'extra' parties, since it would mean having to share power with more parties and thus reducing each party's share. Nevertheless, 'there was a clear propensity among Dutch coalition builders to extend the cabinet's support beyond the parties that were numerically necessary for a majority, even if this meant decreasing the number of portfolio's available to each actor that was indeed necessary'[16].

Table 9.1 The compositions of Dutch cabinets, 1946-1978

Date of installation	Prime Minister and coalition parties	Electoral Support	Number of Seats[a]	Relative strength of coalition parties in percentages[b]			
				Electoral	Parliamentary	Ministers	State-Secretaries
07-03-'46	Beel I	59.1%	61	100.0%	100.0%	10 100.0%	inap.
	x KVP	30.8	32	52.1	52.5	6 50.0	
	PvdA	28.3	29	47.9	47.5	6 50.0	
08-07-'48	Drees I	86.9	89	100.0	100.0	15 100.0	inap.
	KVP	31.0	32	35.7	36.0	6 40.0	
	x PvdA	25.6	27	29.5	30.3	5 33.3	
	ARP	13.2	13	15.1	14.6	1 6.6	
	CHU	9.2	9	10.6	10.1	2 13.3	
	VVD	7.9	8	9.1	9.0	1 6.6	
03-13-'51	Drees II	73.7	76	100.0	100.0	16 100.0	5 100.0%
	KVP	31.0	32	42.1	42.1	6 37.5	3 60.0
	x PvdA	25.6	27	34.7	35.5	5 31.3	2 40.0
	CHU	9.2	9	12.5	11.8	4 25.0	
	VVD	7.9	8	10.7	10.5	1 6.3	
09-02-'52	Drees III	77.9	81	100.0	100.0	16 100.0	7 100.0
	KVP	28.7	30	36.8	37.0	6 37.5	3 42.9
	x PvdA	29.0	30	37.2	37.0	5 31.3	4 57.1
	ARP	11.3	12	14.5	14.8	2 12.5	
	CHU	8.9	9	11.4	11.1	3 18.8	
10-13-'56	Drees IV	82.7	85	100.0	100.0	15 100.0	7 100.0
	KVP	31.7	33	38.3	38.8	5 3.3	5 71.4
	x PvdA	32.7	34	39.5	40.0	5 33.3	2 28.6
	ARP	9.9	10	11.9	11.8	2 13.3	
	CHU	8.4	8	10.1	9.4	3 20.0	
12-22-'58	Beel II	50.0	77	100.0	100.0	15 100.0	4 100.0
	x KVP	31.7	49	63.4	63.6	8 53.3	4 100.0
	ARP	9.9	15		19.5	3 20.0	
	CHU	8.4	13	16.8	16.9	4 26.6	
05-19-'59	de Quay	61.3	94	100.0	100.0	13 100.0	11 100.0
	x KVP	31.6	49	51.4	52.1	6 46.2	5 45.4
	ARP	9.4	14	15.3	14.9	2 15.4	1 9.1
CHU		8.1	12	13.8 12.8	2 15.4	3 27.3	
	VVD	12.2	19	19.9	20.2	3 23.0	2 18.2
07-24-'63	Marijnen	59.5	92	100.0	100.0	13 100.0	12 100.0
	x KVP	31.9	50	53.6	54.4	6 46.2	5 41.6
	ARP	8.7	13	14.6	14.1	2 15.4	3 25.0
	CHU	8.6	13	14.5	14.1	2 15.4	2 16.7
	VVD	10.3	16	17.4	17.3	3 23.0	2 16.7

Date	Party								
04-14-'65	Cals	68.6	106	100.0	100.0	14	100.0	13	100.0
	x KVP	31.9	50	46.5	47.2	6	42.9	6	46.2
	PvdA	28.0	43	40.8	40.6	5	35.7	4	30.7
	ARP	8.7	13	12.7	12.2	3	21.4	3	23.1
11-22-'66	Zijlstra	40.6	63	100.0	100.0	14	100.0	8	100.0
	KVP	31.9	50	78.6	79.4	8	57.1	6	75.0
	x ARP	8.7	13	21.4	20.6	6	42.9	2	25.0
04-05-'67	de Jong	55.2	86	100.0	100.0	14	100.0	11	100.0
	x KVP	26.5	42	48.0		6	42.9	4	36.4
	ARP	9.9	15	17.9	17.4	3	21.4	2	18.2
	CHU	8.1	12	14.7	14.0	2	14.3	3	27.3
	VVD	10.7	17	19.4	19.8	3	21.4	2	18.1
07-06-'71	Biesheuvel I	52.5	82	100.0	100.0	16	100.0	13	100.0
	KVP	21.9	35	41.7	42.7	6	37.5	5	38.4
	x ARP	8.6	13	16.4	15.9	3	18.8	2	15.4
	CHU	6.3	10	12.0	12.2	2	12.5	2	15.4
	VVD	10.4	16	19.8	19.5	3	18.8	2	15.4
	DS'70	5.3	8	10.0	9.8	2	12.5	2	15.4
08-09-'72	Biesheuvel II	47.2	74	100.0	100.0	16	100.0	11	100.0
	KVP	21.9	35	46.4	47.3	6	37.4	5	45.4
	x ARP	8.6	13	18.2	17.6	3	18.8	2	18.2
	CHU	6.3	10	13.3	13.5	4	25.0	2	18.2
	VVD	10.4	16	22.0	21.6	3	18.8	2	18.2
05-11-'73	den Uyl	62.9	97	100.0	100.0	16	100.0	17	100.0
	KVP	17.7	27	28.1	27.8	4	25.0	6	35.3
	x PvdA	27.4	43	43.6	44.3	7	43.7	5	29.4
	ARP	8.8	14	14.0	14.4	2	12.5	2	11.8
	D'66	4.2	6	6.7	6.2	1	6.3	3	17.6
	PPR	4.8	7	7.6		2	12.5	1	5.9
12-19-'78	van Agt	49.9	77	100.0	100.0	16	100.0	16	100.0
	x CDA	31.9	49	63.9	63.6	10	62.5	10	62.5
	VVD	18.0	28	36.1	36.4	6	37.5	6	37.5

x Indicates party of Prime Minister.

a) The Second Chamber of Parliament consisted of 100 seats until 1956 and of 150 seats since t
b) Non-partisan Ministers are not included in the percentage base. Only the Beel I, Drees I, and
Drees III cabinets contained non-partisan Ministers (Beel I 4; Drees I 1; and Drees III 1).

From Table 9.1 it is clear that the average support on which a cabinet could count both among the electorate and, more importantly, in parliament, is far from minimal[17]. De Swaan's explanation for this seemingly non-rational behaviour is again game-theoretical; the Catholic party (KVP, now part of the CDA) has always occupied the centre of the Dutch political spectrum – a comfortable, and above all pivotal position, enabling it to play the parties to its left and to its right off against each other. This has ensured the Catholics' uninterrupted participation in all governments since 1918. When the KVP would enter a government with, for example, one or more parties on its right, it would find itself on the extreme left within such a coalition. De Swaan argues that, in order to extend the advantage of being in the centre and holding the balance into the cabinet, it was sometimes necessary for the KVP to insist on adding 'unnecessary' parties to the coalition. However, this hypothesis does not explain why the Catholics have preferred large coalitions, including at least one of the secular parties, over smaller coalitions with one of the Protestant parties to the right, and the other to its left.

Another explanation for the more-than-minimal size of many Dutch government coalitions is that coalition parties not only share benefits, but also share costs – a feature that is somewhat neglected in the game-theoretical models. As we have seen, the theory of 'minimal winning' coalitions rests on the assumption that the parties want to share power with as few coalition partners as possible. Parties in a government coalition do not only share power, but also responsiblility, and they may be less anxious about letting extra parties share in their responsibility. Having to share the benefits may cause the parties to restrict participation in government to those that are necessary to obtain a majority, but having to share the costs might prompt more extensive coalitions. It is common practice in Dutch electoral campaigns for a party to claim all the credit for the popular policies and the successes while putting all the blame for the failures and unpopular measures on the coalition partners.

9.3.2 The Politics of Accommodation

The Dutch predisposition towards large coalitions (albeit not 'grand coalitions' including all major parties) can also be accounted for by the exigencies of the politics of accommodation.

Only a decade ago, the Netherlands was still a strongly segmented society, divided into four subcultures – a Protestant, a Catholic, a socialist, and a liberal one – rather hostile towards and isolated from one another. Each sub-culture had its own organisational infrastructure with the main parties acting as the political branches of these organisational 'pillars' (*zuilen*). Pillarisation (*verzuiling*) was prevented from destabilizing Dutch society through co-operation between the leaders of the pillars. Lijphart has formulated a number of 'rules of the game' that seem to have governed this process of elite accommodation: depoliticisation and a business-like approach to politics, tolerance, summit diplomacy, secrecy, proportionality, and a considerable degree of restraint on the part of parliament in dealings with the government[18]. This last rule is highlighted by the constitutional provision, discussed above, that Ministers cannot be members of parliament at the same time.

The cabinet-formation process, epitomising elite co-operation in a segmented society, is clearly moulded by these standards for political behaviour. Even after hotly contested elections the leaders always sat down together in secret meetings to build a new coalition. Burning issues were reduced to technical problems, delegated to *ad-hoc* committees of 'wise men', or simply postponed – 'iceboxed' as this last practice is known. Respect for the other party's convictions ran so deep that coalition partners have occasionally 'agreed to disagree': when a prospective coalition partner was unable to concede on a given issue, it was sometimes allowed 'to fall out of the boat' – to vote against the government on that issue – without risking a cabinet crisis. Conflicts concerning the distribution of cabinet positions were avoided by extending the principles of proportional representation from the elections into the government; each coalition-partner's share of the seats was determined by its parliamentary strength relative to the other partners (see Table 9.1). Occasionally, the number of Ministers and State-Secretaries has actually been expanded to permit a proportional apportionment of positions. It is evident that cabinet formations in the Netherlands have been prime examples of elite co-operation in a segmented society. There is no gainsaying that elite accommodation and the construction of 'concurrent majorities' is greatly facilitated when most of the pillars are represented in the government itself. Hence the more-than-minimal size of so many Dutch government coalitions.

9.4 Recent developments

9.4.1 Social Change

The late sixties and early seventies have been turbulent years throughout the Western world, but in Holland the commotion was not confined to occasional riots and campus turmoil. The whole fabric of pillarisation started to come apart. People no longer took it for granted that they should be confined to their own segment of society from cradle to grave. As has been described at length in the previous chapter, depillarisation (*ontzuiling*) profoundly upset the hitherto stable patterns of voting behaviour. The proportions of Protestants voting for either ARP or CHU and of Catholics voting KVP declined sharply, and the secular parties did not remain unscathed. The ranks of floating voters subsequently swelled and a number of new parties profited in proportion.

The widespread electoral dealignment was accompanied by a waning of deference towards those in authority and a growing interest in more participatory forms of democracy. Again, this was not an exclusively Dutch phenomenon; even before the students started to march, Dahl had warned that the modern welfare state, the 'Democratic Leviathan', was susceptible to opposition from young intellectuals because 'in their view, it is not democratic enough: this new Leviathan is too remote and bureaucratized, too addicted to bargaining and compromise, too much an instrument of political elites and technicians with whom they feel slight identification'[19]. Dahl was writing about Western democracies in general, but his words seem particularly applicable to the Dutch case. In this wake of neo-democratic interest the elitist politics of accommodation, with its secrecy, its depoliticisation, and its indifference to the masses, could not but evoke protest and calls for reform. Being of central importance in Dutch politics, government formations could not fail to be affected by depillarisation and attempts at democratisation.

9.4.2 The Effects of Depillarisation

As noted above, new parties flourished at the expense of the traditional Big Five, whose share of the vote dropped from 92 percent in 1959 to a relatively meagre 73 percent in 1972. Although many of the new entrants never had any coalition potential, some have even been involved in government coalitions. In 1971 DS'70, a one-year old party of rather conservative former Social Democrats, joined the three religious parties and the Conservative Liberals in a short-lived coalition. In the 1973-1977 Den Uyl-government two of the newer parties participated: the PPR, a leftist party founded by ex-members of the KVP and ARP, and Democrats '66, (D'66), a progressive-liberal party set up to press for political reform. D'66 also took part in the abortive negotiations between PvdA and the federation of the three religious parties, CDA, in 1977. Although the present Van Agt-coalition does not contain any Ministers from the smaller parties, an unprecedented formal attempt was made to enlist the support of these parties. We may conclude that, even though the 1977 elections reduced the importance of most of the newer parties, government formations are no longer a private affair of the traditional major parties.

A second effect of depillarisation has been the erosion of electoral support for the religious parties. Not only did the number of religious persons diminish, but those remaining in the churches began to turn away from the religious parties, eventually stimulating the merger of KVP, ARP and CHU into the CDA. As noted above, the Christian Democrats lost their majority in Parliament in 1967[20], and one might expect that such a dramatic loss of support would have reduced the central role in coalition-building that the Christian-Democrats and especially the Catholics, had hitherto played. However, because the Social Democrats and the Conservative Liberals have excluded each other from coalition partnership since the beginning of the sixties, the Christian Democrats are still needed to procure a parliamentary majority for any cabinet. Thus they continue to enjoy their pivotal position in government formations, despite their heavy losses.

One of the most important effects of depillarisation results from the increase in the number of floating voters, in that the parties can no longer rely on a loyal constituency to turn up at the polls, particularly following the abolition of compulsory voting in 1970. The parties had previously regarded elections as 'awkward interruptions of their daily affairs'[21], but now election campaigns became serious fights for votes instead of rather folkloric rituals. In two-party electoral contests, the parties try to capture the middle ground because a vote won in the centre is also a vote lost for the competition. Such parties do not have to worry about the voters on the extremes, because they have nowhere else to go, there being in general more voters in the centre than on the extremes anyway. However, in a multi-party system such as the Dutch one, there is no sense in competing centripetally. The distribution of the voters along the left-right scale, is seldom single-moded in a multi-party system; there are usually several modes. Hence a party does not necessarily find more voters in the centre. Besides, the parties cannot neglect their extreme voters because all of the parties, except two, must face competition on that flank as well. As Downs pointed out, in order to maximize votes 'parties in a two-party system deliberately change their platforms so that they resemble one another; whereas parties in a multi-party system try to remain as ideologically distinct as possible'[22]. The consequent polarisation may be an electoral necessity, but as no party even comes close to a majority, the parties still have to co-operate after the elections in order to form a government. During the era of pillarisation the voters were loyal enough to make too much polarisation unnecessary, and deferential enough to accept post-election compromises. Today they are neither loyal nor deferential, and the subsequent incompatibility between centrifugal forces before and centripetal forces after the elections has brought the government-formation process under considerable stress.

9.4.3 Calls for Reform

Cabinet formations, threatened by the centrifugality of heated electoral competition, have come under fire from neo-democrats as well. These critics note that the Dutch political system not only falls short of the 'classical' ideal of participatory democracy, but it does not even meet the standards of 'revisionist' democracy, which is, in Schumpeter's famous definition 'that institutional arrangement for arriving at political decisions in which individuals acquire the power to decide by means of a competitive struggle for the people's vote'[23]. In Holland, however, there is only a tenuous link between elections and government selection. This is best illustrated by the fact that on occasion in the past the governing coalition has been radically altered without resort to new elections. On the basis of the 1963 general election, for example, a government consisting of the three religious parties and the VVD was formed. When this coalition broke up in 1965, due to disagreement about a reorganisation of the broadcasting system, a new cabinet was constituted comprising KVP, ARP, and the Social Democrats. In 1966, this government lost its majority when one of its participants, the KVP, sided with the opposition in denouncing a budget deficit. A third government containing only KVP and ARP then served as an 'interim-cabinet' until the general election of 1967. The timing of these reshufflings could not have been better suited to the cause of the neo-democrats. The dismantling of old and compilation of new coalitions regardless of election results epitomised the unresponsiveness of government formations, and, in the words of Gladdish, became 'a kind of Gethsemane in the litany of the evils of the system'[24]. The numerous suggestions for reform that have been put forth in an attempt to make the Dutch system of government more responsive, can be roughly divided into three groups.

The first strand of reform-plans involved technical constitutional changes[25]. Most of these originated from the ranks of D'66, a party founded with the express purpose of 'exploding' the existing political structure. Their most drastic proposal called for a separate election for the office of Prime Minister, akin to U.S. presidential elections and terminating the mutual dependency of government and parliament. D'66 made a tremendous impact, not only electorally – 7 seats in the 1967 election meant a landslide – but it also prompted the institution of a Government Advisory Commission on Constitutional and Electoral Law. This Cals-Donner Commission, named after its two chairmen, advised against an elected Prime Minister for the very reason that this would in effect replace the present parliamentary system with a presidential one. Albeit not unanimously, the Commission did recommend the institution of a separate election for *formateur* to be held concurrently with parliamentary elections. However, if no candidate won an absolute majority of the votes, the existing procedure would remain in effect[26]. Through these elections for *formateur* the electorate would be given an opportunity to influence the government formation, and the parties would be stimulated to combine forces with other parties in order to nominate a joint candidate who would stand a better chance of winning. Such pre-election coalitions would counter the present centrifugal tendencies of polarisation and give the voters an even greater say in government selection.

A second line of thinking about political reforms, inspired more by the British than by the American political system, stressed the need for pre-election coalitions irrespective of constitutional change. A leading social-democratic politician, Ed van Thijn, argued that, because of the multitude of political parties, the displeasure of the voters is not channeled into 'turning the rascals out', and opposition votes are fanning out over many parties. In such a system, according to Van Thijn, an inherent tendency exists for the extremes to grow at the expense of the centre, until the centre is crushed between extremist anti-system parties. To avoid such a show-down he advised a remodelling of the party-system along the lines of the British one, in which the pendulum of power could freely swing back and forth between two parties according to the electorate's preference. Since in Holland there are more than two parties, the existing parties ought to form blocs or pre-election coalitions, so as to offer the voter a clear choice between two competing alternatives. It was hoped that eventually these blocs would transform themselves into parties[27].

Finally, a third approach to the problem of government unresponsiveness concerned the outcomes in terms of policy. Like the other types of reform proposals, this too arose in one of the leftist parties. A group of young intellectuals within the PvdA, 'New Left', argued that coalition politics had proven to be unsuccessful in changing the socio-economic structure, and that it had diluted the working-class image of the party, thus blurring a clear choice for a leftist policy by the voters. A new emphasis on party ideology was needed, stressing issues such as nationalisation, workers' councils, development aid, etc[28]. In other words, their remedy was to increase polarisation and politicisation. After the elections the party should stick to its guns, preferring the opposition benches or a minority cabinet to murky compromises in coalition-formations[29].

9.4.4 The Results

The other political parties never showed much interest in the nostrums for government unresponsiveness proposed by the Left. The Cals-Donner Commission's recommendations have been shelved and never acted upon. In 1970, D'66, together with PvdA and PPR, introduced a parliamentary initiative pertaining, among other things, to the institution of an elected Prime Minister. They found little support outside their own ranks, and the initiative was defeated. In 1974 the Den Uyl-government submitted the proposal once again as a white paper, but this attempt was ill-fated as well[30]. A more lasting result of the 1963-1967 cabinet formations and the subsequent calls for constitutional reform, has been the tacit acceptance of an unwritten rule that, whenever a coalition breaks up, irrespective of whether this is due to a rift within the government or a conflict with Parliament, new general elections must be called.

Meanwhile, within the PvdA, the 'New Left'-movement succeeded in gradually taking over most of the positions of the old party elite, and many of their policy proposals were written into the party platform. At the same time, negotiations had begun to create a leftist pre-election coalition following Van Thijn's recommendation mentioned above. In the 1971 election campaign, PvdA, D'66 and PPR presented a shadow-cabinet, but they fell no less than 24 seats short of a parliamentary majority. They did not want to negotiate with the Christian Democrats, however, and because the religious parties did not command a majority even together with the VVD, the débutant DS'70 was asked to join the coalition. This coalition soon foundered because of disagreements between DS'70 and the other parties, and new elections had to be called according to the new rule banning partner exchange in between elections.

In the 1972 election campaign the three leftist parties continued their electoral coalition with an elaborate programme ('Turning Point '72') and the promise not to bargain about this programme after the elections. The outcome of the 1972 elections made the formation of a new cabinet look like 'mission impossible'; the leftist combination was still far from a majority and refused to govern with the Christian Democrats unless the latter would fully endorse the leftist election platform. The Christian Democrats' electoral losses had not been sufficiently offset by VVD-gains to create a majority for this combination, and there was no point in calling back DS'70, since this party had caused the rift in the previous coalition. Ultimately, after an unprecedentedly long interregnum (163 days), a new cabinet was sworn in. The solution of the seemingly complete deadlock was provided primarily by *formateur* Burger (PvdA) who managed to convince the leftist alliance that some bargaining was indeed necessary despite electoral promises. Moreover, he succeeded in enlisting the support of two prominent ARP-politicians who agreed to accept Ministerial posts without the consent of their parliamentary party. Although 'Burger's burglary', as this last move became known, was to leave deep scars in the Christian Democrats' pride, it did lead to the formation of the Den Uyl-government, consisting of the leftist combination and members of ARP and KVP. The government programme was a deliberately vague formula, stipulating that in case of incompatibility between the leftist and christian-democratic platforms, the conclusions of the *formateur* would prevail. The KVP and ARP did not wholeheartedly support the new cabinet, but agreed to 'suffer' it; the third religious party, CHU, joined the Conservative Liberals in the opposition[31]. Despite its laborious birth the Den Uyl-government did serve a full four-year term. A cabinet crisis occurred in March 1977, but since elections had already been called for the following May, this conflict merely signaled an early start of the election campaign.

In 1977, the leftist parties did abandon their pre-election coalition strategy. D'66 had suffered heavy losses, probably because the close alliance with the Social Democrats had resulted in a loss of identity. In order to survive, the party returned to the sound Downsian multi-party strategy of emphasizing its ideological distinctiveness. The PPR also left the alliance because after the March-crisis it ruled out a future coalition with the Christian Democrats. The PvdA recognised that it would have to bargain with the newly formed CDA in order to prolong Den Uyl as Prime Minister, but on the other hand, the Social Democrats still clung to their reform aspirations. To ensure that the voters would be able to influence government selection and to recognize themselves in the end result, the PvdA developed its so called 'majority strategy'. According to this plan, the Social Democrats would participate in a new government only if they were to occupy at least half of the cabinet positions, including the office of Prime Minister. Besides, the PvdA would enter coalition-formation negotiations only if the party gained seats and came out of the elections with more seats in parliament than the Christian Democrats. This 'majority strategy' was presented as a last endeavour to make the government-formation process more responsive. A voter for the PvdA could know in advance what the party planned to do with his or her vote – a coalition with the CDA in which the Social Democrats were to have a slight edge, thus more or less ensuring continuation of the Den Uyl-government's policies. The CDA refused to leave its comfortable centre position and did not explicitly state a preference for either PvdA or VVD. It would not have been rational for them to do so, since any sign of preference for the left might have cost them votes on the right and vice versa. The PvdA's 'majority strategy' was interpreted by the Christian Democrats as a sign of distrust; moreover, it added to the frustrations of both Burger's burglary and of having had to play, in their view, second fiddle to the leftists during Den Uyl's reign.

The May 1977 elections gave the PvdA a landslide 10-seat gain and a 4-seat lead over the Christian Democrats, whose CDA-merger apparently had stopped a series of heavy losses. The outcome of the election was generally interpreted as indicating a popular preference for a second Den Uyl-government, and it was expected that a short interregnum would suffice to put such a coalition together. No one expected at that time that the negotiations would be of record length and result in a centre-right cabinet rather than a centre left coalition. The talks between the Christian Democrats and PvdA and D'66 stalled repeatedly and ultimately broke down completely. The CDA demanded a proportional distribution of seats in the new cabinet, amounting to equal representation for PvdA and CDA, the office of Prime Minister being, in their opinion, sufficient reward for the Socialists' extra four seats. The PvdA, however, stuck to its 'majority strategy' in order to translate its electoral victory into the new government's composition. Against the express wishes of the CDA, *formateur* Den Uyl decided to first negotiate a government programme before tackling the apportionment of positions. However, the widely publicised arduous programme negotiations did anything but mellow the Christian Democrats, and when the distribution of seats was finally put on the agenda, it was the PvdA that eventually had to consent to a 7-7-2 arrangement (seven Ministers for the PvdA, including the Prime Minister, seven Ministers for the CDA, and two for D'66). This turned out to be totally unacceptable to the PvdA's left-wingers, who occupy important positions in the Party Executive and Party Council. A special PvdA Party Congress was called to resolve the conflict between the leftist Party Council opposing the 7-7-2 arrangement and the moderate parliamentary party that approved of the deal. In the meantime, Den Uyl as *formateur* tried to appease the upcoming Party Congress by finding suitably 'leftist' Christian-Democratic candidates for Ministerial posts. The CDA did not take kindly to the PvdA taking its nominees' measure, especially because its select list of candidates already was a precarious compromise between the federation's constituent parties. Intransigence on both sides about one candidate led to the final break-down. For the Conservative Liberals this conflict came as an unexpected windfall, and they readily accepted most of the CDA proposals. The CDA-VVD negotiations were once again held in secret, and the seats were apportioned proportionately[32].

9.4.5 *Voters Propose, Politicians Dispose*

We have described these recent government formations rather extensively because they vividly illustrate the current predicament of coalition building in the Netherlands. The results of the drive for constitutional reform have been meagre indeed. The other efforts to provide the voter with influence in government have been watered down from a shadow cabinet, via an unkept promise not to bargain, to the 'majority strategy'. None of these panaceas has actually worked and has only succeeded in further encumbering the government-formation process, already under considerable stress because of increased electoral polarisation.

The most recent government formation has been aptly likened to a match between a soccer team and a rugby team. Both sides play the ball, but they do so according to widely differing sets of rules. In 1977 the PvdA tried to play by the rules of 'Schumpeterian' democracy; their election posters read: 'Elect the Prime Minister, vote for Den Uyl', and they vowed to enter a coalition with the CDA only under specified conditions. The CDA, on the other hand, observed different rules of the game, those of the politics of accommodation in which tolerance, proportionality, and depoliticisation are important, rather than the responsiveness of government formations.

For one party to reject the old rules of the politics of accommodation and to embrace the new ones of responsive democracy, as the PvdA has done, is equivalent to disqualification in a system in which no party can govern on its own. True, the Christian Democrats have also adhered less strictly to Lijphart's rules. In the last government formation, for example, they have deliberately politicised the abortion-issue, while the old rules would have called for postponement or devolution of this delicate problem to some special commission. However, the CDA can afford deviations from the rules, since as long as PvdA and VVD continue to exclude each other, the Christian Democrats will be needed to furnish the votes necessary for a parliamentary majority. To stay within our sports metaphor, the present role of the CDA is the uncommon one of a playing referee.

9.4.6 *Duration*

One of the symptoms of the stress brought upon the government formations by electoral polarisation and the attempts at reform, is undoubtedly the increased longevity of recent formations. However, even though 163 and 207 days are extraordinary to Dutch standards as well, long interregnums are a common feature of Dutch politics.

Table 9.2 Number of days a Dutch cabinet was *demissionair* because of:

year	a. elections	b. crises between elections	
1918	68		
1922	75		
1923		73	
1925	34		
1925		117	
1929	38		
1933	30		
1935		6	
1937	29		
1939		26	
1939		14	
pre-war total:	274	236	(510)
1946	47		
1948	31		
1951		50	
1952	69		
1955		16	
1956	122		
1958		10	
1959	68		
1960		10	
1963	70		
1965		46	
1966		38	
1967	49		
1971	69		
1972		23	
1972	163		
1977		65	
1977	207		
post-war total:	895	258	(1153)
Total 1918-1977:	1169	494	(1663)

Source: G. Kuypers, *Het politieke spel in Nederland*, Meppel, 1967 and own additions.

Dutch government formations have always taken considerably longer than in most other countries that are governed by coalitions. One reason for the long formations is that Dutch government coalitions tend to comprise more parties than those in other countries. It would seem logical that negotiations between 5 parties would take longer than between 2 parties, as for example in West Germany. Another time-consuming factor in Dutch government formations is the tendency to formulate very elaborate government programmes, covering as many contingencies as possible. In many other countries the emphasis in the formation negotiations is on the distribution of cabinet positions rather than on policy plans[33]. As much as possible, political conflicts between coalition partners are taken care of before, not during, their joint reign. For these reasons, most Dutchmen would probably agree with Gladdish, who noted that 'these delays are scarcely a pathological feature, since the system depends upon the patient reconciliation of the ambitions of a number of minority parties; and they do not connote the kind of government instability associated with the French Fourth Republic'[34]. Moreover, once they are formed, Dutch governments tend to be remarkably stable. Between 1884 and 1967, Holland was governed by the same number of governments as Britain (28), which compares favourably with other coalition-governed countries such as France or Italy, or even Belgium.

Nevertheless, recent cabinet formations have taken disquietingly longer than previously, and this trend deserves serious consideration. If we average the duration of the interregnums over all years between the First and Second World War, Holland was ruled by a caretaker government for an average of 23 days a year because of formation negotiations. Even if we assume that the Van Agt-government will serve a full four-year term, this average is now more than a month per year (33 days) for the Post-war period. From Table 9.2 it is evident that the most recent cabinet formations have contributed disproportionately to this increase. If we confine ourselves to the last interregnum – the longest yet – we may well ask whether these 207 days are due to specific but accidental circumstances, or whether they reflect some ongoing development.

There are indeed a number of 'coincidences' that may account for some of the delay. For example, finding a compromise on abortion took considerable time. The issue was not new on the agenda, but several attempts to pass new legislation to regulate this emotional problem had foundered. The CDA, and particularly its leader, Van Agt, had championed the anti-abortion cause, while PvdA and VVD formed an *ad-hoc* coalition in favour of liberalisation of abortion. As abortion is a matter of ethics rather than of politics, it is extremely difficult to find a common ground between the two opposing sides. Thus the final PvdA-CDA compromise, reached only after tedious negotiations and later adopted by the CDA-VVD government, was procedural rather than substantive[35]. More important than the delicate problem of abortion, however, was the psychological climate in which the negotiations took place. After the difficult government formation in 1972 and a long series of collisions during the Den Uyl-government, CDA and PvdA no longer fully trusted each other. CDA-leader Van Agt, who professes to dislike politics, and his PvdA counterpart Den Uyl, who relishes it, were constantly looking askance at each other, reading and rereading all the small print, constantly on the alert for hidden traps. This atmosphere of suspicion and distrust necessitated a fairly comprehensive government programme and substantially slackened the pace of the negotiations. Finally, two other factors responsible for some of the 207 days delay have already been mentioned in another context – the incompatibility between the PvdA's 'majority strategy' on the one hand, and the CDA's adherence to the old rules of the game on the other hand, and the federal nature of the CDA, making it mandatory to have time-consuming 'shadow formation' negotiations between KVP, ARP and CHU.

In spite of the wide array of accidental causes that may well be unique to the 1977 interregnum, we would argue that the extraordinary length of the last government formation is not entirely coincidental. The increased number of floating voters and of people who decide what to vote, if to vote at all, only on the spur of the moment, will continue to necessitate fierce electoral competition and polarisation. After the election, the parties cannot be too eager in making concessions on their electoral promises without even putting up a fight. Long formations may be necessary for the parties to save credibility, and, in the long run, to save votes.

It is also unlikely that the long established trend towards more openness and greater responsiveness of the principal negotiators vis-à-vis their own parties will be reversed. Since Ruys de Beerenbrouck first asked for the approval of the formation results by the parliamentary parties in 1922, the influence of the MPs has grown to such an extent that today the parliamentary leaders of most parties are mere agents of their party's MPs. In some parties the party chairman and members of other party organisations have become active participants. At the same time the smoke-filled rooms in which the 'King-makers' of the past conducted their secret negotiations, have been replaced with glaring television lights, interviews, and instant publication of every compromise and disagreement. That intra-party consultations take time goes without saying, but publicity too can be the cause of considerable lag. When a negotiator appears on radio or television, he will address both his opponents and his own constituency at he same time, prompting him to speak more simplistically and belligerently than he would normally do at the conference table. However, once a politician has dug in his heels in front of the television cameras, concessions could easily result in a loss of face. The subsequent inflexibility is exacerbated by the fact that ordinarily a new government programme is negotiated stepwise rather than as a package deal. Every partial agreement is publicised and comment- ed upon; winners and losers are pointed out. This causes the negotiators to seek compensation for their ascribed losses in the next 'round' by being even more intransigent. In other words, today's instant publicity carries the polarisation from the elections over into the government formations, resulting in ever more difficult and time-consuming negotiations. True, the CDA-VVD negotiations were conducted fairly swiftly and in almost total concealment, but it is highly unlikely that the negotiators could have neglect- ed the press, the public, and their own parties, to the same extent, had their negotiations taken place immediately after the elections and without the hangover of 163 days wasted in trying to put together a centre-left coalition.

On the basis of these factors (polarised electoral competition, increased openness and intra-party responsiveness), we would argue that future government formations may very well take long, even though the 207 days of 1977 may remain unmatched for some time.

9.5 Summary and prospect

As long as no party or bloc of parties succeeds in winning a majority in Parlia- ment, coalition governments and cabinet formations will remain central features of Dutch politics. The procedures and outcomes of Dutch govern- ment formations do not differ much from those in other polities ruled by coalition, but they do have a special flavour, the flavour of the politics of accommodation. This is evident in the mutual respect the parties have for each other's convictions and in their adherence to the principle of proportionality in most policy decisions. The Dutch penchant for slightly over-sized coalitions may also be explained by the exigencies of elite co- operation in a segmented society.

Depillarisation has profoundly rocked the stable boat of the politics of accommodation. Swelling numbers of floating voters have prompted the parties to more electoral competition and polarisation, which has impeded post-election co-operation and government formation. At the same time neo-democratic criticism of the rather elitist politics of accommodation has resulted in a number of reform proposals directed at a more responsive way of government selection than the secretive cabinet formations. None of these proposals has been successful and the efforts of the leftist parties to offer the voters a clear choice by, among other things, refusing to bargain after the elections, have only resulted in putting the government formation process under more stress. One of the symptoms of this stress is the increased longevity of recent cabinet formations, culminating in the 207 days interregnum of 1977. Although many accidental factors have contributed to this latest record, increased electoral competition and openness of the formation process can be expected to slow down the compilation of future coalitions as well.

The most interesting question about the future of Dutch government formations is whether the PvdA and VVD will stop barring one another from co-operation in government. On ethical or life-style issues, the two parties are often in agreement, with the Christian Democrats opposing most efforts at liberalisation of abortion, pornography, etc. On most socio-economic issues, however, the two parties have widely divergent views, with the CDA somewhere in between. There have been a few signs of an improving relationship between the Socialists and the Conservative Liberals. The two parties apparently enjoyed working together on a joint parliamentary initiative to liberalise abortion (which was defeated in the First Chamber). During the 1977 interregnum the VVD repeatedly recommended the formation of a 'national government' consisting of CDA, PvdA, and VVD, which would have brought an end to the latter parties' mutual exclusion. In the aftermath of the installation of the Van Agt-government, members of both PvdA and VVD have balked at their 'obligatory mating' with the CDA that is the consequence of precluding a PvdA-VVD government. In 1979, it was discovered that leading politicians from PvdA, VVD and D'66 were regularly and secretly meeting in a hotel in The Hague to discuss the possibilities of future co-operation. After the 1978 local elections a few municipalities have instituted PvdA-VVD administrations, but whether these local coalitions are the harbingers of co-operation on the national level still remains to be seen. We might add though, that the co-operation of KVP, ARP, and CHU also started in local and provincial governments and gained such momentum that the national federation into the CDA could no longer be stopped. If the Dutch Social Democrats and Conservative Liberals were to follow the example of their Danish colleagues[36], coalition politics in the Netherlands would become a different ballgame altogether. The Christian Democrats would be forced out of their luxurious centre position and into the opposition. They would no longer be able to determine the rules of the game and the CDA would become 'just another party'.

At the moment, the prospects for such a PvdA-VVD coalition are still dim, but if it ever comes about, the practical and theoretical consequences will be great, and a thorough revision of this chapter would be in order.

* We are indebted to Galen Irwin, Hans Daalder, Peter Mair, Geoffrey Roberts and Paul Schoemaker for their valuable comments and suggestions regarding both substance and grammar.
[1] A few caveats are in order, since very few (if any) 'pure' two-party systems actually exist. Sometimes third parties in what, for all practical purposes, has always been considered a two-party system, come to be the tail that wags the dog (e.g. the 'Lib-Lab Pact' in Britain). Sometimes the electoral system distorts the popular vote to such an extent that the party with most of the votes gets fewer seats and is unable to form a government (e.g. Britain in 1951 and in 1974).
[2] Our condensed translation of Romme as cited in H. Daalder (ed.), Parlement en Politieke Besluit-vorming in Nederland, Alphen aan den Rijn, 1975, p. 28.
[3] H.A. van Wijnen, Van de Macht des Konings, Amsterdam, 1975, pp. 51-59. Cf. J.F. Lachaume, 'Le Rôle du Chef d'Etat dans les Monarchies Parlementaires d'Ajourd'hui', Politique, vol. 41, 1968, p. 87 seq.
[4] Article 86 of the Constitution.
[5] Hermerén, in a study of such appointments in Belgium, Denmark, Finland, Norway, Sweden, and the Netherlands found that the appointment of someone from a smaller party can usually be explained by that party's greater potential for co-operation. See H. Hermerén, 'Government Formation in Multiparty Systems', Scandinavian Political Studies, vol. 11, 1976, pp. 131-146.
[6] The office of informateur was first instituted in 1951 when a conflict between the VVD parliamentary party and its own Minister of Foreign Affairs, Stikker, led to a cabinet crisis. According to the informal rule 'qui casse paie', Stikker was called upon to form a new cabinet, but because of the conflict with his own party he did not want to become formateur. For these purely tactical reasons he was appointed the first informateur. In the cumbersome cabinet formation of 1956, informateurs first performed the same tasks they have now. See G. Ringnalda, 'De Kabinetsformatie', in A. Hoogerwerf (ed.), Verkenningen in de Politiek I, Alphen aan den Rijn, 1971, pp. 139-140.
[7] For a description of past government formations, see: G. Ringnalda, idem, pp. 132-158; F.J.M.F. Duynstee, De Kabinetsformaties 1946-1965, Deventer, 1966; H. Gruyters and J.J. Vis, 29-11-'72, Verkiezingen, Utrecht, 1972, ch. 3.
[8] See H. Hermerén, op. cit., pp. 137-140. The Dutch procedure seems to deviate only with respect to the office of informateur, unknown in other countries except Belgium, and with regard to the fact that in other countries the head of state sometimes specifies the political parties from which a cabinet is to be formed, whereas in the Netherlands some standard formula, asking the formateur to form a government that is supported by parliament, is used.
[9] Dutch constitutional law does not require a formal vote of confidence.
[10] Article 106 of the Constitution stipulates that a Minister can remain a member of Parliament for three months after election. This provision can be of some importance in cabinet formations that take longer than three months, since it may cause politicians who head a Department in the outgoing cabinet to choose between their cabinet position and the negotiation table.
[11] This does not mean that the dissidents have always supported the government. In 1980 a

number of dissidents supported a motion of the opposition calling on the government to resist the stationing of nuclear weapons on Dutch soil. However, when the government later threatened to resign rather than execute this policy, the dissidents soon joined the government in order to prevent a cabinet crisis.

[12] A. de Swaan, *Coalition Theories and Cabinet Formations; a study of formal theories of coalition formation applied to nine European parliaments after 1918*, Amsterdam, 1973, p. 131.

[13] G. Sartori, *Parties and Party Systems; a framework for analysis; Vol. I*, Cambridge, 1976, pp. 122-123.

[14] A. de Swaan, *op. cit.*, p. 226. For a comparative perspective on coalition formations, see also S. Groennings et. al. (ed.), *The Study of Coalition Behavior; theoretical perspectives and cases from four continents*, New York, 1970, and L.C. Dodd, *Coalitions in Parliamentary Government*, Princeton, 1976. This latter study also contains references to Dutch coalition politics and an extensive bibliography.

[15] *Ibid.*, p. 225.

[16] *Ibid.*, p. 226. See also H. Daalder, 'Cabinets and party systems in ten smaller European democracies', *Acta Politica*, vol. 6, 1971, p. 289.

[17] We would like to thank the computerised archive of the Parliamentary Documentation Centre in The Hague, and particularly N. Cramer jr., for giving us access to these figures.

[18] A. Lijphart, *The Politics of Accommodation; Pluralism and Democracy in the Netherlands*, (second edition), Berkely, 1975, ch. 7. Of course we do not only borrow these 'rules of the game' from Lijphart, but rather our entire description of pillarisation and elite accommodation.

[19] R.A. Dahl (ed.), *Political Oppositions in Western Democracies*, New Haven, 1966, p. 400. See also A. Lijphart, 'Kentering in de Nederlandse Politiek', *Acta Politica*, vol. 4, 1968-1969, pp. 238-243.

[20] KVP, ARP and CHU had an absolute majority of the seats until 1967, except for the 1959-1963 period, when they commanded exactly 50 percent (75 seats) of the seats in the Second Chamber.

[21] E. van Thijn, 'Een Moderne Verkiezingscampagne', *Socialisme & Democratie*, 1966, p. 707 (our translation).

[22] A. Downs, *An Economic Theory of Democracy*, New York, 1957, p. 115.

[23] J.A. Schumpeter, *Capitalism, Socialism and Democracy*, New York, 1947, p. 269.

[24] K.R. Gladdish, 'Two-Party vs. Multi-Party, The Netherlands and Britain', *Acta Politica*, vol. 7, 1972, p. 344.

[25] In this paragraph we confine ourselves to proposals aimed directly at reforming the government selction process. Actually these plans were combined with suggestions for changes in the electoral system. Plants to institute a multi-member district system and to introduce a higher electoral threshold were discussed. These proposals were aimed at a reduction in the number of parties represented in parliament which was believed to simplify the voters' choice and to facilitate the cabinet formation process. See H. Daalder, 'Extreme Proportional Representation: The Dutch Experience' in S.E. Finer (ed.), *Adversary Politics and Electoral Reform*, 1975, London, pp. 242-246.

[26] *Staatscommissie van Advies inzake de Grondwet en de Kieswet, Eerste Rapport*, 1968; *Tweede Rapport*, 1969; *Eindrapport*, 1971, The Hague.

[27] E. van Thijn, 'Van Partijen naar Stembusaccoorden', in E. Jurgens et. al., *Partijvernieuwing? Open Brief 2*, Amsterdam, 1967, pp. 54-73.

[28] See for example H. van den Doel et. al., *Tien over Rood: uitdaging van Nieuw Links aan de PvdA*, Amsterdam, 1966.

[29] In 1969 for example, New Left succeeded in getting a motion passed at the PvdA party congress barring a coalition with the KVP in the immediate future.

[30] The 1970 initiative did lead to the passing of a parliamentary motion, introduced by Kolfschoten (KVP), suggesting that Parliament should convene immediately after the elections to vote on a nomination for *formateur* to be submitted to the Queen. Such a 'parliamentary election' for *formateur* was held only once, in 1971, but he experiment was a failure as all MPs voted for their own party's candidate, and no common nomination could be agreed upon.

[31] For an account of the 1973 government, see J.J. Vis, *Kabinetsformatie 1973; De Slag om het Catshuis*, Utrecht, 1973.

[32] For an account of the 1977 government formation, see R.B. Andeweg, K. Dittrich and Th. van der Tak, *Kabinetsformatie 1977*, Leiden, 1978.

[33] In Norway, in 1965, the formation of a government programme was even left to the parliamentary parties' secretaries, which would be unthinkable in the Netherlands. See S. Groennings, 'Patterns, Strategies and Payoffs in Norwegian Coalition Formation' in S. Groennings et. al., *op. cit.*, p. 75.

[34] K.R. Gladdish., 'Two-Party vs. Multi-Party' p. 344

[35] According to this procedural compromise the government would try to introduce new abortion-legislation to parliament. If the government would not succeed in sending proposed legislation to the Second Chamber before January 1st, 1979, the coalition partners would then be free to introduce or support parliamentary initiatives. Although the government failed to meet this deadline and although the legislation is still pending, no parliamentary initiatives have yet been introduced.

[36] In 1978 the Danish Social Democrats and Liberals have ended an even longer period of mutual refusal to govern together. See for an assessment of the probability of a PvdA-VVD coalition: L.G. Gerrichhauzen and J.G.A. van Mierlo, 'De Weg naar de Regeringsmacht, maar met welke strategie? De PvdA in coalitieland', *Beleid & Maatschappij*, 1978, pp. 191-206.

Select Bibliography

English language texts

H. Daalder, 'Cabinet and Party Systems in Ten Smaller European Democracies', *Acta Politica*, vol. 6, 1971, pp. 282-303.

L.C. Dodd, *Coalitions in Parliamentary Government*, Princeton, 1976.

A. Downs, *An Economic Theory of Democracy*, New York, 1957, chapter 9 (Problems of Rationality under Coalition Governments).

K.R. Gladdish, 'Two-Party vs. Multi-Party, the Netherlands and Britain', *Acta Politica*, vol. 7, 1972, pp. 342-361.

S. Groennings et. al., *The Study of Coalition Behavior; theoretical perspectives and cases from four continents*, New York, 1970.

H. Hermerén, 'Government Formation in Multiparty Systems', *Scandinavian Political Studies*, vol. 11, 1976, pp. 131-146.

A. de Swaan, *Coalition Theories and Cabinet Formations; a study of formal theories of coalition formation applied to nine European parliaments after 1918*, Amsterdam, 1973.

M. Taylor and M. Laver, 'Government Coalitions in Western Europe', *European Journal of Political Research*, vol. 1, 1973, pp. 205-248.

Dutch language texts

R.B. Andeweg, K. Dittrich, and Th. van der Tak, *Kabinetsformatie 1977*, Leiden, 1978.

J.Th.J. van den Berg, 'De Kabinetsformatie 1977 en het gebruik van het begrip 'meerderheid', *Acta Politica*, vol. 13, 1978, pp. 505-530.

F.J.F.M. Duynstee, *De Kabinetsformaties 1946-1965*, Deventer, 1966.

L.G. Gerrichhauzen and J.G.A. van Mierlo, 'De Weg naar de Regeringsmacht, maar met welke strategie? De PvdA in coalitieland', *Beleid & Maatschappij*, 1978, pp. 191-206.

A.K. Koekkoek, *Partijleiders en Kabinetsformatie. Een rechtsvergelijkende studie over de rol van partij-leiders bij de kabinetsformatie in Engeland, West-Duitsland, België en Nederland*, Deventer, 1978.

G. Ringnalda, 'De Kabinetsformatie' in: A. Hoogerwerf (ed.), *Verkenningen in de Politiek I*, Alphen aan den Rijn, 1971, pp. 132-158.

J.J. Vis, *Kabinetsformatie 1973, de slag om het Catshuis*, Utrecht, 1973.

10 The Legacy of Empire

W. Brand

10.1 Introduction

It seems rather strange that a small country like the Netherlands (35.000 km²) stumbled into an empire in Asia (1.9 million km²) and Latin-America (165.000 km²), but history is full of surprises to the rational mind. When at the end of the 16th century (1596) Dutch seafarers sailed to the East Indies, conquest was not their goal. As the foremost traders in Europe, they were interested in obtaining a part of the spice trade then monopolized by the Portuguese. The Republic of the United Provinces was then engaged in the 80-years' war (1568-1648) against Spain, which in 1580 also obtained the hegemony over Portugal, thereby closing the Portuguese ports to Dutch trade. After several skirmishes the Portuguese were successfully evicted from the Moluccas and thus a considerable part of the trade in cloves, mace and nutmegs from the Indies went henceforth through Dutch hands. On the way to the Moluccas à foothold was also acquired on the island of Java (Banten) where several tropical products (e.g. pepper and sandelwood) were traded and many competitors (e.g. the English) also possessed trading posts. From here, a little more eastward, through playing one native ruler against the other, land for a real settlement (Jacatra) was annexed, so that a fortress could be built which subsequently became Batavia and the nub of all Dutch activities in Asia. Batavia served in following years as the springboard for territorial extension along the coast and further inward.

In 1602 the United East Indies Company (V.O.C.) was established which received from the States-General of the Republic exclusive rights in trade matters and further administrative and military authority in its ventures. The V.O.C. was actually a mercantile company with a capital subscribed by the 'chambers' of merchants in the participating towns (Amsterdam, Zeeland – Middelburg, Vlissingen and Veere –, Rotterdam including Delft and Dordrecht, Hoorn and Enkhuizen) in which Amsterdam was by far the most important member. The capital of the V.O.C. amounted to £ 650,000 compared with £ 30,000 of the English East Indies Company founded in 1600. The share in the capital determined the number of directors on the board ('De Heeren XVII' or 'the Seventeen Gentlemen') on which also a representative of the States-General sat and which was responsible for decision-making.

It was no mean feat to bring the individualistic merchants together and the reward of a monopoly seemed the only means of securing their co-operation. Such a co-operation was, of course, also necessary to combine the knowledge required for the hazardous voyages to still largely unknown areas and to ward off the foreign competitors who were similarly organized. Further economies of scale dictated the amalgamation of the diverse interests as the cost of wars against intruders had to be paid out of the profits of the V.O.C. and could only be borne by a relatively large group. 'You cannot have trade without war or war without trade' – was a saying of Jan Pieterzoon Coen, one of the first governor-generals of the V.O.C. and the founder of the Dutch empire in the East. This dictum reflected the circumstances under which trade could be and was conducted at that time. It should also be remembered that Euro-Asian trade before 1800 consisted mainly of luxury products which could bear the high transport costs involved.

Another element needs to be touched upon. In the beginning of the 17th century the Dutch possessed about three-fourths of mercantile tonnage in Europe, conveyed an important part of the trade in the Mediterrean and the Baltic and thus transported the imports and exports for many countries. In order to acquire an optimal load of their ships, the V.O.C. was eager to duplicate this story to some extent in Asia and being able to out-trade and out-war its rivals, it obtained in due time a sizeable share in the inter-Asian trade (e.g. from China: pottery, silk and porcelain, from India: cotton cloth, calico, and silk clothing, from Persia: rugs, etc.). From Arabia coffee was bought, but from imported beans cultivation of this product was also initiated in the mountainous area of the Preanger (south of Batavia) by the V.O.C., so that after 1720 this crop came mainly from Java. The motivation for diversification was strong as non-industrialized Europe had, as far as commodities were concerned, little to offer Asia, so that ships on their outward voyage generally carried considerable amounts of silver and gold in minted and unminted form as payment for the tropical goods to be acquired.

En route to the Indies, a Dutch settlement was also started in South Africa (near the Cape of Good Hope) following the establishment of a hospital and supply post in 1652 to receive sick seamen and to deliver food to the Dutch seafarers on their long journeys between Europe and the Indies. It could hardly have been foreseen that the descendants (speaking 'Afrikaans' which is an offshoot of Dutch) of this settlement imbued with the old Calvinistic spirit are now the self-proclaimed protectors of Western culture among a majority of other races (Bantus, Coloured – kin of the Malaysians and Indonesians imported during the reign of the V.O.C. – and Indians brought over in the 19th century as manpower for the building of the infrastructure and for the sugar estates) in a seething continent. Further, already in 1640 the island of Ceylon (now Sri Lanka) had come under the wing of the V.O.C. The island was formally transferred to England in 1820 together with the South African colony whilst most of the other possessions taken over by the English during the Napoleonic interlude (1798-1815) were returned to Dutch hands. The appellation of some of Sri Lanka's citizens as 'burghers' still forms a reminder of the early Dutch influence.

The empire in the West Indies was acquired as a by-product of the hope of finding a route to the Indies by sailing West. Thus the colony of New Netherland and the city of New Amsterdam (now New York) were founded following the discovery of Manhattan (a mispronunciation by the Dutch of what they thought to be an Indian name of one of the tribes living nearby) and its environment in 1609 by the English captain H. Hudson who was in the employ of the V.O.C. In 1621 the West Indies Company (W.I.C.) was established with a capital of £ 700.000 which (as the V.O.C.) was given a monopoly of trade and administrative and military responsibilities under the aegis of the States-General of the mother country. In the W.I.C., besides the already mentioned chambers of commerce of the V.O.C., also the northern provinces (Groningen and Friesland) participated and thus a group of 'Nineteen Gentlemen' ('de Heeren XIX') chosen by the share-holders directed daily affairs. In the W.I.C. the 'chamber' of Zeeland originally played first fiddle. When in 1664 New Netherland was surrender-ed to the English (the names of the boroughs (Harlem - the capital of the province of North Holland, Brooklyn – a corruption of the Dutch village Breukelen and many other landmarks along the Hudson and East rivers still echo the distant past), the W.I.C. had in the period 1634-48 taken possesion from the Spanish of the three so called Leeward islands Curaçao, Aruba and Bonaire near the coast of South America (now Venezuela) and the much smaller three so called Windward islands St. Eustatius, Saba and St. Maarten at a distance north of about 900 km from the others, together now known as the Netherlands Antilles (1000 km²). Furthermore, already between 1595 and 1600 Dutch merchants sent out ships to trade with the 'Wild Coast' – the name for the region between the rivers Orinoco and Amazon – and as a result of the activities of the W.I.C.

after the defeat of the Portuguese, settlements were established in parts of now Brazil (Pernambuco and Recife) in 1624. Here they were again evicted by the Portuguese in 1654 (the name of the present bishop of Olinda (Portuguese for Holland) and Recife, Dom Helder Camara (Den Helder was and is the naval port of the Netherlands) reminds us of the formal Dutch presence), but in the meantime footholds had also been obtained in the Guyanas. In 1667 the part now Surinam (on the left flanked by settlements on the rivers Berbice, Demarara and Essequebo, until 1814 also Dutch colonies but then transferred to England and becoming British Guyana and on the right since 1750 French Guyana or Cayenne) was firmly established as a Dutch possession. In Brazil the Dutch learnt through the Portuguese the large-scale cultivation of export crops and the need of importing labour from Africa in view of the scarcity or unwillingness of the Indians to work on the estates. Thus the W.I.C. felt the compulsion to attain two ports (Elmina in 1637 and Luanda in 1641) in West Africa to purchase slave labour.

This brief sketch does not do justice to the ups and downs of Dutch colonization, but for our purpose it may suffice to say that after several conflicts with its rivals the position of the Dutch in the East Indies, in the Netherlands Antilles and Surinam became secured through treaties concluded at the end of the 17th century. That the English ceded these territories again to the Dutch after the Napoleonic wars, can probably be explained by the wish to have the Dutch join in an overseas policy parallel to English strategy and in any case not antagonistic as that of other continental powers.

In retrospect, it seems clear that the Dutch were foremost interested in trade and not in the settlement of territories with its own citizens. The Dutch population (around 0,7 million in 1700 and about 1 million in 1800) was on the one hand too small for large-scale emigration and on the other hand not inclined to settle overseas in view of the relative prosperity in the mother country. As soon as the cost of military adventures exceeded the potential profitability of future exchanges in the eyes of the merchants and the States-General, the Dutch withdrew as in Brazil and New Netherland. The fact that the second-in-command after the Governor-Generals of the colonies was the Director-General of Trade and that the officials of the V.O.C. and W.I.C. were designated as upper-merchants, merchants, junior merchants, book-keepers or assistants mirrors the mercantile character of the then Dutch overseas settlements.

10.2 Economic and social forces in the Netherlands

10.2.1 Events until 1800

Before attempting to describe some of the legacies of colonialism, it is necessary to go somewhat deeper into what happened in the odd 350 years that Dutch rule prevailed in parts of the East and West Indies. In this respect it should be kept in mind that until the 20th century colonies were considered as regions to be exploited for the benefit of the mother country while the potential exploitation depended, of course, on available natural resources and on inherent political and social constraints.

The great difference between the colonization in Asia and in the Americas was that in the first area one encountered relative densely populated territories with old and established civilizations, while in the latter the indigenous population was scarce and its level of development rather primitive. When the Dutch arrived in the Indies, the size of their ships and their economic activities were not too different from those of Chinese, Indian and other traders who had plied the area for centuries. But the Dutch traders held an advantage over most of their competitors. They were better organized and disciplined since the V.O.C. had been established. The capital of the company was largely used to purchase ships while the cost of each trip' was financed proportionally through the chambers of the company. The proceeds upon return served first of all to pay off the debt incurred to the bankers. Annually it was decided how many ships would sail to the Indies and agents of trading posts would assure that sufficient cargo was available when the ships arrived. Thus shipping through the V.O.C., became a continuing business and not a one-trip affair as most of the voyages by its rivals were organized. Originally, the Dutch traded (or probably better raised tribute) through local rulers who in exchange for protection against intruders were obliged against payment to deliver the commodities required in certain quantities. Gradually, more trading posts and fortresses were established on Java as it was found that treaties with native rulers were insufficient to secure regular supplies of export products (spices, coffee, cotton, indigo, etc.) and also of food and other wherewhithal especially labour to build and maintain the Dutch settlements. Thus a Dutch reign of peace and quiet was slowly expanded, but even by 1900 the extent of Dutch influence was mainly restricted to Java. In the so-called Outer Regions (Sumatra, Kalimantan or Borneo, Sulawesi or Celebes and a host of other islands) Dutch dominance with few exceptions (e.g. the Moluccas) existed foremost in the form of treaties with native sovereigns to obtain their loyalty in exchange for protection against local adversaries. Until the 20th century Dutch power in the archipelago outside Java 'was represented merely by officials planted out as animated coats of arms ('levende wapenborden' in Dutch) to warn off trespassers.

The apex of the V.O.C.'s influence fell in the 17th century when Dutch sea power was supreme in Europe and which era is rightly called the 'golden age' in Dutch history as it coincided with an outburst of political and artistic energies. The 18th century saw a decline of Dutch power as other European countries especially England started to build up their maritime fleets. By that time most of the other territorial positions in Asia had been lost to especially England and France so that the V.O.C. became mainly the importer of tropical produce from the Indies. According to prevalent opinion the decline of the V.O.C. was further accelerated by a) improper bookkeeping as no distinction was made between revenue from trading and government (tolls, taxes and customs duties) and administrative and real cost (transport, agents), b) the increasing burden of payments for civilian and military personnel and c) corruption among the colonial officials which always had been a latent tendency on account of the low remuneration they received. However, these reasons are now considered to be of a relative nature. The main causes were the decisive English wars in the 1780's as a result of which the source of the rich return freight stopped and the debt of the V.O.C. to Dutch bankers jumped by leaps and bounds so that the V.O.C. had to suspend payments to its creditors. Thus by 1799 the States-General felt obliged to take over the assets and liabilities of the V.O.C., thereby assuming political and administrative responsibilities for the settlements in Asia.

Trade with the Americas was from the outset of an entirely different order. In New Netherland furs and hides were purchased from the Indians in exchange for cheap ornaments and bright coloured cloth. Though this seems like a profitable undertaking, it should be realized that the colonists had to struggle to earn a living while the W.I.C., and not they, gained from the unequal exchange. It explained why the colonists in general were not eager to defend Dutch interests. The advantages seemed to be more evenly distributed at least among the Whites involved in the West Indies. Once plantations were opened up on the mainland and the slave trade (including also trade in gold and ivory) was established, a triangular trade developed. In West-Africa slaves were bought through native agents against textiles, household articles, guns, gunpowder and liquor. The proceeds of the slaves in the West Indies were used for the purchase of sugar, coffee, cocoa and hides as homeward cargo for Europe. In addition, the plantations in Surinam required relatively large investments which were financed by

Dutch bankers. Moreover land also had to be reserved for the growing of food crops and cattle grazing for local needs of the colonists and their slaves.

On the Netherlands Antilles because of the quality of the soil and scarce rainfall, plantations remained unimportant. Here mostly food and meat were produced so that the slaves after their sea-journey (between 15 and 20 percent of them died during the trip) could be rested and fed and thereby their price presumably enhanced on the mainland. On some of the islands (St. Maarten especially) salt was obtained which was needed for the curing of the herring or large-scale fishing which in the 17th century was still considered the mother of all trade in the Netherlands and made the West-frisian towns on the Zuyderzee as Hoorn, Medemblik and Enkhuizen prosperous. On Curaçao some phosphate was mined and still is, while on Aruba (Ora huba, i.e. there is gold) gold mining was originally practised but this has since disappeared. Gradually some of the islands (Curaçao and St. Eustatius) became transit ports for the mainland and for some of the Carribean territories held by the English or French though trade was normally monopolized by the mother countries. However, as private and national interests did not always converge, it was sometimes advantageous to circumvent the monopoly for the sake of private profits. Besides such smuggling the islands served also as ports of sally for Dutch ships which were trying to pirate the Spanish vessels laden with tropical produce and precious metals during the 80-years' war. The most spectacular feat was the conquest of a Spanish silverfleet in 1628 by Piet Heyn. This event is still celebrated in the only song ('Peter Heyn, his name is short, but his deeds are big', etc.) which all Dutchmen are able to sing together.

According to estimates, the Dutch were responsible during the 17th and 18th centuries for some 5 percent of the total Atlantic slave-traffic (involving some 500.000 slaves of a total of 10 million transported) and thus stood in third place after England and France. Around 1800 there were about 500 plantations in Surinam of which some 450 were cultivating export crops (coffee, sugar, cocoa and cotton). Most of the plantations had by that time been taken over by Dutch creditors (only 20 percent of the plantations belonged to inhabitants of Surinam), and this absentee-ownership led to a decline in efficiency and production. Moreover, the role of the W.I.C. had by then become restricted to the slave traffic as most of its trade with Europe had been taken over by so called 'interlopers' i.e. independent shippers who undermined the position of the W.I.C. Shareholders in the W.I.C. reaped in the period 1676-1720 as an average only about 2½ percent annually on their investment compared with about 30 percent for those of the V.O.C. Actually the statute of the W.I.C. lapsed in 1791 and colonial rule then reverted to the

States-General of the United Provinces.

From the above it will be clear that until 1800 Surinam was more important than the East Indies for the mother country. Yearly, some 60 to 70 ships sailed regularly from Surinam to the Netherlands while only some 25 to 30 ships arrived from the Indies.

It is difficult to gain an idea of the profitability of the colonies to the mother country. There seems no doubt that the building and equipping of ships provided a boon for the economy as did the trade in tropical products for which Amsterdam became the staple market and as a result the most important financial centre in Europe gradually. Colonial trade was, however, only a small part of total Dutch trade and according to the scarce data available not more remunerative than normal mercantile shipping. Around 1780 it was estimated that the share of ships sailing under the flag of the V.O.C. was only 4 percent of total volume of freight entering Dutch harbours while amounting to about 13 percent of total value of foreign trade confirming that the import from the Indies consisted of products with a high value. As the number of ships annually from Surinam was on the average 3 times larger than those under the V.O.C., it may be roughly assumed that about 15 percent of total traffic conducted by Dutch ships originated from the colonies and that its value was about 25 percent of total imports in its hey-day.

10.2.3 Events from 1800 till 1940

At the end of the 18th century the Republic of the United Provinces after having taken over the V.O.C. and W.I.C. had no time to initiate a policy for the colonies as the mother country came under the influence of the French republic, later empire (the so called 'continental system' restricted all overseas trade) and most colonies fell in the hands of the English. When in 1815 the home country became free again and around 1820 the colonies returned (whereby slave trade became forbidden), the Republic had become a Kingdom with William I of Orange the first king. Under the proclaimed constitution the King had supreme authority over the colonies, but this seemed an empty gesture as the Netherlands had become disinterested in the colonies. Being practically cut off from them since 1795, the colonies appeared like a bankrupt estate, the East Indies having been taken over from the V.O.C. at a large cost (Fl. 135 million) while the West Indies largely languished as a decaying plantation economy. Moreover, the dismal state of the Dutch economy precluded any great effort on behalf of the colonies. The Treasury being empty, there were only some general ideas on the part of the

King's advisers on how to attempt to make the colonies solvent again. The general ideas consisted of a reliance on private European enterprise along the lines of Adam Smith's thinking and the thoughts of the French revolution (liberty, equality and fraternity) based on the self-interest of the individual peasant who if motivated by suitable incentives would greatly enhance production of export crops. The first approach faltered upon the apathy of Dutch entrepreneurs who 'could not be beaten out of their homes with sticks' (W.F.M. Mansvelt), as it was said. A policy of relying on the individual peasant (through a land tax or otherwise) failed because of the sway village headmen and native rulers held over the countryside. Moreover, the Dutch discovered upon their return that most of the exports and imports were carried in English (and American) ships because they were faster than Dutch vessels. Also the English were able to bring on their outward journeys large quantities of cotton goods for which an effective demand existed making it possible to offer a higher price for the tropical produce in exchange. Thus the number of English firms in Batavia outnumbered that of Dutch enterprises for a considerable time, while the sale of produce occurred on Java instead of in Europe.

In 1824 the Netherlands Trading Company (N.H.M.), of which the King guaranteed a fixed dividend on a capital of Fl. 37 million, was launched which served as an export and import agency for the Indies. Further a textile industry was started through subsidies in the eastern part of the country (Twente) which could match the English supply of cotton goods for the Indies. None of these measures promised an early success, but then financial difficulties as a result of the Java-war (1825-30) when the whole island was brought under Dutch rule and insufficient revenue of the land-tax, forced the issue. The governor-general J. van den Bosch, appointed in 1830, who had been instrumental in the foundation of the N.H.M. and the textile industry, initiated the so called 'culture system'[1]. Under this system the peasants under their headmen were forced to devote some of their cultivable areas to export crops which had to be delivered at a fixed price to the Government. The N.H.M. was charged with shipping to and sales of produce in the Netherlands for a fee, while the main profits went to the Dutch Treasury. This scheme was extremely successful. The exports from Java of e.g. coffee, sugar and indigo soared and in the period 1830-50 fetched some fl. 450 million at the Amsterdam auctions. About half of this amount went into the Dutch Treasury. Thus in the period 1830-50 annually some fl. 10-15 million was added to State revenue while in the period 1851-73 this amount had increased to fl. 25 million or about 25 percent of total State revenue. It was at that time that the slogan often repeated afterwards that the Indies were 'the cork (or life-belt) on which the Netherlands was kept afloat' was born. The sums received were used for the redemption of State debt, the reduction of taxation and the construction of railways and other public works in the Netherlands.

Van den Bosch was the first to reveal to the Dutch that Java could be made into a profitable field of enterprise though it was run for a long time as 'one large State business concern' (H. Colijn). The cultivation of coffee and indigo could largely be left to the indigenous peasants, but for sugar and later tobacco and tea arrangements had to be made with individuals to supervise production and processing. Initially Van den Bosch had to find such contractors among the English, French, Chinese and even Indians, but under his successors gradually the number of Dutch citizens increased. Aroused by the profit motive, they were the first ones to criticize the culture system as bringing a one-sided benefit to the Dutch state. Instead the 'planters' wanted to have more money devoted to railways, irrigation and also schools plus sanitary facilities for themselves in the Indies, services which could only be provided by the State. As liberal influences in the Netherlands were gaining (some of the 'planters' became cabinet ministers) and the culture system came in to disrepute as tending to neglect food production for the native peasants, the time became ripe for a retreat by the State. From 1870 up to 1900 some fl. 250 million of the 'spoils' (called 'batig slot' or credit balance in Dutch) was spent by the government in the Indies on railway construction, harbour extensions, etc. In 1870 the Agrarian Law was adopted making it possible for entrepreneurs to obtain long-term leases (75 years) of State land (i.e. not cultivated by peasants) and peasant land on short-term leases against adequate payments and arrangements. The opening of the Suez Canal in 1869 served as another catalyst in firing private initiative. From 1870 onward all the big companies which later became prominent in plantation agriculture, trade and banking were founded. Around 1885 scientific cultivation came into its own and besides sugar and coffee a rich variety of other tropical produce (among which tobacco, rubber, palm oil and sisal) made its appearance. Apart from the normal cyclical fluctuations, private capital became the spearhead of the expansion of the economy of the Indies, as it did in the mother country where finally industrialization was taking root. Only then were Dutch shipping lines established, a field which until 1870 had been largely left to the English. After 1900 the Outer Regions (in 1852 the Billiton Company had already been granted a concession to mine tin on this island, while in 1863 tobacco cultivation was initiated by private interests on Sumatra's East Coast), where large tracts of land were State domain, were also opened up for large-scale agriculture and apart from tin mining which had been mined on Bangka since V.O.C.-times, also petroleum and mineral exploration and exploitation. Labour for these activities had often to be imported from outside (from China and Java). In the 1920's exports from the other islands (mainly petroleum and rubber) started to surpass in value those of Java and this process has continued ever since. It is worthwhile to note that in petroleum prospecting originally English capital had to be sought. As a result the Royal Dutch Company co-operated for the trade of its products with an English company with which it subsequently merged into the Royal Dutch Shell of which 60 percent of the capital was Dutch and 40 percent English. It needs also to be stressed that the government of the Indies remained active in agriculture (e.g. quinine, teak), mining (coal and tin), in transport (railways) and communications (post, telephone and telegraph) but was anxious not to compete with the private sector.

In 1938 about one-sixth (£ 400 million) of Dutch national wealth (£ 2.2 billion) was invested in the East Indies. For the same year it was calculated by J.B.D. Derksen and J. Tinbergen[2] that income from the Indies contributed about 8 percent to the national income of the Netherlands and up to 13 to 14 percent if all secondary effects were taken into account. Most of the growth of colonial investment had, as was also the case in the experience of other countries, not taken place in the form of capital migration from the mother country, but as a result of reinvested local earnings. The Dutch, as a small nation, having reached competitive equality with its potential rivals (through initially providing protection and subsidies to its own citizens), was eager to follow an open-door policy resulting in relatively large-scale investments (£ 100 million) by English, American, French, Japanese, German, Italian and Belgian capital in that order of importance.

Meantime, in Surinam things had gone from bad to worse. The number of viable plantations declined and the abolition of slavery in 1862 (reluctantly under the moral pressure of the English and French which had liberated their slaves in 1833 and 1848 respectively) seemed to the 200 then remaining plantations the final blow. It appears somewhat ironic that the official compensation given to the slave holders in the West Indies for the loss of their 'assets' was paid from the profits of the Culture system in the East Indies. Through the import of contract labour, some from China (in 1970 there were some 6500 Chinese in Surinam) but larger numbers from British India (some 34.000 Indians in the period 1873-1916, called Hindustanis in Surinam) and the East Indies (about 33.000 Javanese in the period 1891-1939) it was hoped to replace the negroes (called Creoles in Surinam), who were unwilling to continue working as free labourers in estate agriculture.

But Surinam's products could not compete with more efficiently produced Asian goods, though the lowering of transport cost due to the Suez Canal and faster ships also contributed to their problems. So gradually the majority of the labour force from India and the Indies drifted into subsistence agriculture. In 1913 only 80 plantations remained. A windfall occurred when in 1916 bauxite was discovered and the Aluminium Company of America (Alcoa) started its exploitation in 1922. In 1939 also the Billiton Company (prominent since 1852 in tin mining on Billiton, but also exploiting bauxite and nickel in the Indies) acquired a bauxite concession and subsequently the income from the bauxite industry provided a large share of state revenue in Surinam. Thus in 1942 a balanced budget was obtained for the first time after virtually a century of subsidies (from the Culture System) by the home country. Also the Netherlands Antilles had become a stagnating economy, but here the new impetus was provided by the refineries built in 1920 on Curaçao by the Royal Dutch Shell (daughter company named Curaçao Petroleum Industry) and in 1928 on Aruba by the Standard Oil company of New Jersey (Lago Oil and Transport Company) based on petroleum from Venezuela. These companies caused a boom on the islands through their demand for labour which even had to be met by migration from the other islands and neighbouring countries (including Surinam). Average income rose at a remarkable speed and government revenue increased proportionally so that here as well, subsidies from the Netherlands were no longer necessary.

The spurt of colonial activities in the latter part of the 19th century especially in the East Indies affected only a small part of the population in the mother country. The governing élite though paying lip service to humanitarian ideals was imbued with a materialistic or selfish spirit. When a protestant minister W.R. van Hoëvell, who had worked in the Indies, proclaimed in 1849 prior to his election to the Dutch parliament that the Dutch should place the welfare of the Indies and of the indigenous population above considerations of trade and profit, an official explanatory statement (annex to the budget of 1854) stated quite flatly that the Indies were a conquered region and 'save for the welfare of the natives, must continue to furnish the Netherlands with those material benefits for which they were acquired'. In 1860 a book appeared called 'Max Havelaar' by E. Douwes Dekker (using as penname Multatuli) who as a former civil servant in the Indies described his experience in West-Java. Though because of its style (he was the one to depict the Indies or the beautiful realm of Insulinde, as he called it, as a girdle of smaragds slung around the equator) it worked as a bombshell and opened for the first time the eyes of a larger public to the practice of colonial policy. It is in my view not an accusation against Dutch colonial administration, but rather against the native rulers who abused their power through excessive demands of forced labour and personal services of their people. Only indirectly the Dutch are charged by condoning these practices but one wonders how they could have done otherwise with only a handful of civil servants (about 175 on a population of 12 to 13 million). It is interesting to observe that neither at that time nor earlier was there a rejection or a questioning of the colonial relationship as such or of slavery in the West Indies in particular[3]. From the Biblical notation (Genesis IX: 25, 26) that negroes as descendants of Cham were cursed by Noah and thereby doomed to servitude, it was easy to rationalize the idea that 'slaves were created to plant sugar and cotton'. Even when socialist representatives entered parliament at the end of the 19th century, the responsibility of the white man's burden appeared to be implicitly accepted whatever criticism they raised against particular policies. However, around 1900 a shift in thinking occurred. In 1899 another former civil servant in the Indies, C.Th. van Deventer, who became a parliamentarian, wrote an article entitled 'A Debt of Honour' in which he pleaded that the money taken from the Indies through the cultural system in the period 1867-77 (after 1878 no remittances had been made to the Dutch treasury) should be returned to raise the welfare of the native population. Such repayment was never made (except in 1904 a debt of the Indies of fl. 40 million was cancelled, while in the depression of the 1930's fl. 25 million was granted as a gift) but sentiment had changed and in 1901 in the Speech from the Throne (the annual message delivered by the King to outline Government policy), it was stated that as a Christian nation the Netherlands was obliged to perpetrate in its policy for the Indies the idea that it had an ethical calling to fulfill towards its people. Thus the so-called ethical policy was born as a combination of freedom of enterprise and a paternalistic welfare policy for the benefit of the population of the Indies. From then onward the Dutch mission was perceived as a 'dual mandate', namely the opening up of the natural resources of the country for the benefit of the world and the raising of the human wealth entrusted to it so that the population of the Indies would be able to cope with its introduction into a rapidly changing world.

Though one can have misgivings whether the Dutch have lived up to these ideals, there seems to be no doubt that it became the flame which fired the civil service[4]. Those in the civil service (including those in fields as food agriculture, industrialization, transport, public health, etc.) became the social engineers or the introducers of modern science, technology, law and organization in a society still steeped in tradition and conservatism.

Through persuasion and patience, differentiated according to needs and local varieties of culture in line with the training they had received first in Delft and later in Leiden and Utrecht (from 1922 onward on an academic level), the credo of the civil service sounded like the guidelines now provided to development experts under which even the promotion of 'self-reliance' could be claimed. Peace and stability remained the goal of rather a method of gradualness intended not to upset the local loyalties and venerated beliefs which provided the basis of security. The preservation of the native social order had always been the loadstar of Dutch policy. Still, though the dedication of this group was sincere, it was part and parcel of (and paid for by) an economic structure bent on exploiting the natural resources of the Indies also for the benefit of non-autochthonous minorities (Europeans and Chinese). The ideal of a synthesis between the various races, so dear to Dutch thought, was a reflection of a Eurocentric policy and not necessarily of the striving of the native population. In 1938 about 7 percent of those with a Dutch university degree resided in the Indies, mainly working in the public sector but increasingly also in the private sector (e.g. lawyers, medical doctors and biologists working on the experimental stations of estate agriculture). Their study and experience fertilized academic life in the home country and several chairs at the universities were manned by people who had earned their laurels in the Indies. Thus, the Netherlands became a depository of knowledge on history, languages, cultural anthropology, agriculture, forestry, etc. of tropical areas which still prevails.

10.2.3 Events beyond 1940

When the Netherlands was overrun by the German armies in May 1940, the colonies were left to function on their own. In the Indies a relative boom occurred until March 1942 (when the country was occupied by the Japanese) as a result of the demand of the Western world for some of its strategic raw materials required for the preparation of war. In May 1945 when Germany surrendered, the Netherlands was anxious to resume its role as colonial power. Though the Queen who had fled in 1940 with her cabinet to London had promised in a radio speech in 1942 to re-organize the political structure so that the separate parts, the Netherlands and the East and West Indies, would each be responsible for its internal affairs based on their own powers and the will to co-operate with each other, the Dutch wanted to re-establish peace and quiet before negotiations about a new political order were to be held.

It was recognized from the outset that the advantages from the possession of the Indies would no longer flow to the same extent and thus in the Netherlands an intensive industrialization policy needed to be launched so that the required imports of food and raw materials could be paid for by domestic exports. On the contrary, it seemed certain that the funds required for the rehabilitation of the Indies, devastated by the Japanese occupation and its aftermath, would jeopardize the reconstruction of the mother country. Thus the then Lieutenant Governor-General Van Mook said in a talk in 1947 with one of the Indonesian leaders (M. Hatta, later vice-president) that if the economic ties with Indonesia were severed, the recovery of the Netherlands would be more rapid. His words proved to be prophetic, but at the time nobody foresaw such events.

The English, who in July 1945 had assumed responsibility for the liberation of the Indies, were not in a position to provide the arms to the Dutch for the re-establishment of peace and quiet when Japan surrendered in August 1945 (they had first to liberate their own colonies, there was a Labour Government in power unwilling to be instrumental in restoring Dutch rule and thirdly they possessed only British Indian troops in the area which they could not use to put down a nationalistic revolution then raging in parts of the Indies). In August 1945 the independence of Indonesia was proclaimed by a group of Indonesian leaders. The English wanted the Dutch to negotiate with this group, which the Dutch were unwilling to do as most of the most prominent Indonesian leaders were considered to be Japanese collaborators. It should be stressed that the Netherlands, having been cut off from the stream of events during the German occupation, had little appreciation for the acute nationalism then reigning in part of the colonial world. Though prodded by England and the United States (on account of its anti-colonial background pressing all European powers to relinquish their colonies after World-War II) to discuss the new political landscape with the Indonesians, the Dutch felt themselves twice compelled to take military action because the Indonesians did not live up to the agreements reached. The actions as such were successful[5], but the Dutch were twice rebuffed by the United Nations Security Council which forced the Dutch to retreat. It finally dawned upon the Dutch that there was no alternative than to transfer sovereignty over the Indies to the Republic of Indonesia. This eventually occurred in December 1949. However, in the agreement reached with the Indonesians, the Dutch held back New Guinea (now called West-Irian) – a large island in the eastern part of the archipelago of which the other half belonged to Australia – because as it was said it was not really an integral part of Indonesia from a geographic, ethnological and political viewpoint[6]. Moreover the Dutch had insisted that Indonesia was to form a federal state in view of the great cultural diversity existing on the many islands which meant that the original Republic mainly based on Java would be only one of several states. Such states, about 16 in number, had been established by the Dutch in the territories under their control since 1947. Moreover, Indonesia was to conclude a union with the Netherlands, with the Queen at its head, through which joint consultation on economic and cultural matters were to be conducted. These provisos were considered necessary by the Dutch in order to obtain the two-thirds majority in parliament required for the indispensable change in the constitution. After a brief euphoria the Indonesians established an unitarian or central state and the parliaments of the various regions were dissolved nor did they show any inclination in making the union with the Netherlands effective. This in turn hardened the attitude of the Netherlands towards the eventual return of New Guinea and large sums of money were spent to develop the meager resources of this island.

Meanwhile the Dutch private sector had, in spite of its material and human losses suffered during the Japanese occupation and subsequent fighting, achieved a remarkable economic recovery of Indonesia. Though the scope of its activities was restricted (some part of the islands remained inaccessible) it restored production as far as possible. With the aid of the Government, transportation channels were re-opened and in view of the unlimited demand for raw materials in the post-war World exports were renewed to the well-known industrial markets. However, some of the business groups involved were anxious to improve the atmosphere between Dutch and Indonesian negotiators. Among them there had hardly ever been any concern with New Guinea and they felt in general that the territory should be ceded to Indonesia. They were aware that conditions for the conduct of their affairs in an independent Indonesia had changed (they trained Indonesians for staff positions on a large scale and were willing to accept Indonesian capital in new and old ventures, etc.), but unless the bone of contention of New Guinea was removed, they realized that there would be no chance for an accommodation between their interests and those of Indonesia. It is noteworthy that they never represented their views to the Dutch public which appears to be a reflection of the rather apolitical character of Dutch enterprise. Instead, their efforts were mainly directed in the form of personal contacts to prominent politicians of various complexions, but their message fell on deaf ears. The Netherlands, or rather the parties then co-operating in the governing coalitions, needed time to reconcile themselves to the painful withdrawal from a country and commitment to a people amounting then to about 70 million to which they felt deeply attached. The attitude of the Dutch Government became even more recalcitrant due to the constant raising by Indonesia of the New Guinea-issue in the organs of the United Nations. The whole problem seems a perfect example of how economic considerations which are assumed to be preponderant in Western industrial states can be overwhelmed by outmoded political principles. New Guinea became the provocation for Indonesia to sever relations with the Netherlands in 1957 as a result of which practically all Dutch property was confiscated and Dutch personnel forced to repatriate.

Prior to 1957 and since the proclamation of Indonesian independence in 1949, an estimated number of 210,000 Dutch subjects returned to the Netherlands which together with the 40,000 departing in 1957 and 1958 brings the total to 250,000. The majority of them (about 200,000) were Eurasians or Indo-Europeans who had never seen the Netherlands before but did not want to take out Indonesian citizenship or later changed their mind (the so called 'spijtoptanten' or those regretful of their original option) about their status as Indonesians. In general this group became well-integrated into Dutch society partly on account of the post-war prosperity which facilitated the absorption of additional manpower but also because this group had always adhered to Dutch values, spoke Dutch after a fashion and was anxious to adapt itself to its new-found fatherland[7]. In the relevant literature a great deal has been written about the cleavage between the Dutch-born and Indonesian-born Netherlanders and the discrimination which the latter suffered during the colonial period. Without minimizing these differences it needs to be pointed out that Dutch society in Indonesia had never been colour-conscious to the same extent as the British in English colonies. Under Dutch law legitimate and legitimized children of European fathers by native mothers had always been reckoned among the Europeans. There had always been cabinet ministers, governor-generals of mixed blood and a large percentage of high posts in the colonial administration and military establishment had been occupied by Indo-Europeans. The seat of Government, the Hague, especially had for a long time had an Indonesian flavour and a German author[8] who I came across in the '30's had called the Netherlands 'a Javanized Rhine-delta' implying that many of the Dutch élite had Indonesian blood in their veins. This is probably true though the matter has for obvious reasons never been thoroughly investigated.

An exception to the successful integration of the stream of immigrants needs to be made for the Amboinese. They came from a group of islands in the Moluccas where the first settlement of the V.O.C. was established. From this area (which was largely Protestant and loyal to Dutch rule though not speaking Dutch) came a substantial part of the former Royal Dutch Indies Army. Due to various circumstances this group, together with their families and other Amboinese opting for Dutch citizenship, came to the Netherlands. In retrospect, it seems clear that the military segment should have been amalgamated into the Dutch army, but it was then thought that their stay in the Netherlands would be of short duration and that their eventual return to their own country was only a question of time. Unfortunately, this proved to be an illusion and as no adequate measures were taken for their assimilation (they were herded in separate settlements emphasizing their isolation and kindling their nationalism), they or rather their descendants (in 1951 their number was about 13,000 but now they total about 35,000 because of their high birth rate) were responsible for various terrorist actions and kidnappings (in 1975, 1977 and 1978 as a result of which several Dutch citizens were killed) to protest against the lack of interest of the Dutch government in the fate of the Republic of the South-Moluccas. This had been established in April 1950 when the state of East Indonesia was abolished, but had subsequently been suppressed and incorporated into the Republic Indonesia. Though this rebellious group consists probably of less than 5 percent of the Moluccan segment, it finds a great deal of sympathy among the Moluccan community and has been able to raise a furor about its assumed neglect far beyond its numbers. It is well-known that a small group bent on making its voice heard can play havoc with a democratic society especially if such a society has a feeling of doubt about the justice of its past behaviour.

In the meantime it had become evident that the Dutch opposition against the return of New Guinea had become untenable and in 1962 a complete transfer to Indonesia was agreed upon after heavy pressure from the United States. By then it had been realized that New Guinea was a liability, with no raw materials, few investment opportunities and no possibilities for immigration of Indo-Europeans as originally thought. However, these economic considerations played only a small part in the final decision. More important was that the continuing success of Dutch recovery (making a myth of the often quoted slogan that the loss of the Indies would be a calamity for Dutch prosperity) and the lapse of time (almost 12½ years after Indonesian independence) had softened the principles of moral and national rectitude plus all those other elements of frustrated pride which are often a hindrance to international decision-making. Since then relations with Indonesia have been re-established with no hard feelings on either side.

The traumatic Indonesian experience had, of course, also its repercussions on relations with Surinam with about 350,000 inhabitants and the Netherlands Antilles with about 250,000 inhabitants, though nationalist feelings there were never antagonistic. In 1954 after many preliminaries a new Statute of the Realm was proclaimed after consultation with these territories as a result of which they obtained almost full autonomy in internal matters. However, nationalistic stirrings occurred here as elsewhere, while in the Netherlands there was a strong sentiment towards divesting itself of the rest of the colonial empire. Thus at the end of 1975 Surinam, which until that date had received a sizeable share of Dutch aid, declared its independence. However due to the fear of political upheavals, because of the precarious relations between the Creoles, Chinese, Hindustanis and Javanese, and the beckoning fleshpots of social security some 60,000 persons from Surinam (largely Creoles, but also Hindustanis) who still held Dutch citizenship, migrated to the Netherlands. In 1974 and 1975 about 20,000 people of Surinamese origin already lived in the Netherlands, mainly belonging to the upper- or middle-class (there are more Surinamese doctors in the Netherlands than in the mother country) who after their education here had stayed because of the limited capacity of absorption of highly-qualified labour in their home country. Now also the lower classes with little education or other qualifications came en masse and their assimilation still forms a problem. Their rate of unemployment is twice as high as of the average Dutch worker while their share in such social evils as prostitution, drug-use and -traffic is proportionally large. The event of the separation of the Republic of Surinam was 'celebrated' with a Dutch gift of fl. 3,5 billion guilders to be spread over a period of 10-15 years partly to cancel some debts but mostly to finance hopefully productive and infrastructural investments to strengthen the economic base of Surinam. So far there have been no signs of Dutch money being wisely spent, but fortunately the political tensions in this segmented society have not lead to any serious explosions.

In the Netherlands Antilles there seems no prospect of an early release from colonial ties, though a Dutch parliamentarian has said that if they are not going to ask soon for their independence, it will be sent to them by registered letter. The six islands hardly form a homogenous community being separated geographically and even more divided on racial and other grounds. The economic situation has deteriorated because of the mechanisation in the petroleum industry which has resulted in a large reduction of the labour force. Through substantial Dutch aid, the tourist industry plus a supplementary infrastructure has been built up on the basis of abundant sunshine and white beaches, but this can only be considered a mixed blessing because of its unfavourable side-effects (gambling, prostitution, smuggling and the false aspirations raised by the luxurious life style of foreign tourists). The efforts at industrialization have had little success because of the lack of indigenous raw materials and the relatively high wage level (based on the oil-boom and now anxiously defended by trade unions) compared with the neighboring islands. Thus the ruling class at least at Curaçao (the largest island with about 160,000 inhabitants of which the majority is black and the élite non-negroid) tends to decline independence until a better economic structure (there is an estimated 20 percent unemployment rate on this island) for a more secure future is in place. This appears like an indefinite postponement of separation, but on the most important island Aruba (60,000 inhabitants of which about 80 percent is non-negroid) there is an one-sided demand for autonomy especially from the central government at Curaçao which if granted might also lead to a call for political decentralization of the other islands. None of the islands wants to lose the annual aid provided by the Netherlands Government and it appears likely that the Netherlands Antilles will for a long time remain 'the lice in the pelt of the Dutch Realm' as one of its prime ministers has stated. If independence is granted, perhaps due to Dutch prodding, it is likely that a sizeable migration of Antilleans will occur (since 1976 a stream of about 3000 people per annum to the Netherlands has occurred, bringing the total of Antilleans to about 30,000) because of the fear of a further economic decline even though the Dutch Government will probably provide a 'diamond handshake' as in the case of Surinam.

The financial sustenance (largely gifts and soft loans) extended by the mother country has made Surinam and the Netherlands Antilles the countries with the largest aid received per head in the world according to the standards of the Development Assistance Committee of the Organization for Economic Co-operation and Development (OECD). Though the assistance provided has in my view been excessive given the relatively high income levels (average national product per capita in Surinam was $ 1380 and in the Netherlands Antillis even $ 1680 in 1975), political determination on this matter has never been influenced by such rational thinking. It can be partly explained by the special relations with these territories, but it has further to do with the reaction in the Netherlands when development assistance of the industrial countries came to the fore in the 50's. For those familiar with the subject it is evident that the Netherlands has played a substantial role in this field considering its size and wealth. There appears no other European country where the call for aid of the United Nations or other international organizations to combat poverty in the world has fallen on more fertile ground. The reason in my opinion is apart from ordinary human motivations, a general guilt complex not in a pejorative sense but as a general emotion that so often shapes our goodness and generosity. Another cause is probably also that the mission in the Indies having been interrupted, it is now felt that Dutch wealth and knowledge has to be spread to the whole developing world. The Dutch fervour has, of course, its limits, but in 1977 the Netherlands Government provided $ 900 million dollars in public aid amounting to 0.85 percent of its gross national product. All political parties share this enthusiasm for development aid and hardly ever are any questions raised about its effectiveness. It is , moreover, interesting to note that the Netherlands has since 1967 when the Inter-Governmental Group for Indonesia (IGGI) was instituted to co-ordinate aid efforts by the industrial countries under the aegis of the World Bank, assumed the chairmanship. No doubt the Netherlands was more or less eager to assume this position because of its traditional relationship with Indonesia. This desire has so far cost the Dutch taxpayer fl. 1,774 million in the period 1967-79 of which about 45 percent in the form of gifts and the rest in soft loans, definitely a much higher amount than if the Netherlands had just joined the club or abstained from its membership. This commitment should be seen in the light of the value of Dutch investment estimated at fl. 3.7 billion and confiscated by Indonesia in 1957 of which only a small part is now going to be repaid over the period 1979-2000 in depreciated guilders.

Epilogue

The physical remnants of the colonial empire are visible for all to see in the Netherlands. There are houses bearing outlandish names (in my own village Voorschoten a mansion called 'Berbice' being erected probably by a sugar-'baron' from the Guyanas) showing that their original owners gained their fortunes in the Indies. In every city streets or quarters bear names of islands in the East Indies and of prominent men (J.P. Coen, J.B. van Heutsz, etc.) in colonial history. Among the firms which started their business in Indonesia and now still active, the Royal Dutch Shell stands out as one of the large transnationals with branches engaged in production and distribution of petroleum products all over the world. The other large transnational enterprises in the Netherlands – Philips, State Mines, General Royal Salt Company (AKZO) and Unilever – did originate in the home country, though some of them have daughter plants now in Indonesia. It will be evident that among the firms formerly active in Indonesia and whose properties were confiscated in 1957, the possibilities of transferring operations or applying their knowledge elsewhere must have been widely different[9]. Some of them, such as those operating public utilities, did not accumulate any liquid capital which could be easily converted into foreign exchange. Those enterprises engaged in estate agriculture had only a limited potential for transferring their assets. Two of the largest – the Trading Company Amsterdam (HVA) and Amsterdam Rubber – did shift some of their resources to Africa and elsewhere, where they learnt to their dismay that on account of poorer soil and less adaptable labour, conditions for production were not as favourable as in Indonesia. The HVA by now a much leaner organization (a workforce of 330 compared with 800 executive staff with 170.000 labourers in 1928) became heavily involved in Ethiopia, where again most of its property has been taken over by the Government for which as yet no compensation has been received. The banks working in Indonesia among which the Netherlands Trading Company (N.H.M.) was the largest, have all merged with Dutch banks and are no longer visible except for the building of the N.H.M. (now the General Bank Netherlands) which in its exterior shows some of the characteristics of its former field of operations. The large shipping companies have also disappeared and have amalgamated with other shipping lines on a much smaller scale. The best to have thrived are the large trading corporations which have prospered due to the expansion of World trade especially within the European Common Market. In general, it can be said that most of the companies which tried to engage in ventures in the developing world, overestimated the significance of the experience gained in Indonesia or rather its transferability to other countries with a different social and economic climate.

There are no signs any more on the macro-economic level of the gains or losses of empire. In the balance of payments proceeds of Dutch capital (a large part of foreign assets were also liquidated in connection with the war effort) no longer forms a significant item and are in any case compensated by transfer of dividends and otherwise on behalf of foreign capital invested in the Netherlands. This implies that exports of goods and services now cover for a much larger part than before World-War II the imports of raw materials and other wherewithal for a resource-poor small country like the Netherlands. In overall trade Indonesia is rather unimportant, about 0.5 percent (fl. 510 million) of total imports and 0.6 percent (fl. 624 million) of total exports in 1977. Surinam and the Netherlands Antilles as small markets are of even less consequence; their exports and imports are largely directed to and derived from the Americas. In recent years the Netherlands Antilles have become a heavy importer of Dutch capital, but this is caused as in other Caribbean islands to the rather lenient tax facilities offered and not by investment opportunities.

The post-war Dutch experience seems a perfect illustration of the recognition that human resources are much more important in development than material capital. Despite the destruction of material assets in the

Netherlands during the German occupation and the losses in Indonesia due to the Japanese occupation and the subsequent confiscation, the Netherlands were able to make a quick recovery because of its possession of a highly trained labour force and the necessary institutions enabling this manpower to make full use of its capabilities. The European personnel returning from Indonesia made a significant contribution. Though for the most part they had to seek other functions, their absorption went smoothly and the greater range of responsibility which they had encountered in Indonesia compared with those who stayed home, proved an advantage in adapting to the greatly changed post-war circumstances in the Netherlands.

Among the 'expatriates' coming home, there is still nostalgia about the 'lost paradise' and some of them maintain that they spent the best part of their lives in Indonesia. The large number of restaurants in even smaller towns serving tropical dishes are a sign of the taste acquired for spiced food by those who sojourned there and also their offspring. In this group should also be included the about 100.000 Dutch soldiers who were in Indonesia in the years 1945 to 1949. Apart from material aspects, the Dutch language betrays, of course, some remnants of colonial history. Almost everybody uses now and then words such as 'toko' (Malay for shop), 'susah' (Malay for trouble), 'tabeh' (Malay for good-bye), 'pasar' (Malay for market), etc. while those who have lived in Indonesia intermingle in their speech many more Indonesian expressions. That the colonial past lingers on is even more manifest by the sizeable number of books published dealing with Indonesia which by far surpasses the amount issued in the pre-war period even considering the general increase in reading matter. Even among students there has in recent years sprung up an increasing interest in colonial history. Though the academic output seems on the whole critical (I am thinking of publications by W.F. Wertheim and J. Pluvier) of colonial administration, it appears doubtful whether these opinions have coloured official thinking on foreign policy. As far as I can judge the responsible strata in the Dutch population consider such critical attitudes as anti-historic or based on the benefit of hindsight. Most of the dominant social classes still feel in my view a certain somewhat subdued pride about what their countrymen, contemporaries and forefathers, accomplished and share the opinion that the fate of the former colonies was determined by external and not internal forces. The Netherlands never possessed a defense policy against foreign agressors and were reckoning on the English, who controlled the sea lanes from Gibraltar to Singapore, and on the Americans who became a world power in the Pacific after World-War I. When the allies failed them, the empire status suffered, but now official spokesmen are boasting that the Netherlands is number 10 on the world scale as far as the value of its international trade (value of exports and imports combined) is concerned. This is true and this dependence on foreign trade and a World order free from protectionist tendencies explains the Dutch role as a proponent of a new international system whereby accommodation is sought for the developing countries to be more fully integrated into the World economy.

It appears to be part of Dutch character to judge itself by its motives and others by their actions. The motives surrounding colonial policy and practice were sound according to the Dutch view, but other tendencies less noble or evil have thwarted Dutch action. This attitude is also reflected in the seldom passed up opportunity by Dutch spokesmen or newsmedia to point an admonishing finger at real or fancied weaknesses in the policies of other nations. This attitude of believing oneself righteous and therefore right is no doubt a reflection of the Calvinist make-up which has tainted not only the Dutch Reformed, but also the Roman-Catholics, the Socialists (the latter the two largest parties) as well as those who profess not to be religious. Pragmatic considerations rule politics here as elsewhere but despite the national and colonial experience the supreme test of any decision remains whether it can be based on a principle of higher order, preferably a quotation from the Bible.

[1] The 'culture system' has been thoroughly described by C. Fasseur, *Kultuurstelsel en Koloniale Baten, De Nederlandse exploitatie van Java 1840-60* (The Culture system and Colonial Profits, The Dutch exploitation of Java 1840-60), Leiden, 1975.

[2] See J.B.D. Derksen and J. Tinbergen, Berekeningen over de economische betekenis van Nederlandsch-Indië voor Nederland (Calculations on the economic significance of the East Indies for the Netherlands), *Monthly of the Central Bureau of Statistics*, 1945.

[3] The slavery question is treated by J.M. van Winter, De openbare mening in Nederland over de afschaffing van de slavernij (Public opinion in the Netherlands about the abolishment of slavery), *West-Indische Gids*, 1953, pp. 61-107 and M. Kuitenbrouwer, De Nederlandse afschaffing van de slavernij in vergelijkend perspectief (The Netherlands' abolishment of slavery in comparative perspective), *Bijdragen en mededelingen betreffende de geschiedenis der Nederlanden*, October 1978, pp. 69-99.

[4] The philosophy of the civil service has been elaborated upon by A.D.A. de Kat Angelino, De Ontwikkelingsgedachte in het Nederlandse Overzees Bestuur (The Development Thought in Dutch Overseas Rule), in H. Baudet and I.J. Brugmans (ed.), *Balans en Beleid* (Balance Sheet of Government), Assen 1961, pp. 35-65. See also S.L. van de Wal (ed.), *Besturen Overzee* (Governing Overseas), Franeker, 1977.

[5] Some of the aberrations resulting from these military actions are described by J.A.A. van Doorn and W.J. Hendriks, *Ontsporing van Geweld* (Derailment of Force), Rotterdam, 1970. According to the authors, the excesses committed by the Dutch forces (partly as a result of the frustration and humiliation suffered during the German occupation and the wish to show its

mettle after the liberation on another battlefield) are officially swept under the carpet of colonial history and memory.

[6] The subject of New Guinea has been thoroughly investigated by A. Lijphart, *The Trauma of Decolonization: The Dutch and West New Guinea*, New Haven/London, 1966.

[7] The integration or assimilation of those and other immigrants has been described by H. Verwey-Jonker (ed.), *Allochtonen in Nederland* (Allochtones – those born outside (W.B.) – in the Netherlands), The Hague, 1971.

[8] I am thinking here of a study I wrote while living in the Indies entitled 'Duitschers in Nederlandsch-Indië' (Germans in the Netherlands Indies), *Mensch en Maatschappij* (Man and Society), 1939, pp. 180-200.

[9] The subject has been treated somewhat more thoroughly in my article 'Reorientation of the Netherlands concerns formerly working in Indonesia', H. Baudet (ed.), *Trade World and World Trade*, Rotterdam, 28 August 1963, pp. 135-164.

Select bibliography

In English

Blussé, L. and F.S. Gaastra (eds.), *Companies and Trade, Essays on Ancien Régime Trading Companies and their Impact on Asia* (Comparative Studies in Overseas History Vol. III), Leiden 1980.

Creutzberg, P. (ed.), *Changing Economy in Indonesia* 1. *Indonesia's Export Crops 1816-1940,* 2. *Public Finance 1816-1939,* 3. *Expenditure on Fixed Assets,* 4. *Rice Prices,* 5. *National Income,* 6. *Money and Banking 1816-1940,* The Hague. Publications on *Trade Statistics 1821-1940* and on *Balance of Payments 1816-1940* are to be issued shortly.

Emmer, P.C. and H.L. Wesseling (eds.), *Essays on Post-war Historiography about European Expansion* (Comparative Studies in Overseas History Vol. II), Leiden, 1979.

Fieldhouse, D.F., *Economics and Empire, 1813-1914*, London 1973.

Furnivall, J.S., *Netherlands India*, London/New York 1944.

Ross, R. (ed.), *Colonialism and Racism* (Comparative Studies in Overseas History Vol IV) to be published in 1981.

Wels, C.B., The Colonies as a Constant Factor in Dutch Foreign Policy, in: Mrs. Yang Aisyah Mutallib (ed.), *Proceedings of the Second Dutch-Indonesian Historical Conference*, Ujung Pandang 1978, 1980.

Wesseling, H.L. (ed.), *Expansion and Reactions in Asia and Africa* (Comparative Studies in Overseas History Vol. I), Leiden 1979.

Wesseling, H.L., Post-Imperial Holland, *Journal of Contemporary History*, Vol. 15, No. 1 (1980), pp. 125-143.

In Dutch

Baudet, H. and C. Fasseur, Koloniale bedrijvigheid, in: J.H. van Stuijvenberg (ed.), *De Economische Geschiedenis van Nederland*, Groningen 1977, pp. 309-350.

Burger, D.H., *Sociologisch-economische geschiedenis van Indonesië*, two parts, Wageningen/Amsterdam 1975.

Encyclopedie van de Nederlandse Antillen, Amsterdam/Brussel 1969.

Encyclopedie van Suriname, Amsterdam/Brussel 1977.

Gonggrijp, G., *Schets eener economische geschiedenis van Nederlandsch Indië*, fourth edition, Haarlem 1957.

11 THE NETHERLANDS AND THE EEC

R.T. Griffiths

This chapter will attempt to describe the implications for the Netherlands of membership of the European Communities from both political and economic standpoints. Because of limitations of space, it has proved necessary to restrict discussion on many items and, unfortunately, to omit others altogether. Thus it has proved impossible to say anything about the Dutch position on regional or social policy, on energy or development aid. The inclusion of such issues would undoubtedly have provided a more rounded picture of the Netherlands' role within the Communities but it would have been at the expense of what this author, at least, felt to have been more central concerns.

11.1 Introduction: Towards the Treaty of Rome

The experience of the depression and the Second World War had forced the Dutch to abandon policy positions that might otherwise have precluded participation in experiments at regional co-operation. Economically, the rising wall of protectionism of the late 1920s and 1930s led the government to reverse its free trade policy, which had been held since the 1840s, and to protect vulnerable sectors of the economy. At the same time the government tried, unsuccessfully, to co-operate with other nations in establishing havens of relative economic stability to which other countries might be drawn. In the political sphere, foreign policy since 1815 could be described as one of passive neutrality coupled with a belief in the efficacy of international law. This passivity was seen as the best way of avoiding conflicts potentially damaging to both trade and colonial interests. Faith in the continued utility of such a policy did not long survive the landing of the first German paratroopers in May 1940.

During the war there was much soul-searching both inside and outside the Netherlands over the future world order and, more importantly, over the

Dutch position within it[1]. Within the European context this led to an agreement, signed in September 1944, to form a Benelux customs union[2]. Although the Benelux initiative was soon to be overshadowed by developments of wider European significance, the experience yielded a number of important lessons. It demonstrated that, notwithstanding the relatively low level of existing tariffs and the complementarity of the two economies[3], the stimulating effects on intra-area trade were far greater than originally anticipated. Moreover, it showed the economic dislocation expected to follow in the wake of tariff dismantling to be relatively slight. It also proved that trade liberalisation could proceed without the necessity for complex arrangements for the co-ordination of economic policy. Finally, it demonstrated to the countries themselves that they could fruitfully co-operate at a political level, thus dispelling much of the mutual antipathy that existed before the war[4]. This co-operation was to lead later to a number of significant initiatives in the tortuous path towards closer European co-operation.

However, the Dutch did not view Benelux purely as an end in itself. With substantial trading links overseas and with the German hinterland, Dutch economic interests lay in co-operation in the widest possible field[5]. Thus in 1949 Foreign Minister Stikker (1948-1952) proposed a plan for tariff reduction among members of the Organisation for European Economic Co-operation (OEEC), the establishment of a fund to help smooth out possible dislocation and provision for a higher measure of inter-governmental co-operation[6]. These proposals were rapidly overtaken by discussions on the Schuman Plan to establish a European Coal and Steel Community (ECSC).

Whilst Dutch policy in the economic field represented a measure of continuity with the initiatives taken in the 1930s, politically there was a complete change of stance. Security was now perceived to lie not in an aloof independence but in the closest possible co-operation with other countries[7]. The practical expression of this policy lay in full-hearted support for the North Atlantic Treaty Organisation (NATO) and, within NATO, unwavering support for the American nuclear monopoly[8]. Whilst it is outside the scope of this chapter to discuss it further, this 'Atlanticist' trend in Dutch foreign policy is vitally important in understanding Dutch attitudes towards European questions.

Thus Dutch policy after the war lay in encouraging the re-establishment of a stable economic and political order on the widest possible scale whilst fostering initiatives to that end in Europe in particular. Another policy consideration was how best to defend national interests within any new institutional framework which was to evolve. This last factor was to assume immediate importance in the negotiations for the ECSC which began in 1950. In the course of these Stikker proposed that a Council of Ministers be created to provide an intergovernmental check on the independence of the High Authority in order to avert the danger that sectoral policies on coal and steel might get out of step with general economic policy[9]. Interestingly, there is no sign, at this early stage, of the belief in supranationalism that was later to become the hall-mark of the Dutch approach.

The Netherlands was rather less enthusiastic over the next steps towards European integration. It participated reluctantly in talks for a European Defence Community (EDC) only because it would serve to rehabilitate West Germany and it made it known that participation in a European Political Community (EPC) was contingent upon greater progress in the area of economic co-operation[10]. In September 1952, Beyen (1952-1956), one of the two foreign ministers at the time[11], proposed an all-embracing customs union among members of the ECSC but his suggestions were received with little enthusiasm. However, when the movement towards EDC and EPC came to grief, Beyen, together with the Belgian foreign minister Spaak, in a memorandum to other members in May 1955 relaunched proposals for a common market in trade, agriculture, energy and transport under the guidance of a communal authority. The intense co-operation among the Benelux countries in elaborating the proposals played no small part in securing their acceptance at the Messina Conference in June 1955[12]. The rest is history. Whereas earlier federalist approaches towards integration had failed, this broad-based functionalist initiative was to culminate in the signing of the Treaty of Rome in 1957.

Within the Netherlands there were certain apprehensions about ratifying the Treaty. There was uneasiness about the protectionist momentum which the upward revision of tariffs implied[13] but against this the government set advantages of trade security. There were also fears that the EEC might lead to the creation of antagonistic trade blocs, partly reflecting disappointment that the market was not wider in scope, and there were allied fears that it might weaken NATO. However, the ultimate defence of the government was political – that the creation of a Common Market would terminate intra-European rivalry and promote the cause of peace and stability on the Continent. In the event the Treaty was ratified in the Second Chamber by an overwhelming majority[14].

11.2 Shaping the European communities

11.2.1 Policy Content

As we have seen, Dutch enthusiasm towards European integration was tempered by a preference for a wider and more liberal concept of economic relationships and, politically, by unswerving allegiance to the idea of Atlantic co-operation. Nearly three years after the signing of the Treaty of Rome, new initiatives were taken which appeared not only to undermine both of these principles but to threaten the effective representation of Dutch national interests at a European level as well. De Gaulle's proposals for 'political union' launched at the Rambouillet summit in July 1960 involved regular meetings of heads of government and foreign ministers backed up by a permanent secretariat. Four other permanent commissions were to be established to deal with foreign policy, defence, economic and cultural affairs and a European assembly was to be created with membership nominated by national parliaments. Throughout the so-called Fouchet negotiations which lasted from February 1961 to April 1962, the Dutch maintained an implacably hostile and often isolated opposition[15].

It is difficult to unravel the exact logic behind the Dutch position but it would seem to rest on two basic objections. Firstly, there was a relative lack of interest in the Netherlands in developing a political community. More than the other nations, the Dutch interpreted their membership of the Community primarily in welfare terms and, thus, tended to adopt a more functionalist approach to questions of closer co-operation. Secondly, the Dutch were deeply suspicious of French motives since Franco/American relations were at a low ebb in this period. There was a very deep concern that in going along with de Gaulle's plans, the country would eventually be forced to choose between the Atlantic connection and closer European ties. Luns (Foreign Minister 1952-1971) expressed both these sentiments in the following way, 'Europe is not and cannot be the Europe of the six either economically or politically . . . . . I much prefer the outline of political integration in Europe which would be rather vague, including as many countries as possible, to an extremely elaborate political integration which would exclude other countries of Europe and which would be limited to the Six alone'[16].

At first the Dutch tried to defuse the issue by urging that consultations on de Gaulle's proposals should take place in the wider forum of the Western European Union (WEU) of which Great Britain was a member. When this failed, the Dutch insisted outright that they would not proceed towards political union without British participation. Bodenheimer has argued that the Dutch commitment towards an open community was all along nothing more than a rationalisation of a preference for British membership and that this, in turn, stems primarily 'from the Dutch perception of substantive British policy regarding the Atlantic alliance and the effect a British presence would have upon Europe's position withing the Alliance'[17]. Other observers have commented that British membership was viewed in terms of power politics, as a useful counter to the threat of Franco/German hegemony within an inter-governmental framework[18].

Alongside the issue of British membership, a second policy stance was adopted by the Dutch government. Given the distinctly cool attitude hitherto demonstrated towards the question of supranationalism[19] it was ironic that the Dutch should now adopt the standpoint that they would be willing to participate in closer integration if existing supranational institutions were strengthened and if new supranational elements were introduced into the union[20]. Bodenheimer has interpreted Luns' conversion as a negotiating manoeuvre – Knowing in advance that any such proposals would be unacceptable to the French, playing the supranational card was tantamount to saying 'no' to an inter-governmental Europe[21]. There was also a power-politics logic to the Dutch position in that strengthened Community institutions, which would be relatively free from nationalistic considerations and therefore more amenable to the force of rational (i.e. Dutch) arguments, would also serve to provide a counter to the danger of large power hegemony[22]. Whatever cynicism may have lain behind the government's new found enthusiasm for a policy of strengthening the position of supranational institutions, its conversion brought it into line with a significant stream of political feeling within the national parliament which was to have important consequences later on.

The Fouchet negotiations were finally deadlocked in the spring of 1962 and well-meaning attempts by other nations to revive them floundered on the mutual intransigence of the French and Dutch. Whether it was good for Europe or not, the outcome represented a successful defence of Dutch interests. In the course of the negotiations, two new planks of European policy had emerged – a determination to secure British membership of the Communities and a desire to strengthen and democratise Community institutions. Progress in realising the first of these aims received a temporary setback with de Gaulle's veto of British entry in January 1963 and the announcement in 1964 by the British that they would not be making any new moves towards joining the Community. With the issue of British membership removed, albeit temporarily, from the political limelight, Dutch policy emphasis switched to the need to democratise the Communities and strengthen supranational elements in Europe.

The occasion for the manifestation of this new stance was the negotiations for a common agricultural policy (CAP). After much protracted discussion, punctuated by marathon sessions of the Council of Ministers, the Six had made quite considerable progress. In December 1963 the machinery for the CAP had been agreed and by December 1964 the common price levels had been accepted. The only issue remaining on the agenda, for June 1965, was to settle the financial regulation for the policy, under which it was envisaged that the Community would eventually receive its own revenues and would be exclusively responsible for administering the expenditure associated with the policy.

Within the Netherlands these negotiations coincided with an increasing resolve in Parliament to assert greater control over foreign policy and, in particular, to secure budgetary powers in favour of the European Parliament[23]. Sensing this change in mood, in December 1964, Luns signalled to the Council of Ministers, for the first time, the Dutch intention of strengthening the powers of the European Parliament[24]. The following February, the Dutch parliament unanimously adopted a motion to accord the European Parliament a central position in the decision-making process of the European Communities[25]. In June 1965 Luns was forced to accept a motion, sponsored by all the major parties, to support the European Commission's proposals in the forthcoming negotiations[26], effectively constraining his room for manoeuvre unless the Commission should change its position. The proposals contained, *inter alia*, provision for the Parliament to alter the budget by simple majority vote and that, if supported by the Commission, these amendments could only be altered by the Council of Ministers by a 5:1 majority[27]. The negotiations which took place in June 1965 eventually reached deadlock over the manner of financing the CAP, the timing of its introduction as well as the new decision-making structure. They culminated in the French walk-out and boycott of Community institutions. When the French returned to the fold, negotiations continued, though it was not until December 1969 that the final details of the package establishing the CAP were locked into place and when they were, precious little of the proposals for democratic control of the budget or qualified majority voting in the Council of Ministers remained. Given that there was little sympathy outside the Netherlands and Italy for such developments, progress in this direction was effectively blocked. In the Dutch parliament, Luns reaffirmed the governments's commitment to democratisation but that, given the political realities of the moment, it was unable to guarantee any positive outcome[28].

One of the outcomes of the crisis into which the French walk-out plunged the Community was a renewed Dutch enthusiasm for the British candidature. When the application was finally made in May 1967 it received the full backing of the Dutch government which, at the same time, declared itself opposed to further discussions on closer European integration until the issue of British membership had been settled[29]. The second French veto (November 1967) was greeted with open hostility in the Netherlands and, in concert with the other Benelux countries, the Dutch announced their intention of continuing the discussions outside the Community framework. For this to work, the Benelux plan required the adhesion of Italy and Germany but the Germans were anxious to avoid too open a confrontation with France. They were, however, willing to participate in discussions with Britain within the framework of the WEU on closer co-operation in foreign policy, technology, defence and monetary policy (France immediately boycotted these meetings)[30]. The determination of the five EEC members, led by Benelux, not to allow the momentum of the second British application to peter out, coupled with the departure of de Gaulle in April 1969 helped to weaken French resolve. At the Hague summit in December 1969 it was decided to reopen negotiations with Britain and the other candidates; negotiations which were to culminate successfully in the signing of the Treaty of Accession in Brussels in January 1972.

The resolution of the issue of British membership removed Dutch objections to participating in discussions towards closer integration. The Hague summit had witnessed agreement not only on the question of enlargement but also on the need to accelerate progress towards economic and monetary union (EMU) and European political co-operation (EPC). It is convenient to examine these two issues separately.

The decision to proceed towards EMU had been taken in the absence of any consensus on the ultimate objectives of such a union or the mechanisms by which it would be attained. In the debate which followed, two basic schools of thought emerged. The Dutch standpoint initially coincided closely with that of the Germans in what may be called the 'economist school'. They believed that closer policy co-ordination and convergent economic development should precede the tighter linking of currencies and the introduction of an element of supranational decision-making. The 'monetarist school', which embraced the Commission and the other member states, especially France, believed that exchange rates should be irrevocably fixed as soon as possible in order to provide the discipline to enforce policy co-ordination. They also believed that a supranational element should become important far earlier in the process[31].

In 1971 the Six were able to agree on the Werner Plan which envisaged that EMU be attained by 1980. Its first phase was something of a compromise whereby permitted exchange rate fluctuations were to be confined to a narrow band (the famous 'snake'), the co-ordination of national budgets was to be achieved at the level of Council of Ministers and a Community Fund was to be set up to iron-out exchange rate fluctuations. Only the first part of this package was ever implemented and by 1975 the shocks of unstable world currency markets, accelerating inflation and different national responses to the oil crisis had reduced even this to a total shambles. That same year a special advisory commission, set up by the government to advise on the problem of European union, published its report (called the 'Spierenberg Report' after its chairman). At the heart of its advice was a 'monetarist' argument that 'the introduction of the monetary union can take place in accordance with a schedule . . . comprising a number of coercive stages'[32]. Surprisingly the government now did a complete *volte-face*, accepted the advice and declared its willingness to enter into binding commitments for the implementation of EMU[33]. Given the strong objections of other countries, notably Great Britain, to the surrender of sovereignty which EMU would imply, there was little that the Dutch could do to accelerate progress in the direction they desired. It was to take a Franco-German initiative in 1978, to strengthen the mechanism of exchange-rate co-ordination, to establish the European Monetary System (EMS) and even this fell a long way short of what the Dutch would have wished.

Turning to the question of EPC, in 1970 the Belgian diplomat Davignon suggested that regular meetings of the foreign ministers be held to harmonise the European position on foreign policy issues. Dutch antipathy towards the idea was strong. It reawakened all the fears apparent during the Fouchet negotiations that the standing of Community institutions would be diluted and that the integrity of NATO might be jeopardised. However, unlike the Fouchet negotiations, the Dutch did not block progress towards closer co-operation. In the first place, the participation of Great Britain appeared to ensure that the Atlanticist views would not be ignored. Secondly, the new arrangements did not automatically imply operating outside the Community institutions, although they, initially, did nothing to strengthen them[34]. However, Foreign Minister van den Stoel (1973-1977) was able to extract some concessions in this direction which helped to reduce hostility to the idea[35]. It has also been suggested that, notwithstanding the constant Dutch insistence on suprantionalism, intergovernmental processes (whether non-binding consultations in EPC or unanimous decision-making in the Council of Ministers) actually helped guarantee against small-power domination by larger partners[36]. Finally, whatever Dutch feelings about the course of developments, a 'yes', however reluctant, was better than a refusal which might have led to an even less acceptable alternative – bilateral co-operation between the larger powers[37].

A final theme of Dutch policy has been continued pressure for a transfer of powers to supranational Community institutions and a strengthening of democratic control within the Community. In theory these policies represent the means towards the ultimate goal of federal European state. In practice it is doubtful whether the Dutch are any more willing than other governments to countenance the massive transfer of powers which this would imply. Indeed, under the centre-left den Uyl cabinet (1973-1977) there has been some distancing from this concept[38]. In public statements on belief in a federal Europe it would appear that Dutch parliamentarians have become prisoners of their own success at having made the issue virtually a national religion[39]. If one accepts that Dutch policy objectives are somewhat less ambitious than they often appear, pressure from the Netherlands has had some limited success. In December 1974 agreement was reached on a democratically elected European Parliament (elections for which were held in June 1979) and in 1975 it was agreed that the European Parliament have the final say over the adoption of the budget. Beyond that very little progress has been made and the focus of the struggle for democratic control has now shifted to the Parliament itself.

11.2.2 Policy-making process

Membership of a large international organisation, whose range of competences embraced many areas of economic and social interest hitherto the preserve of domestic rather than foreign policy, created new problems for Dutch policy-makers. At the highest level the problem of policy co-ordination was complicated by the system of coalition government. Problems of coalition-balancing tend to give individual ministers a large measure of personal responsibility for policy and it was rare for the portfolios for major departments to be held by members of the same political party. The problem of inter-departmental co-operation was further accentuated by the relatively weak position to which the Foreign Ministry had been reduced after the war. During the 1930s, the intense diplomatic activity over economic questions meant that the implementation of foreign policy had devolved increasingly to the Ministry of Economic Affairs. After the war this position was reinforced by the fact that the newly created Directorate General for Foreign Economic Affairs, BEB (*Directoraat-Generaal voor*

Buitenlandse Economische Betrekking), intended to foster interdepart-
mental co-operation, was made responsible to the Economics Ministry.
With negotiations for the EEC, the struggle for ministerial competence
intensified[40]. In 1958 a new co-ordinating body was established under the
Foreign Ministry, DGES (*Directoraat-Generaal voor Europese Samenwerking*)
but BEB was still left in existence. Since there were now two ministerial
co-ordinating bodies in existence a formal co-ordinating committee
was set up, the CCEIA (*Co-ordinatie Commissie voor Europese Integratie en
Associatie Problemen*), with a chairman supplied by BEB and the secretariat
provided by DGES. Since, not surprisingly, conflicts still remained
unresolved within the CCEIA, a cabinet-committee was formed in
1961, the REZ (*Raad voor Europese Zaken*) under the chairmanship of the
Prime Minister[41]. All this accomplished was to institutionalise the forum
within which the struggle for ministerial competence between the Foreign
Ministry and the so-called 'technical' ministries (especially the Economics
Ministry) could play itself out.

Thus the ability of successive Dutch governments to formulate and
present policy effectively at a European level has been hampered by this
continuous tension between Departments. Valuable ministerial time has
been wasted in resolving blistering inter-departmental rows over both
policy-content and departmental competence. Furthermore, in order to
accommodate various departmental interests, the size of Dutch delegations
at international negotiations has often proved large, unwieldly and cumber-
so. Finally, and most importantly, the continuous squabbling has seriously
weakened attempts to impart some unity to the overall direction of
European policy[42]. The classic, oft-quoted, example was the occasion of the
negotiations in 1964 over Nigeria's association with the EEC at which two
rival delegations arrived both claiming the right to represent the Dutch point
of view[43]. More recently, the Agricultural Ministers agreed to a temporary
ban on meat imports into the EEC from third world countries to which the
Dutch minister assented (seeing it as a technical question) without considering this action in conflict with Dutch policy on aid to less developed
countries (a political question)[44].

In 1971 a government commission reported on the problem of inter-
departmental responsibility and co-ordination (the van Veen Report). It
rejected the possibility of a separate Ministry for European Affairs, arguing
that it would carry too little political weight and that it would lack the
necessary expertise for all the matters with which it would be confronted in
Brussels. However it did recommend that the position of the Ministry of
Foreign Affairs as co-ordinator of European policy be strengthened[45]. In

1972 the government acted to implement some of the recommendations of the van Veen Report. Although the delineation of ministerial responsibility still left room for a certain ambiguity[46] ex-Secretary of State for Foreign Affairs, Professor Brinkhorst (1973-1977) has claimed that the new arrangements have worked very well. Pivotal to their success the fact that the Secretary of State for Foreign Affairs took over the chairmanship of the CCEIA. As a political chairman of an inter-departmental committee of civil servants, he felt he had been able to influence policy-making at the preparatory stage before Departmental decisions had hardened. He had been able to exercise his political authority to 'encourage' the settlement of inter-departmental differences and when unresolved were discussed at the REZ, his position amongst his colleagues was enhanced by his overall view of the issues and his practical experience in being able to advise on the feasibility of realising different policy options in Brussels[47]. Whilst, as an outsider, this analysis seems a little too perfect, one must accept Professor Brinkhorst's statement that the practical results of the new arrangements have proved encouraging.

11.3 The economics of the Common Market

11.3.1 Trade

We have already suggested that part of the Dutch reluctance to support proposals for closer political co-operation within the Community stemmed from a tendency to view the potential benefits of membership primarily in welfare terms. In this section we shall examine some of the more tangible economic benefits of community membership, starting with trade. In July 1960 the EEC took the first step towards the abolition of tariffs on intra-area trade and the erection of a common external tariff and it completed the process in July 1968. As a nation highly dependent on foreign trade, the Netherlands was among one of the most enthusiastic proponents for this policy.

At first sight the figures would seem to confirm the expectation that trade within an area in which tariffs were being eliminated would grow faster than trade with the rest of the world where progress in this direction was more modest. Between 1958 and 1972 the value of Dutch exports to other EEC states increased at a rate of 14.8 percent per annum compared with a rate of 7.6 percent for exports to the rest of the world (the corresponding figures for imports were 12.0 and 7.6 respectively)[48]. The question arises how far this difference was attributable to EEC tariff policies as opposed to other factors as the relatively faster growth of continental European markets or changes in the structure of trade in favour of manufactured goods both of which would have served to deflect Dutch trade towards EEC member states without the extra fillip of tariff reduction.

It is necessary then, to attempt to isolate the 'EEC-effect' in promoting intra-area trade. A recent Dutch survey has claimed that between 1956 and 1969, Dutch exports of manufactured goods to member states were 80 percent higher than they would have been in the absence of the EEC (the corresponding figure for imports was 26-35 percent)[49]. Leaving aside the problem of the accuracy of these calculations, another question arises as to how far this increase in Dutch intra-area trade has been at the expense of trade with the rest of the world. It might be that as a result of the common external tariff, the Netherlands switched its source of imports from low cost countries outside the EEC to higher cost countries within it. Far from benefitting either the economy or the consumer, this situation would penalise them. This is known as 'trade diversion'. On the other hand, the elimination of intra-area tariffs may well have promoted trade previously none had been possible, in which case the effect will be beneficial. This is known as 'trade creation'. It would seem likely that the 'EEC-effect' observed above contains elements of both 'trade creation' and 'trade diversion' and, as can be imagined, the exercise of distinguishing between the two is fraught with difficulties.

Before we progress; a word of caution is appropriate. One economist, surveying the techniques for measuring trade creation and trade diversion, concluded that, 'all estimates of trade creation and diversion by the EEC which have been presented in the empirical literature are so much affected by *ceteris paribus* assumptions, by the choice of the length of pre- and post-integration periods, by the choice of benchmark year (or years), by the methods to compute income elasticities, changes in trade matrices and relative shares and by structural changes not attributable to the EEC but which occurred during the pre- and post-integration periods .... *that the magnitude of no single estimate should be taken too seriously*'[50] (my italics). Very few of the studies on this problem disaggregate their findings by individual countries and, of those that do, even fewer present their findings in comparable form. Two studies which do, come to apparently contradictory conclusions. The calculations of Verdoorn and Schwartz are based on trade in manufactured goods only for the years 1956-1969. Their most favourable estimate is that the Netherlands experienced net trade creation equivalent to 16.9 percent of the 'normal' value of imports in 1969 (i.e. the level of imports in the absence of integration). Their less favourable estimate reduces this figure to 1.1 percent[51]. Prewo's calculations cover all physical trade over the period 1959-1970. He estimates that the Dutch economy experienced net trade diversion equivalent to 8 percent of the 'normal' value of imports in 1970[52]. Both studies are in complete agreement, however, that the Netherlands benefitted less than any of the other member states from the net trade creation effect of EEC tariff policies.

The reasons for this relative failure to gain from the Community tariff policy are not hard to find. Because the Dutch had a relatively low tariff level in 1959, on the eve of the creation of the EEC, their economy stood to gain relatively less from the trade creating effects of mutual tariff reduction. Similarly, the high degree of openness of the economy prior to 1959 suggests that the Netherlands had already achieved a high degree of international specialisation to meet the needs of foreign markets. On the other hand, the fact that the common external tariff implied an upward revision of Dutch levels of protection, accentuated the trade diverting effect on the economy. Finally the fact that the trade preferences agreed within Benelux had to be extended to other members meant that the Dutch lost ground in that market – a case of negative trade creation or 'trade erosion'[53]. It is perhaps too easy to allow these econometric studies to shape our appreciation of what would have been the case had no integration occurred. This, of course, was not a realistic policy option. What the calculations do not tell us is what would have happened had the EEC been formed and the Netherlands left outside it![54]

11.3.2 Transport

As the only net exporter of any significance in intra-Community transport services, one would have expected the Netherlands to have a vested interest in seeing the abolition of national descrimination in transport policies and the establishment of a common Community market. Yet progress to this end has proved painfully slow, due in no small measure to Dutch intransigence towards the proposals of other member states (particularly Germany) and even towards those of the Commission. It was not that the Dutch were against a common policy *per se* but against the form of policy that was being suggested.

As a long-established provider of European transport services it was natural that the Netherlands should expect to fare well in a relatively free and uncontrolled market which would give free rein to their competitive advantage. Indeed it was argued that if logic demanded the abolition of restrictions on trade as being in the interests of the development of the Community as a whole, then the same considerations should apply to the transport of those goods. In opposition to those other states which emphasised the social or strategic position of transport, the Dutch pressed for the adoption of a relatively liberal policy. In particular they strenuously opposed suggestions for the compulsory publication of freight rates and the imposition of national quotas on Community transport licences, both of which, it was felt, would serve to strifle free competition and lead to the suboptimal utilisation of resources[55].

Dutch opposition towards regulation in the transport sector was rewarded in 1960 when the European Court ruled against the interpretation of the High Authority of the ECSC that freight rates should indeed be published. However this minor success was short-lived for in 1962 the decision was reversed[56]. The same year the Commission published its Action Plan envisaging that countries adopt a so-called 'fork-rate system' (i.e. published minimum and maximum freight rates between which competition would occur) and that a system of quotas be established for Community licences. Both of these proposals were bitterly rejected by the Dutch for the next three years but eventually internal division within the Netherlands and the increasingly isolated negotiating position undermined the government's stance. In 1964 agreement was reached on the principle of quotas and in 1965, after the French boycott made it even more difficult, politically, for the Dutch to resist the pressures of the other parties in the negotiations, the government was forced to agree to the implementation of a fork-rate system. Both of these were seen as 'temporary' measures. Even then their introduction was to be delayed until 1968 whilst the ramifications of these agreements were worked out[57].

The Dutch attitude towards a common transport policy is revealing because it further demonstrates that the government is perfectly capable of a tenacious defence of national interests in the face of the opposition of other member states and even of the Commission. Although eventually forced to compromise, the Dutch have succeeded in stalling progress towards a co-ordinated and comprehensive policy in this sphere. It is also interesting that this defence is structured not in terms of national self-interest but in an appeal to a higher principle – that a relatively free and liberal policy is economically more efficient than a highly regulated regime. Perhaps in terms of neo-classical economics the Dutch position has much to recommend it but it is instructive to reflect that when it comes to discussions on agriculture this principle does not seem to apply!

11.3.3 Agriculture

In agriculture, as in transport, the Netherlands possessed a sector of the economy which provided an important share of national income (in 1968 agriculture comprised 7.2 percent of national income, transport 10.2 percent) and a significant surplus contribution to the balance of payments (in 1968 agriculture had a net export surplus of 2.7 billion guilders, transport 1.5 billion)[58]. In contrast with transport, however, the Dutch had little difficulty in agreeing to a common policy in agriculture, the CAP. Indeed, the system of artificially supported, high domestic prices, coupled with export rebates and intervention buying, bore a close resemblance to the schemes already operating within the Netherlands before the inception of the CAP. When this national system of market regulation was applied at a Community level, it could be expected to confer extra benefits both on the agricultural sector and on the economy as a whole.

The most obvious observation to make is that it seems probable that the sheer magnitude of the costs of administering such a policy at a purely national level would have prohibited such a generous measure of protectionism. Under the CAP these costs were reduced. Firstly, the policy was funded at a Community level and because of the methods by which the funds were collected and dispersed, this places less of a strain on the exchequer than would have been the case with a national policy (this will be illustrated below). Secondly, the costs of the policy itself were reduced because, since the high Community price level prevails throughout the EEC for national production and traded produce alike, there is no necessity for export rebates on Dutch exports to member states to make Dutch produce competitive with world prices[59]. This second point leads to a benefit or cost for the balance of payments insofar as exports to member states will earn more foreign exchange than those to the rest of the world (RoW), because of the differences in prices, though, conversely, imports from within the Community will cost more. Whether this works out as a gain or a loss depends on the net trade flows inside and outside the EEC and the structure of the export and import packages. Finally, the fact that there is an element in the CAP expenditure to finance improvement schemes, it could be expected to contribute towards increasing levels of agricultural efficiency.

With the increasing isolation of the Community market from world competition and the attraction of relatively high prices within the EEC, it is not surprising to see Dutch agricultural exports (and, at a lower level, imports) concentrated increasingly on other member states.

This is clearly shown in Table 11.1. This table also demonstrates that the

Table 11.1 Value of Dutch Trade in agricultural products
(annual averages, billion guilders)

	1956-59	1960-63	1964-67	1968-71	1976-78[1]
Exports to EEC	2.0	2.8	4.2	7.3	21.0
Imports from EEC	0.5	0.7	1.2	2.4	7.8
Balance	+ 1.5	+ 2.1	+ 3.0	+ 4.9	+ 13.2
Exports to RoW	2.2	2.4	2.8	3.5	6.0
Imports from RoW	3.3	3.6	4.6	5.7	12.4
Balance	− 1.1	− 1.2	− 1.8	− 2.2	− 6.4
Overall Balance	+ 0.4	+ 0.9	+ 1.2	+ 2.7	+ 6.8

[1] EEC of 9 members

Source: Figures 1956-59 to 1968-71, J. de Hoog, 'De gemeenschappelijke landbouw-markt en de Nederlandse economie' *Jaarverslag Landbouw-Economisch Instituut*, Den Haag, 1975, p. 12.
Figures 1976-78 calculated from *Landbouw-economisch Bericht*, 1979, pp. 82-83.

Dutch earned growing surpluses on its agricultural trade with the EEC which more than offset increasing deficits with the RoW, yielding an ever growing surplus contribution to the balance of payments as a whole. It is impossible to say just how far privileged access to Community markets was responsible for this 'balance of payments effect' since it must be noted that this trend was already apparent before the CAP began. It is possible, however, to measure a specific 'food gain' contribution to the surplus which derives from the form in which European agriculture is protected. Thus the Dutch balance of payments benefitted because, on balance, agricultural produce was sold on markets at which the high Community price prevailed whilst, on balance, agricultural purchases were obtained at lower world prices. This 'food gain' (the difference between Dutch agricultural trade with the EEC measured at Community and at world prices) has been estimated for 1978 at between £ 312 million[60] and £ 441 million[61]. At a rate of 4.2 guilders = £ 1 this would represent a not inconsiderable contribution to the balance of payments of between 1.3 and 1.8 billion guilders.

It is difficult to establish precisely what the implications of guaranteed access to high price markets were for Dutch agricultural production partly because agriculture is a sector of the economy rarely characterised by dramatic changes in direction and partly because it is impossible to state how it would have developed outside the CAP. The average annual rate of increase in the volume of gross agricultural production improved marginally from 4.3 percent p.a. in 1960-1970 to 4.4. percent p.a. in 1970-1975. In terms of net production (gross production minus inputs of goods and services) the tempo of improvement certainly increased from an average growth of 2.7 percent p.a. in the 60s to 4.4 percent p.a. in the first half of the 70s[62]. This increase in production was accompanied by a shift in the structure of production away from arable produce towards animal products. In 1962-64 the ratio between the two was 35:65 whereas by 1973-74 it stood at 32:68[63]. Whilst this change in the pattern of production undoubtedly confirmed the Dutch natural advantage in intensive production given the relative scarcity of land, it might feasibly have been reinforced by the fact that levels of protection in animal products such as butter and milk (where EEC prices were as much as five times the world price) were higher than for grains (where EEC prices were between one and a half and two times world prices)[64]. Although one cannot state exactly how far these developments were attributable to the CAP, an intuitive guess can be made as to the alternative of life outside the CAP when one looks at Danish agriculture which presents a picture of relative stagnation from the mid-60s to her entry in 1973[65].

When one comes to examining the impact of the CAP on levels of agricultural efficiency, the discussion becomes even more difficult. The tempo of improvement in productivity accelerated in the period 1970-75 compared with the previous decade with the average annual increase in net productivity (the relationship between net production and the costs of land, labour and capital) improving from 5.2 percent p.a. to 7.1 percent p.a.[66]. One factor within the CAP which might have contributed to this development is the structural shift in the pattern of output observed in the previous paragraph but only insofar that this shift in the concentration of production towards areas in which the Dutch were relatively more efficient was caused by differential prices within the EEC.

Another factor one could isolate are the funds for improvement received from the Guidance Section of the European Agricultural Guidance and Guarantee Fund (EAGGF). However Table 11.2 shows that until 1975 the sums received from this source were small compared with the outlays of the Dutch government itself. On the other hand, opponents of the CAP would argue that agricultural improvements were inspite of, and not because of, the policy and that indiscriminate protection is likely to deter rather than foster a climate of innovation and improvement. They would attribute the increase in productivity in agriculture more to the relatively greater attraction of non-agricultural forms of employment 'pulling' labour from

Table 11.2 Expenditure on projects for agricultural improvement
in the Netherlands 1968-1978 (million guilders)

	National Government	Community funds
1968	227	2
1969	218	7
1970	240	15
1971	241	10
1972	246	30
1973	209	40
1974	181	60
1975	260	100
1976	315	80
1977	218	100
1978	263	120

Source: National Government – Data supplied by Directoraat-Generaal voor de Landbouw en de Voedselvoorziening afdl. Landinrichtingsdienst, Utrecht.
Community Funds – Data supplied by Centraal Bureau voor de Statistiek, afdl. Nationaal Rekening, Ref. no. 07317-79-E8; 18-10-79.

the land, the outlays by national governments and the general improvements in the economic infrastructure of the country.

There can be little doubt that the CAP has served Dutch national interests both in its contribution to the balance of payments and in funding a sectoral/social policy intended to ensure those working in agriculture a reasonable standard of living. Whether it has actually benefitted the development of the agricultural sector, or, even, whether the economy might not have gained more with fewer resources tied into agriculture, are both open questions. It will be interesting to see how the Netherlands fares as the United Kingdom, Denmark and Ireland challenge for agricultural markets and what position the government will take when the whole question of agricultural protectionism is re-examined in the light of the current unwillingness to countenance unlimited expansion in the Community budget.

11.3.4 Budgetary transfers

It is appropriate to conclude this discussion on the economic benefits of Community membership with a brief reference to the net transfer of funds through the Community budget. In almost complete contrast with Great Britain, where this question has proved a burning political issue, virtually nothing has been publicised in the Netherlands on the matter. As an official at the Ministry of Finance said to me, 'When one feels one is doing well out of a thing, then one does not look too hard'.

Table 11.3 Outlays and receipts of the Dutch Government to and from the European Communities (million guilders)

	1968	1969	1970	1971	1972	1973
Outlays	164	130	248	950	1150	1580
Receipts	131	243	518	1350	1440	2250
Balance	− 33	+ 113	+ 270	+ 400	+ 290	+ 670

	1974	1975	1976	1977	1978	
Outlays	1410	2340	2550	3090	3450	
Receipts	1690	2000	2870	3450	3760	
Balance	+ 280	− 340	+ 320	+ 360	+ 310	

Source: Centraal Bureau voor de Statistiek, afdl. Nationaal Rekening. Ref. no. 07317-79-E8; 18-10-79.

The main component in Dutch outlays to the Community in recent years have been the taxes and levies on production and imports (the ECSC levy, customs duties, levies on agricultural imports, MCAs levied on exports and imports, sugar production and storage levies and the corresponsibility levy on milk). In 1978 this category accounted for 68.7 percent of government outlays to the Community. Most of the remainder (30.14 percent) is accounted for by the Dutch contribution for financing that part of expenditure not covered by the Community's own resources and funds to cover expenditure under the EAGGF Guidance Section. The residual is made up of the contribution to the European Development Fund. Turning to receipts from the Communities, the lion's share (95.5 percent in 1978) is made up of intervention and refund payments from the Guarantee Section of the EAGGF and the MCAs granted on imports and exports. The remainder is accounted for by transfers from the Social Fund, the Regional Development Fund and the Guidance Section of the EAGGF.

The figures in Table 11.3 confirm that the Netherlands have been almost continuous beneficiaries of the European Budget, the only exceptions being the years 1968 and 1975. Any attempt, however, to reform the CAP would almost certainly place this position in jeopardy.

11.4 The future of the European Community

11.4.1 The Dutch vision

In July 1979 the first elections were held for membership of the European Parliament, elections in which most Dutch political parties took part. The occasion, therefore, provides an ideal opportunity for assessing the degree of agreement or disagreement within the Dutch body politic towards the future development of European integration[67]. The fact that the individual election programmes ranged over many issues outside the competence of the new parliament makes them useful documents for this purpose since they reflect party feeling over the entire spectrum of European Community affairs. Their utility in this direction is only marginally affected by the fact that the confessional parties, CDA (*Christen Democratisch Appel*) and the liberal VVD (*Volkspartij voor Vrijheid en Democratie*) both fought the elections on the platforms of their respective European Federations.

The most striking conclusion from a study of the election programmes is the remarkable consensus among the major political parties towards the central European issues. The only dissenting voices over the need for closer European co-operation were the minor parties of the extreme left and the extreme right which all laid stress, instead, on the need to defend national sovereignty (though, obviously, for different reasons). Among the major parties, the socialist PvdA (*Partij van de Arbeid*) were the coolest in their enthusiasm for closer co-operation, continuing the stance adopted by den Uyl in 1973 (see p. 285). The party was willing to see closer co-operation at a European level only if Europe develops in a socialist/democratic character and does not compromise the socialist programme at a national level. At the other extreme the VVD sought the ultimate goal of a European government and in between the two were to be found the CDA and the important neo-liberal party D'66 (*Democraten '66*), whose programme as a whole was closer to the VVD's than that of the PvdA.

On the question of democratisation of the Communities, the consensus among the major parties was even stronger. All four political parties were in favour of an extension of the European Parliament's budgetary powers and all were in agreement over the need to introduce majority decision-making into the Council of Ministers. All parties except the CDA stated explicitly in their programmes that the Parliament be given legislatory powers whilst D'66 aspired to the Parliament eventually becoming the centre of 'opinion-forming' within the Community. This consensus applied equally on the question of further enlargement with no dissenting voices to be heard over the desirability of further expansion of the Community.

Turning to economic policies, the CDA, VVD and C'66 all declared themselves in favour of economic and monetary union. The PvdA added an
important caveat that closer monetary was to be viewed as an end in itself
and not as a motor for European integration. It was also emphasised that
member states should retain responsibility over their own economic
policies. On the question of the CAP, it will come as no surprise that there
was no discussion of wholesale reform of the policy although all the major
parties were concerned to tackle the problems of surpluses and their
implications for Third World trade.

It is difficult to ascertain from the results of the European parliamentary
elections exactly what impact these appeals of the political parties had on
Dutch voters. In the first instance the fact that the poll was disappointingly
low (57.8 percent as opposed to 87.5 percent in the 1977 Parliamentary
elections and 79.1 percent in the 1978 provincial elections) may well have
distorted the results since it was especially low in areas where the socialists
might have expected to draw support. Secondly, it was impossible to have
a poll on one sector of Dutch policy and not expect it to reflect, at least in
part, the popularity of government and opposition parties. Of the major
parties the PvdA and, to a lesser extent, the VVD lost support compared with
the 77 and 78 elections whilst the CDA and D'66 increased their share of the
vote. The latter showed a remarkable jump in popularity from 5.44 percent
of the poll in 1977, 5.20 percent in 1978 to 9.03 percent in 1979. Interesting
also was the fact that the four 'rejectionist' parties that participated in the
elections marginally increased their joint share of the vote from 5.74 percent in 1977, 6.05 percent in 1978 to 6.77 percent in 1979, though this might
say more about the voting behaviour of 'supporters of the minority parties'
than anything about the attitude of voters as a whole. In the event, however,
the most important election statistic was the 42 percent abstentions.

The reason for the low turnout may well lie in boredom with the
campaign, in the 'credibility gap' between the issues raised and the existing
powers of the Parliament or in total bewilderment with the whole affair.
There is evidence, however, that the politicians' view of Europe is not shared
quite so fully by Dutch citizens. Although the Commission's publication
Euro-barometer has consistently shown that the overwhelming majority of
Dutchmen questioned felt that membership of the EEC was 'good' for the
country (in April 1979 84 percent felt this way, in October 78 percent;
corresponding figures for those who felt it a 'bad' thing were 2 and 3 percent
respectively)[68], when asked more specific questions this enthusiasm begins
to dissipate. A poll conducted for the Dutch news service in October 1978

showed that of those questioned only 46 percent felt that further integration would be good for the economy (14 percent, bad) and only 26 percent that it would make the struggle against unemployment easier (33 percent, more difficult)[69].

11.4.2 The Dutch role[70]

By any standards of comparison, against France, Germany and Italy, the Netherlands was, and still is, a small country. Yet it played a surprisingly large role in shaping the Community of the Six. This was largely attributable to the fact that for much of the 1950s France was preoccupied by instability at home and decolonialisation problems abroad. As French self-confidence increased, the Germans proved reluctant to translate their growing economic power into political power and Great Britain, of course, remained outside the Community. It was in the circumstances of this relative vacuun that Dutch influence was able to express itself. Even at this time, however, our study has demonstrated the largely negative power of Dutch intervention – the ability, for example, to block French proposals during the Fouchet negotiations and to delay the implementation of the Commissions' plans for transport. Its positive influence, to move the Community in a direction it desired, could only succeed if the large powers were in agreement – as witnessed by progress towards mutual tariff reduction and the CAP and equally by the relative failure to move the other member states in the direction of democratisation of the Communities.

By the 70s, the Dutch were already being reduced to a smaller, though no less active, role within the EEC. On the one hand Germany began to play a larger role in the Community whilst, on the other hand, Britain's entry to the Community in 1973 decreased the relative role of the Netherlands in sustaining Atlanticist interests. However the expectation that in Britain the Dutch would find a powerful ally for democratisation within the EEC was soon rudely shattered. As the inter-play between the larger powers assumed more importance, so the 'blocking-power' of the Dutch diminished. Indeed, as negotiations for the new EPC demonstrated, reluctance to compromise might lead to the Netherlands being by-passed altogether. For the smaller powers this danger of being left-out of limited bilateral contacts between the larger powers has assumed a very real dimension as was almost the case at the Tokyo economic summit. Dutch policy must also take cognisance of the fact that without the agreement between the larger powers, further progress towards European integration will be impossible. Yet differences in interests between them make it extremely unlikely that any relatively permanent consensus will spontaneously be reached. If European co-operation is not to be blocked by total impasse, the smaller powers must attempt to participate in preparing the ground for consensus in a manner best exemplified by the Benelux co-operation in relaunching the Beyen Plan in 1955. The Europe of the 1980s, the Europe of ten, or even of twelve, will need such qualities of vision and political adroitness again if it is to overcome the economic, social and political problems confronting it.

* The research for this chapter was undertaken in the Netherlands in the summer of 1979 and was made possible by a grant from the British Academy for which I would like to express my sincerest appreciation.

[1] H. Daalder, 'Nederland en de wereld, 1940-1945', *Tijdschrift voor Geschiedenis*, Vol. 61 (1953), pp. 170-200.

[2] Immediately after the war the agreement linking exchange rates came into effect. Because of problems of reconstruction, the Dutch dragged their feet over further progress so that it was not until January 1948 that the agreement to abolish tariffs on trade between the two areas was implemented. H.A. Schmitt, *The Path to European Unity. From Marshall Plan to Common Market*, Baton Rouge (1962), pp. 29-30.

[3] Belgium and Luxembourg had already formed an economic union in 1921 and are, for convenience, treated as a single economic unit.

[4] F. Hartog, *Nederland en de Euromarkt*, Leiden (1971), pp. 10-19.

[5] This desire did not, however, prevent the Dutch torpedoing initiatives to extend the Benelux union to embrace France and Italy (christened FRITALUX by the French) or a later initiative to include Germany (GERBENELUX). Their rejections were motivated by fears that the new unions would be dominated by the larger partner(s).

[6] D.U. Stikker, *Memoires. Herinneringen uit de lange jaren waarin ik betrokken was bij de voortdurende wereldcrisis*, Rotterdam, The Hague (1966), pp. 161-166.

[7] S. Bodenheimer, *Political Union: A Microcosm of European Politics*, Leiden (1967), p. 166 has argued that this did not, in fact, imply a change in policy but a continuation of the same policy within a different context '. . . membership in a western bloc dominated by one Super-power has permitted a continuation of traditional Dutch neutrality within a new framework and has relieved them of the need to develop an ambitious foreign policy of their own'.

[8] R.W. Russell, 'The Atlantic Alliance in Dutch Foreign Policy', *Internationale Spectator*, Vol. 23, No. 13 (8-6-1969), pp. 1189-1208. J.J.C. Voorhoeve, *Peace, Profits and Principles. A Study of Dutch Foreign Policy*, The Hague (1979), pp. 101-109 *et seq*. This was written before the decision of the Dutch government not to sanction the stationing of cruise missiles on Dutch soil.

[9] W. Diebold, *The Schuman Plan. A Study in Economic Co-operation, 1950-1959*, New York (1959), pp. 61-63.

[10] I. Samkalden, 'A Dutch Retrospective View on European and Atlantic Co-operation', *Internationale Spectator*, Vol. 19, No. 7 (1965), pp. 634-637. Voorhoeve, *Peace, Profits and Principles*, pp. 110-112.

[11] Because of difficulties in allocating portfolios in the fourth Drees cabinet, two ministers of foreign affairs were appointed; J.W. Beyen in charge of European issues and J.M.A.H. Luns to take care of the rest. Once asked to explain the situation, Luns quipped, 'Because our country is so small, abroad is so large'.

[12] H.J.M. Aben, 'Plannen en werkelijkheid', *Europa Onderweg. Ooggetuigen brengen verslag uit*, ed.

H.J.M. Aben, Amsterdam (1967), pp. 20-26. This article was written in collaboration with ex-minister Beyen.

[13] Luns proposed that the external tariff of the EEC be cut by 20 percent but this was opposed as serving to weaken the central discipline of the Common Market. A similar fate met his proposal that the EEC and the European Free Trade Association (EFTA) should extend their tariff cuts to all signatories of the General Agreement on Tariffs and Trade (GATT). Voorhoeven, *Peace, Profits and Principles*, p. 163.

[14] For a discussion on the trends of opinion within the Netherlands on the eve of the inception of the Common Market see R. de Bruin, *Les Pays Bas et l'Integration Européenne*, 1957-1967, Ph.D. Thesis, Paris (1978), pp. 415-443.

[15] For an account of the Fouchet negotiations see Bodenheimer, *Political Union*, de Bruin, *Les Pays Bas et l'Integration Européenne* and A. Silj, *Europe's Political Puzzle: A Study of the Fouchet Negotiations and the 1963 Veto*, Harvard University Centre for International Affairs, Harvard (1967).

[16] Silj, *Europe's Political Puzzle*, p. 57.

[17] Bodenheimer, *Political Union*, pp. 159-160.

[18] Russell, 'The Atlantic Alliance', p. 1204, J.J. Schokking (ed.), *Nederland, Europa en de Wereld: ons buitenlands beleid in discussie*, Meppel (1970), p. 71.

[19] Silj, *Europe's Political Puzzle*, pp. 49-51, Bodenheimer, *Political Union*, p. 161.

[20] During the negotiations concessions were made in this direction. In January 1962 the draft-treaty provided for a quasi-independent Secretary-General 'whose office would constitute a Community feature that could develop at later stages of the Union'. Later, in June 1962, Spaak proposed establishing a political commission to represent a 'Community interest'. The Dutch rejected both formulae (though the latter was also rejected by de Gaulle). Bodenheimer, *Political Union*, p. 156.

[21] *Ibid.*, p. 159.

[22] 'A supranational co-operation can serve the interests of a small country, allowing it to throw the weight not of power, but of intellect, into a bigger whole', L.G.M. Jaquet, 'The Role of a Small State within Alliance Systems', *Small States in International Relations*, ed. A. Schou and A.O. Brundtland, Stockholm (1971), p. 61. 'Supranational institutions preserve the sovereign equality of the smaller nations by artificially imposing constraints upon the larger countries roughly similar to those practical considerations which have always limited the actions of smaller nations', Bodenheimer, *Political Union*, p. 158.

[23] 'L'action du Parlement néerlandais n'est explicable quesi l'on tient compte de la frustration qu'a provoquée la politique d'intérêt national menée par M. Luns depuis 1959. Durant six ans, les fédéralistes du Parlement ont eu l'impression d'être en face d'un Ministre habile, certes mais sans convictions européennes profondes; ils estiment aussi que le Parlement manque d'influence réelle sur la politique étrangère du gouvernement' de Bruin, *Les Pays Bas et l'Integration Européenne*, pp. 659-660.

[24] *Ibid.*, p. 673.

[25] *Ibid.*, pp. 694-697.

[26] *Ibid.*, pp. 708-716.

[27] J. Newhouse, *Collision in Brussels. The Common Market Crisis of 30 June 1965*, London (1968), p. 61.

[28] De Bruin, *Les Pays Bas et l'Integration Européenne*, pp. 774-775.

[29] *Ibid.*, pp. 793-794.

[30] Voorhoeven, *Peace, Profits and Principles*, p. 171.

[31] See L. Tsoukalis, *The Politics and Economics of European Monetary Integration*, London (1977).

[32] D.P. Spierenberg, *Europese Unie: Rapport van de Adviescommissie Europese Unie*, The Hague (1975), p. 34. Spierenberg criticised the Tindemans Report published a little later for its belief that the Community would develop naturally towards closer co-operation and for its failure to suggest concrete measures to achieve EMU by 1980. D.P. Spierenberg, 'Het Rapport-Tindemans. Een Kritische beschouwing', *Internationale Spectator*, Vol. 32, No. 3 (1976), p. 148.

[33] *Nota inzake de Europese Unie*, Handelingen van de Tweede Kamer der Staten-Generaal, Zitting 1975-1976, 13 426, No. 4.

[34] See W. Wallace and D. Allen, 'Political Co-operation: Procedure as Substitute for Policy', *Policy-Making in the European Communities*, eds. H. Wallace, W. Wallace, C. Webb, London (1977), pp. 227-247.

[35] In 1973 it was agreed that political aspects of problems dealt with by the Community could be put on the EPC agenda, that the European Commission would be represented at meetings where discussions might impinge on community work and that more meetings be held between EPC Ministers and the Political Commissions of the European Parliament. Voorhoeven, *Peace, Profits and Principles*, p. 179.

[36] J. Boehmer, *Het Nederlandse beleid met betrekking tot de Europese samenwerking*, 1971-1975, Ph. D. Thesis, Leiden, 1976, p. 100.

[37] *Ibid.*, p. 120.

[38] In October 1973 den Uyl stated 'the question of what sort of society we wish to create in the Community is more important than the tempo at which the process of European unity is completed'. The statement caused much consternation in the Netherlands at the time since no Premier before him had so openly distanced himself from the concept of integration as such. W.J. Veenstra, 'De Partij van den Arbeid en Europa', *Internationale Spectator*, Vol. 33, No. 4 (1977), p. 249.

[39] Boehmer, *Het Nederlandse beleid met betrekking tot Europese samenwerking*, pp. 103-105.

[40] E.H. van der Beugel, *Nederland in de westelijke samenwerking. Enkele aspecten van Nederlandse beleidsvorming*, Brill, Leiden (1966), pp. 16-19. Indicative of the relative ministerial importance at the time was the fact that negotiations for the formation of Benelux and the ECSC were conducted by the Economics Ministry.

[41] See H. Wallace, *National Governments and the European Communities*, London (1973), pp. 33-35, and C. Sasse, *Decision Making in the European Community*, New York (1977), pp. 24-27.

[42] Van der Beugel, *Nederland in de westelijke samenwerking*, pp. 21-22.

[43] De Bruin, *Les Pays Bas et l'Integration Européenne*, pp. 299-300.

[44] L.J. Brinkhorst, 'Coordinatie van Europees beleid in Nederland', *Sociaal-Economische Wetgeving*, Vol. 26, No. 12 (1978), p. 823.

[45] *Bestuurs-organisatie bij de Kabinets-formatie 1971. Rapport van de Commissie Interdepartementale Taakverdeling en Coordinatie*, The Hague (1971), pp. 33-34, 75-78.

[46] Sasse, *Decision-Making in the European Community*, pp. 22-23.

[47] Brinkhorst, 'Coordinatie van Europees beleid', pp. 815-828.

[48] G.M. Taber, *Patterns and Prospects of Common Market Trade*, London (1974), p. 54.

[49] P.J. Verdoorn, 'Economische gevolgen der handelspolitiek integratie binnen de EEG 1956-1970', Spierenberg, *Europese Unie*, pp. 121-127. These findings receive confirmation from another study which attempts to measure the trend development of trade intensities. M. Lefeldt and A. Schneider, 'Structural Changes in EC Trade Intensities', *Intereconomics*, Hamburg, Vol. 12, No. 11/12 (1977), pp. 293-296.

[50] W. Sellekaerts, 'How Meaningful are Empirical Studies on Trade Creation and Diversion?', *Weltwirtschaftliches Archiv*, Kiel, Vol. 109, No. 4 (1973), pp. 519-548.

[51] P.J. Verdoorn and A.R.N. Schwartz, 'Two Alternative Estimates of the Effects of EEC and EFTA on Patterns of Trade', *European Economic Review*, Vol. 3, No. 3 (1972), pp. 291-335.

[52] E.W. Prewo, 'Integration Effects in the EEC', *European Economic Review*, Vol. 5, No. 4 (1974), pp. 379-405.

[53] *Ibid.*, pp. 396-397.

[54] It is too early yet for detailed studies to have been published on the effects of the enlargement of 1973 on patterns of Dutch trade. An exception is W.F. Smits, 'De Nederlandse concurrentiepositie binnen de EG', *Economisch-Statistische Berichten*, 9-5-1979, pp. 457-461 which suggests that the Dutch market share of the new member states declined between 1974 and 1977. Since his calculations, however, exclude trade in energy and agriculture some care should be taken in drawing any conclusions.

[55] Hartog, *Nederland en de Euromarkt*, pp. 113-117. See also D.C. Oort, 'Het vervoer in de Europese Gemeenschap. Algemene Inleiding', eds. C.J. Oort *et al*, *Het vervoer in de Europese Gemeenschappen*, Deventer (1969), pp. 9-39.

[56] K. Vonk, 'The Transport Sector. A Struggle for Balance and Mobility', *Internationale Spectator*, Vol. 19, No. 7 (1965), pp. 611-612.

[57] De Bruin, *Les Pays Bas et l'Integration Européenne*, pp. 829-888.

[58] Hartog, *Nederland en de Euromarkt*, p. 113.

[59] The widespread incidence of 'green currencies' and MCA's in the 1970s does not fundamentally affect this premise since, for virtually the entire decade, prices within the EEC remained firmly above world prices.

[60] *The Economist*, Vol. 270, No. 7074, 31/3-6/4-1979, p. 38.

[61] *Ibid.*, Vol. 270, No. 7080, 12/18-5-1979, p. 63.

[62] *Landbouwverkenning*, Ministerie van Landbouw en Visserij, The Hague (1977), pp. 20-21.

[63] *Ibid.*, p. 18.

[64] Commissie, Europese Economische Gemeenschap, *De toestand van de landbouw in de Gemeenschap.* Verslag 1979, Brussels, Luxembourg (1980), pp. 222-223.

[65] J. de Hoogh, 'De gemeenschappelijke landbouwmarkt on de Nederlandse economie', *Jaarverslag, Landbouw-Economisch Instituut*, Den Haag, 1975, pp. 15-17.

[66] *Landbouwverkenning*, p. 21.

[67] The information for this section is derived from Y.H. Berghorst and P.M. Hommes, *Europese Verkiezingen. Programma's en analyse*, The Hague (1979) and from a study of the election programmes and information sheets of the individual Dutch political parties.

[68] Commission of the European Communities, *Euro-barometer. Public Opinion in the European Community*, Vols. 11 and 12 (1979). See also Voorhoeven, *Peace, Profits and Principles*, pp. 184-186.

[69] N.O.S. *Publiek-en Programma- Onderzoek. Intern Bulletin. Nederlanders over Europa*, October 1978.

[70] See L.J. Brinkhorst, 'Nederland in de Europese Gemeenschap: terugblik en vooruitzicht', *Internationale Spectator*, Vol. 38, No. 12 (1978), pp. 760-770.

Select Bibliography

In English

Baehr, P.R., 'The foreign policy of the Netherlands', *The Other Powers. Studies in the foreign policies of small states*, ed. R.P. Barston, London, 1973.

Bodenheimer, S.J., *Political Union: A Microcosm of European Politics, 1960-1966*, Leiden, 1967.

Deboutte, J. and Staden, A van, 'High Politics in Low Countries: A study in foreign policy-making in Belgium and the Netherlands' *Foreign Policy-Making in Western Europe*, eds. W. Wallace and W. Patersen, 1977.

Leurdijk, J.H. (ed.), *The Foreign Policy of the Netherlands*, Alphen aan de Rijn, 1978.

Newhouse, J., *Collision in Brussels. The Common Market crisis of 30 June 1965*, London, 1968.

Sasse, C. (ed.), *Decision-making in the European Community*, New York, 1977.

Silj, A., *Europe's Political Puzzle: A study of the Fouchet Negotiations and the 1963 veto*, Harvard, 1967.

Voorhoeve, J.J.C., *Peace, Profits and Principles. A study of Dutch foreign policy.* The Hague, 1979.

Vonk, K., 'The Transport Sector. A struggle for balance and mobility' *Internationale Spectator* vol. 19, No. 7, 1965.

Weil, G.L., *The Benelux Nations: The politics of small-country democracties*, New York, 1970.

In Dutch

Aben, H.J.M. (ed.), *Europa onderweg. Ooggetuigen brengen verslag uit*, Amsterdam, 1967.
Berghorst Y.H. en Hommes, P.M., *Europese Verkiezingen. Programma's en analyse*, The Hague, 1979.
Boehmer, J., *Het Nederlandse beleid met betrekking tot de Europese samenwerking 1971-1975*, Ph. D. Thesis, Leiden, 1976.
Brinkhorst, L.J., 'Coördinatie van Europees beleid in Nederland' *Sociaal-Economische Wetgeving*, vol. 26, No. 12, 1978.
Brinkhorst, L.J., 'Nederland in de Europese Gemeenschap: terugblik en vooruitzicht' *Internationale Spectator*, vol. 32, 12, 1978.
Europese Unie, *Rapport van de adviescommissie Europese Unie* (Rapport Spierenberg), The Hague, 1975.
Hartog, F., *Nederland en de Euromarkt*, Leiden, 1971.
Hommes, P.M., *Nederland en de Europese Eenwording*, 's-Gravenhage, 1980.
Hoogh, J. de, 'De Gemeenschappelijke landbouwmarkt en de Nederlandse economie' *Jaarverslag Landbouw-Economisch Instituut*, Den Haag, 1975.
Oort, C.J., Stavenow, W. and Raven, H. (eds.), *Het vervoer in de Europese Gemeenschappen*, Deventer, 1969.
Schokking, J.J. (ed.), *Nederland, Europa en de Wereld*, Meppel, 1970.
Spierenberg, D.P., 'Het Rapport Tindemans. Een kritische beschouwing' *Internationale Spectator*, vol. 30, No. 3, 1976.

INDEX

NOTES ON CONTRIBUTORS

Rudy B. Andeweg (born in Leiden, February 28th, 1952) studied government at the University of Leiden and political science at the University of Mitchigan, Ann Arbor, USA. Since 1976 he has been a lecturer in political science at the University of Leiden. He teaches Dutch politics and political behaviour and is currently preparing a dissertation on the causes and processes of post-war change in the Dutch electorate. Among other publications he has co-authored a book on the 1977 Dutch cabinet formation.

Jos de Beus (born in Utrecht, November 27nd, 1952) studied political science at the Catholic University of Nijmegen. Since 1977 he has been a lecturer in the Department of Economics at the University of Amsterdam. His field of lecturing concerns public choice. He has written articles about guided wage policy, the theory of the state and enterprise in the People's Republic of China. His current research concerns the relationship between economic order and freedom.

Willem Brand (born in Amsterdam, 1910) obtained his doctorate in economics from the University of Amsterdam. Between 1937 and 1946 he worked for International Business Machines Inc., managing a subsidiary in the East Indies. He spent the years 1942-1945 as a Japanese prisoner of war. In 1946 he joined the United Nations as an economist and in 1956 he became professor of development economics at the University of Leiden. He is author of several books and articles related to development problems and economic and social questions related to rich countries and the Third World.

Karl Dittrich (born in Maastricht, July 9th, 1952) studied government at the University of Leiden. From 1975 to 1978 he was a research assistant in the Department of Political Science at the University of Leiden where he completed a dissertation on Dutch municipal elections. Having spent a year as a Fellow at the European University Institute in Florence, Italy, he is currently a lecturer in political science at the University of Leiden. Among other publications he has co-authored a book on the 1977 Dutch cabinet formation.

Hans van den Doel (born Zierikzee, April 4th, 1937) studied economics at the Free University of Amsterdam and he was awarded his Ph.D. by the Erasmus University, Rotterdam in 1971. Between 1966 and 1973 he was a member of parliament (Tweede Kamer) for the Dutch labour party. From 1973 to 1975 he was professor of political science at the Catholic University of Nijmegen and since 1975 he has been professor of economics at the University of Amsterdam. He has published a number of books and articles on economic systems and economic policy.

Wim Driehuis (born Utrecht, June 22nd, 1943) studied economics at the University of Amsterdam and received his Ph. D. from the Erasmus University, Rotterdam in 1972. Between 1967 and 1972 he worked in the Central Planning Bureau in The Hague. In 1973 he became reader and in 1975 professor of macro-economics at the University of Amsterdam. His current research interests include labour market analysis, wage and price formation and macro-economic models.

Cornelis J. van Eijk (born Amsterdam, October 5th, 1923) studied economics at the University of Amsterdam. He is currently professor of economics at the Erasmus University, Rotterdam. His current research interests lie in recent developments in model building for the design of economic policy in the countries of the EEC.

Richard T. Griffiths (born Twickenham, Middlesex, U.K. 7th April 1948) studied economic history and Russian studies at the University College of Swansea and received his Ph. D. in 1977 from Cambridge University. From 1973 to 1979 he was lecturer in European Studies at the University of Manchester Institute of Science and Technology. He is currently professor in social and economic history at the Free University Amsterdam. He has published in the area of 19th and 20th century Dutch economic development.

Galen A. Irwin (born Joplin, Missouri, USA January 14th, 1942) studied at Joplin Junior College, the University of Kansas and received his Ph. D. in 1967 from the Florida State University. he has taught at the Florida State University and the University of Iowa, USA. He is currently professor in political behaviour and research methods at the University of Leiden. In 1977 he was Director of the Dutch National Election Study and co-editor of *De Nederlandse Kiezer '77.* He has published various articles on political participation and voting behaviour.

Peter W. Klein (born Vienna, December 12th, 1931) studied economics at the Nederlandse Economische Hoogeschool, Rotterdam. He received his Ph. D. in 1965. Between 1969 and 1974 he was extraordinary professor in economic history at the Erasmus University, Rotterdam. He has published books and articles on Dutch economic history spanning the 17th to the 20th century. At the moment he is professor in the history of society at the Erasmus University, Rotterdam.

Gerbertus A. van der Knaap (born Rotterdam, July 16th, 1944) studied human geography at the University of Utrecht. In 1970 he was appointed lecturer in economic geography at the Erasmus University, Rotterdam lecturing on research methods in economic geography and regional development problems in Western Europe. He received his Ph. D. in 1978. His current research interests are in urban and regional planning with special emphasis on population migration.

Cornelis Lemckert (born The Hague, November 21st, 1941) studied economics at the Nederlandse Economische Hoogeschool, Rotterdam. Since 1969 he has worked for the Ministry of Economic Affairs, first in the division for general economic policy and, at present, in the Directorate General for energy policy. He has contributed 'à titre personnel'.

Ruud Lubbers (born Rotterdam, May 7th, 1939) studied economics at the Nederlandse Economische Hoogeschool, Rotterdam. He worked as secretary for the Board of Directors of Lubbers' construction plant and machinery mill, Hollandia B.V., from '63-'65. In 1965 he became one of the Directors. Mr. Lubbers was member of the board of the Netherlands' Christian Employers Federation (NCWB). From 1973-1977 Mr. Lubbers was Minister of Economic Affairs. At the moment, as Member of Parliament (Tweede Kamer) he leads the parliamentary fraction of the Christian Democratic Party. He published regularly, mainly on economic policy issues.

Theo van der Tak (born Rotterdam, February 21st, 1948) studied government at the University of Leiden and then worked as a journalist. Since 1975 he has been a lecturer in public administration at the Graduate School of Mangagement in Delft where he teaches Dutch politics and policy processes. His main research interests are in the field of public administration and public policy. Amongst other publications he has co-authored a book on the 1977 Dutch cabinet formation.

Pieter de Wolff (born Amsterdam, May 25th, 1911) studied Mathematics at the University of Amsterdam. He held various appointments at the University of Amsterdam, the Central Bureau of Statistics, Philips and the Amsterdam Municipal Bureau of Statistics until, in 1957, he became director of the Netherlands' Central Planning Bureau which he remained until 1966. Between 1953 and 1975 he was professor in Mathematical economics at the University of Amsterdam. He is currently vice-chairman of the Advisory Council on Science Policy. Current research interests are in economic planning, mathematical economics and growth theory.